# A Heavenly Craft

# A HEAVENLY CRAFT

## THE WOODCUT

## IN EARLY PRINTED BOOKS

ILLUSTRATED BOOKS PURCHASED BY LESSING J. ROSENWALD
AT THE SALE OF THE LIBRARY OF C. W. DYSON PERRINS

*Edited by Daniel De Simone*

*Curator, Lessing J. Rosenwald Collection,*

*Library of Congress*

GEORGE BRAZILLER, INC., NEW YORK

*in association with the*

LIBRARY OF CONGRESS, WASHINGTON

2004

*A Heavenly Craft: The Woodcut in Early Printed Books,* a book and exhibition, was supported by generous gifts from the Fellowship of Bibliophilic Societies (www.fabsbooks.org), Jonathan A. Hill, the Berkley Foundation, Inc., Ray and Lorraine Perryman, and Donna L. and Robert H. Jackson.

*Published for an exhibition at the*
Grolier Club, New York, New York, December 2004
Library of Congress, Washington, D.C., April 2005
Bridwell Library, Southern Methodist University, Dallas, Texas, September 2005

LIBRARY OF CONGRESS
*Director of Publishing:* W. Ralph Eubanks
*Editor:* Evelyn Sinclair
*Photographer:* James R. Higgins

*Index:* Kate Mertes, Mertes Editorial Services, Alexandria, Virginia
*Typography:* Duke & Company, Devon, Pennsylvania
*Book design:* Patricia Inglis, Inglis Design, Galesville, Maryland

Printed in China

For information, please address the publisher:
George Braziller, Inc.
171 Madison Avenue
New York, NY 10016

*Library of Congress Cataloging-in-Publication Data*

A heavenly craft : the woodcut in early printed books, illustrated books purchased by Lessing J. Rosenwald at the sale of the library of C.W. Dyson Perrins / edited by Daniel De Simone. — 1st ed,
    p. cm.
Includes bibliographical references and index.
ISBN 0-8076-1536-6 (alk. paper)
  1. Wood-engraving, Renaissance — Exhibitions.
  2. Illustration of books — 15th century — Exhibitions.
  3. Illustration of books — 16th century — Exhibitions.
  4. Early printed books — Europe — Exhibitions.
  5. Rosenwald, Lessing J. (Lessing Julius), 1891–1979 — Art collections — Exhibitions. 6. Wood-engraving — Private collections — Washington (D.C.) — Exhibitions.
I. De Simone, Daniel. II. Library of Congress. III. Title.

NE1052.H43   2004
761'.2'09024074753 — dc22
2004007145

FRONTISPIECE: Crucifixion, canon woodcut illustration, with passe-partout border, from *Missale secundu[m] ordinem carthusiensium,* printed in Ferrara, Italy, at the Carthusian Monastery, April 10, 1503 (see item 41, LC/R744).

PAGES i (detail), viii: Woodcut from Saint Birgitta's *Revelationes,* printed in Nuremberg, by Anton Koberger, Sepember 21, 1500 (see item 6, LC/R 205).

ENDPAPERS: Woodcut, with sacred monogram and Saint George, produced in Ferrara to decorate the binding of Battista Fregoso's *Anteros, sive Tractatus contra amorem* printed in Milan in 1496, item 21, LC/R313.

SPINE: Detail from Mary of the Apocalypse, woodcut from Miquel Pérez, *La Vida y excellencias y milagros dela sacratissima Virgen Maria,* Toledo, November 29, 1526 (item 74, LC/R1284).

See Library of Congress online collections at

# CONTENTS

# FOREWORD

THE LESSING J. ROSENWALD COLLECTION on the History of the Illustrated Book has stood at the center of the Library of Congress's vast collections from the day Lessing Rosenwald's magnificent gift arrived at the Library. As a collection, it is an unsurpassed revelation, documenting the history of the book and the power of the pictorial image. Having lived and worked with this collection over the past few decades, Library of Congress curators and specialists, as well as its visiting researchers and scholars, have discovered that it is indeed much more. The images found in Lessing Rosenwald's books, we have all learned, are windows that open onto grand as well as mundane subjects, providing a notion of the past and a glimpse into the future.

The accomplished exhibition and catalogue for *A Heavenly Craft: The Woodcut in Early Printed Books* bring us to yet another level in understanding the riches that form Mr. Rosenwald's legacy by exploring the power and meaning of woodcut images in the earliest European illustrated printed books. Here we witness the transformation of Europe as it moved from the medieval world into the Renaissance. With its three excellent essays by scholars and its detailed item descriptions, *A Heavenly Craft* invites the reader to contemplate the meaning of these vital images and to understand how they were conceived and how they entered the visual world of everyday life in medieval and Renaissance Europe. We are introduced to the vision of the artist and how it is transformed by the extraordinary craft of the block cutter and the printer, producing a vibrant vocabulary of iconic and familiar images.

Another, equally important insight is to be gained from *A Heavenly Craft*. In highlighting Lessing J. Rosenwald's acquisition of the books of another great collector, C. W. Dyson Perrins, this catalogue underlines the fundamentally important work of book collectors and bibliophiles. Great libraries are lifted up by the power of great collections. Lessing J. Rosenwald understood this and fervently believed that he could impart his own passion and respect for these great books through this unparalleled gift to the American people. It is through his grand beneficence that these images can be brought to life in a manner that allows us to see the past with compassion and understanding.

JAMES H. BILLINGTON
*Librarian of Congress*

# PREFACE

THE INSPIRATION FOR THE EXHIBIT AND CATALOGUE *A Heavenly Craft: The Woodcut in Early Printed Books* came as a near instantaneous response to the discovery of a set of auction catalogues in the Lessing J. Rosenwald Archive. This set of four octavo volumes stood out from the rest of the modern auction catalogues in the archive, most of which, bound in wrappers, are fairly nondescript in appearance. Three of these volumes are bound in cloth, each in a different color, and the fourth has its original blue wrappers. The set is Lessing Rosenwald's marked copy of the auction catalogues for the sale of the illustrated books collected by C. W. Dyson Perrins, heir to the Lea & Perrins fortune. The catalogues were marked by Rosenwald in purple pencil, as was his custom, and contain bid information and questions about the condition of the books. Buyers' names, prices realized, and condition reports are noted in the hand of Rosenwald's agent, who previewed the books in London and attended the sale.

The Dyson Perrins sale was one of the first important book auctions to take place after World War II, and from it Lessing Rosenwald purchased eighty-four titles, making him its most important buyer. Much of the history of the sale is recorded in this set of auction catalogues, which document a significant event in the history of international book collecting and in the formation of Lessing J. Rosenwald's outstanding collection of early illustrated books.

C. W. Dyson Perrins had a passion for English porcelain as well as for illuminated manuscripts and books. The noted English collector and philanthropist decided to sell his collection of printed books, many of which he had owned for nearly fifty years, to save the financially troubled Royal Worcester Porcelain Factory. To avoid bankruptcy after the devastation wrought by the war, the eighteenth-century firm needed capital. The monies raised by the sale of Dyson Perrins's collection of books in 1946 and 1947 stabilized the porcelain manufacturer and saved for the English people one of the few remaining companies that had survived from the early years of Great Britain's industrial revolution.

Lessing J. Rosenwald, like Dyson Perrins, was not only a formidable collector but also an important philanthropist. In 1943, Rosenwald signed the first in a series of deeds of gift that would divide his collection of illustrated books and prints between the Library of Congress and the National Gallery of Art. Along with the collection of illustrated books he gave to the Library, he included part of his archive of personal papers that related to his business and governmental career, and most of his reference library. All the quotations, invoices, and correspondence pertaining to the purchases of books and prints accompanied his collection of prints to the National Gallery of Art. Included in the National Gallery's Rosenwald Archive is a series of files documenting events surrounding the Dyson Perrins sale.

Woodcut from Saint Birgitta (1302–1373), *Revelationes,* printed by Anton Koberger in Nuremberg, September 21, 1500. See item 6, LC/R 205.

These papers document Rosenwald's personal involvement in every aspect of this auction sale. They demonstrate his working relationship with the Philadelphia bookseller A. W. S. Rosenbach and the auctioneer, Sotheby & Company, which resulted in the purchase of almost 15 percent of what was offered at the sale. In "Lessing J. Rosenwald and the 'Magnificent Library' of C. W. Dyson Perrins," Paul Needham, Scheide Librarian at Princeton University, traces the history of the auction and in the process describes highlights of the Dyson Perrins collection. Using Rosenwald's set of marked auction catalogues, the Rosenwald Archive at the National Gallery of Art, and his vast knowledge of early books and book collecting, he discusses the part played by Rosenwald in the auction sale and how his purchases complemented his growing collection of illustrated books.

Peter Parshall, curator of old master prints at the National Gallery of Art and coauthor with David Landau of *The Renaissance Print, 1470–1550,* was particularly helpful in suggesting essay topics for this book. When I approached him, I learned that he was organizing an exhibition on the single-leaf woodcut for the National Gallery, scheduled to open in the fall of 2005. The prospect of two exhibitions with catalogues devoted to medieval and Renaissance woodcuts, opening in Washington during the same year, stimulated broad discussion of the subject. Much of this discussion revolved around the different approaches taken by bibliographers and art historians in their study of the early woodcut. Peter Parshall offered valuable advice about recent studies published by art historians on the single-leaf woodcut.

A review of basic sources for the study of the medieval and Renaissance woodcut in early printed books reveals that much of the research bibliographers rely on today was published between 1885 and 1935. Systematic studies of German, Italian, French, and Dutch illustrated books were carried out over decades by scholars dedicated to establishing a proper chronology of the use of the woodcut in printed books. Arthur M. Hind's book, *An Introduction to a History of the Woodcut,* published in 1935, was an attempt to create a synthesis of this research, and a close look at his general bibliography shows the breadth of research done over a fifty-year period.

The facsimile reproductions of woodcuts that accompany these analytical texts have provided a remarkable resource. Found in the published work of Paul Heitz, W. L. Schreiber, Albert Schramm, Alfred W. Pollard, Paul Kristeller, Anatole Claudin and Paul Lacombe, M. J. Schretlen, and Conrad Haebler and in the collection catalogues of the prince d'Essling, Dyson Perrins, Charles Fairfax Murray, and J. Pierpont Morgan, these facsimile reproductions were critical to the advancement of research on the origins and development of early book illustration. They offered scholars the opportunity to systematically examine series of woodcuts and chronicle their use in various editions of a given title and by various printers during the incunable period. Along with the study of printing types, the study of the use of wood blocks brought about a tremendous advance in understanding the spread of printing in its first century.

Beyond establishing a systematic arrangement and chronology for woodcut images, some early scholars attempted to determine their local origins and define national styles. Most woodcuts were designed and cut by anonymous artists and craftsmen, and attributions were often made based on the imprint information that was sometimes found in the printed book. The date, printer's name, and place of publication were useful tools to suggest an attribution, but not all books carried this information and even when they did, it proved difficult to determine the origins of a woodcut design based solely on a book's imprint or on physical evidence. Although much of the work of this group of early bibliographers was sound, many of the qualitative judgments and attributions they made can no longer be supported. The fact is, since the 1930s, bibliographical research on the woodcut in early printed books has slowed considerably, and though today's scholars must consult the work of early bibliographers, it is essential that they realize that this research is incomplete and, in the worst event, misleading.

Such has not been the case for the study of the single-leaf woodcut. Art historians have been studying and writing about early woodcut prints with very fruitful results for the past four decades. The exhibition catalogues devoted to late medieval and early Renaissance prints, many of which are cited in the catalogue entries in this book, are a testament to the recent work of this group of scholars. With an emphasis on technique, artistic innovation and influence, and iconography, art historians have contributed a new understanding of the development of the early woodcut print and, in consequence, to its closest relative, the woodcut in early printed books. In their methods of analysis, art historians offer a lesson for those of us interested in advancing the study of the early illustrated book and an opportunity to combine traditional bibliographical skills with a greater emphasis on art historical techniques.

With this revelation in mind, it seemed imperative to invite an art historian to write an essay focusing on early books illustrated with woodcuts. An example of creative research that combines art historical techniques with bibliographical description is the work of Lilian Armstrong, Mildred Lane Kemper Professor of Art History at Wellesley College. Her research, a model of its kind, stems from thirty years' experience identifying the style, technique, and iconography of manuscript illuminators. Recently, she has devoted much of her research to analyzing woodcut designs printed in late fifteenth- and early sixteenth-century Venetian books. Comparing them with illuminated manuscript paintings from the same period, Professor Armstrong has been able to attribute woodcut designs to a number of known miniature painters.

In her essay "Venetian and Florentine Renaissance Woodcuts for Bibles, Liturgical Books, and Devotional Books," Lilian Armstrong examines images from some of the most famous books that Rosenwald purchased at the Dyson Perrins sale. Beginning with Giunta's edition of *Biblia italica,* Venice, 1494; Dante's *La Commedia divina,* printed by Bernardinus Benalius and Matteo Capcasa, Venice, 1491; and a number of early sixteenth-century illustrated liturgical books printed in Venice by LucAntonio Giunta, she demonstrates her method by describing the woodcuts, comparing design elements, and attributing the work to three Venetian miniaturists, the Pico Master, the Rimini Master, and Benedetto Bordone. Shifting her attention to Florence, she describes the most important Italian book Lessing Rosenwald acquired at the sale—the 1495 Florentine edition of the *Epistole et Evangelii* printed by Lorenzo Morgiani and Johannes Petri for Piero Pacini. In examining its woodcuts, Lilian Armstrong shows how knowledge of Florentine paintings and illuminated manuscripts can be used to suggest attributions for anonymous woodcut designs. Although the attributions for these Florentine images are not as definitive as those for the Venetian cuts, such work points the way for future research into the origins of Florentine woodcut design.

Tracing an arc of European history, Daniela Laube places in perspective the northern European books from the auction and provides an informed overview of German woodcut design in the late fifteenth century. A second-generation print seller from Zurich, she is the owner of Daniela Laube Fine Arts in New York, specializing in old master and modern master prints, drawings, and rare books. In "The Stylistic Development of German Book Illustration, 1460–1511," she focuses on the evolution of the illustrated book in Bamberg, Augsburg, Ulm, Nuremberg, Strasbourg, and Basel and describes the development of the woodcut from the first German illustrated book, *Der Edelstein,* 1461, to Albrecht Dürer's monumental images and the work of contemporary artists who absorbed his stylistic influences. Included in her careful analysis are descriptions of woodcut designs created for the most important printers and publishers working during the incunable period, among them Günther and Johannes Zainer, Conrad Dinckmut, Erhard Ratdolt, Johann Grüninger, Bernard Richel, and Anton Koberger.

The entries for items described in this catalogue are organized in the same manner as are the entries in *The Lessing J. Rosenwald Collection: A Catalog of the Gifts of Lessing J. Rosenwald to the Library of Congress, 1943 to 1975* (Washington: Library of Congress, 1977) and in the four-part auction sale catalogue titled *The Catalogue of the Magnificent Library Principally of Early Printed and Early Illustrated Books Formed by C. W. Dyson Perrins* (London: Sotheby & Co., 1946–47). In both these catalogues, items are arranged by century, country of origin, and date.

Following the same arrangement, *A Heavenly Craft* begins the catalogue descriptions with fifteenth-century books, first those printed in German-speaking regions, then Italy, France, the Low Countries, England, and Spain, and from there continues with books printed in the sixteenth century in the same geographical order. We hope that by using this arrangement, the development of the art of the woodcut in Europe during the late medieval and early Renaissance period will be more readily apparent.

The Rosenwald number (for example, "Rosenwald 126," or, in references, "LC/R 126") that appears at the head of each item's description corresponds to the number of the item in the *The Lessing J. Rosenwald Collection.* In the heading, the Rosenwald number is followed by the lot number given in the Dyson Perrins sale catalogues. Throughout the text, Rosenwald numbers (from LC/R 126 to LC/R 1286) identify specific books from the Rosenwald Collection, provide the source for illustrations, and specify works cited in notes. Item numbers locate specific catalogue descriptions (item 1 through item 75). Standard works of scholarship and bibliographic reference are cited by commonly used abbreviations, such as Hind, Schramm, Pollard, and so on, in notes and text. These abbreviations are noted in the bibliography, and readers should consult it for full information for such reference works.

At the initiation of Winston Tabb, then Associate Librarian of the Library of Congress, Mark Dimunation, chief of the Rare Book and Special Collections Division, proposed to Peter Kraus, chair of the Exhibitions Committee of the Grolier Club, an exhibit of early illustrated books that Lessing Rosenwald purchased at the Dyson Perrins sale. Given its size, its provenance, and the fact that the collection documents part of the history of the development of woodcut in western Europe, this group of books seemed a perfect fit for both institutions. The opportunity to celebrate the vision of two distinguished collectors in a single exhibition and to display seventy-five rare fifteenth- and sixteenth-century illustrated books was enthusiastically endorsed by the Grolier Club. Irene Chambers, chief of the Library's Interpretive Programs Office, Ralph Eubanks, director of publishing, Diane Kresh, then director of Public Services Collections, and Winston Tabb supported the idea and thought it an excellent opportunity for the Library of Congress to expand its partnership with the Grolier Club and to display some of the treasures from the Rosenwald Collection in both New York and Washington. As the exhibition took shape, Valerie Hotchkiss, director of the Bridwell Library, Perkins School of Theology, at Southern Methodist University, and Eric White, rare book curator at the Bridwell, saw that the content of the exhibition of the Rosenwald/Dyson Perrins books was an excellent match to their recent exhibition program, and a third exhibition venue was established for Dallas, Texas.

A project the size of *A Heavenly Craft,* with its three exhibition venues and illustrated catalogue, would not be possible without the support and dedicated help of scores of people. The interest in this project taken by Librarian of Congress James H. Billington and by the staff of the Office of the Librarian of Congress, headed by Jo Ann Jenkins, was crucial to its success.

The Exhibitions Program Review Committee, headed by Deanna Marcum, Associate Librarian of Congress, and Charles Stanhope, director of development, and his staff in the Development Office offered significant support as well.

Special recognition goes to Irene Chambers, for from the beginning, her faith in this project and her determination to see it through inspired others to support it when troubles threatened its completion. Ralph Eubanks and Evelyn Sinclair of the Publishing Office, with the collaboration of Patricia Inglis of Inglis Design as the book's designer and Duke & Company as typographer, are responsible for producing a beautifully illustrated volume, a testament to their dedication to this project. Without their patience, help, and support, this catalogue would never have achieved the status of reference work, which was the intention of the Publishing Office from the beginning. Hopefully, the content of the catalogue meets their high expectations.

The help of the administrators and staff of the Rare Book and Special Collections Division (RBSCD) was crucial to the completion of the exhibition and catalogue. Mark Dimunation piloted the project through the Library's bureaucracy and held firm when funding became more difficult as budgetary restrictions caused all programs in the Library to be reexamined. George Chiasson, special assistant to the chief of the division, and Clark Evans, Walter Walden, Tamika Epperson, and David Robinson, members of the reference staff who manage the Rare Book Reading Room, were especially helpful with research questions and finding obscure reference sources. Elizabeth Gettings and Shirley Liang, the RBSCD digital team, worked seamlessly with Dominic Sergi, Karl Rogers, and Jade Curtis of the Digital Scan Center of Information Technology Services of the Library. James R. Higgins, senior photographer in the Library's Photoduplication Service, was a pleasure to work with, and his photographs provide a key element in any success this catalogue achieves.

The staff of the Interpretive Programs Office, including Kim Curry, Betsy Nahum-Miller, Martha Hopkins, Tambra Johnson, and Margaret Brown demonstrated their creative approach to the exhibition side of the project. Their interaction with their counterparts at the Grolier Club and the Bridwell Library made for a beautifully designed and efficiently managed exhibition. Rikki Conden of the Conservation Division ensured that the books that went on exhibition were fit for travel and that the exhibit areas where the books would be displayed met the Library of Congress's requirements for preservation of the collections.

As personal acknowledgments, I would like to thank my wife, Angela Scott, for allowing me the freedom to take this position as curator of the Rosenwald Collection at the Library of Congress and for encouraging me to fulfill the dream that brought me to Washington. Writing about the books in the Rosenwald Collection was a part of that dream, and her support over the past two years was essential to my completing this project. Jerry Wager, whose unfortunate death in February 2004 kept him from seeing its completion, was my most consistent champion as I worked my way through the complicated process of writing catalogue descriptions. His help as proofreader, fact-checker, and friend was indispensable, and his contribution to whatever is good about this catalogue cannot be overstated. Michael C. Lang also read much of the manuscript and made helpful suggestions that clarified some of the more complicated points about the books I was describing. Finally, I would like to thank Paul Needham, Lilian Armstrong, and Daniela Laube for the important contributions they made to this book. Their essays bring life to the catalogue descriptions and provide the context in which they can be better understood.

# Lessing J. Rosenwald and the "Magnificent Library" of C. W. Dyson Perrins

## Paul Needham

Lessing J. Rosenwald's joint gift of his book and graphic art collections to the Library of Congress and the National Gallery of Art, initiated in March 1943 in the depths of World War II and completed at his death in 1979, is one of the great acts of cultural philanthropy in the history of the United States. The Library of Congress has had no greater benefactor. Although this was a gift divided by intention between two national institutions, Rosenwald himself saw the prints and printed books as parts of a unified collection, formed according to his developing tastes and preserved as such in his lifetime in his home, Alverthorpe, in Jenkintown, Pennsylvania.

The scale of the gift can be expressed concisely. Rosenwald gave about twenty-six hundred rare books to the Library of Congress, about twenty-two thousand prints to the National Gallery, and a fine reference library divided between the two. But this does not remotely indicate the importance of the donation. As many exhibitions in Rosenwald's lifetime and after have demonstrated, even small samples and relatively narrow themes selected from the whole are invariably of interest and of imposing quality. Had Rosenwald made only much smaller gifts to either institution—only the block books, or only the Blake collection, or only the fifteenth-century prints—still their rarity is such that these would have been milestones of quality. The present exhibition catalogue reinforces the point, based as it is only on Rosenwald's purchases at the 1946–47 auction sales of the printed books of C. W. Dyson Perrins. One valuable feature of this selection is that it enables us to observe Rosenwald as an independent collector, exercising his own judgment.

Most accounts of Rosenwald's book collecting have been dominated by the story of his relations with his great "mentor and tempter," A. S. W. Rosenbach, fifteen years his senior and the preeminent American book dealer of his age. The Rosenbach connection was unquestionably the sine qua non for Rosenwald's book collecting. In his decades on the stage, Rosenbach sold books to a galaxy of major American book collectors—Henry Huntington, Henry Clay Folger, Herschel Jones, Arthur Amory Houghton, Frank Hogan, Estelle Doheny, the J. Pierpont Morgans, father and son, and their formidable librarian Belle da Costa Greene, and many others. With an incomparable talent for publicizing himself, Rosenbach often seemed to stand at the center of the galaxy. Among these many figures, Rosenwald was Rosenbach's favorite customer and valued friend. Rosenwald was, indeed, one of the few among his clients—Frank Hogan was another—who was truly a friend, with whom Rosenbach could relax and show the most attractive, least assertive side of his oversize personality.

By the time of the Dyson Perrins sales, however, Rosenbach was on the decline: seventy

Figure 1. Lessing J. Rosenwald. Portrait by Gardner Cox, 1955. National Gallery of Art, Washington, D.C. Image © Board of Trustees, National Gallery of Art.

years old, in ill health, and generally low in spirits. The Rosenbach firm handled Rosenwald's bids at the sales as it had done at all major auctions for many years, but Rosenbach in his own right played no leading role. At this stage, Lessing Rosenwald had already formed a great library, and well knew it; and had himself gained a considerable knowledge of the history of book illustration from the fifteenth century to the twentieth. When the Dyson Perrins catalogues reached him—in four sales from June 1946 to June 1947—Rosenwald was able to study them with care, and consider which items, among many treasures, would add most to his collection, a collection already promised as a national gift.

Rosenwald never met Dyson Perrins, and it is impossible to say what the two would have thought of each other. Nonetheless, there are undeniable broad similarities between them. Both were unassuming gentlemen endowed with a strong sense of public responsibility. The wealth of both came from enterprises that are, in the English-speaking world, household names. For both, the personal pleasures of collecting were joined to a lifelong philanthropic spirit.

## ANTECEDENTS

Lessing Julius Rosenwald was born in Chicago on February 10, 1891, the eldest of five children of Julius Rosenwald (1862–1932) and his wife Augusta Nusbaum (1869–1929). Julius, born in Springfield, Illinois, in a house just a block away from Lincoln's house, was the son of a German-Jewish cloth merchant who had emigrated from a small town in Westphalia. His father had begun as a peddler and then bettered himself by marriage into the family of the Hammerslough Brothers, clothiers in Baltimore. Julius, too, went into the clothing business at an early age, not completing high school. His wife's family was in the same trade. It is said that Lessing was named in honor of Julius's good friend Lessing Rosenthal, a young civic-minded lawyer, later a trustee of the Brookings Institution and of Johns Hopkins University. At about the time Lessing was born, Julius told a friend that his ambition was eventually to earn $15,000 a year, dividing it by thirds between family expenses, savings, and charity.[1]

The remark was presumably made while Julius's crystal ball was still cloudy, before he descried in it the emerging figure of Richard Warren Sears, the young president of the Sears, Roebuck Company. Sears, a native of Stewartville, Minnesota, showed a remarkable salesman's talent from the time of his first job as a local station agent for the Minneapolis and St. Louis Railroad, where he developed a sideline in selling inexpensive watches. As the sideline grew, Sears moved to Chicago and in 1887 he took in as junior partner Alvah Curtis Roebuck, a young watchmaker from Indiana. In the early 1890s, Sears extended his catalogue sales line from watches and jewelry into broader areas: sewing machines, saddlery, wagons and buggies, and the new craze, bicycles. The company developed, somewhat chaotically, into a general mail-order business focused especially on America's expanding farming community, similar to that of the slightly older company of Aaron Montgomery Ward. The Sears, Roebuck catalogue of 1891 was a pamphlet of 32 pages; that of 1894, a close-packed book of 322 pages; and of 1895, of 507 pages. Sears's genius was for advertising. He wrote his copy with a kind of apostolic fervor, aimed and able to convince his rural readers of his determination to bring them good quality, returnable merchandise at prices far below what their nearest general stores, with much smaller stocks, could offer. Efficient order fulfillment was not his strength.

Julius Rosenwald first met Sears when the latter came to his shop to make bulk purchases of men's suits, one of the new special promotions of Sears, Roebuck. Julius's brother-in-law Aaron Nusbaum, who had made considerable money from a soda and ice cream concession at

Chicago's Columbian Exposition of 1893, also knew Sears. In the summer of 1895, Alvah Roebuck, who was worried about his health, wanted to cash in his share of the business. Sears, Rosenwald, and Nusbaum made an agreement whereby the three of them would each buy one-third shares in the company, valued at $50,000 each. Julius's investment came not from cash, but from the writing down of Sears, Roebuck's unpaid bills for clothing ordered from Rosenwald and Company. Roebuck retired, content with a payment of $25,000 for his share, which, if he had held on to it, would have soon grown to many millions.

In the next decade, from the powerful combination of Sears's marketing talents and a much-improved management overseen by Rosenwald, the company expanded dramatically, from net sales of $2.8 million in 1897 to more than $50 million in 1907, and more than $100 million in 1914. In 1901, Sears and Rosenwald combined to buy out Nusbaum's share of the company, at twenty-five times the original investment. In 1906 Sears, Roebuck went public, and through Lehmann Brothers and Goldman, Sachs, some $9 million in common and preferred stocks was sold. Over the course of a dozen years, Julius Rosenwald became a man of great wealth.[2]

Rosenwald's early stated belief in the obligation of charity had not been pro forma. He increasingly gave his time and money to an endless stream of good causes, both in Chicago and nationally. His greatest single interest was in creating opportunities for education and improved public health for southern African Americans, who were disenfranchised from the political arena of their states and suppressed in countless other ways. Eventually, his financial support, joined with much local support, led, for instance, to the construction of some five thousand "Rosenwald schools," as they were unofficially called, in the South. Julius Rosenwald did not have the wealth of a Carnegie or a Rockefeller, though it is said that he gave away more than $60 million in his lifetime. It was his practical philosophy of giving that marks him out as perhaps the most original and independent-minded of America's great philanthropists.

On one hand, Julius Rosenwald did not believe in anonymous donations, for announcement of the names of donors could encourage emulation from others. When he had a good cause to promote, he was tireless in soliciting help, sometimes bluntly, from his many friends in the business world. On the other hand, he did not approve of permanent monuments and was insistent that buildings and institutions not be named after him. Even more strongly, he argued, with many examples, that permanent charitable foundations brought in almost as many problems as they solved, that their mission and ability to respond to new needs deteriorated under the desire to nurture their endowments prudently. Each American generation, he believed, would bring forth new philanthropy, and we should not try to lay a dead hand on the future. The Julius Rosenwald Fund was instructed to spend its endowment within twenty-five years of his death, and it succeeded in less than twenty. Now, more than two generations later, the visible footprints of Julius Rosenwald's extraordinary public spirit have been mostly erased.

Lessing Rosenwald acknowledged his father as the formative influence on his own life. He studied at Cornell for several years but left before graduation to join the Sears, Roebuck Company, where he began in the shipping department, on his way to learning at first hand every facet of the complex company. When only twenty-one, he married Edith Goodkind, who became his partner in every endeavor. They had five children, and in almost sixty-seven years of marriage lived to see many grandchildren and great-grandchildren. In World War I Rosenwald served as a seaman in the navy. In 1920, he and his family moved to Philadelphia, where he took charge of a new branch plant.[3]

To this point, Sears, Roebuck had been based in Chicago with branch distribution plants only in Dallas and Seattle. The move to Philadelphia was in part a response to the changing demographics of America. An ever greater proportion of the population lived in urban areas, and the Northeast was the most urbanized region of the country. A larger company response to the same demographic change in the course of the 1920s was a movement to open retail stores, a move paralleled by Sears's now smaller competitor, Montgomery Ward. When Julius Rosenwald died in early 1932, Lessing was named chairman of the board. He directed the company for seven years before taking early retirement in 1939, giving himself more time to devote to a wide variety of philanthropic activities. All five of Julius's children inherited the charitable spirit of their parents.

## The Beginning Collector

It appears that Lessing Rosenwald first visited the Rosenbach book firm on Walnut Street in Philadelphia in 1922, when he acquired a couple of "modern firsts" by Stephen Crane, and several reference works on prints. It was about six years before Dr. Rosenbach (he had a Ph.D. in English literature from the University of Pennsylvania) was able to tempt Rosenwald into serious collecting. He declined to buy a Crane autograph manuscript offered him at $175, nor did he bite when Rosenbach sent him catalogues of major book sales.[4]

Rosenwald's print collecting, at first his dominant interest, likewise developed slowly. By his own memory, his first serious art print was a 1916 etching of the newly built Royal Scottish Academy by the artist D. Y. Cameron, who later designed Rosenwald's first bookplate. Until about 1928, Rosenwald concentrated on fashionable and accessible British, French, and American artists of the late nineteenth century and after: Cameron, James McBey and Muirhead Bone; Charles Meryon, Jean-Louis Forain, Francis Seymour Haden, and Whistler. Some purchases were made from Rosenbach, whose older brother Philip maintained a stock of prints, but more came from Charles Sessler's Walnut Street shop. (Despite their proximity, Philip imposed an iron curtain between the Rosenbach and Sessler firms.)

In the years from 1928 to 1930 Rosenwald began to give attention to the old masters, including, of course, Dürer and Rembrandt. He became an avid buyer at a series of important European print sales that presented unusually rich opportunities, where Charles Sessler's son Dick represented him. Later that year, Rosenbach finally succeeded in his reasonable argument that the collector of single-leaf prints should also collect important illustrated books, and he sold to Rosenwald a group of some dozen German woodcut-illustrated incunables (fifteenth-century printed books), including a good, tall copy of the most profusely illustrated of all incunables, the 1493 *Nuremberg Chronicle*. None was of high rarity, but together they began to create a foundation.

Shortly after this, Lessing Rosenwald came down with—in the words of Rosenbach's biographer, Edwin Wolf II—"a most virulent case of bibliomania." Over the course of 1929, Rosenwald's purchases from A. S. W. Rosenbach totaled well over $1 million, with a concentration on rare illustrated incunables and block books (the latter from the Holford collection) and on William Blake's illuminated books (from the collection of William A. White). This was in addition to continuing purchases of fine prints. In November and December 1929, Rosenwald's Dürer and Rembrandt prints were publicly shown for the first time at the Baltimore Museum of Art in two successive exhibitions. The stock market crash of October 1929 did not put an immediate end to Rosenwald's buying: on the last day of the year he spent— more precisely, committed himself to spending—almost $300,000 in Rosenbach's shop for a beautiful group of illustrated incunables.

Dr. Rosenbach's spell continued to work into the New Year. In early 1930, under the encouragement of Representative Ross H. Collins of Mississippi, the U.S. Congress was considering the purchase for its Library, at a price of $1.5 million, of Dr. Otto H. F. Vollbehr's collection of some three thousand incunables, including a complete copy of the Gutenberg Bible printed on vellum. But passage of Collins's bill was far from certain, and Vollbehr himself, who had been trying to find an American buyer for his collection for several years, was overextended and anxious. He had borrowed $25,000 from Rosenbach, putting up a select group of his incunables as collateral. Rosenbach suggested that Lessing's father might want to buy the collection as a gift to some Chicago institution, but this was not remotely the kind of idea to appeal to Julius Rosenwald.

In March 1930, Rosenbach and Lessing Rosenwald evolved together another plan. Vollbehr did not actually own the Gutenberg Bible: he held a long-term option to buy it for about $300,000 from its owners, the monks of Sankt Paul im Lavanttal, in Austria. Rosenbach and Rosenwald took out an option on the option: if the Library of Congress did not purchase the Bible, Rosenwald would buy it for $400,000. As the year went on, however, the value of Sears, Roebuck stock steadily declined from its 1929 high of nearly $150 per share, and Lessing Rosenwald's personal finances worsened accordingly. (The stock's decline bottomed out in 1932 at about one-seventh the value of its 1929 peak.) It must have been a great relief to Rosenwald in the early summer of 1930 when the great Vollbehr purchase was finally approved by Congress and the appropriations bill was signed by President Herbert Hoover. Nonetheless, Rosenwald still had notes due to Rosenbach of hundreds of thousands of dollars which he could not immediately pay. Sessler similarly held overdue notes from Rosenwald.

For five years Rosenwald remained in debt to the firm of Rosenbach; his final obligations were not discharged until the end of 1935. It is the strongest evidence of the two men's friendship that it continued throughout and beyond this difficult period, when it would have been so easy, and even expected, for mistrust and embarrassment to have developed. Not until 1936 did Rosenwald's serious collecting begin again, but now with a greater degree of self-control. There can be little doubt that this debt and forced suspension of collecting, brought on by his own enthusiasm, were never forgotten, and made him consider more closely how he could justify his expensive avocation. His 1945 essay "The Formation of the Rosenwald Collection" puts the matter thus:

> Strange as it seems, the collector must be forever rationalizing what he does, not to someone else, but to himself. Rationality is to collecting what conscience is to life. He knows that for any number of reasons his scope must be kept within reasonable bounds, and he also knows that his acquisitive propensities will not recognize limits and boundaries.

One may hazard a guess that for Rosenwald, there remained an aura of moral danger in the great private pleasure he derived from collecting and from studying his acquisitions. He was conspicuously generous in exhibiting his books and prints and in making them available to students at all levels from school groups to scholars, but some necessary rationale remained to be found.

In 1939, the year of his retirement from Sears, Roebuck, the Rosenwalds' new house, Alverthorpe, in Jenkintown, was completed, with a separate gallery carefully designed for the storage, viewing, and study of the print and book collection, which were brought into one place for the first time. In connection with this, Rosenwald realized also that he needed a curator, and on the recommendation of his longtime friend Paul Sachs of the Fogg Art Museum, he hired a young Bryn Mawr graduate, Elizabeth Mongan, whose older sister Agnes was on the staff (and eventually became director) of the Fogg. It was a more than happy decision. Elizabeth, who like her sister became a distinguished and productive art historian, remained at Alverthorpe as curator until 1963.

In 1940 the Free Library of Philadelphia held an exhibition commemorating the (supposed) 500th anniversary of the invention of European printing; the catalogue was written jointly by Elizabeth Mongan and Edwin Wolf II of Rosenbach's shop. Apart from Joseph Widener's copy of the Gutenberg Bible (donated to Harvard in 1944), all the exhibits except nine anonymous loans came from Rosenwald's shelves. The anonymous loans were Rosenbach stock, and the two finest among them—the 1459 Durandus of Fust and Schoeffer and the 1460 *Catholicon* of Johann Gutenberg—were bought by Rosenwald a few years later.

Nineteen forty marked the beginning of the blackest years in Europe's history. May saw the retreat of the British Expeditionary Forces from their last foothold, Dunkirk; June, the collapse of the French army; and the rest of the summer, the air Battle of Britain, as Hitler and his general staff planned for an imminent invasion of the island. Germany and the Soviet Union were still "friends" under the 1939 Nonaggression Pact. In these months, Rosenwald joined the board of the anti-interventionist America First Committee, whose most prominent spokesman was Charles Lindbergh.

Rosenwald was virtually the only prominent Jew on the committee. He may have been partly influenced by his longtime colleague and friend General Robert E. Wood, the committee's chairman. Wood, who had been quartermaster general of the army in World War I, was a brilliant businessman whom Julius Rosenwald had recruited from Montgomery Ward in the 1920s, as Sears, Roebuck expanded into retail. Wood became president of Sears, Roebuck in 1928 and succeeded Lessing Rosenwald in 1939 as chairman of the board.

Rosenwald's involvement with America First was brief; he resigned from the board before the end of 1940. The committee dissolved in December 1941 immediately after the Japanese attack on Pearl Harbor, and the declaration of war against Japan, Germany, and Italy. Like most other America Firsters, once war was declared, Rosenwald was determined to contribute his services, just as his father had done in the First World War. He joined the War Production Board, where he was named as director of the Bureau of Industrial Conservation. In 1942 and after, he began to spend much of his time in Washington, D.C.

Rosenwald's new responsibilities caused a temporary slowing down in his book acquisitions. In 1941 he added twenty-seven important incunables. Among these was the illustrated edition of William Caxton's *Game of Chess,* which had been in the library of his and Rosenbach's mutual Philadelphia friend A. Edward Newton, a genial bibliophile and enthusiastic chronicler of *This Book-Collecting Game,* in whose pages Rosenbach was prominently featured. Photographs of Rosenbach and Rosenwald sitting together at the first Newton sale at Parke-Bernet in New York on April 16, 1941, have been reproduced several times. In 1942 and 1943, the number of incunables Rosenwald acquired dropped to eight and six respectively.

Still, it was in 1941 that a new and important element in Rosenwald's collecting began. He began to meet German-Jewish dealers who had been able to emigrate to New York and, under difficult conditions, resume their careers there. At least so far as early printed books are concerned, all of Rosenwald's acquisitions from 1941 until the end of the war were made either from Rosenbach or from various of these "gentle invaders," in the phrase of Bernard M. Rosenthal. Among them were Bernard Rosenthal's father, Erwin Rosenthal (1889–1981), a brilliant art historian; William H. Schab (1888–1975); Otto Ranschburg (1899–1985); and H. P. Kraus (1907–1988), all of whom became important figures in the American rare book world.

In these early years, they were struggling for customers. Kraus, a man of driving ambition who in the postwar period became the nearest equivalent to Rosenbach in the generation before him recalls in his memoirs that in 1941, two years after his arrival in New York, he found it almost impossible to make money as a bookdealer. He was recently married, and his wife's father, a prosperous businessman, was not reluctant to express doubts about the new son-in-law. But in November 1941, Lessing Rosenwald agreed to see Kraus, who drove down to Alverthorpe with an assortment of good books, mostly taken on consignment from other dealers. During the visit, his wife Hanni stayed outside in the car. Rosenwald looked through the pile, examined each quickly and put aside a group of interest, asked their price, and immediately wrote a check for $4,500. The sale was the first real success of Kraus's American career.

During his time in Washington, Rosenwald became more closely acquainted with both the National Gallery of Art and the Library of Congress. The National Gallery, the gift to the nation of Andrew Mellon (1855–1937), was a new institution. Its stately building opened in 1941, and apart from Mellon's own magnificent collection of paintings, its holdings were at that time sparse. There was hardly a print collection at all, save for scattered individual gifts, including, already, some from Rosenwald. But Rosenwald was impressed by the museum's director, David E. Finley. The Library of Congress, by contrast, was a venerable library and a great one in many collecting areas, including early printing, especially since the 1930 purchase of Otto Vollbehr's incunables. On the other hand, the Library's holdings were relatively weak in just the area where Rosenwald's library was extraordinary: book illustration. The acting chief of the Rare Book Collection, Frederick R. Goff, was only in his mid-twenties, and looked even younger, but he had a considerable knowledge of early printing and an informed enthusiasm about rare books of all periods. Goff and Rosenwald soon became friends, and Rosenwald later wrote that Goff shared with Rosenbach "the major credit for bringing to me the great pleasure of collecting books and learning about them."

It was surely Rosenwald's confidence in both Finley and Goff, in addition to a more abstract patriotism, that led to his decision, formalized in March 1943, to give his prints to the National Gallery—essentially creating an important new department—and his books to the Library of Congress. All parties benefited from the arrangement that Rosenwald would keep the collections at Alverthorpe during his lifetime, where they would be available to scholars, whose visits Rosenwald always welcomed. The collections would be exhibited in Washington. Thus Rosenwald was able to maintain the full pleasure of the collector who builds on the context of his library and to add to this the sense of purpose he had been searching for. His collecting would also be for the permanent benefit of the United States.

From this time on, Rosenwald bought only books not already in the Library of Congress. The terms of the original gift envisioned, but of course could not require, that Rosenwald would add to his gift. Periodically, as his acquisitions continued, Rosenwald made more donations, the final gift being made in the spring of 1978. The first gift of between four and five hundred books was immediately celebrated with a joint exhibition of Blake material at the National Gallery.

In 1944 and 1945 Rosenwald added another twenty-seven significant incunables to his collection and, in the first months of 1946, an additional fifteen, continuing to rely on Rosenbach and the gentle invaders. Then, in May 1946, he received the Sotheby's catalogue for part 1 of "the Magnificent Library principally of early printed and early illustrated books, formed by C. W. Dyson Perrins, Esq.," to be sold in London on June 17–18. The first sale was devoted to Italian books, with future sales announced of early books, mostly illustrated, from other countries.

## C. W. DYSON PERRINS

Charles William Dyson Perrins, born in 1864, is not, outside book collecting circles, a name widely known in America. And yet, as Rosenwald once pointed out, his name is in another sense highly familiar, for he was by descent the Perrins of Lea & Perrins, creators in the early nineteenth century of the "truly authentic" Worcestershire Sauce (in Britain called Worcester Sauce) with its mystery ingredient, a condiment whose bottle has for more than 160 years been seen in restaurants and on kitchen shelves. Though this was the source of the family's considerable wealth, Dyson Perrins had a much greater involvement in another local firm of high reputation, the Royal Worcester Porcelain Company. After education at Charterhouse in London and at Queen's College, Oxford, and four years as an officer in the Highland Light Infantry, Dyson Perrins returned to Worcester and joined the board of Royal Worcester.

By every account, Dyson Perrins was a shy and quiet man, devoted to country sports and to art. He was also a steady, generous benefactor to many communities and institutions. In Oxford, his name lives in the Dyson Perrins Laboratory, a major center of scientific research. Without Dyson Perrins, the Royal Worcester factory would perhaps no longer be in business. Several times over the decades he made substantial loans to the company when there were financial crises. In 1926, he bought at a large figure the company's fine collection of old Worcester porcelain, but left the collection in place (both it and Dyson Perrins's personal collection are preserved in Worcester's Porcelain Museum by his gift). More than once, when business slowed, he made up the wages of Royal Worcester employees out of his own pocket. Finally in 1934, when the company went bankrupt, he bought it outright. The proceeds of the sale of his printed books in 1946–47 went toward re-equipping the factory, which in World War II had been converted mostly to manufacturing insulators, resistors, and other electrical parts necessary to the war effort.

Dyson Perrins assembled his collection of early printed-book illustration and of illuminated manuscripts primarily between the ages of forty and sixty. He had been seriously collecting for at least several years before he made two foundational en-bloc purchases in May 1906 and January 1907 that brought the library to a new level, both of which were negotiated by Thomas Hodge of Sotheby's. The first was some 650 or more illustrated books collected by Richard Fisher and his son of the same name, the second a group of about 30 illuminated manuscripts collected by Charles Fairfax Murray (1849–1919), a self-made artist and close friend of William Morris who had an exceptional eye in many areas of collecting but was perennially overextended.[5]

After World War II, it was not difficult for Dyson Perrins to decide to part with his printed books but to retain his manuscripts. He wrote to his friend Dr. Eric Millar of the British Museum that for him "illuminated manuscripts are living things . . . and are of constant interest, whereas printed books are dead!" His manuscript collection, grown to 135 volumes of highest quality, was sold after his death by Sotheby's in three sessions, 1958–60, still remembered as one of the most spectacular manuscript sales in the firm's history. Dyson Perrins bequeathed to the British Museum what was perhaps his finest medieval manuscript, the early fourteenth-century Gorleston Psalter, together with a Persian calligraphic masterpiece created for the Mogul emperor Akbar in 1595.

Little has been written about the collector Richard Fisher (1809–1890), of Midhurst, Sussex, but in his lifetime he was a highly respected print connoisseur, active in London's Burlington Fine Arts Club, where socially accepted artists and respectable collectors met. He had the doubtful honor of being secretary of the club in 1867, the year Whistler was elected, then lobbied against by his brother-in-law Francis Seymour Haden (who accused him of personal assault), asked to resign, and finally expelled. In 1879 Fisher issued a privately printed *Catalogue of a Collection of Engravings, Etchings, and Woodcuts,* an unusually handsome and well-made volume for its time. He included among the lists of his prints a selection of his early illustrated books, most of which can be identified two generations later in the Dyson Perrins sale catalogues.

Even less seems to be known about the son Richard C. Fisher (1841–ca. 1907?), who sold his father's prints at Sotheby's on May 23, 1892, but retained and added to the printed books. R. C. Fisher was married to Kate Cobden. Kate's father was the English reform politician Richard Cobden, born in 1801 near Midhurst. Cobden had gone bankrupt in the 1840s, but his popular reputation was so great that large public subscriptions were raised in his relief and comfortable portions were set aside for each of his five daughters. One daughter was married to the publisher T. Fisher Unwin (no relation to Richard Fisher), another to the artist Walter Sickert, and another to T. J. Sanderson, who after the marriage took the name Cobden-Sanderson and found his métier as a fine bookbinder and printer.[6]

It is unclear whether it was the senior or junior Fisher to whom Sickert referred in a letter to Whistler of the late 1880s, giving a little warning to "Dear Jimmy" that "Mr. Fisher of Hill Top, Midhurst" had recently bought two proofs of a Whistler etching for one pound and then resold them for more than seventy pounds.

When R. C. Fisher went to Sotheby's to sell his books, an auction catalogue was issued, announcing the sale for May 21–24, 1906. Several months before that date, an article in the London *Times*—which must have been in fact a paid advertisement—spoke glowingly of the collection, of its interesting heritage, and of R. C. Fisher as "himself a bibliophile of fine taste." The owner, however, hoped throughout that a private sale would be made. Hodge had already shown his skill as a private negotiator. His greatest coup had come in 1902, when he sold Richard Bennett's medieval manuscripts and early printed books, including a major portion of William Morris's library, to Pierpont Morgan at a price of £130,000, providing a considerably greater profit to Sotheby's than the total of all its auctions that year had done.

In these years, the British fine art and rare book community was increasingly vexed with the idea that Americans like Morgan and Henry Huntington were buying up the national heritage. Put another way, when Britons had heritage to sell, their hopes turned increasingly toward America. It is likely that both the owner and Hodge at one time had an idea that an American buyer for the Fisher books would be found. It has been recorded that Fisher "bombarded" Hodge with anxious letters, first fearing that the books would after all go to the uncertainties of an auction, and then, after the sale to Dyson Perrins was fixed at something over £10,000, claiming that Sotheby's had taken too large a commission, a point on which Hodge was able to put him right.

Dyson Perrins did not make a full catalogue of his printed books as he had, in 1920, of his illuminated manuscripts—a scholarly, lavish, and now rare and expensive work. He did, however, engage A. W. Pollard of the British Museum to undertake the Italian section. *Italian Book-Illustrations and Early Printing . . . in the Library of C. W. Dyson Perrins* was published by Oxford University Press in 1914 in a limited edition of 125 copies. Like everything Pollard turned his pen to, it is at once scholarly and so beautifully written that all the labor of learning that underlies it is thoroughly disguised. Lessing Rosenwald, of course, owned and was well acquainted with Pollard's monograph, and at least the Italian section of Dyson Perrins's library would have been well known to him many years before the sale was announced.


## AFTER WORLD WAR II

The Dyson Perrins sales were the first truly major book auctions to be held in England in the post–World War II era. During the war years, Sotheby's had continued to hold sales of books and of works of art, but under restricted conditions of all kinds. Many of the staff were in war service—the highly capable book cataloguer A. N. L. Munby, later librarian of King's College, Cambridge, and eminent historian of book collecting, had been captured at Calais in the days before the Dunkirk evacuation, and spent the war in a German camp outside Eichstätt. The owners of valuable property had little incentive to send their works to auction during the war years when, among other discouraging elements, American participation was much reduced.

Thus, the giant "Hawking, Hunting, and Fishing" library of Colonel C. F. G. R. Schwerdt had been offered by Sotheby's in four sales in May to July 1939, but the final portions were deferred until the war was over, being sold in March and July 1946. At the March session, Rosenwald bought one important but imperfect book for £640, the woodcut-illustrated *Livre du Roy Modus* printed in Chambéry in 1486, of which the only other copies surviving are at the British Library, the Morgan Library, and the Musée Condé in Chantilly. Rosenwald had also successfully bid on an important Ulm woodcut book at a Sotheby's sale of May 1942, but it stayed in London until 1946, when it was shipped together with his Dyson Perrins purchases.

Against the background of the sales of the five or six preceding seasons, the Sotheby's reference to the "Magnificent Library" of Dyson Perrins was both a publicity statement and a species of fact, for there was a house tradition of trying to be reasonably careful with adjectives, according to an implicit hierarchy: "interesting" and "rare" meant little, nor did "famous" commit to much. "Valuable" meant more, and "important" much more. "Magnificent" stood above all.

Rosenwald had previously done relatively little bidding at auctions, although he did recall with pleasure attending, with Rosenbach, the first Clumber Library (Duke of Newcastle) sale at Sotheby's on June 21, 1937. On that day, immediately after lunch, he succeeded in capturing five of the thirty-four lots, including a block book *Ars moriendi* and Valturius's *De re militari* printed in Verona in 1472, one of the most visually powerful of all incunables—spending close to $24,000 in just a few minutes. That sale too had been "magnificent" in the semiofficial Sotheby's nomenclature, and the word was accurate.

The Dyson Perrins sales were the first auctions since Rosenwald had begun his serious collecting that offered precisely the kind of books he most wanted to buy, many of which were rare enough that this was the first time he had seen them on the market. Various records in the Rosenwald archives, including his carefully marked copies of the catalogues themselves, enable us to follow in some detail the process by which Rosenwald assessed each sale and worked out his priorities and bids. That the first portion in particular, the Italian books, caught his imagination is indicated even on the cover, where he wrote in purple pencil "Lessing J. Rosenwald, His catalog."[7]

In what seems to have been the first stage, Elizabeth Mongan made notes on the majority of the lots, including a separate listing of all the Savonarola editions and their woodcuts, with references to A. W. Pollard's catalogue and to Paul Kristeller's *Early Florentine Woodcuts* (1897). A number of these editions were already at Alverthorpe, some were in the Library of Congress, and those without woodcuts were set aside. Mongan occasionally suggested "bid?" and Rosenwald added "Bid" or "Bid?" to others, but all this was tentative. Shortly after, through Rosenbach, Rosenwald requested estimates on about sixty-five of the lots, almost a quarter of the sale. The Anglo-American auction houses at this time did not print estimates, which were supplied on request. Not until the early to mid-1970s did the major auction houses, first Sotheby Parke-Bernet in New York, in the fall of 1972, and then Sotheby's and Christie's in London, in fall 1975, begin to print auction estimates either in their catalogues or as inserted leaflets.

The Dyson Perrins estimates reached Rosenwald in the form of an unsigned typed copy of a telegram from London. The source would have been the Sotheby's cashier, Henry Rham, a longtime employee who for some years had been Rosenbach's liaison on Sotheby's matters: a demanding responsibility. After the war, when Munby was asked if he wanted to take over the job from Rham, he replied, with a few other pointed words, "Never!"

The telegram to Rosenbach from Rham began: "CONDITION OF PERRINS BOOKS DISAPPOINTING ON THE WHOLE AND THERE ARE NO RESERVES STOP MANY COMMISSIONS RECEIVED FOLLOWING ESTIMATES ON THE LOW SIDE." The wording indicates the complexity of Rham's dual role. No auction house employee should ever comment on the lot reserves, that is, the amounts, set by the consignor, below which the lots would not be sold. These first estimates seem to have been Rham's own, not those of the book department, and many were so low as to be unhelpful. It appears that Rosenbach did not go into details on their source, for Rosenwald treated them in other of his notes as "outsider" estimates.[8]

The mediocre condition of Dyson Perrins's printed books has become so much a part of their continuing reputation among bookdealers and collectors that it is worth adding that this was not a universal feature. There were also many books in unusually fine condition, including important historical bookbindings. Generally speaking, the poorest copies were those that had been collected by the elder Richard Fisher, and the best, those purchased by Dyson Perrins as individual items. For Richard Fisher senior, early illustrated books had been an interesting and, for his time, enterprising comparative supplement to his single-leaf prints, which he held to a much higher standard. When Fisher was buying his early printing he would not have had heavy competition, for the dominant taste among British incunable collectors was for classical editions, early presses, and Caxtons. William Morris is often thought of as the pioneer British collector of early woodcut books, but Fisher preceded him by a full generation.

In one respect, the tradition of collecting of Fisher's day undoubtedly damaged the books. It was accepted that the "right" binding for a gentleman's library was full morocco by Zaehnsdorf, Riviere, or one of the other fashionable London binderies. Many incunables were disbound, the leaves bleached and heavily pressed ("thorough chemical laundry-work," in John Carter's phrase), and margins trimmed to produce smooth edges that could be gilded. Signs of ownership from the earlier bindings and their endleaves were typically lost. At the stage of rebinding, it was common for any missing leaves to be supplied in either expert pen facsimiles or, increasingly, photographic reproductions printed on antique papers, which might be artificially "aged" to blend in better with the authentic leaves. As a very rough rule, the Dyson Perrins books in pre-1800 bindings were decidedly better copies than those in nineteenth-century bindings.

Curiously, at the time the Dyson Perrins Italian sale was approaching, A. N. L. Munby wrote anonymously about the "Role of the Book Auctioneer" in the *Times Literary Supplement* (March 23, 1946). An earlier anonymous reviewer, the London dealer Percy Muir, had written scathingly about the Parke-Bernet cataloguing of Frank Hogan's library, and Parke-Bernet had answered with an injured defense, to which Munby's contribution was an independent supplement. Munby's letter is a brilliant distillation of good advice, and those with experience in auction cataloguing will undoubtedly find their ears burning at some point or another as they read it, for instance, "Except in the case of almost unknown books, comment is usually best confined to the particular copy, its provenance, &c.: literary disquisitions and promotional hyperbole are out of place." He summarized the central responsibility of the book auction catalogue as "to enable the potential purchaser to identify the book without fear of error and to give as accurate a picture as possible of the condition of the copy offered."

The Dyson Perrins catalogue tried to do just this: besides notices of missing leaves, there are numerous notes of "leaves remargined," "many leaves defective," "many of the plates shaved," woodcuts "slightly defaced," "water-stained," "shaved at fore-edge and mended," and so on. There are relatively few "blurbs," or footnotes, as they were called at Sotheby's. One of Rosenwald's eventual purchases, lot 236, is a collection of four Florentine *rappresentazioni,* of which the earliest, possibly of 1500 or before, is unique. That is, still, in 2004, it seems to be unique. (See item 26.) But the catalogue does not remark on this, in accordance with Munby's dictum, "to describe a book as 'unique' is the surest way of conjuring up a second copy within six months." Still, practically speaking it is impossible for every lot of a sale to be given a fully detailed condition report, nor is it a simple matter to use words to convey the factor that contributes most to the "life" of a copy: the quality of its paper, including the size of its margins. At any book sale, no matter how detailed the catalogue's condition notes, there is no substitute for close examination by an experienced dealer. Rham summarized this as "MOST OF DEFECTS NOTED BUT USUALLY A FEW OMITTED."

Rosenwald always tried to maintain a high standard of condition in his books, and he credited Rosenbach for enforcing this. Yet it is clear that in the Dyson Perrins sales, and particularly the first sale of Italian books, he decided to go below his standard in acknowledgment of the great rarity of many of the books. He adjusted for condition primarily by the limits he put on his bids. One book in particular was for Rosenwald a highest desideratum: lot 106, the September 1, 1495, Florence folio edition of the *Epistole et Evangelii et lectioni volgari,* that is, Gospels and lessons of the mass, heavily illustrated with woodcuts mostly commissioned specifically for the edition. It is said that it was the presence of this book in the Fisher collection that had determined Dyson Perrins to make his en bloc purchase, rather than risk losing it at auction.

The Fisher copy of the *Epistole et Evangelii* had all the defects noted above — washed and ironed and trimmed for gilt edges by the binder Riviere, with a leaf missing, the title leaf mounted, and other leaves with defects. But it is the major "anthology" of Florentine book illustration of the fifteenth century, and one of two surviving copies, and here Sotheby's so committed itself in its footnote in large and small capital letters: "ONE OF ONLY TWO COPIES KNOWN. The other, in the Bibliotheca Corsiniana at Rome, is also imperfect, wanting the last two leaves." (In fact, that copy lacks four leaves.) Dyson Perrins had published a facsimile of the woodcuts in his copy, with a preface by Pollard, through the bibliophile Roxburghe Club in 1910. Rham's estimate on the lot was £3,000, equivalent to $12,000. On her first list Elizabeth Mongan had noted "defective, but bid?" and Rosenwald added "Bid."

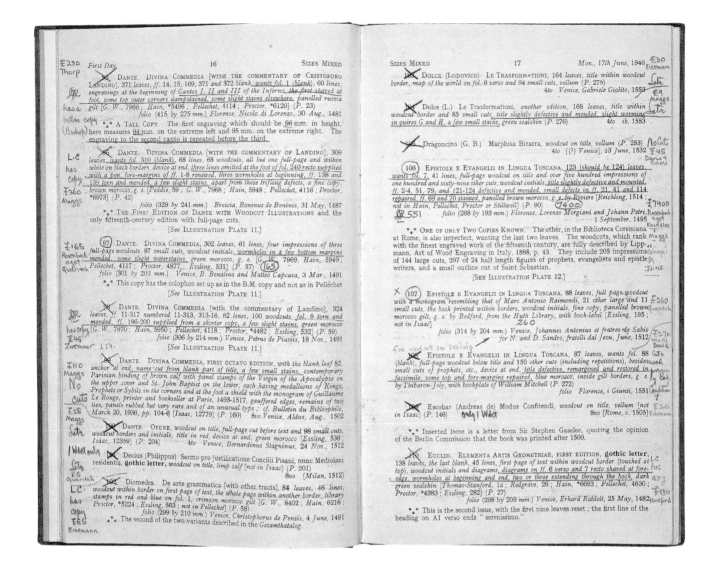

A complication in the process of decision arose at the end of May 1946 when the collector Philip Hofer wrote to Rosenwald, via Elizabeth Mongan, suggesting that "the New York Public, you and ourselves . . . avoid overlapping bids in the Dyson Perrins sale." He wrote Karl Kup, curator of the Spencer Collection at New York Public Library, to the same effect, and further suggested, "I don't think that the Morgan Library or the Metropolitan Museum are likely to be large competitors." Hofer was a Harvard graduate who, after some years in the family coal business, was financially able to devote himself to the collecting of art and books, though never with the ample means of Rosenwald. At his twenty-fifth Harvard reunion, a week before the Dyson Perrins sale, he wrote, "My hobby, books, has turned into a profession." Hofer planned that his book collections should go to Harvard's Department of Printing and Graphic Arts—in fact, his personal department, to which he had already made important gifts —though the arrangements were and continued to be much more complex than Rosenwald's with the Library of Congress.[9]

Hofer's eye was legendarily sharp, and so was his personality. Rosenwald was happy to place his trust in dealers whom he liked, fully understanding that they—and Rosenbach in particular—often made strong profits on their sales to him. When, as happened a few times, he came to believe that a dealer did not deserve his trust, Rosenwald simply stopped buying from him. Consciously or not, he was following the advice of the seventeenth-century jurist

FIGURE 3. Pages 16–17 from the *Catalogue of the Magnificent Library Principally of Early Printed and Early Illustrated Books Formed by C. W. Dyson Perrins, Esq.*, the first portion, Sotheby & Company, London, June 17–18, 1946. Lessing J. Rosenwald Archive, Library of Congress.

and collector John Selden: "The giving a *Bookseller* his price for his *Books* has this advantage, he that will do so, shall have the refusal of whatsoever comes to his hand, and so by that means get many things, which otherwise he never should have seen." (To which Selden added, "So 'tis in giving a Bawd her price.")

Hofer was more adversarial. A dealer's fixed price acted on him like a gadfly's sting. When dealers saw him entering their shops, they knew he would ferret out, rapidly judge, and per- haps buy their most interesting books, but they did not necessarily discover that they had a song in their hearts. Rosenwald admired Hofer and was agreeable to trying to work out some noncompetitive arrangement, but he would have well understood that there was more in this for Hofer than for himself. In principle, curbed only by his own "rationality," Rosenwald could buy any lot he wanted. If he laid off a lot in favor of Hofer, that was a real advantage to the latter: one of the world's wealthiest collectors would not be bidding. If Hofer laid off a lot in Rosenwald's favor, that would not necessarily affect Rosenwald's chances.

Rosenwald appears to have suggested consulting also with the Morgan Library, for in a letter Hofer sent him by special delivery on June 6, that library was still much on Hofer's mind. "I have had one thought," he wrote, ". . . I doubt if the Morgan Library will do anything at the sale if they aren't stirred up by the feeling that others are being very active. Miss Greene is ill and tired, as you know. The Morgans haven't been buying much and only a spirit of compe- tition would arouse them now. Wouldn't we be wiser to let 'sleeping dogs lie?' This may be the wrong psychology and yet after working there three years I honestly think that maybe it isn't." Unstated is that Hofer's years as assistant director at the Morgan Library, 1934–37, had been stormy ones. He may have expected that Belle Greene would soon retire as director; she had no such intention. Finally there was a crisis. Its details are unknown and perhaps in essence amounted to no more than the clash of two exceptionally strong wills, but Greene more or less forced Hofer to leave, and the unpleasant incident stayed with him.

By Saturday, June 8, Rosenwald had received notice of the lots in which Hofer and the New York Public Library expressed interest. Hofer had also contacted Henry Rossiter, curator of prints of Boston's Museum of Fine Arts, who was keen on two lots. Rosenwald's own desid- erata created eleven conflicts with Hofer, six with the New York Public Library, and one with the Museum of Fine Arts. Rosenwald and Hofer talked on the phone, and decided who would lay off which lots in roughly even division. The most significant of these were the 1495 *Epis- tole et Evangelii* and the Venice 1494 illustrated *Italian Bible* (lot 46), both which were left to Rosenwald; and the Florence 1568 edition of Boccaccio's *Ninfale fiesolano* (lot 51), for which Hofer's bids would have priority. Rham had treated this last as a minor book, with an estimate of £30, and the official book department estimate was even less. But as Hofer and Rosenwald well knew, it is a work of high interest. Its woodcut series was cut in the late fifteenth century, strongly implying that there had been a now-lost illustrated incunable edition of the same work. (The surviving incunable editions of the *Ninfale,* all rare, are without illustration.)

By Monday, Hofer wrote Rosenwald again, somewhat apprehensively. He told Rosenwald "in deepest confidence, of course" his bid-limits on the lots Rosenwald had ceded to him. He was worried, however, that if Rosenwald gave higher bids on these to Rosenbach to be exe- cuted only when Hofer's limit had been surpassed, Rosenbach might "feel inclined to keep the bidding open," that is, to bid earlier against Hofer so as to get to Rosenwald's bids. Hofer also reported that Henry Rossiter was upset to learn of the conflict with Rosenwald on lot 285, the 1484 Rome edition of the *Meditationes* of Juan de Torquemada (or, Johannes de Turrecremata; see item 9). This very rare edition is of great importance: its woodcuts were first used in an even rarer Rome edition of 1467 that is one of the first illustrated books to be printed in Italy.

Hofer's remarks on lot 8 are also of interest. One of the finest lots in the sale, it was a collected volume in contemporary Florentine binding of an Italian edition of the *Imitatio Christi* and of twenty-one Savonarola tracts. Rosenwald had been tempted by this wonderful survival, but his notes indicate that he finally decided not to bid, apparently because the Library of Congress already owned several of the tracts, he owned several others, and yet others were without illustration. The Savonarola volume appeared, however, on the New York Public Library's want list and Hofer wrote, "I am now trying to get a private collector to stay off #8 Savonarola for the New York Public Library! . . . (I, of course, ceded it to them some time ago.)"

Rosenwald had his own conflict with the New York Public in lot 53, a Venice 1487 edition of the Italian *Meditationes vitae Christi*. This rare work, which Dyson Perrins had added to his Fisher purchase, uses woodcuts from an Italian block book that survives in a single imperfect copy in Berlin. Rosenwald's notes, apparently written after discussion with Karl Kup, indicate that in this case he would not defer. Rosenwald was also in close touch about the sale with Fred Goff at the Library of Congress. Very unusually, the Library of Congress put in bids on various lots through Rosenbach—surely one of the few times the Library had bid at auction —and succeeded in acquiring seven items that closely complemented Rosenwald's acquisitions. In fact, all of Rosenbach's purchases at the first Dyson Perrins sale were on commission from either Rosenwald or the Library of Congress except one lot that he bought for the history of science collector Harrison D. Horblit.

Shortly before the sale, Rosenbach cabled Rosenwald's bids and instructions to Rham for execution. Rosenwald gave in bids on fifty-six of the lots, and succeeded in buying twenty-six of these. Rosenwald's notes show that he went through several stages of estimating his bids, increasing those on a half-dozen major items. In principle—that is assuming he succeeded in each bid at its maximum—he was prepared to spend, including his 10 percent commission to Rosenbach, about $115,000 at the first sale. Rosenwald did not rely to any very great extent either on Rham's estimates or on the official estimates from the Sotheby's book department. Among the lots he lost, a number of the bids were quite modest, suggesting that he would not and did not seriously regret their absence from his library.

The bidding at the first Dyson Perrins sale proved to be very strong and broad-based. The sale total came to just under £46,000, that is, something over $180,000 (the exchange rate was four dollars to the pound), which was surely well beyond Dyson Perrins's most sanguine expectations. Rosenwald's buying was the single greatest factor: the hammer price of his purchases came to 30 percent of the sale total, and he was the underbidder on four or five other significant lots. The *Times Literary Supplement*'s reviewer, anonymous but almost certainly John Carter, was censorious, writing in the July 5, 1947, issue: "There was a great deal of wild and ill-informed bidding, especially in the first (Italian) section." Such normative comments on auction sales tend to age very quickly. In the nature of things, book and art auctions do not operate according to pure reason and cool calculation; the expectation that they should is unrealistic. It is true that, as the reviewer notes with regard to relatively common books, imperfect copies at this sale sometimes sold for considerably more than perfect copies had before the sale. But it should also be noted that the "wild and ill-informed bidding" came almost entirely from the most respectable and experienced bookdealers, and part of the presumed obligation of these dealers, if they bid on behalf of customers, was to give good advice. In any case, this particular point did not apply to Rosenwald's purchases: whatever he paid for them, none of the books he bought can be called common.

By far the highest price of the sale, and Rosenwald's most important acquisition, was the 1495 *Epistole et Evangelii*. Rham's original estimate had been £3,000, but in view of the wide

| Number | AUTHOR | TITLE | PUBLISHER | Year | Cost | REMARKS |
|---|---|---|---|---|---|---|
| 51 | Benedetti, Elpidio | Essequie di Anna d'Austria | Rome: 1666 | | ARX LR | Kraus |
| 52 | Justiniano, Leonardo | Laude Devotissime | Venice: Bernardin di Vidali | 1517 | EOX RO | " |
| 53 | | Speculum Humanae Salvationis | Lyons: Husz | 1483 | OLWN WE | " |
| 54 | | Horae | Paris: Pigouchet | 1498 | RXAYnA | Kraus Rötte — |
| 7/1/46 55 | J. Simon after J. Verelst | Four Kings of Canada | | | JKnz | Rosenbach. |
| 56 | Ligne, Prince de | Fantaisies Militaires | | 1780 | SKZ | " |
| 7/13/46 57 | Pulci, Luca de | Pistole in rima al Lorenzo de' Medici | Florence: Piero Pacini | n.d. | RNX | Schab |
| 58 | Aesop | Fabulae | Venice: manfredis de Bonellis | 1483 | RWEO | Djoon Perrins |
| 59 | | Apocalipsis Jesu Christi | Venice: Alexander de Paganinis | 1515 -1516 | | LWW. |
| 60 | Ariosto | Orlando Furioso | Venice: Francesco de Franceschi | 1562 | | JJJ- |
| 61 | Augustine | Sermoni devotissimi in lingua Fiorentina | Florence - Miscomini | 1493 | OJX. AL | |
| 62 | Berlinghieri | Protesto alla Signoria di Firenze | Florence: B. dei Libri | [1495] | RAR. XN | |
| 63 | | Biblia Italica | Venice: Johannes Rubeus | 1494 | OOOX LS | Perrins |
| 64 | Bonaventura | Meditazioni sopra la Passione del nostro Signore | Venice: Lazarus de Soardis | 1497 | RNN SW | " |
| 65 | Cometus de Latis | Anuli per eum compositi | [Rome: Andreas Freitag. 1493] | | JEE SS | " |
| 66 | | Breviarium Romanum | [Venice: Giunta 1507] | | JWW NE | " |
| 67 | Calandri, Filippo | Aritmetica | Florence: L. Morgiani | 1491 | JEJY XK | " |
| 68 | Alighieri, Dante | Divina Commedia | Venice: Benalius, Capcasa | 1491 | WOK Az | " |
| 69 | | Epistoli e Evangeli in Lingua Toscana | Florence: Lorenzo Morgiani Johann Petri | 1495 | ORA NE. AE | " |
| 70 | | Evangelium Sanctum Arabica | Rome: Medici | 1591 | SSS JK | " |
| 71 | Fantis, S. de | Theorica et Pratica de Modo Scribendi | Venice: Johannes Rubeus | 1514 | ANN XS | " |
| 72 | Qualla, Jacobus | Sanctuarium | Pavia: Jacobus de Burgofrancho | 1505 | RJX US | " |
| 73 | Guillermus | Postilla super Epistolas et Evangelia | Venice: J. Pentius | 1505 | JWW NE | " |
| 74 | Fregoso, Baptista | Anteros | Milan: L. Pachel | 1496 | OJLNU WX | " |
| 75 | Jerome | Vita di sancti padri | Venice: Otino de Luna | 1521 | SAA | " |

interest it attracted, either Rham or the book department increased this to £5,000. In his notes, Rosenwald steadily increased his planned bid, from £5,600 to £6,750 to £7,600. When it fell to him at £7,400 (the underbidder was the art dealer Knoedler & Company), he had come close to his stated limit. From other lot results it is clear, however, that Rham had a certain discretionary power to go beyond Rosenwald's maximum. This was probably looked on as "overage" from the notional savings on lot 46, the 1494 *Italian Bible* printed in Venice, which Rosenwald got at £750, well under the Sotheby's estimate of £1,200. He had been ready, if necessary, to bid up to £2,750, his highest bid after the *Epistole et Evangelii*. Here there probably was a benefit from the consultation with Hofer, for both men were interested in this very rare book. No copy has appeared on the market since the Dyson Perrins sale.

A word or two should be said about the Dyson Perrins prices of 1946–47. It is natural to wonder how those figures compare to what the same or similar copies would bring today, but there is no simple answer. There is, in fact, a fair amount of information available in the form of Dyson Perrins copies that have come back to the market in more recent auction sales, but each book has its own result, and it is far from clear that averaging a number of such results produces a meaningful multiple. The most conspicuous comparison is Dyson Perrins's copy of the Gutenberg Bible, the first volume only but in wonderful condition. This was offered in the third sale, March 10–11, 1947, and brought the highest price of the sales, £22,000 or $88,000. A few years later it was acquired by Estelle Doheny, who left it by bequest to St. John's Seminary in Camarillo, California. In 1987, when the seminary sent the Doheny books to Christie's in New York, the volume sold for just under $5.4 million, a multiple of sixty times the 1947 price. On the other hand, a well-preserved Paris book of hours that in the second Dyson Perrins sale, November 1946, was sold for £120 or $480, eventually passed into the collection of Otto Schäfer (1912–2000) of Schweinfurt. When it was offered in London in June 1995, with a low estimate of £8,000 or $12,800, it attracted no bidding at all. The following year, reoffered in New York, it sold for $4,600, less than ten times what it brought in 1946. In this case, the feature that its 1995 cataloguer found most interesting, that it was the only copy known printed on paper rather than vellum, was almost eccentrically arcane and had no resonance whatever with potential buyers.

In preference to attempting an extrapolation into the present, it may be more helpful to give an orientation according to book prices and wages of the time. The time in Great Britain was not an easy one: under the new Labour government and its mandate of a "planned social democracy," wartime restrictions were increased, not loosened. Queues were long, shop shelves notoriously empty. A month after the first Dyson Perrins sale, rationing on bread was introduced, partly the result of obligations to ship wheat for the German population in the British occupied zone. The continuing restrictions made themselves visible even in the Dyson Perrins catalogues, with their cramped layouts on cheap paper, stapled together, though in the limited illustrated issue, the plates are fine velvety collotypes on good stock.

Two New York auction prices of 1946–47 for books very different in nature from Dyson Perrins's provide yardsticks on the larger scale. In April 1946, Parke-Bernet sold a copy of the 1623 Shakespeare First Folio, in the final portion of its Frank Hogan sale, for $50,000. This copy, now in a European private collection, is exceptionally large-margined and fresh, one of the finest among the more than two hundred surviving copies. The price was high, and yet was notably less than the same copy had brought at Sotheby's in the Earl of Rosebery sale in June 1933, where Hogan, through Rosenbach, had paid $72,500 plus commission. No other copy of comparable condition has since appeared at auction; a lesser but complete copy was sold at Christie's, New York, in October 2001 for nearly $6.2 million.

FIGURE 4. Rosenwald Inventory Book, dated July 1946, showing purchases at the Dyson Perrins sale. Lessing J. Rosenwald Archive, Library of Congress.

In January 1947, Parke-Bernet offered a copy of the so-called *Bay Psalm Book,* published in Cambridge, Massachusetts, in 1640, the first book printed in British North America. It went to Rosenbach, who was bidding for Yale University, for $151,000, an auction record for a printed book that held up for many years. The episode caused considerable unhappiness. The book would have been Rosenbach's at about $92,000, but then Cornelius Vanderbilt Whitney, one of the trustees of the consignor, entered the bidding, something that today would not be allowed. Because Rosenbach exceeded Yale's limit by so much, he ended by making, in effect, a gift of more than $45,000 to the university. *The Bay Psalm Book* is of great rarity, and no copy has been on the public market since then, to test the 1947 result.

These figures, gigantic for their time, might be compared at the lower end of the scale to British librarians' salaries—salaries that were, for that matter, comparable to those of most employees of Sotheby's in these same years. Contemporary advertisements show library assistant positions being offered at annual salaries of from £180 to £260, sometimes with a cost of living bonus depending on location, and sometimes with the rate reduced if the applicant was a woman. Cambridge's public library sought a deputy librarian at £420, a chief librarian for Great Yarmouth was offered £480 plus a cost of living bonus, and a particular plum was the librarianship of the Royal Institute of British Architects, at £750. In various town boroughs, professional and senior clerk's positions were posted at salaries around £440, and assistant solicitor's positions at £535. The Public Record Office sought an assistant keeper with an honors degree for £250, and "somewhat lower" for women. The chancellor of the exchequer, Hugh Dalton, recommended that stipends of members of parliament should be increased from £600 to £1,000 per annum.

After the first Dyson Perrins sale, Hofer sent his results, through Betty Mongan, to Rosenwald. He had succeeded in getting ten lots, plus "a better copy of No. 72 from the man who did the bidding for me." It is worth noting that this menial-sounding personage was E. P. Goldschmidt (1887–1954), generally accepted as the greatest of all scholar-bookdealers. Both Hofer and Rosenwald failed on lot 51, the 1568 *Ninfale fiesolano.* Rosenwald deferred to Hofer up to the latter's limit of £310, and then began his own bids, but ended up as underbidder to the firm of Davis & Orioli, which got it at £440. Both men later succeeded in finding copies: Rosenwald acquired a copy (not Dyson Perrins's) from Davis & Orioli in 1950 and Hofer, a very fine copy, formerly the Prince d'Essling's, from Tammaro de Marinis in 1957.

At the New York Public Library, Karl Kup, bidding through Maggs, succeeded with three good incunables for the Spencer Collection, none of which had conflicted with Hofer's or Rosenwald's want lists. Boston's Museum of Fine Arts had no chance with lot 285, the 1484 Rome *Meditationes* of Torquemada. It went to Rosenwald at £1,750, his second highest figure at the sale. It is doubtful that if he had stayed off the lot, the museum could have bid at this level. With regard to the Rosenwald-Hofer-New York Public Library plans, the fate of two other lots must be noted. Lot 8, the Savonarola tract volume, had been perhaps the most attractive single item on the library's want list, and Hofer volunteered that he was trying to dissuade another American collector from going after it. The lot went to the New York Public Library's agent, Maggs, at the high figure of £1,400, but as it turned out, the bidder was not the New York Public, it was the institution Hofer was most eager to freeze out, the Pierpont Morgan Library. An annotation in the Morgan Library's accession book indicates that the bid was made more or less clandestinely with the aid of the New York Public Library, that is, of Karl Kup, who had very friendly relations both with Belle Greene and with the Morgan's keeper of printed books, Curt F. Bühler.

Also prominent on the New York Public Library's want list was lot 53, the 1487 Venice

*Devote meditatione sopra la passione* with woodcuts cut up from an earlier block book. In this case, Rosenwald did not defer to the library. He bid strongly but lost as underbidder to E. P. Goldschmidt, to whom it was knocked down at £1,300—again, as it turned out, on behalf of the Morgan Library. It is likely that when Rosenwald discussed the conflicting wants with Karl Kup, the latter discreetly indicated, without giving a name, that he knew of other interest in the lot, for in Rosenwald's notes next to this lot is written "Another Bidder." The Morgan Library also apparently put in a strong bid on lot 285, the 1484 Rome Torquemada, where Rosenwald's notes indicate "Another 'Stout' Bidder." The lot went to Rosenwald at £1,750, far above the Sotheby's estimate, but in this case the Morgan Library would not have had a chance: Rosenwald's limit was many bids above that figure. Nor was it a tragedy for the Morgan, which already owned the Rome editions of 1473 and 1478, both using these same woodcuts. Belle Greene may have been "ill and tired," but she was still a clever and powerful presence in a world that operated mostly as a men's club, and she was fiercely devoted to the Morgan Library.

The 1487 *Devote meditatione* is very rare. In 1967 another, slightly inferior copy came into the hands of H. P. Kraus. It may have been offered to Rosenwald, but by that time, in view of his responsibilities to his many grandchildren, he had considerably moderated his collecting (when he told this over lunch one day to Fred Goff, the latter offered to pick up the tab). In any case, it was purchased rather by Otto Schäfer, whose refined taste as a collector almost uncannily mirrored Rosenwald's. Schäfer, too, had begun with prints, and then gradually moved into early illustrated books after he bought a copy of the 1493 *Nuremberg Chronicle*. When Schäfer's copy was sold at Sotheby's, New York, in December 1994 (where it was mistakenly identified as the Dyson Perrins copy), it brought over $250,000 and returned to Italy.

One book that Rosenwald lost stayed in his mind: lot 197, a rare and richly illustrated 1497 Venice edition of Ovid's *Metamorphoses* in Italian, of which there was no other American copy. This lot was not on Hofer's want list, perhaps because he knew that by this point in the sale, if he had had any earlier significant success, he could not have afforded it. Rosenwald at first planned a very strong bid which would perhaps (taking into account Rham's license to advance one or two bids beyond the maximum) have been successful. Then a post-catalogue announcement notified bidders that the first leaf, with title page and preface, was a facsimile, and Rosenwald reduced his bid by several hundred pounds. In the salesroom the copy went to Maggs at £1,600. There must have been residual regret, however, for in 1949 Rosenwald bought an even more imperfect copy from Rosenbach, a very unusual occurrence, and one that Rosenbach himself would not have recommended. Equally curious—for the 1497 Ovid truly is a very rare book—is that in 1948 Hofer found another, complete copy at Davis & Orioli in London and was able to acquire it for about two-thirds of what the inferior Dyson Perrins copy had brought. He kept it in his private collection until his death, when it went to Harvard by bequest. As for the Dyson Perrins copy, it seems to be currently lost from sight.

Three Dyson Perrins sales followed: part 2, November 4–5, 1946, with Spanish, French, and Netherlandish books; part 3, March 10–11, 1947, with German books; and part 4, June 9, 1947, with a small group of English books. Rosenwald made significant additions from all three, although none, nor even the three together, had the importance for the development of his library that the Italian books had. Nor, it seems, did Rosenwald get involved again in the complicated arrangements and calculations that the coordination with Philip Hofer had required for the first sale.

At the first sale, including commission to Rosenbach, Rosenwald had spent just short of $68,000 for twenty-six lots. At the three remaining sales combined, he spent a little over $61,000 for a total of forty-three lots. In the second sale, among thirty lots acquired, Rosenwald's most costly purchase at £1,350 hammer price was an illustrated *Bible historiée* published in 1517 by the heirs of Antoine Vérard, described in the sale catalogue as unique and hitherto unrecorded. In fact, in partial confirmation of Munby's dictum, it survives also in copies at the Rylands Library in Manchester, the Bibliothèque de l'Arsenal in Paris, and two French provincial libraries. In terms of enriching the range of Rosenwald's early book illustration, the second sale's greater interest was in its twenty-five lots of Spanish book illustration, of which Rosenwald was able to get eight lots at the sale and one, for which his bid was unsuccessful, the following summer. Rosenwald's bids allowed Rosenbach to make a very respectable showing at the sale; he had no other customers. Maggs Brothers spent a little more, £8,660 to Rosenbach's £8,500, but this was spread over some seventy-eight lots.

Rosenwald had no need to be concerned with the two most expensive lots in the second sale. A very rare Paris 1492 *Danse macabre* went to Maggs, who were bidding for the Swiss collector Martin Bodmer, at £2,800. But Rosenwald already owned an immaculate copy of the 1490 Latin version, from the same press and using the same woodcuts, which he had bought from Rosenbach in 1937. The second highest price was a copy of the Paris 1488–89 first edition of the *Mer des histoires,* which was sold to Maggs at £1,650, but in this case there was already a copy at the Library of Congress in the John Boyd Thacher collection.

It should be kept in mind that the Dyson Perrins sales by no means consumed all of Rosenwald's book-buying interests or budget in 1946–47. In the area of early printing, he continued to acquire important individual books from dealers, almost exclusively Rosenbach and the gentle invaders. Most striking of all was his purchase of a book he would have had in his eye for many years, an early sixteenth-century London binding containing, in unusually fine condition, four Caxton folios printed between 1479 and 1481, which, immediately after he learned the results of the second Dyson Perrins sale, Rosenwald finally resolved to buy from Rosenbach.

This volume had first come to light at a Sotheby's auction in 1909, where it was captioned as the property of a "Gentleman living in an old Manor House in the North." It later was owned by the Chicago coal magnate James W. Ellsworth, father of the dashing polar explorer Lincoln Ellsworth. In 1923 Rosenbach bought Ellsworth's library, including a Gutenberg Bible that he sold to John H. Scheide. He quickly passed the Caxton volume on to Charles W. Clark of San Francisco, son of Senator William Andrews Clark, the Montana mining millionaire. When C. W. Clark died in 1933, Rosenbach arranged to sell his fine collection on consignment from his widow, a long-drawn out process. Many former C. W. Clark books remained on the shelves until after Rosenbach's death, in 1952. Even in the late 1970s, some were in the stock of the Rosenbach Company's successor, John F. Fleming.

The price Rosenwald paid for the Caxton volume, $37,500, almost exactly equaled that of his thirty lots from the second Dyson Perrins sale. It was a favorite book of his, and Rosenwald delighted in showing it to visitors to Alverthorpe. Unfortunately, only after his death and the removal of the books to the Library of Congress was it discovered that the volume also contained, as sewing guards, fragments of several copies of a previously unknown vellum indulgence that Caxton had printed in 1480 to benefit the nearby hospital of St. Mary Rounceval in what was then the village of Charing Cross. No one would have taken greater pleasure in learning of the Caxton bonus.

The third Dyson Perrins sale, of early German books, an area in which Rosenwald already had great strength, did not, with some significant exceptions, include books of great rarity. Rosenwald spent a little over £2,000 in acquiring twelve lots, but a number of these were books that in principle he could have already acquired elsewhere or which would become available in years to come. A definite exception is lot 608, his most expensive acquisition at a hammer price of £420. It was a 1491 Ulm edition of a German vernacular book of hours, *Dye Siben Cursz,* formerly in the library of Franz Trau, auctioned in Vienna in October 1905. These German-language versions, of which only a handful of editions survive in a handful of copies, are of highest rarity. The 1491 Ulm edition is recorded in only one other copy, in the city library of Ulm, and that copy lacks all seven leaves with woodcuts. Rosenwald already owned a unique copy of *Dye Siben Cursz* printed in Reutlingen in 1492, which he had bought from Rosenbach in 1930. His two copies are the only incunable German books of hours in the United States—or for that matter, anywhere outside Germany. (See item 4.)

Two books that Rosenwald decided not to bid on should also be noted, for both touch on his collecting interests. Lot 564 was the first volume of the Gutenberg Bible, mentioned above, which Dyson Perrins had purchased at a hammer price of £2,050 at the Sotheby's auction of Lord Amherst of Hackney's library, in December 1908. Because Congress had purchased the complete vellum copy sold through Otto Vollbehr in 1930 and Rosenwald's library was itself now promised to the Library of Congress, he needed no longer to be tempted by Gutenberg Bibles. Rosenbach succeeded in interesting Estelle Doheny, but her bid of £19,200 fell short of being the underbid to Maggs's winning bid of £22,000—itself well under the Sotheby's estimate on the book. Maggs's customer was Sir Philip Frere. The Times Literary Supplement's reviewer of the sales, while noting that many of the finest items had gone to Rosenwald, was pleased to single out the Gutenberg Bible as one of the "rarities of the first rank that have remained in this country." It did not remain there for very long. Frere lost interest and in October 1950, through Maggs, the Bible was sold to Doheny for $70,000. Because of the 1949 devaluation of the pound sterling from $4.00 to $2.80, she paid less than if her 1947 bid had been successful, and Frere got his money back.

But the book in the sale that in principle would have interested Rosenwald most was lot 646, *Der Ritter vom Turn,* Basel, 1493. This German-language version of Geoffroy de La Tour Landry's fourteenth-century moral tales in French, which Caxton had translated into English and published in 1484, contains more than seventy very fine woodcuts that are generally accepted as being Albrecht Dürer's first series of book illustrations. The Dyson Perrins copy lacks a leaf, but the book is of high rarity. All other known copies are in Germany. Why did Rosenwald not bid? In this case, to reject it as imperfect would have made little sense. There are hints that he deferred out of friendship for Belle Greene and the Morgan Library. In his marked copy of the catalogue, Rosenwald first noted the lot with a question mark, which he later crossed out. At the sale, the book was knocked down to Rosenbach at £1,500, but on the commission of the Morgan Library, whose expected London agent at this time would have been E. P. Goldschmidt.

The Dyson Perrins books marked the most extensive auction buying ever done by Rosenwald, and they featured prominently in two exhibitions of Rosenwald's "Important Recent Acquisitions" that Fred Goff mounted at the Library of Congress in June 1947 and June 1948. The catalogue of the first exhibit contained a preface by A. S. W. Rosenbach. The central theme of Rosenwald's *Recollections* is that for him the friendships he formed with other collectors, dealers, scholars, and curators were the greatest pleasure of collecting. The Library of Congress is fortunate that Goff, whose knowledge and personality were so closely in harmony with Rosenwald's, was its head of rare books at the time of Rosenwald's first gift.[10]

The Library benefited from more than the gift of the books themselves. From 1943 onward, there are many signs that Rosenwald and Goff planned together and together looked to the long term. At the first Dyson Perrins sale, Rosenwald did not bid on the Savonarola titles, but the Library of Congress acquired two. In the next few years, Rosenwald bought a number of significant Savonarola editions, of finer quality than those in the Dyson Perrins sale, and the Library of Congress itself added many other less expensive Savonarola titles. As a result, today the Library's collection of Savonarola is second in this country only to Harvard's, which had the unsurpassable advantage of buying in 1921 the large collection formed in Florence in the nineteenth century by the American expatriate painter Henry Roderick Newman. Again at the Dyson Perrins sales, Rosenwald acquired three rare Aesop editions, while the Library of Congress added another.

It is to be hoped that this tradition continues. Book collectors well know that the acquisition of any one book almost always gives a reason why some other book, not previously thought of, should also be acquired. This continuing engagement with the implications of Lessing Rosenwald's choices is one of the important ways by which his unparalleled gift remains alive.

NOTES

*I am grateful to Daniel De Simone for constant help; to Dr. Hope Mayo (Department of Printing and Graphic Arts, Houghton Library) for answering several questions about Hofer's acquisitions; and to Dr. Roland Folter for searching out, from his own massive holdings of auction catalogues, the history of printed lot estimates in New York and London book auctions.*

1. See M.R. Werner, *Julius Rosenwald: The Life of a Practical Humanitarian* (New York and London: Harper & Brothers, 1939); Edwin R. Embree and Julia Waxman, *Investment in People: The Story of the Julius Rosenwald Fund* (New York: Harper, 1949).

2. For the Sears, Roebuck Company, see Boris Emmet and John E. Jeuck, *Catalogues and Counters: A History of Sears, Roebuck and Company* (Chicago: University of Chicago Press, 1950).

3. On Lessing J. Rosenwald, see his writings *Recollections of a Collector* (Jenkintown, Pa.: Alverthorpe Gallery, 1976); "The Formation of the Rosenwald Collection," *Library of Congress Quarterly Journal of Current Acquisitions* (hereafter *LCQJ*) 3, no. 1 (October 1945), pp. 53–62 (and other articles in that issue); and "The Mirror of the Collector," *LCQJ* 22, no. 3 (July 1965), pp. 160–69 (and other articles in that issue). See also Frederick R. Goff, "A Catalog of Important Recent Additions to the Lessing J. Rosenwald Collection . . . ," with a fore-

word by A.S.W. Rosenbach," *LCQJ* 4, no. 3 (May 1947), pp. 3–56, and Goff, "A Catalog of Important Recent Additions to the Lessing J. Rosenwald Collection . . . ", *LCQJ* 5, no. 3 (May 1948), pp. 3–51; William Matheson, "Lessing J. Rosenwald, A Splendidly Generous Man," *LCQJ* 37, no. 1 (Winter 1980), pp. 1–24; and Ruth E. Fine, *Lessing J. Rosenwald: Tribute to a Collector* (Washington: National Gallery of Art, 1982).

4. On A.S.W. Rosenbach (1876–1952), including his relations with Rosenwald, see Edwin Wolf II with John F. Fleming, *Rosenbach: A Biography* (Cleveland and New York: World Publishing Co., 1960); Kathleen T. Hunt (Mang), *Rosenwald and Rosenbach: Two Philadelphia Bookmen* (Philadelphia: Rosenbach Museum and Library, 1983); and Leslie A. Morris, *Rosenbach Abroad* (Philadelphia: Rosenbach Museum and Library, 1988).

5. On C.W. Dyson Perrins, see the entry in *Dictionary of National Biography, 1951–1960,* pp. 808–10 (David Rogers), and a brief memoir by Sir Eric Millar in the *Book Collector,* Summer 1958, pp. 118–20; see also Henry Sandon, *Royal Worcester Porcelain from 1862 to the Present Day* (London: Barrie and Jenkins, 1973).

6. Little has been written about Richard Fisher and Richard C. Fisher, but there is a brief entry on the former in Frits Lugt, *Les Marques de collec-*

*tions de dessins & d'estampes* (Amsterdam, 1921), nos. 931, 2204–5, and some further information can be found on the Web site of the Centre for Whistler Studies, University of Glasgow <http://www .whistler.arts.gla.ac.uk/>.

7. Lessing Rosenwald's accession book and marked copies of the Dyson Perrins sale catalogues are at the Library of Congress; his invoices from Rosenbach, correspondence with Philip Hofer, and other notes he made on the Dyson Perrins sales are at the National Gallery of Art.

8. On Sotheby's, including the private sale of the Fisher Library to Dyson Perrins, see Frank Herrmann, *Sotheby's: Portrait of an Auction House* (London: Chatto and Windus, 1980).

9. On Philip Hofer (1898–1984), see *Philip Hofer as a Collector* (Cambridge, Mass.: Houghton Library, 1988), with memoirs by William Bentinck-Smith, Lucien Goldschmidt, Charles Ryskamp, and Arthur Vershbow.

10. Frederick R. Goff (1916–1982) became assistant to the curator of the Rare Book Collection of the Library of Congress, Arthur A. Houghton Jr., in 1940. In 1941, Goff was named assistant chief and in 1943, acting chief. On March 1, 1945, he was appointed chief of the Rare Book Division, and he retired with that title in 1972.

# Venetian and Florentine Renaissance Woodcuts for Bibles, Liturgical Books, and Devotional Books

## LILIAN ARMSTRONG

IN ITALY IN THE LATE FIFTEENTH AND EARLY SIXTEENTH CENTURIES, there was an extraordinary outpouring of woodcuts designed to illustrate books of all kinds. Not least of these were the hundreds of woodcuts created for Christian Bibles and for devotional and liturgical books. Because these texts all center on events told in the Hebrew and New Testaments, the Renaissance illustrations produced for them in diverse centers show many similarities. Nevertheless, it is fascinating to study the traits that distinguish illustrations produced in two important Renaissance cities, Venice and Florence, with the goal of understanding their stylistic differences, while also appreciating their communality of religious intent.

FIGURE 1. *Epistole et Evangelii et lectioni volgari in lingua toscana,* printed in Florence by Lorenzo Morgiani and Johannes Petri for Piero Pacini, 27 July 1495. Title page with Saint Peter and Saint Paul in a central roundel. (See item 18, LC/R 298.)

## THE *BIBLIA ITALICA,* VENICE, 1494

Primary among all Christian texts is of course the Bible. One of the first books to be printed with movable type was the *Biblia latina* (Latin Bible) printed in Mainz around 1455 by the famed Johannes Gutenberg, and numerous Latin Bibles followed from presses in Germany and in Italy. In Italy, the first Latin Bible was printed in Rome in 1471 by the German printers Conrad Sweynheym and Arnoldus Pannartz. Bibles were also printed in vernacular languages in the late fifteenth century, especially translations into German and Italian. Interestingly, it is these editions of the Bible in vernacular languages that were the earliest to be illustrated with woodcuts.[1]

The first Bible printed in Italy that was fully illustrated was an Italian translation by the monk Nicolò Malerbì (Malermi, in the earlier scholarly literature), the *Biblia italica* printed in Venice in 1490 by Giovanni Ragazzo for the publisher LucAntonio Giunta.[2] This 1490 illustrated edition proved popular and was reprinted in 1492 and again in 1494. Fortunately, the Rosenwald Collection includes a rare copy of the 1494 edition, printed in Venice, this time by Johannes Rubeus, also for the publisher LucAntonio Giunta.[3] Observation of the woodcuts in this wonderful book can reveal the aesthetic qualities that were valued by Venetian patrons in the early period of book illustration.

The 1494 *Biblia italica* is printed in two columns of roman type as can be seen in the illustrated opening of the first chapter of Genesis (see item 17). At the beginning of the text is a square woodcut illustration of God the Creator, seated, surrounded by angels and holding an orb while he raises his right hand in a gesture of blessing. Partially obscured behind him is a capital letter *N,* the first letter of the words *Nel principio* (In the beginning [God created the

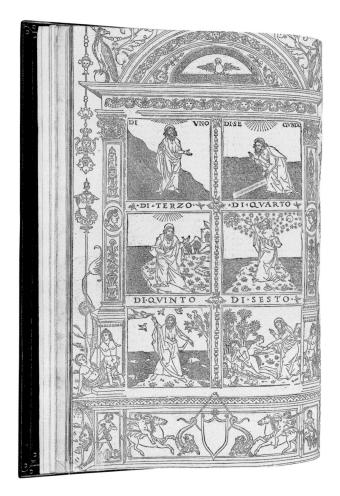

FIGURE 2. *Biblia italica,* printed in Venice by Johannes Rubeus for LucAntonio Giunta, June 1494, fol. a8v: Architectural frontispiece with Six Days of Creation, woodcuts designed by the Pico Master. (See item 17, LC/R289.)

heaven and the earth]). On the facing page (fig. 2, fol. a8v) are six small woodcut scenes representing God's work on the first six days of Creation. Framing both pages is an identical architectural structure, also a woodcut.

As these pages are analyzed, it is good to remember the processes of creating a woodcut.[4] An artist must first make a drawing on a sheet of paper sized to whatever area he wishes his design to fill. The drawing is traced onto a flat wooden block. A cutter then carves the block, cutting away everything except the thin ridges of wood that are the lines drawn by the designer. To produce an image, the surfaces of the raised ridges are inked and a piece of paper is pressed onto the inked surface. When removed, the paper will have received an image that is in reverse from the original design. For book illustration, the advantage of this process is that it is similar to that of printing type. The woodcut relief lines resemble the raised forms of the individual letters of type, and the block can be fitted into the same matrix that holds the lines of type. The type and the woodcut can be inked and printed simultaneously. Additionally, the woodcut can be reused on any page where there is a similarly sized area not filled with text.

With this brief technical explanation in mind, we can appreciate how sophisticated the printing of these two pages of the 1494 *Biblia italica* really is. The most striking duplication is the architectural frame, which has clearly been combined on the left-hand page with scenes of Creation, and on the right with columns of text.[5] Its parts are elegant. In the side margins are slender rectangular piers decorated with antique heads in profile. The piers terminate in scrolling capitals and support an entablature in turn crowned by a curved pediment. Eagles standing on spheres rest at the ends of the cornice, and dolphins slide down the sides of the curved pediment. Within the framing pediment is the image of a dove, the Holy Spirit, hovering over the waters. Strings of beads and fruit, punctuated with tiny heads, dangle beside the piers. Fanciful creatures, part human and part lion, perch before the tall bases; their dragon tails curl around the torsos of men who hold aloft poles that support Roman cuirasses. The entire structure rests on a broad base decorated with still other antique motifs. Satyrs play musical instruments, boys ride horses while blowing horns, and dragons flank an empty shield.

This description of the architectural border already indicates some predilections of Venetian patrons. To frame the beginning of Christianity's most sacred text with a plethora of motifs derived from classical (Greco-Roman) antiquity presumes that the buyer would not find the pagan allusions offensive. The Renaissance revival of classical culture was well enough established so that readers could enjoy classical art as a complement to their own education in classical literature and history, while still considering the religious content to be of supreme importance.

Within the woodcut frame on the left-hand page (fig. 2) are representations of traditional religious figures, God the Creator, Adam, and Eve. The viewer is directed to understand the images both through God's actions and by brief titles, *DI VNO, DI SEGVNDO, DI TERZO* (Day One, Day Two, Day Three), and so on. God the Creator is a slender figure dressed in long robes that nevertheless reveal the position of his body. The outlines of his figure and drapery are indicated with single, rather short lines, often set at sharp angles. The design and cutting make understandable the designation of such an image as an "outline woodcut." There are no curving modeling lines to suggest three-dimensionality or the fall of light. Movement is indicated by God's stance and gestures—bending over when he separates the waters from the heavens on Day Two, reaching to heaven when he creates the sun, moon, and stars on Day Four, actively grasping the arm of Eve to draw her from the side of sleeping Adam on Day Six. The surrounding ambience is created with a bare minimum of features. Closely cut wavy lines suggest the waters, a few tufts of grass indicate vegetation, and only when the effect of a verdant Eden is required are curiously sprouting trees included. The fragile nude figures of Adam and Eve are echoed by the nude boys on horseback in the base below. The overall effect is open and harmonious.

The style of the woodcuts of the 1494 *Biblia italica* and in many other books printed in Venice in the 1490s was called, by A. M. Hind, the "popular style," to distinguish it from other woodcuts in what he called the "classical style." More recently, the Popular Designer has been identified as the prolific book illuminator known as the Master of the Pico Pliny, or in shortened form, the Pico Master. The Pico Master was one of several artists working in Venice in the late fifteenth century who began their careers as illuminators of manuscripts, then turned to decorating individual copies of printed books, and finally became designers of woodcuts.[6]

FIGURE 3. *Biblia italica*, printed in Venice by Antonio di Bartolommeo Miscomini in 1477 (copy in Vienna, Österreichisches Nationalbibliothek, Inc. 5.D.22, fol. 11r); Architectural frontispiece with Six Days of Creation, drawn in pen and ink and tinted with watercolors by the Pico Master. Courtesy Bildarchiv d.ÖNB, Vienna.

The Pico Master's experience in decorating individual copies of printed books must have helped him in imagining designs for woodcuts in the 1494 *Biblia italica*. For the opening of Genesis in one copy of a *Biblia italica* printed in 1477, the Pico Master designed a similar combination of classical architectural motifs and scenes of the Creation (fig. 3).[7] The frontispiece is drawn in pen and ink and subsequently lightly tinted with watercolors, creating a delicate and almost impressionistic effect. In the side margins are columns that support an entablature, above which are semicircular elements flanking a central rectangular unit, in turn capped with a curved pediment. Within the areas defined by architectural elements are scenes of Creation. In the upper central scene of the Second Day—in which God separates the heavens above from the waters beneath—the standing figure of God clearly anticipates the 1494 woodcut image of God in Day Five. God stands erect, raising his right hand to point at the heavens and lowers his left to point to the waters, a pose appropriate both for the separation of the heavens from the waters (Day Two) and for the Creation of Birds and Fishes (Day Five).

Other strong similarities exist between the drawing of the Creation of Eve in the lower margin of the 1477 Bible and the woodcut counterpart in the 1494 Bible. By the late Middle Ages, artists had conflated the activities of God on the Sixth Day as described in Genesis 1:25–31, that is, the Creation of Animals and of Man, with the subsequent description of the Creation of Eve in Genesis 2:21–23. Both the 1477 frontispiece and the 1494 woodcut show God bending toward the sleeping Adam to draw Eve out of Adam's side. Not forgetting the animals, however, the Pico Master includes a rabbit and a deer in both compositions, tucking a lion's head into the edge of the woodcut as well.

Only one other opening in the 1494 *Biblia italica* rivals the illustrated Genesis opening. The same architectural border frames a woodcut scene and the text of the beginning of Proverbs

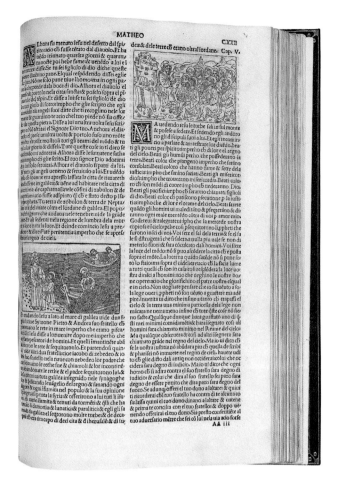

(fol. A1r). In the large woodcut, King Solomon is shown asleep, and again at his desk writing, both representations somewhat oddly appearing in a beautiful hall inscribed on its back wall, *AVDIENTIA* (Audience). The page demonstrates the versatility of the architectural woodcut border, used in the same book to frame a sequence of scenes, a page of text, and a page half filled with text and half occupied with another Hebrew Testament personage.

These elaborate pages are different in overall effect from several hundred other pages in the 1494 *Biblia italica* that have woodcut illustrations. There are 330 small woodcut scenes, each the width of one column of text, usually not more than one per page. It has been pointed out that 110 of the narrative scenes derive from the woodcuts of a German Bible printed in Cologne by Heinrich Quentell in the 1470s.[8] Although the Venetian designers certainly emulated the German compositions, they completely redesigned the figures, transforming their style from German to Italian. Furthermore, the remaining two hundred and more compositions do not depend on the Cologne prototypes and owe instead to the originality of the Venetian designers.

At least two miniaturists provided designs for the small woodcuts, the Pico Master and a more whimsical artist named the Master of the Rimini Ovid.[9] Turned over to cutters who were not yet always skilled at translating the designs into woodcuts, the images are sometimes crude, though vivid. On the page illustrated here, there are two such scenes: Christ Calling Peter and Andrew to be his disciples (Matthew 4:18–20) and Christ Preaching the Sermon on the Mount (Matthew 5–7), both designed by the Master of the Rimini Ovid (fig. 4, fol. AA3r). A single black line frames the scenes, and the figures are represented in the same outline style as in the Creation scenes. The narrative is made clear by the gestures and poses of the figures. Peter and Andrew are fishermen, so it is important to show their boat, or at least enough of it to be understood. The cutter's inexperience is shown in the blotchy effect of the fishing net, flatly blotting out the boat and visually clashing with the sea behind it.

In the Sermon on the Mount, Christ sits with his back to a jagged rock formation facing the tightly packed group of apostles from whom he is separated by a bit of landscape. Characteristic of the artist's style are the curiously rounded beards and the shaggy hair of the apostles, making their heads appear to be capped by piles of tiny twigs. Regardless of their unkempt air, the apostles gaze lovingly at Christ, demonstrating the artist's ability to convey emotion. The important point is made: Christ is speaking and the crowd is attentive. The reader in the fifteenth century would understand the image as an assist in finding his or her place in the sacred text, and also as an adequate evocation of the essential meaning of the event.

The decoration of another Venetian book in the exhibition is closely related to the 1494 *Biblia italica,* namely, Dante Alighieri's *La commedia divina* printed in Venice by Bernardinus Benalius and Matteo Capcasa, March 3, 1491 (see item 10).[10] A full-page woodcut faces a text page on which are the last lines of the *Purgatorio* and the beginning of the prologue of the humanist Christoforo Landino's commentary on the *Paradiso* (fols. B6v–C1r). The Pico Master designed both the Paradiso illustration and its architectural border, which is similar in style to that of the 1494 *Biblia italica* frontispiece.

In the *Paradiso* woodcut, Dante is first depicted walking on the ground toward a wooded area. Delicately outlined above the earth-bound poet, Dante is represented again with Beatrice, floating upward under the arching band of zodiac signs. Beatrice, alone at the upper left, ascends heavenward, about to pass through the spheres, which are symbolized by the zodiac signs and the stars (fig. 5). She is surrounded by an aureole of fine lines that announce her beatific state. The same unshaded outline style is used to delineate the architectural forms: columns support seated nude youths who hold classical vases and appear like caryatids on whose shoulders rests the cornice. Above the cornice are a handsome pair of seated lions and a pediment, which curves above a half-length image of God the Father. Dragon-tailed sphinxes, dolphins, profile busts, and winged putti all recall motifs found in the Pico Master's miniatures and other woodcut designs. Thus, the outline style of the 1494 *Biblia italica* frontispiece may be understood as one that printers easily adapted for works of secular literature as well as for more purely religious texts.[11]

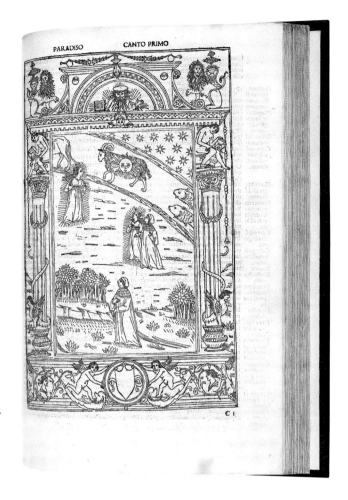

FIGURE 5. Dante Alighieri, *La Commedia divina*, printed in Venice by Bernardinus Benalius and Matteo Capcasa, 3 March 1491, fol. C1r: Architectural frontispiece for the *Paradiso,* with Dante and Beatrice, woodcut design by the Pico Master. (See item 10, LC/R260.)

## EPISTOLE ET EVANGELII, FLORENCE, 1495

The services or public rites of the Catholic Church are called the liturgy, and liturgical books are the books used by priests and monks for these services. All liturgical books contain excerpts from the Bible along with prayers, other devotional texts, and sometimes music, arranged for use throughout the year. Missals contain the texts for the mass; and breviaries contain the texts for the Divine Office, that is, the cycle of daily devotions performed by monks and clergy. Yet another liturgical book is called an epistolary and evangeliary (or lectionary), and contains the readings (lections)—from the Epistles and Gospels of the New Testament and from the Hebrew Testament—that were read at mass throughout the year.[12]

The Rosenwald Collection in the Library of Congress possesses an extremely important example of an epistolary and evangeliary, one of only two surviving copies of the *Epistole et Evangelii* in Italian, printed in Florence by Lorenzo Morgiani and Johannes Petri for the publisher Piero Pacini in 1495 (see item 18).[13] This 1495 *Epistole et Evangelii* is profusely illustrated with 144 narrative woodcuts, plus 24 smaller woodcuts with half-length images of saints and prophets, and a full-page frontispiece with standing figures of Saints Peter and Paul. All writers agree that the 1495 *Epistole et Evangelii* is the greatest Florentine illustrated book of the fifteenth century, yet surprisingly it has been little discussed in the recent scholarly literature.[14] Comparing the layout and woodcuts in this rare edition with those of the 1494 Venetian *Biblia italica* can help in understanding the differences between Florentine and Venetian illustrated books.

In contrast to the two-column layout of the 1494 *Biblia italica,* the Florentine *Epistole et Evangelii* text is laid out in a single block of handsome roman type (see item 18). A header in capital letters indicates the liturgical season, QVARESIMA (Lent), when the passages on those

FIGURE 6. *Epistole et Evan-*
*gelii,* printed in Florence
by Lorenzo Morgiani and
Johannes Petri for Piero
Pacini in 1495, fol. g4v
(XXXXVIv): The Fall of
Manna (text of Exodus 15),
Christ's Entry into Jerusa-
lem, and Saint Matthew
(text of Matthew 21);
fol. g5r (XXXXVIIr):
Christ Teaching the Apostles
(Matthew 26), woodcuts by
an anonymous Florentine
designer. (See item 18,
LC/R 298.)

pages should be read, and folio numbers are also shown in capital roman letters, hence XXXXVII
(47) on the right-hand page. Indented lines preceded by curved paragraph markers give the
precise book and chapter of the reading that follows and indicate the day on which it should
be read. Thus, in the middle of the right-hand page we can see: *Epistola di sancto Paulo a Philip-*
*pensi nel seco[n]do Capitolo: Dicesi ladomenica delle palme alla messa* (Epistle of Saint Paul to the
Philippians in the second chapter: Say [Read on] the Sunday of Palms [Palm Sunday] at mass)
(fig. 6, fols. g4v–g5r [46v–47r]).

Further emphasizing each reading is a large or small woodcut, or both. Each small square
woodcut contains a half-length figure of the saint who is the author of the following text, accompanied by an animal, figure, or object that identifies him. Saint Matthew's symbol is an
angel, and so Saint Matthew may be recognized by the presence of a small figure standing at
his shoulder (fig. 6). The evangelist appears twice in these pages, on the left holding a closed
book and on the right, an open book. Also on the right-hand page is Saint Paul, holding a
book and the sword with which he was martyred. Typical of Florentine woodcuts are the black
ground against which the saint is shown and the quatrefoil shape defined by a white line that
surrounds the saint, a shape echoing the frames of Andrea Pisano's and Lorenzo Ghiberti's famous bronze reliefs on the doors of the Florentine Baptistry.[15]

Most characteristic of Florentine woodcuts, however, are the narrative scenes in rectangular frames that illustrate the *Epistole et Evangelii.* Three of these scenes appear on the illustrated
opening: The Fall of Manna (Exodus 15; fol. 46v [g4v]), Christ's Entry into Jerusalem (Matthew
21; also fol. 46v), and Christ Teaching the Apostles (Matthew 26, Palm Sunday; fol. 47r [g5r]).[16]
All three scenes are enclosed by borders that are a hallmark of Florentine book illustration,
narrow bands of black edged with white lines and decorated with repeated white motifs. Fourteen different versions of these borders appear in the 1495 *Epistole et Evangelii.* Many of them
are variations of three-lobed leaves or buds, whereas others are more geometric, as in the angular ribbons around Christ's Entry into Jerusalem. Yet others appear to be strings of beads, either
circular disks or squares (figs. 6, 7). A variety of motifs fill the corners of the frames—square

crosses, rosettes with three, four, or six petals, and so on. It may seem that describing these subsidiary visual elements is excessive, but in fact, these borders provide one of the chief ways of identifying a woodcut illustration made for a Florentine book in contrast to one made in Venice or elsewhere in Italy.[17]

The narrative episodes of the 1495 *Epistole et Evangelii* woodcuts are also recognizably Florentine in style. Most distinctive are the figures outlined in fine black lines. Their white bodies and draperies contrast to the black backgrounds, and this contrast of white and black areas can be seen in all of the illustrated scenes. In the Fall of Manna, the overall composition is divided diagonally from lower left to upper right, with most of the figures set against the black ground. Moses stands at the right and five men and women kneel to collect the manna that miraculously falls from heaven. A standing woman closes the composition on the left. The black ground itself is patterned by white bits of manna in the lower half and by thin white parallel horizontal lines on the hill behind Moses.

The apparition in the heavens is created with thin curving black lines against the white ground. These delineate the half-length image of God, the clouds from which he emerges, and the oval shapes of the falling manna; and a few lines indicate distant mountains. A small detail suggests that the artist who drew the composition did not fully consider that it would be reversed when it printed from the carved wood block. God blesses the Hebrews with his left hand, when traditionally, the right hand would be held up in blessing. The "error" would occur, however, unless the artist had already reversed the position of the blessing hand before giving the design to the cutter.

The hill behind Jesus in the scene Christ Teaching the Apostles is similar to that behind Moses. The otherwise solid black is patterned with a web of parallel horizontal white lines, a pattern that extends all the way down to the area where Jesus and the apostles sit and stand. A technical reason helps to explain the practice of breaking up solid areas of black with lines of white. On close inspection, the handmade papers on which these books were printed show the lines of the fine wire sieve used in producing the paper. When a flat inked area of the wood block is printed on handmade paper, the shallow hollows between the ribs of paper do not receive the ink evenly, and an unwanted pattern of white lines appears. Modifying the wood block's surface with delicately carved lines mitigates the unwanted effect. In the woodcut Christ Entering Jerusalem, there are some small areas of solid black in the hills behind Christ, but even here the cutter has introduced a few white lines to avoid any problem in printing.[18]

It has long been recognized that some of the 1495 *Epistole et Evangelii* narrative scenes had already been printed in earlier publications. Eight of them, for example, were created for an edition of Saint Bonaventura's *Meditationes* in Italian, printed in Florence by Antonio Miscomini about 1493.[19] The illustrated pages include one of these slightly earlier narrative woodcuts, Christ's Entry into Jerusalem, and two that were created for the *Epistole et Evangelii* itself. The figure style of the earlier design shows somewhat stockier figures with cruder facial features and stiffer shocks of hair than in the two other woodcuts. The apostles behind Christ huddle together in a mass that is less well-defined than the clearly positioned figures in Christ Teaching the Apostles. The dimensions of the Entry into Jerusalem are also larger than the other two woodcuts, and the scene projects down into the lower margin to accommodate its larger size. These features verify the observation that the woodcut was originally planned for another text.

The figures in the Fall of Manna and in Christ Teaching the Apostles are more gracefully composed than those in the Entry into Jerusalem. All are outlined with black lines and most contrast to a dark ground. Drapery folds are elegantly indicated with gently curving lines, occasionally sharply angled for emphasis. Tiny loops enliven the ends of lines at elbows and knees.

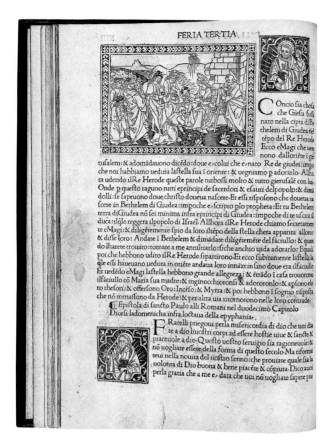

In the Fall of Manna, the designer has successfully shown a variety of kneeling positions. The young woman in front of Moses kneels on her left knee, keeping her right leg bent as she leans forward, her lovely profile outlined against the dark ground. The older men at each side kneel on both knees, each with one arm stretched toward the ground, one of them eagerly eating a bit of manna. Finally, the younger man in the dark hat appears in a foreshortened pose, his lower legs projected back as he leans forward.

These subordinate figures accentuate the commanding figure of Moses, who stands in an easy counterpoised position, his weight falling on his straight right leg, and his relaxed slightly bent left leg clearly suggested through the folds of his garment. The woman at the far left balances a basket of manna on her head. The pose is derived from classical figures but more immediately recalls one of the women at the left of Lorenzo Ghiberti's bronze relief of the Story of Isaac for the East Doors of the Florentine Baptistry, completed in 1452.[20]

In Christ Teaching the Apostles, the artist's challenge is to give authority to Christ while suggesting some individuality for the apostles. The first goal is accomplished by isolating Christ's head in profile against the dark hillside, and by representing his outstretched arm more rigidly than any other gesture in the scene. Six apostles stand in a semicircle around five seated peers, and one young apostle is more isolated behind Christ. The young apostle at the left and a long-haired apostle near the far right are both seen from behind, and in both cases the artist shows that their weight falls primarily on the right leg. These men hold up bunches of drapery under their right and left arms respectively, providing variety in the forms. The presence or absence of beards further individualizes the men, all but two of whom stare intently at their teacher. Thus the biblical messages are conveyed with conviction, and the compositions testify to the great skill of the designers, however anonymous they remain to us today.

Writing in 1897, Paul Kristeller sought to associate many Florentine woodcuts with the styles of great contemporary Florentine painters, for example, Domenico Ghirlandaio (1449–1494), Alessandro Botticelli (1445–1510), and Filippino Lippi (1457–1504). Specifically excluding any stylistic relationship to contemporary manuscript illuminators, Kristeller limited

FIGURE 7. *Epistole et Evangelii,* printed in Florence by Lorenzo Morgiani and Johannes Petri for Piero Pacini in 1495, fol. b5v (XIIIv): Adoration of the Kings and Saint Matthew (text of Matthew 2) and Saint Paul (text of Romans 12), woodcuts by an anonymous Florentine designer. (See item 18, LC/R298.)

FIGURE 8. Filippino Lippi and Alessandro Botticelli, *The Adoration of the Kings,* ca. 1470. (London, National Gallery, NG 592). Copyright © National Gallery, London.

himself to noting a very few figures in Florentine woodcuts that imitated a specific painted or sculpted figure by these artists, and otherwise spoke in broad generalizations. Now, more than a century later, Kristeller's observations can be both supported and modified by the intervening years of art historical research.[21]

Regarding the dependence of the *Epistole et Evangelii* compositions on monumental painting, it is useful to consider a specific comparison. One example is the woodcut of the Adoration of the Kings (fig. 7, fol. 13v [b5v]) that precedes the Gospel reading for Epiphany (Matthew 2). Many elements of the composition can be found in an Adoration of the Kings earlier attributed to Botticelli and currently considered to have been begun by Filippino Lippi and continued by Botticelli (fig. 8).[22] The most striking analogies between the woodcut and the panel painting are found in the figures of the Virgin and Child, Saint Joseph, and the kneeling oldest king. In both scenes, Joseph stands behind Mary, leaning on a staff. Mary is posed in profile, bending slightly as she holds the Christ Child, who in turn bends forward and blesses the kneeling king with his right hand. The bearded king reaches to kiss the extended foot of Christ, his precious golden gift on the ground nearby.

Other figures in the woodcut suggest knowledge of the painting but are not so directly derivative. The youngest king in the woodcut reveals an elegant long leg and gestures with an open hand, both details that are found in the youth who gazes up to the star, isolated beyond the kneeling oldest king in the painting. The stately figure in a turban contrasted to a kneeling figure behind him is a combination found in the Lippi/Botticelli painting as well. Thus, although the woodcut does indicate that its designer was imbued with detailed knowledge of contemporary Florentine painting, he has found new combinations of motifs to provide his own original interpretation.

Renaissance manuscript illumination was much more intensely studied in the second half of the twentieth century than it had been at the time of Kristeller's writing.[23] What may be profitably gleaned from these studies is a new appreciation of Florentine artists who not only painted frescoes and panels but also illuminated manuscripts. For example, Domenico Ghirlandaio and Francesco Rosselli (1447–1513?) did both.[24] The sharp distinction that earlier scholars made between these two activities can no longer be maintained. Domenico Ghirlandaio signed and dated a miniature for a choir book in 1473, and both he and Francesco Rosselli were among the artists who designed narrative miniatures in the great manuscript Bible of Federico da Montefeltro.[25]

The two-volume Bible of Federico da Montefeltro was illuminated in Florence for the Duke of Urbino between 1476 and 1478. In it, each book of the Bible begins on a folio decorated with a large narrative miniature in a horizontal rectangular format that stretches over two columns of text (fig. 9), an innovative layout that is distinctively Florentine. Before this time, illustrated manuscript Bibles in Italy normally included smaller miniatures fitted into one column of text. The biblical characters of the Montefeltro Bible miniatures appear in landscape and architectural settings, with important figures often contrasted to attendant groups. In a Judgment of Solomon whose design is attributed to Domenico Ghirlandaio, Solomon and the threatening executioner are contrasted to a crowd of bystanders.[26] The young king is emphasized

FIGURE 9. Design attributed to Domenico Ghirlandaio, miniature of Judgment of Solomon and text of Proverbs in Bible of Federico da Montefeltro, 1476–1478 (Vatican City, Biblioteca Apostolica Vaticana, MS Urb. Lat. 2, fol. 31v). Copyright © Biblioteca Apostolica Vaticana.

by his isolation on a raised throne and the executioner by his violent pose. Like the framing apostles in the *Epistole et Evangelii* woodcut of Christ Teaching the Apostles, the "false" mother who stands at the right is seen from behind. Both the executioner and the striding young man at the left recall the men throwing stones in another woodcut of the *Epistole et Evangelii,* the Stoning of Saint Stephen (fol. 9r [b1r]).[27] Thus while not exact counterparts, the figures, compositional groupings, and horizontal format of the miniatures in the famous Montefeltro Bible suggest that the woodcut artists of the 1495 *Epistole et Evangelii* could draw on manuscript prototypes for their compositions as well as looking at monumental paintings for inspiration.

The printers of the 1495 *Epistole et Evangelii* were justifiably proud of their achievement. A long colophon at the end of the book argues that the greatest care was taken with the choosing and editing of the texts. Aware that the cost of paper was any printer's greatest expense, the printers also point out that no expense was spared on the number of pages of their book: *Et per farla piu copiosa & piu aperta alectori non habbiamo perdonato alla spesa de fogli: ma. Come tu uedi sono Carte. C.xxiiii* (And in order to make it more copious and more open to the readers, we have not spared any expense of the pages: but as you see there are 124 pages).[28]

Moreover, they declare that the illustrations provide both spiritual and physical consolation for the reader, thereby demonstrating remarkable sophistication about the role of images. To quote the colophon again:

*Et p[er] dar dilecto allocchio de co[m]peratori: habbiamo / posto leproprie historie ordinatam[en]te come tu uedi aluoghi suoi: accioche esse[n]do / lanima spiritualme[n]te co[n]solata: il corpo sia anche partecipe di qualche co[n]solatione* (And in order to give pleasure to the eye of the buyers, we have placed the proper stories [woodcut illustrations], arranging them as you see in their places: so that the soul is spiritually consoled: the body also may participate in some consolation.)[29]

Consideration of another Florentine religious book can serve to demonstrate the effective contrast of Florentine black-ground borders with a scene composed in outline, the type of woodcut found in the 1495 *Epistole et Evangelii.* This is Saint Augustine's *Sermones ad heremitas* (in Italian) printed in Florence by Antonio di Bartolommeo Miscomini, June 28, 1493,[30] a book that is in fact more typical of fifteenth-century Florentine books with woodcuts than the *Epistole et Evangelii.* It is smaller in its dimensions, measuring twenty-four by fourteen centimeters, and it comprises thirty-four folios, illustrated with only one woodcut. This format is similar to that found in other Florentine books described in this catalogue: Landino's *Formulario di lettere* (see item 12); and Berlinghieri's *Protesto alla signoria di Firenze* (see item 19).

The opening folio of the *Sermones* contains the title and an almost square woodcut of Saint Augustine in His Study (fig. 10, fol. a1r). Seated at a desk, the saint looks at an open book propped up in front of him as he writes on a sheet of parchment with a slender pen. On the desk is his bishop's miter, and behind the desk a curtain is pulled aside to show books and an hourglass on a shelf. The image is rendered entirely in outline, except for the small black rectangle of the window. The curving and looped lines of Saint Augustine's drapery recall similar passages in the drapery of Christ Teaching the Apostles in the 1495 *Epistole et Evangelii* woodcut (see item 18; fig. 6). Likewise, his strong profile and intent gaze bring to mind the figure of Christ. The black-ground borders stand in striking contrast to the open effect of the saint in his austere cell, sharply isolating him from the page and indeed from the world around him.

The image of a scholarly saint in a study is frequently found in Florentine Renaissance manuscripts and in monumental fresco paintings as well. Botticelli's *Saint Augustine's Vision of Saint Jerome* and Ghirlandaio's *Saint Jerome in His Study* were painted in rivalry with each other in 1480 for the Ognissanti Church in Florence.[31] Both portray the saints seated at writing desks in closed rooms filled with scholarly objects—many books, pens and inkpots, an armillary sphere, a twenty-four-hour clock. However well-known these frescoes may have been, the pose of Saint Augustine in the *Sermones* woodcut even more closely resembles saints in Florentine manuscript illuminations. For example, in a manuscript of Saint Augustine's *Epistolae* (Letters) destined for Matthias Corvinus, king of Hungary, the dark-bearded saint sits at his desk and gazes intently at an open book (fig. 11).[32] As in the *Sermones* woodcut, a second book is propped above the angled lectern for reference, and on a shelf by the window are other books. In the miniature, Saint Augustine wears his bishop's miter, which like the miter in the woodcut assures the reader of his identity. Many miniatures such as these would have been readily available to the designer of the Saint Augustine woodcut, possibly himself also an illuminator.

## VENETIAN RELIGIOUS WOODCUTS IN THE EARLY SIXTEENTH CENTURY

In Venice, a marked change in the style of woodcuts began to manifest itself in the late 1490s and fully emerged after 1500. Most distinctively, forms from this period appear to be more three-dimensional, because they are shaded with series of parallel lines. This has led, not surprisingly, to naming the style, the "shaded style."[33] Simultaneously, figures and costumes begin to resemble more closely the classical art of Greece and Rome than was the case in the Pico Master's compositions. Both these characteristics—shading of objects with closely placed parallel lines and an emphasis on classical form—show the influence of the great North Italian painter and printmaker Andrea Mantegna.[34] As noted earlier, A. M. Hind designated the principal designer of this style the Classical Designer, seeing him as an artist who initially designed outline woodcuts and later turned to the shaded style.[35] Scholars have sought to identify this artist with various known contemporary painters, and recently several have accepted the idea that many woodcuts by the Classical Designer should be attributed to the Paduan book artist, author, and cartographer Benedetto Bordon (ca. 1450–1530).[36]

In the Rosenwald/Dyson Perrins collection, three liturgical books and one book of saints' lives show woodcuts in the shaded style, and many, but not all, of these images reflect designs by Bordon. The earliest is a small *Missale romanum* (Missal, Use of Rome), printed in Venice

FIGURE 11. Attavante, Saint Augustine in His Study, illuminated initial. In Saint Augustine, *Epistolae,* 1485–1490 (Vienna, Österreichisches Nationalbibliothek, MS Lat. 653, fol. 1r). Courtesy Bildarchiv d.ÖNB, Vienna.

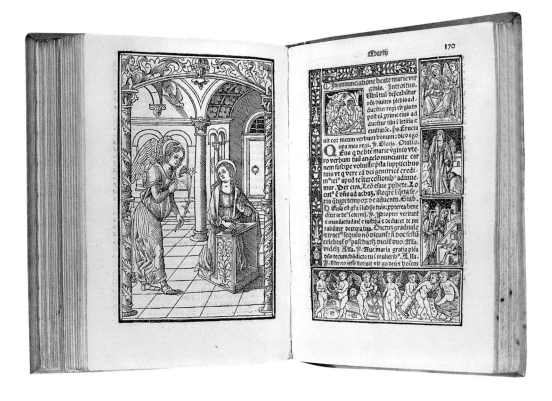

FIGURE 12. *Missale romanum,*
printed in Venice by
LucAntonio Giunta,
20 November 1501, fols.
169v–170r: Annunciation;
and text of Mass for Feast
of the Annunciation with
woodcuts in margins of
Virgin and Child, Standing
Female Saint, Three Marys
at the Tomb of Christ, and
Cherubs with the Symbols
of the Passion, woodcuts
by anonymous Venetian
designer. (See item 39,
LC/R738.)

by LucAntonio Giunta, November 20, 1501 (item 39).[37] Of its eighteen full-page woodcuts, nine had first been used in an *Officium beatae Mariae virginis* printed by Giunta a few months earlier, on June 26, 1501.[38] The text pages in the *Missale* have complex borders: on the pages illustrated here (fig. 12) are three small woodcuts in the outer margin—the Virgin and Child, a Standing Female Saint, and the Three Marys at the Tomb of Christ. In these, the figures are shaded and seen in front of black backgrounds dotted with white dots, known as *criblé* grounds. In the lower margin, a long horizontal woodcut contains putti, or cherubs, holding the implements of the passion; and in the narrow inner and upper margins are borders with delicate vases, flowers, and leaves in white on black grounds. In addition to the full-page and border woodcuts, there are numerous smaller woodcuts scattered throughout the text.

The subjects of the full-page woodcuts are appropriate for the mass they precede: the Adoration of the Kings (fol. 15v), for instance, for Epiphany or the Resurrection (fol. 118v) for Easter. The illustrated Annunciation precedes the mass for the Feast of the Annunciation on March 25 (fols. 169v–170r).

The traditional figures of the Virgin Mary and the Angel Gabriel are set in an elegant Renaissance interior, defined by classical architectural components: a Corinthian column, a coffered barrel vault, and roundheaded windows behind Gabriel. The diagonal lines of the tiled floor converge to suggest the depth of the room. At the edges of the image are decorative columns that appear to support a segmented arch; these act as a frame through which the viewer looks at the holy event. Such framing motifs echo the recommendations in Leon Battista Alberti's treatise *On Painting* (ca. 1435), in which the humanist author and architect defined a picture as "an open window through which the subject to be painted is seen."[39]

The Virgin Mary kneels at a prayer desk decorated with leaf motifs similar to those in the border of the facing page. With one hand on a prayer book and the other raised in welcome, the Virgin turns her head toward the angel. Gabriel walks toward her at a stately pace, dressed in a long tunic, holding a lily and making a gesture of blessing with his right hand. Both figures are idealized and lightly modeled to suggest the volumes of their bodies. Looking again at the Florentine Saint Augustine (fig. 10), one finds the contrast in spatial effects is particularly striking. The Florentine artist stresses simple planes. The side of the desk, the bench on which the saint sits, and the curtained wall are all parallel to the plane of the page. In the Annunciation, on the other hand, Mary and Gabriel appear to be more volumetric and to exist in a deep recessive space. The spacious setting and dignified demeanor of Mary and Gabriel make the composition an early example of Venetian High Renaissance art.

Until Giunta printed the 1501 *Missale romanum,* it was rare to find any narrative woodcuts other than images of the crucifixion in a missal.[40] The small size of the book, the beautiful full-page woodcuts, and the many smaller illustrations and woodcut initials are innovative components in liturgical book design, and this new format contributed to Giunta's great success as a printer of liturgical books.

Similar in size, layout, and use of shaded woodcuts is the *Breviarium romanum* (Breviary, Use of Rome) printed by Giunta in Venice, March 26, 1507 (see item 44).[41] Like the 1501 *Missale romanum,* the *Breviarium romanum* has full-page woodcuts facing text pages. The text pages themselves have complex borders combining woodcuts of Christ and saints on two sides with decorative bars of white leaves on black grounds on the other two. The illustrated pages show the opening of one of the four main sections of a breviary, known as the sanctorale (fols. 232v–233r). This section contains the offices (or services) for saints' days throughout the year. The Feast of Saint Andrew is celebrated on November 30 and is the first office in the sanctorale, although the text also refers to Saint Saturninus, whose feast is celebrated the evening before.

Christ Calling Peter and Andrew (fig. 13, fol. 232v) is a scene frequently used to initiate the sanctorale, and in the 1507 *Breviarium romanum* the episode gives the artist the opportunity to represent monumental figures before a deep landscape. Christ stands on the shore raising his hand in blessing. His robe appears to be pressed against his right leg, an effect that is achieved by the many parallel modeling lines on his thigh and calf that suggest the play of light on a rounded form. The legs, arms, and tunics of the men in the boat, and of Saint Peter, who leaps

FIGURE 13. *Breviarium romanum,* printed in Venice by LucAntonio Giunta, 26 March 1507, fol. 232v: Christ Calling Peter and Andrew, woodcut designed by Benedetto Bordon. (See item 44, LC/R758.)

FIGURE 14. Benedetto Bordon, Christ Calling Peter and Andrew, illuminated initial on folio from an antiphonary for San Nicolò dei Frari, Venice, 1495–1500 (Vatican City, Bibliotheca Apostolica Vaticana, MS Ross. 1195, fol. 28r). Copyright © Bibliotheca Apostolica Vaticana.

out of the boat, are all similarly modeled. The sea is more uniformly patterned with wavy lines, suggesting the texture of water. A sense of great depth is created by the diminished size of buildings and hills that flow in long diagonal lines out into the sea in the upper part of the image.

Although created only about a decade earlier, the Calling of Peter and Andrew in the 1494 Venetian *Biblica italica* (fig. 4) is vastly less sophisticated in composition and in cutting. Likewise, the spatial effects of the landscape in the 1495 Florentine woodcut of the Fall of Manna (fig. 6) are far simpler, despite the elegance of its outlined figures.

The miniaturist Benedetto Bordon painted this scene at least twice in liturgical manuscripts, and the 1507 *Breviarium* woodcut of Christ Calling Peter and Andrew, which echoes these miniatures, was probably also designed by him.[42] Around 1500, Bordon depicted the Calling of Peter and Andrew in a historiated initial painted in an antiphonary for the Franciscan oratory of San Nicolò dei Frari in Venice (fig. 14).[43] As in the *Breviarium* woodcut, Christ stands on the shore addressing Peter and Andrew. Peter is already kneeling on the shore, while Andrew remains in the boat, which he steadies with an oar. Behind them the land stretches out into the sea in narrow promontories. Much later in 1525, Bordon repeated the episode in his documented *Evangeliarium for Santa Giustina, Padua* in a more complex composition.[44] Here, both Andrew and Peter are on the shore before the beckoning Christ, and the detailed landscape includes many water birds and fluffy trees, while in the distance James and John are mending their nets by the shore. The miniatures and woodcut testify to the varied activities of a book artist shifting between the fading art of manuscript illumination and the new demands of book illustration by mechanical means.

Woodcuts in yet another Venetian religious text bear the mark of Bordon's design. These appear in a commentary on the epistolary written by one Guillermus of Paris, the Guilelmus Parisiensis, *Postilla super Epistolas et Evangelia,* printed in Venice by Jacobus Pentius de Leuco, again for the publisher LucAntonio Giunta, and issued on November 6, 1505 (see item 43).[45] The illustrated page shows a text format that was developed for medieval law books with commentaries, in which the text proper in larger type appears in the middle of the page, and the commentary in a smaller font is set in two columns that surround the text proper (fig. 15, fol. XXXIr [31r]).[46] On this folio of the Rosenwald *Postilla,* a small woodcut is set in the column of the text proper. Three Marys at the Tomb of Christ illustrates the reading for Easter from Mark 16. Mary Magdalene, Mary Jacobus, and Mary Salome approach the empty tomb from the left. An angel stands in the dark entrance to a rocky cave and greets them with a gesture of blessing. In the distance are the walls of Jerusalem. The robes and tomb are once again modeled with closely placed parallel lines to suggest light and shade. The composition closely resembles a historiated initial for the San Nicolò dei Frari antiphonaries painted by Benedetto Bordon around 1500 (fig. 16).[47] The cloak of the woman nearest to the angel is draped in similar folds in both miniature and woodcut. The solemn approach of the three women and the poignant gap between them and the gesturing angel are alike in both compositions, and suggest a similar artistic mind at work.

Perhaps the most spectacular book with shaded woodcuts in the Rosenwald/Dyson Perrins collection is an edition of saints' lives whose authorship was traditionally attributed to Saint Jerome. Much larger in scale than Giunta's *Missale* or *Breviarium* (items 39, 44), the Hieronymus *Vita di sancti padri* was printed in Venice by Otinus de la Luna, July 28, 1501, and is illustrated with large circular woodcuts set in magnificent classicizing borders (fig. 17).[48] In the Rosenwald copy, the woodcuts have been colored with red and blue watercolor paint, an unusual but not unknown practice in Italian early printed books.

FIGURE 17. Saint Jerome (Hieronymus), *Vita di sancti padri,* printed in Venice by Otinus de la Luna, 28 July 1501, fols. a4v–b1r: Saint Malchius as a Prisoner of the Ismaelites; and frontispiece to book 1, with Christians Tortured in View of Saint Paul the Hermit, woodcut borders, and initial with Saint Paul the Hermit. (See item 40, LC/R740.)

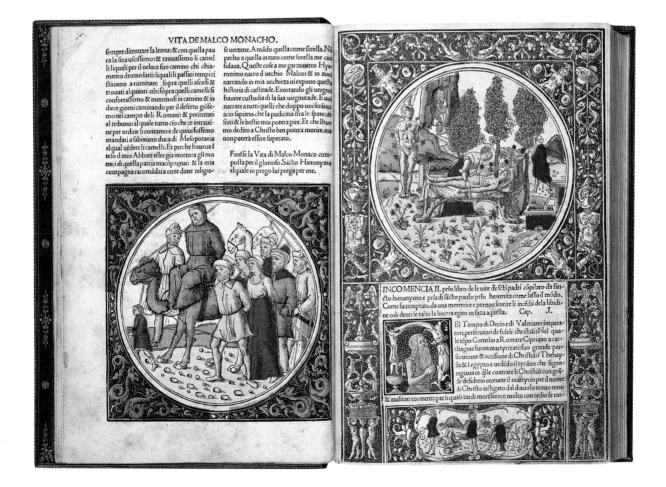

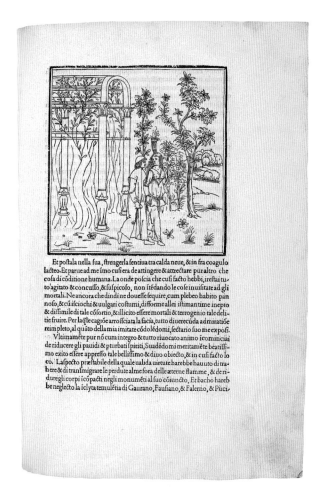

Et poftala nella fua, ftrengerla fentiua tra calda neue, & in fra coagulo lacteo. Et parue ad me fmo cufiera de attingere & attrectare pur altro che cofa di coditione humana. La onde pofcia che cufi facto hebbi, ireftai tutto'agitato & concuffo, & fufpicofo, non itedando le cofe inuifitate ad gli mortali. Ne ancora che dindi ne douelle fequire, cum plebeo habito pannofo, & cu ifciochi & uulgari coftumi, difforme allei iftimantime inepto & diffimile di tale cofortio, & illicito effere mortali & terrogenio tale delitie fruire. Per laqle cagioe arroffciata la facia, tutto diuerecuda admiratioe reim pleto, al quato della mia imitate codolédomi, fectario fuo me expofi.
    Vltimaméte pur no cum integro & tutto riuocato animo icominciai de riducere gli pauidi & pturbati fpiriti, Suadédomi meritaméte beatiffimo exito effere appreffo tale belliffimo & diuo obiecto, & in cufi facto lo co. Lafpecto præftabile della quale ualida uirtute harebbe hauuto di trahere & di tranfmigrare le perdute almefora delle æterne flamme, & deridure gli corpi icopacti negli monuméti al fuo cóiuncto, Et bacho hareb be neglecto la iclyta temulétia di Gaurano, Faufiano, & Falerrio, & Púci-

FIGURE 18. Poliphilus and a Nymph by an Arbor, woodcut in [Francesco Colonna], *Hypnerotomachia Poliphili,* printed in Venice by Aldus Manutius, 1499, fol. i8r, woodcut design by Benedetto Bordon (LC/R 340).

Both scenes on the illustrated pages provide strikingly original effects (fols. a4v–b1r), even though the compositions depend on earlier woodcuts by the Pico Master in an edition of the *Vita* printed in 1490.[49] Saint Malchius is shown with male and female companions, all prisoners of the Ismaelites (see item 40, fol. a4v). He is bound and mounted on a camel, and the forced march moves inexorably toward the left across the stony ground of the desert. Grim expressions convey the serious nature of the captivity.

Several woodcut units make up the handsome blackground criblé border surrounding the text and woodcut roundel on the facing page (fol. b1r). The pairs of putti, dolphins, eagles, and trophies all derive from Roman decorative sculpture. In the roundel are illustrated events in the Life of Saint Paul the Hermit. According to the text, the Emperor Decius had decreed the cruel torture of two Christians, one of whom was stripped, covered with honey, and exposed to be stung by wasps. The second youth was placed in a delectable garden full of white lilies and red roses, murmuring waters and bird songs. There, he was bound to a bed with flowered garlands and then caressed by a beautiful harlot. Refusing to be seduced away from his Christian beliefs, the youth bit off his own tongue, spat it in the face of the woman, and thus won the crown of martyrdom. The artist depicts the event before its gruesome finale, showing the flowering trees, flowing fountain, and curly haired youth tied to the elegant bed over which bends the fashionably dressed temptress. The potential pleasure of this young man's seduction is contrasted to the pain of the other, stung by huge wasps. Saint Paul, frightened by these horrors, flees to embrace the life of a hermit.

The odd scene can be understood in terms of the growing popularity of pastoral imagery in Venice around 1500. In the first decade of the sixteenth century, the painter Giorgione and the humanist poet Pietro Bembo created innovative works invoking the tropes of pastoral poetry.[50] The Saint Paul roundel literally portrays the *locus amoenus,* or "pleasant place" of this genre, with its flowering trees and gentle breezes. The imagery also recalls the arbors and fountains described and visualized in the famous *Hypnerotomachia Poliphili,* or the "Strife of Love in the Dream of Poliphilus," printed in Venice by Aldus Manutius in 1499.[51] In the *Poliphilus,* however, the hero pursues his love rather than rejecting her, and the very secular pleasant places are portrayed with outline woodcuts rather than in the shaded style (fig. 18, fol. i8r). And by 1510, Giorgione's paintings of sensuous nudes in pastoral settings had fixed the genre for which Poliphilus and the tempted youth of the 1501 *Vita* are intriguing preludes.

Doubtless the most problematic of the Venetian and Florentine liturgical books considered here is the *Esposizione sopra evangeli* by Simon de Cassia printed in Florence by Bartolommeo di Libri, September 24, 1496 (fig. 19).[52] Following the normal pattern of evangeliary texts, the author arranges the Gospel readings according to the sequence of services throughout the liturgical year. The commentary follows each reading, preceded by the author's name, FRA SIMONE, and a paragraph marker. The text is laid out in two columns and each reading is preceded by a small woodcut in outline style flanked by a pair of decorative black-ground borders.

The pages illustrated here contain readings for the fourth week of Lent, beginning with the passage in Matthew 21 describing Christ's Entry into Jerusalem, the subject of the woodcut preceding the reading, which is rendered in outline style (fols. LXXXIXv–LXXXXr [89v–90r]). A dense crowd surrounds Christ, who rides toward the left on a long-eared donkey; below him are spread the palms and garments of those who welcome him. The scenes on the facing page are somewhat more open, but still filled with many figures: Christ Expelling the Money Changers from the Temple (two versions) and Christ Teaching through Parables (also from Matthew 21). In the first, a tree with a boy climbing in it divides Christ and the apostles from a second scene of Christ chasing the money changers. The second woodcut on this page repre-

FIGURE 19. Simon de Cassia, *Esposizione sopra evangeli,* printed in Florence by Bartolommeo di Libri, 24 September 1496, fols. LXXXIXv–LXXXXr: Christ's Entry into Jerusalem (Matthew 21), Christ Expelling the Money Changers from the Temple (2 woodcuts), and Christ Teaching through Parables (Matthew 21), woodcuts by anonymous Venetian designers. (See also item 22, LC/R 316.)

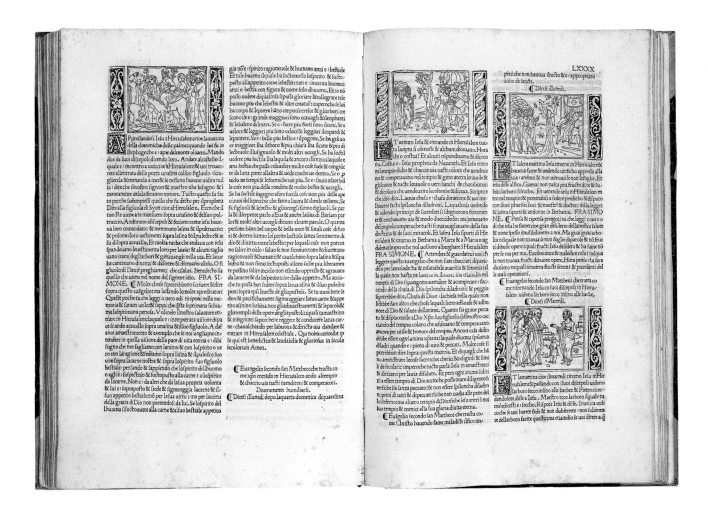

sents the same two scenes, but the figures are more crudely cut, and the apse of the temple is smaller and more distant. The proportions of the figures in the third woodcut are also quite stumpy, and the heads of the apostles touch the upper edge of the frame.

The 1496 Simon de Cassia illustrations have nothing of the elegance of the Florentine woodcuts in the 1495 *Epistole et Evangelii* discussed earlier (see item 18). For example, the lively movement and open effect of Christ's Entry into Jerusalem in the 1495 woodcut (fig. 6) make the event much easier to understand than the undifferentiated mass in the Simon de Cassia woodcut. In fact, the Simon de Cassia woodcuts are transplanted from Venice, where many of them appeared in previously published religious texts. The architectural frontispiece (fig. 20, fol. a2r), with its putti at the vintage and the large woodcut of the Last Judgment, was designed by the Pico Master and was used earlier for the *Legenda di sancti* by Jacopo da Voragine printed in Venice by Manfredo de Monteferrato, December 10, 1492.[53] Its many similarities to the architectural borders in the 1494 *Biblia italica* (fig. 2) and the 1491 Dante (fig. 5) are easy to spot. Many of the smaller woodcuts also first appeared in other Venetian publications, and the style of the illustrated images is related to the less refined cuts illustrating a *Biblia italica* that was printed by Guglielmus de Cereto "Anima

FIGURE 20. Simon de Cassia, *Esposizione sopra evangeli,* printed in Florence by Bartolommeo di Libri, 24 September 1496, fol. a2r: Architectural frontispiece and Last Judgment, woodcuts designed by the Pico Master. (See item 22, LC/R 316.)

Mia" in 1493.[54] The Florentine printer Bartolommeo di Libri must have obtained a variety of Venetian wood blocks with biblical imagery and used them in his publication rather than undertaking the expense of having new wood blocks cut.

Designers and cutters in both Venice and Florence contributed to the creation of magnificent illustrated books that were used for Christian religious services and for private devotion in the Renaissance. In some cases these books survive only in unique or almost unique examples, as some of those in the Rosenwald Collection bear witness. Collectively, however, the huge numbers of these newly printed books that do survive help to refute the notion that Christianity was rejected in the Renaissance in favor of classical ideals. Formally, these two cultures coexisted in the illustration and decoration of Christian books, but the reader would never have mistaken that the messages conveyed were clearly those of the traditional Christian Church.

1. A huge literature exists on Johannes Gutenberg and the Gutenberg Bible. Accessible in English with suggestions for further reading are Janet Ing, *Johann Gutenberg and His Bible* (New York: Typophiles, 1988); Martin Davies, *The Gutenberg Bible* (London: British Library, 1996); and essays in *The Bible as Book: The First Printed Editions,* edited by Kimberly Van Kampen and Paul Saenger (London: British Library, 1999).

On incunable Bibles more generally, see Kristian Jensen, "Printing the Bible in the Fifteenth Century: Devotion, Philology, and Commerce," in *Incunabula and Their Readers: Printing, Selling, and Using Books in the Fifteenth Century,* edited by Kristian Jensen (London: British Library, 2003), 115–38.

2. H 3156; Essling 133; GW 4317; Sander 989; Goff B-644. All discussions of woodcuts in Venetian printed books depend upon [Victor Masséna,] Prince d'Essling, *Les livres à figures vénetiens de la fin du XV^e siècle et du commencement du XVI^e,* 3 parts in 6 vols. (Florence, 1907 and 1914), hereafter Essling, where the 1490 *Biblia italica* is no. 133. Also indispensable are A.M. Hind, *An Introduction to a History of Woodcut* (New York, 1936; reprint, New York: Dover Publications, 1963); and Max Sander, *Le livre à figures italien depuis 1467 jusqu'à 1530,* 6 vols. (New York: G.E. Stechert, 1941–43). On Venetian Bibles in Italian, see especially Edoardo Barbieri, *Le Bibbie italiane del Quattrocento e del Cinquecento,* 2 vols. (Milan: Editrice bibliografica, 1992), with reproductions of the woodcuts of the 1490 edition.

3. See item 17, LC/R289. H 3158; Essling 136; GW 4320; Sander 993; Goff B-647.

4. Hind, *History of Woodcut,* chapter 1.

5. It was long thought that this architectural frame was first used in the *Biblia italica,* Venice, Giovanni Ragazzo for LucAntonio Giunta, October 15, 1490. However, it appeared in a book printed fifteen days earlier which only survives in a single copy, unknown to Essling: *Epistole et Evangeli,* Venice, Theodorus de Ragazonibus, October 1, 1490 (Florence, Biblioteca Nazionale Centrale, Inc. Pal. D.7.5.4; Sander 2564).

6. On the "popular style" and the "classical style," see Hind, *History of Woodcut,* 464–506. For the Pico Master, see Lilian Armstrong, "The Pico Master: A Venetian Miniaturist of the Late Quattrocento," in *Studies of Renaissance Miniaturists in Venice* (London: Pindar Press, 2003), 233–338, esp. 269–314.

7. Venice, Antonio di Bartolomeo Miscomini (HC 3151; GW 4312). The hand-decorated copy is Vienna, Nationalbibliothek, Inc. 5.D.22, fol. 11 (Armstrong, "The Pico Master," pp. 259, 321, no. 41, fig. 20).

8. H 3141; GW 4308; BMC I, 264; Goff B-637. The Cologne Bible has usually been dated to "around 1478," but recently William Sheehan has argued that it must date before 1472. See Essling, no. 133; S. Corsten, "Die Kölner Bilderbibeln von 1478," *Gutenberg Jahrbuch* 1957, pp. 72–93; William Sheehan, *Bibliothecae Apostolicae Vaticanae Incunabula* (Vatican City: Bibliotheca Apostolica Vaticana, 1997), B-296; and *I Vangeli dei Popoli: La Parola e l'immagine del Christo nelle culture e nella storia,* exhibition catalogue edited by Francesco d'Aiuto, Giovanni Morello, and Ambrogio M. Piazzoni (Vatican City, 2000), 385, no. 104 (entry by Christine Maria Grafinger).

9. Lilian Armstrong, "The Master of the Rimini Ovid: A Miniaturist and Woodcut Designer in Renaissance Venice," *Print Quarterly* 10 (1993): 327–63.

10. See item 10, LC/R260. CR 5949; Essling 531; GW 7969; Hind, p. 503, A.(4); Sander 2313; Goff D-32; Armstrong, "The Pico Master," p. 57, W3,a.

11. For woodcuts in many editions of Dante, see *Pagine di Dante,* exhibition catalogue edited by Roberto Rusconi (Perugia: Umbri associati, 1989).

12. A useful survey of major liturgical books is given by Barbara Boehm, "The Books of the Florentine Illuminators" in *Painting and Illumination in Early Renaissance Florence, 1300–1450,* exhibition catalogue edited by Laurence B. Kanter, Barbara Drake Boehm, Carl Brandon Strehlke, et al. (New York: Metropolitan Museum of Art, 1994), 15–23. Also helpful are Michelle P. Brown, *Understanding Illuminated Manuscripts: A Guide to Technical Terms* (London: British Library, 1994), 53–54; John Harper, *The Forms and Orders of Western Liturgy from the Tenth to the Eighteenth Century* (Oxford: Clarendon Press, 1991), 62; and John Plummer, *Liturgical Manuscripts for the Mass and the Divine Office* (New York: Pierpont Morgan Library, 1964), 17–20.

13. See item 18, LC/R298. Reichling 1514; GW 4320; Goff E-94; Sander 2568; Dennis E. Rhodes, *Gli annali tipografici fiorentini del XV secolo* (Florence, L.S. Olschki, 1988), no. 277.

14. Paul Kristeller, *Early Florentine Woodcuts* (London: K. Paul, Trench, Trübner and Co., 1897),

pp. xii, xiv–xv, xxiii, xxx–xxxiii, and no. 135b; and Hind, *History of Woodcut,* 527–58. For a brief recent mention, see David Landau and Peter Parshall, *The Renaissance Print, 1470–1550* (New Haven: Yale University Press, 1994), 38.

15. John Pope-Hennessy, *Italian Gothic Sculpture* (New York: Vintage Books, 1985), plates 46–47 and fig. 39 (Andrea Pisano); Richard Krautheimer, *Lorenzo Ghiberti,* vol. 2 (Princeton: Princeton University Press, 1970), plates 18, 25, etc. (Ghiberti).

16. Christ Teaching the Apostles appears on six other pages in the 1495 *Epistole et Evangelii,* thus proving the versatility of a given woodcut. It illustrates Matthew 13, Fifth Sunday after Epiphany (fol. 16v); Matthew 26 (as described in the text above); John 16, Octave of Ascension (fol. 75v); Matthew 10, Twenty-first Sunday after Pentecost (fol. 92r); Matthew 30, Twenty-fourth Sunday after Pentecost (fol. 93v); Matthew 10 (again), Common of Many Apostles (fol. 110r); and Luke 9, Confessor Saints who are not popes (fol. 117v).

17. Kristeller, *Early Florentine Woodcuts,* ix.

18. On papermaking in relation to Renaissance printing, see Landau and Parshall, *The Renaissance Print,* 15–21. For an illustration showing a detail of a Florentine black-ground woodcut, see William M. Ivins Jr., *How Prints Look* (New York: Metropolitan Museum of Art, 1943; Boston: Beacon Paperback, 1958), 31.

19. CR 1182; GW 4775; Kristeller, *Early Florentine Woodcuts,* p. 45, no. 69a; Sander, 1179; Goff B-911.

20. Krautheimer, *Ghiberti,* plate 94.

21. Kristeller, *Early Florentine Woodcuts,* x, xxx–xxxiii. Among the *Epistole et Evangelii* woodcuts, Kristeller notes that the figures of Christ and Saint Thomas in the woodcut of Doubting Thomas (fols. 71v [l1v] and 95v [o3v]) are borrowed from Andrea del Verrocchio's bronze statues for Or San Michele, Florence; the Beheading of Saint John the Baptist (fol. 104v [p6v]) depends on Antonio del Pollaiuolo's tapestry design of that subject for the Florentine Baptistry; and a figure seen from behind in the Jews Threatening to Stone Jesus (fol. 44r [g2r]) derives from the fresco by Ghirlandaio, Joachim Driven from the Temple in Santa Maria Novella, Florence (pp. xiv, xxxi–xxxii).

22. London, National Gallery, NG 592. See Patricia Lee Rubin and Alison Wright, *Renaissance Florence: The Art of the 1470s* (London: National Gallery, 1999), 290–91, cat. no. 68.

23. Most important for Florentine manuscript illumination is Annarosa Garzelli, editor, *Miniatura fiorentina del Rinascimento, 1440–1525: Un primo cen-*simento, vol. 1, Annarosa Garzelli, *Le immagini, gli autori, i destinari,* and vol. 2, Albinia de la Mare, *New Research on Humanistic Scribes in Florence* (Florence: Giunta regionale toscana, La Nuova Italia, 1985).

24. Garzelli, ed., *Miniatura fiorentina,* 1:145–52, 175–88.

25. Biblioteca Apostolica Vaticana, MSS Urb. Lat. 1 and Urb. Lat. 2. See Annarosa Garzelli, *La Bibbia di Federico da Montefeltro* (Rome: Multigrafica, 1977) and Garzelli, ed., *Miniatura fiorentina,* 1:145–52, 219–22.

26. MS Urb. Lat. 2, fol. 31v (Garzelli, ed., *Miniatura fiorentina,* vol. 2, fig. 461; and Garzelli, *Bibbia di Federico da Montefeltro,* color plate X).

27. Kristeller, *Early Florentine Woodcuts,* p. 67, no. 95.

28. Fol. CXXIIv [122v].

29. Fol. CXXIIv [122v].

30. See item 19, LC/R277. HCR 2010; GW 3010; Kristeller, *Early Florentine Woodcuts,* p. 6, no. 11c; Sander 688; Goff A-1322; Rhodes 74.

31. Ronald Lightbown, *Sandro Botticelli,* 2 vols. (Berkeley: University of California Press, 1978), 1: 49–52 and figs. 22–23.

32. Vienna, ÖNB, Cod. Lat. 653, Augustine, *Epistolae,* fol. 1r: Frontispiece with Saint Augustine in his study, border with arms of Matthias Corvinus, illuminated by Attavante in Florence for Matthias Corvinus, king of Hungary, 1485–90. Closely related is Vienna, ÖNB, Cod. Lat. 930, Jerome, *Expositio Evangelii,* fol. 1r: Frontispiece with Saint Jerome in his study, Corvinus arms and portrait, illuminated by Monte di Giovanni di Miniato. See Garzelli, ed. *Miniatura fiorentina,* 2, figs. 813 (Vienna Augustine), 915 (Vienna, Jerome); and Csaba Cispodi and Klara Csapodi-Gardonyi, *Bibliotheca Corviniana* (Budapest: Magyar Helikon, Corvina, 1981), pp. 270–71, plate XCV, and no. 160, p. 71 (Augustine, *Epistolae*); and pp. 278–79, plate XCIX, and p. 72, no. 164 (Jerome, *Expositio Evangelii*).

33. Essling called the style the *manière ombrée* (part 3, pp. 93ff.); Hind, *History of Woodcut,* 501–2.

34. For a recent discussion of Mantegna's influence on fifteenth-century prints, see Landau and Parshall, *The Renaissance Print,* 65–72.

35. Hind, *History of Woodcut,* 464.

36. Lilian Armstrong, "Benedetto Bordon, *Miniator,* and Cartography in Early Sixteenth-Century Venice," *Imago Mundi* 48 (1996): 65–92, with extensive bibliography.

37. See item 39, LC/R738. Victor Masséna, duc de Rivoli, *Les Missels imprimés à Venise de 1481 à 1600* (Paris: J. Rothschild, [1894]–96) (hereafter

Rivoli), 59; Sander 4786; Paolo Camerini, *Annali di Giunta,* vol. 1, *Venezia* (Florence: Sansoni, 1962), no. 63.

38. Essling 465; Camerini, no. 60; Lilian Armstrong, "Woodcuts for Liturgical Books Published by LucAntonio Giunta in Venice, 1499–1501," *Word and Image* 17 (2001): 65–93, esp. pp. 81–87.

39. Leon Battista Alberti, *On Painting and On Sculpture: The Latin Texts of De pictura and De statua,* edited with translations, introduction, and notes by Cecil Grayson (London: Phaidon, 1972), 55.

40. Rivoli, passim.

41. See item 44, LC/R 758. Essling 937; Sander 1351; Camerini 111.

42. Christ Calling Peter and Andrew first appeared at the beginning of the sanctorale in the 1501 *Missale romanum* (see item 39, LC/R 738, fol. 158v) discussed above. See Armstrong, "Woodcuts for Liturgical Books," 81–87.

43. Bibliotheca Apostolica Vaticana, MS Ross. 1195, fol. 28r. Lilian Armstrong, "Benedetto Bordon, Aldus Manutius, and LucAntonio Giunta: Old Links and New," in *Aldus Manutius and Renaissance Culture,* edited by David S. Zeidberg, with the assistance of Fiorella Gioffredi Superbi, Villa I Tatti: The Harvard University Center for Italian Renaissance Studies, vol. 15 (Florence: L. S. Olschki, 1998), 161–83, esp. 167–76.

44. Dublin, Chester Beatty Library, MS W. 107, fol. 26r. See Armstrong, "Benedetto Bordon, *Miniator,* and Cartography," fig. 2.

45. See item 43, LC/R 750. Essling 194; Sander 3338; Camerini 97.

46. The format of medieval law manuscripts is analyzed in Susan L'Engle and Robert Gibbs, *Illuminating the Law: Legal Manuscripts in Cambridge Collec-*

*tions* (London: Harvey Miller Publishers, an imprint of Brepols Publishers, 2001).

47. Bibliotheca Apostolica Vaticana, MS Ross. 1195, fol. 2; Armstrong, "Benedetto Bordon, Aldus Manutius, and LucAntonio Giunta," 167–83 and fig. 9.

48. See item 40, LC/R 740. Essling 574, Sander 3412.

49. Hieronymus, *Vite di sancti padri,* Giovanni Ragazzo for LucAntonio Giunta, 1491 (H 8624; Essling 568; Sander 3405; Camerini 5; Armstrong, "Pico Master," p. 328, W 2,c.).

50. David Rosand, "Giorgione, Venice, and the Pastoral Vision," in *Places of Delight: The Pastoral Landscape,* exhibition catalogue edited by Robert C. Cafritz, Lawrence Gowing, and David Rosand (Washington: Phillips Collection in association with the National Gallery of Art, 1988), 21–81.

51. H 5501; Essling 1198; GW 7223; Sander 2056; Goff C-767. Normally, Francesco Colonna [Columna] is cited as the author. The literature on the *Hypnerotomachia Poliphili* is enormous, and there are several facsimile editions. See references in *Aldus Manutius,* ed. Zeidberg; *Verso il Polifilo, 1499–1999,* exhibition catalogue edited by Dino Casagrande and Alessandro Scarsella, San Donà di Piave, *Miscellanea Marciana* 13 (1998).

52. See item 22, LC/R 316. HR 4560; Kristeller 135a; Essling 190; Sander 2571; Rhodes 728.

53. Reichling 1424; Essling 678; Sander 7716; Goff J-179; Armstrong, "Pico Master," p. 328, W 5,a.

54. Reichling 838; GW 4314; Essling 135; Sander 992; Goff B-646; Barbieri, *Le Bibbie italiane,* passim.

# The Stylistic Development of German Book Illustration, 1460–1511

## Daniela Laube

THE DAWN OF BOOK ILLUSTRATION is predominated by the German woodcut, and its development is essential to any understanding of the early history of book illustration. This essay will examine the woodcut in printed books as first practiced in Bamberg in the 1460s and explore its stylistic development as the art form spread to Augsburg, Ulm, Strasbourg, Basel, and Nuremberg. The essay is meant to serve as an introduction to the German woodcut in early printed books and to trace its development as it transformed from a medieval craft to Renaissance fine art.

The natural compatibility of wood blocks with movable type was the main attraction persuading printers to illustrate their texts with woodcuts. Letterpress and woodcut are both relief processes. The level of the wood block could be adjusted to the level of the letterpress type. As a consequence, illustrations could be combined with the text and could be printed simultaneously in the same run through the press. Engraving, an intaglio process, requires two separate passes through the press to print the image and the text, resulting in a more expensive and time-consuming operation. This enormous economic advantage proved critical in the early years of printing. Once the printing of letterpress type and wood blocks in one single frame was technically mastered, the woodcut became the leading method for illustrating books.

The actual production of woodcuts involved a complex combination of design and craftsmanship. First, the design was created by a craftsman called the *Reisser* either by drawing an image directly on the wood block or by transferring a drawing onto the wood block by means of transfer paper. The cutting of the wood block was done by a specialist workman, the so-called *Formschneider*. In producing a wood block, the areas that are intended to print stand out in relief, while the surrounding areas are cut away. The lines that print are wedge-shaped ridges whose narrow, flat tops receive the printing ink. A third person in this line of craftsmen was the *Briefmaler,* who colored the prints with watercolor or wash.[1] Coloring the black-and-white image was a common characteristic of the German woodcut and was an integral part of its design as it evolved in northern Europe.

The quality of the woodcut depended to a decisive degree on the craftsmanship of the Formschneider. His ability to translate the designer's drawing into the lines he would cut was paramount, and equally important was his modeling of the ridge-lines that would eventually print the image. In the 1460s, the number of competent Reisser and Formschneider seems to have been limited, and the quality of woodcuts resided at a low level of craftsmanship. In his definitive work on early printing in the south of the German-speaking regions, Peter Amelung suggests that in the early woodcuts the division of labor between Reisser and Formschneider

FIGURE 1. Stephan Fridolin's *Schatzbehalter,* printed in Nuremberg by Anton Koberger, 8 November 1491. Fol. p⁴v (LC/R 154)

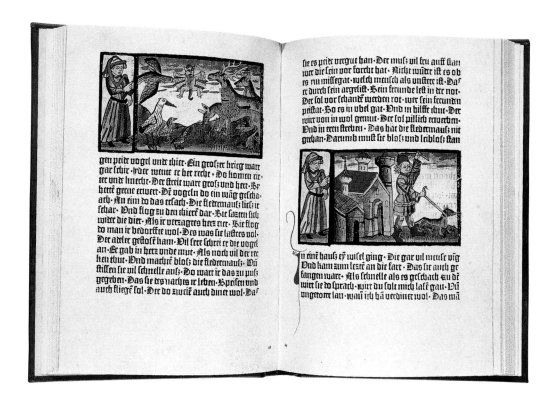

is not entirely clear.[2] This suggests that either one of these workmen could execute both crafts, and that the division of labor and ensuing competence were to develop only later.

## BAMBERG AND THE FIRST ILLUSTRATED BOOKS

German book illustration began in Bamberg less than ten years after the publication of Gutenberg's Latin Bible. Between the years 1460 and 1466, German printers produced the first books to be printed in the German vernacular and the first books, in any language, to contain printed illustrations.[3] Albrecht Pfister of Bamberg, employed as secretary to Bishop Georg I von Schaumburg, was the publisher of five exceptional books, all but one illustrated with woodcuts. In 1461 he published his edition of Ulrich Boner's *Der Edelstein,* followed in 1462 by his *Biblia pauperum* and *Die Vier Historien von Joseph, Daniel, Esther und Judith* and finally, his edition of *Der Ackermann aus Böhmen.* As one might expect, all titles are exceedingly rare.

Albrecht Pfister's woodcuts, recognized as the first printed illustrations in a book, were not sophisticated. His figures are delineated with one clear outline. These outlines are angular and stiff, and thus the figures remain static and motionless. The faces are identical in character, with heavy-set eyelids. Most of Pfister's woodcuts are framed by a double borderline. These first woodcut illustrations were wide spaced, square planed, and almost cubist-like in form. They were intended to be hand colored to resemble miniature painting, albeit on a low level of quality. Text and illustrations were not printed at the same time, but in two press runs per page, first the text and then the illustrations.[4]

However naive and provincial Albrecht Pfister's woodcuts appear from a stylistic perspective, they mark the beginning of graphic art in the book. His printing of Boner's *Der Edelstein* contains the first book illustrations published in Europe. From this point forward, the spread of printing presses and the craft of woodcutting and design was precipitate, if not revolutionary.

For the next three to four decades, printers and woodcutters appeared in towns and cities along the Rhine from the Netherlands, across the southern German-speaking regions, and over the Alps to Venice and Florence.

The demand for illustration in books increased dramatically during the later part of the fifteenth century, and it is estimated that about one-third of all books printed before 1500 contained illustrations. Following the early experiments in Bamberg, several years passed before the next illustrated book was printed in northern Europe. In the 1470s and 1480s Augsburg, Nuremberg, and Ulm became the chief centers for printing illustrated books, soon followed by Basel, Cologne, and Strasbourg.[5]

There remains little documentation recording the names of the northern artists and craftsmen involved in early woodcut illustration. Nonetheless, a stylistic continuity can be discerned for specific regions, and sometimes these characteristics can be localized even to specific workshops. A well-defined style evolved in Augsburg and Ulm in the 1470s, and traits of this style can be found in books printed in the region over the next forty years.

## AUGSBURG, ULM, AND THE ZAINER BROTHERS

Günther and Johannes Zainer, two of the most influential printers of illustrated books, learned their craft in Strasbourg in the early 1460s. Günther Zainer moved to Augsburg in 1468 and established his printing shop, taking with him some of the types he used in Strasbourg. After his arrival, he was apparently forbidden to use woodcut illustrations by non-Augsburg Formschneider in his books. He was granted permission to illustrate his texts under the condition that he only use members of the local guilds.[6] On October 25, 1471, Günther Zainer issued a two-volume edition of Jacobus de Voragine's *Der heyligen leben,* considered the first printed book to be extensively illustrated with woodcuts. Volume 1 was illustrated with 131 woodcuts and volume 2 with 127 woodcuts.[7]

For the first volume, the *Winterteil,* Günther Zainer printed the 131 woodcuts and the text in two different press runs, as Albrecht Pfister had done in Bamberg. Woodcuts and text had obviously not yet been put in one and the same printing frame. These woodcuts have been attributed to the Boccaccio Master, who was also active in Ulm during the early 1470s. The smallish cuts, composed to fit into the columns of text, emphasize the outline and are shaded with scarce, short parallel hatchings. They are all framed with double-line borders.

For the second volume, entitled *Sommerteil,* the cuts are attributed to the Bämler Master and are designed in the same spirit but with the less finesse than those in the *Winterteil.* According to the colophon, this volume was finished on April 27, 1472.[8] The short, compact figures with their oversized heads seem more awkward and exhibit less expression than those of the Boccaccio Master. The faces are mostly delineated in three-quarters view, and the noses often show a second line along the contour. The broad parallel hatching lines evoke a plastic impression, but rather imperfectly. Nonetheless, as Albert Schramm notes, "the numerous variations with which the illustrator de-

FIGURE 3. Jacopo da Voragine, *Legenda aurea sanctorum . . . Das sommerteil der heyligen leben,* printed in Augsburg by Günther Zainer, April 27, 1472. Fol. 112v. (LC/R38)

Rimicp
CFabula·vii·De Pifcatoze quodam·
O nia pzote funt que fuo tpe funt ·
De hoc audi fabulam· CPifcatoz qui
dam pifcandi inexpertus / tibys ac re
the affumptis /iuxta maris littus acce
dit /atcp faxo quodam fuper exiftens /
pzimis rubicinate cepit·putans cantu fe pifces faci
le effe capturum· Verum cantu cum nullum con
fequeretur effectum /depofitis rethe in mari
dimittit·ac pifces cepit perplures·Sed cu ex rethe
pifces extraheret /atcp eos faltantes perfpiceret no
infulfe ait·O impzoba animalia /dum ad tibiaz ce-
cini /faltare noluiftis /nunc quia canere ceffo falte
datis affiduos· Ergo omnia fuo tpe melie fiunt·

CDie·vii·Fabel von ainem fifcher·
lles das zu rechter zyt befchicht /daz be
fchicht löblich. Dar von hör ain fabel·
COin fifcher /dem die kunft def fifch
ens nit wol kundig was /nam zu im
das fifcher garn vñ ain trometen /vñ
gieng zu dem geftad def meres /faß vff ainē ftain

FIGURE 4. Fisherman,
fol. 193, from Aesop, *Vitae*
[after Rinucius] *et Fabulae*
[Lib. I–IV, prose version
of Romulus], printed by
Johannes Zainer in Ulm,
about 1476/77 (PML
23211.1). The Pierpont
Morgan Library.

picts very similar repetitive scenes, especially the many images of beheaded saints, is amazing."[9]

These early woodcut illustrations served a dual purpose: the first was to elucidate a particular text and the second was to decorate it. The flow of reading and contemplation was not to be interrupted by images, but rather their function was to identify and clarify ideas discussed in the text.

After having followed his elder brother Günther to Augsburg at the end of the 1460s, Johannes Zainer set up a printing shop in Ulm at the behest of Heinrich Steinhöwel, a physician and one of southern Germany's important early humanists. Between 1473 and Steinhöwel's death in 1478, Johannes Zainer printed a number of the most famous German illustrated woodcut books.[10] Some of these books were based on classical texts translated into German by Steinhöwel, including Petrarca's *Historia Griseldis* and Giovanni Boccaccio's *De claris mulieribus,* first printed in 1473, and Aesop's *Fables,* which appeared in 1476. Steinhöwel's translations served to introduce classical stories to a growing reading public. Prospering as the city physician in Ulm and married into a patrician family, Steinhöwel dedicated his German rendering of *De claris mulieribus* to the famous patroness Archduchess Eleonora of Austria. Evidence suggests that he not only backed Zainer financially but also collaborated with him on literary matters and perhaps even supervised the layout and the execution of the illustrations in several of Zainer's publications.[11]

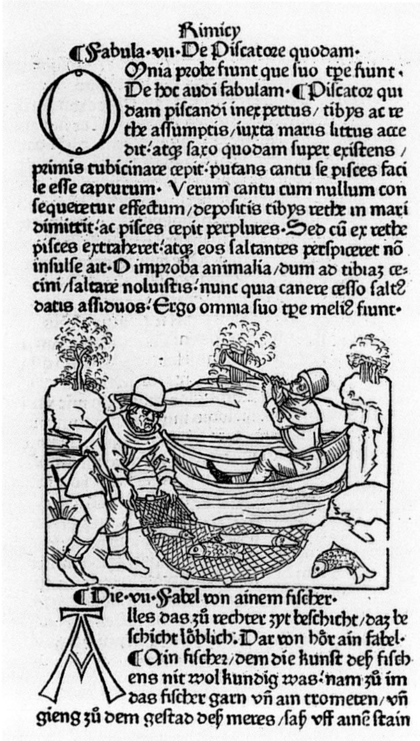

Johannes Zainer's printing of *De claris mulieribus* was his first important richly illustrated text, and it started a tremendous vogue in book illustration. The eighty well-executed woodcuts formed one of the first "picture books," in which the characters, set in lively scenes, are identified by name. The frequent depiction of incidents from classical antiquity, like Pyramus and Thisbe, the Rape of Europa, Lucretia and Tarquin, familiarized late medieval readers with subjects that were to become favorite themes in Renaissance painting. Boccaccio's text became extremely popular and by the end of the century was reprinted in Augsburg, Strasbourg, Paris, Louvain, Florence, and Saragossa in more than ten editions. Johannes Zainer's Boccaccio represents the origin of one of the most popular illustrated texts in the history of printing during the fifteenth century. It was to prove influential also for the revival of printing during the arts and crafts movement at the end of the nineteenth century; William Morris mentions it as one of his favorite books and identifies it as "the first book to give him a clear insight into the essential qualities of 'medieval' design."[12]

The woodcut illustrations in Zainer's *De claris mulieribus,* unmistakable for their clarity of line, represent the inception of the Ulm style woodcut. Iconographically, these cuts borrow some design styles typical of French-Burgundian subjects, of which the pointed feet and shoes would be one indication.[13] Unfortunately, there is no archival or other documentary evidence as to the identification of the artists or woodcutters of these remarkable blocks.

The eighty blocks for Boccaccio's *De claris mulieribus* and nine for *Historia Griseldis,* which mirror in size and design those of the Boccaccio, were most likely cut by different Formschneider, yet they show characteristic similarities of style. The figures, framed by a distinct double borderline, are defined by one clear-cut outline. The sculptural form of the figure's legs and the folds of the draperies is created by use of short, free, simple hatches. The same accents of parallel lines also define space in the surrounding architectural structures or the foreground. As an additional means of accentuating the garments and creating a physical presence beneath the folds, the cutter uses hooked lines and looped lines to delineate form.

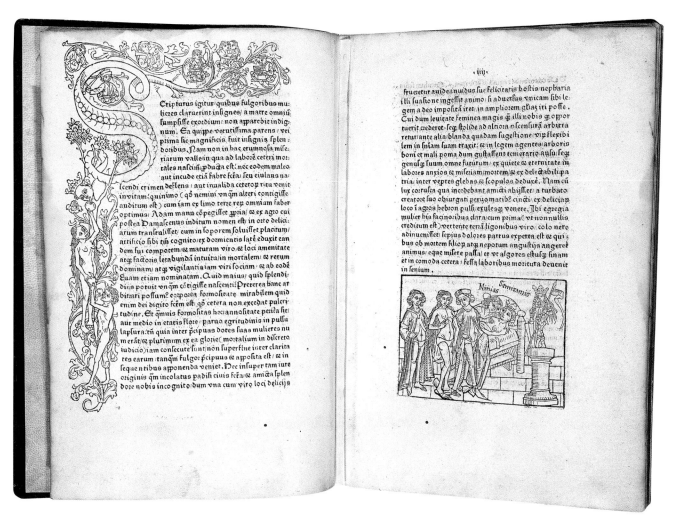

Stylistically, the more than two hundred woodcuts used in Zainer's 1476 edition of Aesop's *Vita et Fabulae* exhibit a distinctly freer feeling than that found in the Boccaccio of three years earlier. The woodcuts still retain a Gothic and somewhat stiff outline, accentuated by the looped and hooked lines, but the rendering of hands and faces is more accomplished, and there is a greater definition of space and perspective in the Aesop woodcuts. The cuts also contain small areas of solid black. Besides feet covered in black shoes, we detect accents in black on the rim of a hat, in the handle of a knife, and in the headdress of a woman, details that add interest and richness to the cuts. One could assume with a certain assurance that artistically trained wood-cutters were employed to produce the Aesop series of woodcuts, and they represent a definite step forward in the evolution of the woodcut.

Zainer's Ulm edition influenced many subsequent printings of Aesop's fables. More than thirty incunabula editions were printed all across Europe following his original model. The Ulm Aesop was dedicated to Duc Siegmund of Tyrol, the husband of Eleonora of Austria. Their coats-of-arms were incorporated into the decorative borders of Zainer's books that are dedicated to them.[14] Both the *Aesop* and *De claris mulieribus,* two of the most significant early German woodcut books, can be associated with Eleonora, Archduchess of Austria.

Peter Amelung asserts that many of the early woodcuts from the 1470s and 1480s were designed in clear outline form to be fully highlighted by color or to receive ornamental touches by the application of color wash.[15] In his exhibition catalogue *Der Frühdruck im deutschen Süd-westen, 1473–1500,* Amelung uses examples from a copy of Zainer's *De claris mulieribus* from the

FIGURE 5. Giovanni Boccaccio's *De claris mulieribus,* printed in Ulm by Johann Zainer, 1473. Fols. iii verso– iv recto. (LC/R47)

Stuttgart Library to demonstrate how the effective use of color can accentuate the foreground and background of a woodcut and turn it into a more powerful image. A number of examples in the present volume that come from the Rosenwald/Dyson Perrins collection illustrate Amelung's point and show the benefit of color in highlighting woodcuts.

Another high point of German woodcut illustration is found in Johannes Zainer's border decorations and in his elaborate woodcut initials. Zainer's border decorations consist of vine leaf borders with floral sprays in different varieties, sometimes interspersed with full or partial figures. The flow of the woodcut is clear and simple, and the image floats freely and gracefully. The border decorating the introduction of *De claris mulieribus* demonstrates this point beautifully, where the serpent in the form of the decorative initial *S,* shown seducing Adam and Eve, is both figuratively as well as conceptually remarkable. This can also be said of Zainer's so-called "erudite border," which appears first in Johannes Gritsch's *Quadragesimale,* dated October 20, 1475.[16] In both cases, the minimal use of parallel lines to shade the border and the delineation of flower petals by cutting one, two, or three simple lines constitute stylistic choices that distinguish Zainer's border style.

The same quality is found in Zainer's woodcut initial letters. The minimal use of lines and parallel hatches for shading, combined with the graceful floating design, results in some of the finest initials in the art of the early German woodcut. The appearance of these elegant initials marks the beginning of a sophisticated design style in German woodcut illustration. No other fifteenth-century German printer had such a wide selection of woodcut borders and initials in his inventory, furnishing his illustrated books with a hitherto unequaled decorative appearance.

FIGURE 6. Thomas Lirer's *Chronik von allen Königen und Kaisen,* printed in Ulm by Conrad Dinckmut, 12 January 1486. Fol. b⁵v. (LC/R 115)

## CONRAD DINCKMUT IN ULM

Ulm's second most important printer was Conrad Dinckmut, whose success began in 1476 when Johannes Zainer descended into financial difficulties. In his editions of the *Schwäbische Chronik* of Thomas Lirer, printed in 1486, we see eighteen full-page woodcuts which represent a clear advance in the style of woodcut illustration. Dinckmut's woodcut designs offer the same clear outlines, Gothic sensibility, simple outline delineation in architectural rendering, and minimal use of parallel hatching in draperies found in Zainer's earlier cuts.

In Dinckmut's woodcuts, however, we see a new stylistic development in the elasticity and movement of the figures. Long-legged soldiers are engaged in more dynamic action than found in the cuts from ten years earlier. The stiffness of Zainer's *De claris mulieribus* figures is replaced by a more developed sense of body and movement. In addition, Dinckmut's designs include a more sophisticated depiction of architecture and interior three-dimensional space. The castles and towers of the *Schwäbische Chronik* exhibit an improved skill in depicting interior space and landscapes. Series of linear contour lines are now effectively used to create background and foreground space in the composition. Curved lines are added to give the illusion of rolling hills, and shaped lines are used to incorporate the foreground into the overall design. It is again worth noting that illustrations from the copy in the Stuttgart Library—one colored, one uncolored—demonstrate the great advantage of the colored specimen over the uncolored.[17]

The depiction of the architectural setting is even more refined in Dinckmut's edition of Terence's *Eunuchus,* also printed in 1486, and illustrated with twenty-eight full-page woodcuts. Here, slender figures in contemporary costumes are identified in the woodcut by name, and these characters seem to move freely within the varied street settings and outdoor scenes. They are now placed in more sophisticated surroundings, whether they be street scenes or detailed interiors within which the action takes place. Facial expression remains limited, but gestures of hands become expressive. The human figures and buildings are accentuated by shadows, cut in fine short parallel lines, and sometimes by cross-hatching. Lively accents appear as black spots in shoes, windows, and doors, and the use of this device is on a much broader scale than in the Ulm Aesop cited above. With the publication of his edition of Terence, Dinckmut extended the high ranking of Ulm as a center for quality production of woodcut illustrations and important woodcut books well into the 1490s.[18]

One fine example that clearly demonstrates the style of the Ulm woodcut is the prayer book *Dye Siben Cursz,* published by Conrad Dinckmut in 1491 (see item 4). In this book, the design of the woodcuts is reduced to one clear outline showing the figures as well as the landscape background, with no cross-hatching or other form of shading to achieve depth in the image. The woodcuts, with their ample white spaces between the outlines, were designed especially and specifically to be colored. The red, green, and pale brown washes give the woodcut the necessary depth and pictorial richness that is so typical of the German woodcut in this period.

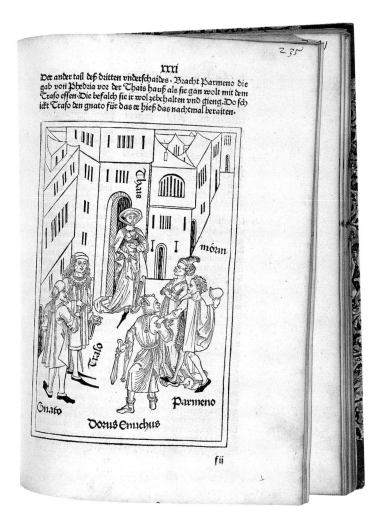

Stylistic similarities can be traced in illustrated editions from both Ulm and Augsburg. We know there was an exchange of texts and woodcuts between the two cities in the 1470s. Toward the end of the century, however, many of the better-trained workmen, printers, Briefmaler, and Reisser had left Ulm for Augsburg or possibly Nuremberg, where more lucrative jobs were then being offered.[19]

Later Augsburg printers, like Anton Sorg or Johann Bämler, successfully used woodcuts with similar stylistic expression. All Augsburg woodcut subjects of the 1470s and 1480s reside within the traditional iconographical pictorial style. Very often the hands of more than one cutter can be discerned in them. The demand for wood-block cutters must have been great, for the quantity of publications increases dramatically during a twenty-year time period. With a few exceptions, the pictorial repertoire and the stylistic characteristics remain unchanged through the end of the century.

In 1480, Anton Sorg issued a series of passion woodcuts for the first time.[20] Nine years later, he had new wood blocks of the same subjects cut considerably smaller in size for his *Horologium devotionis* of 1489. This provides clear evidence of the continuing demand for the same style and expression in woodcut imagery. The next year, Johann Schönsberger used these smaller cuts for his edition of the *Passio,* February 22, 1490. The twenty-four woodcuts in the colored copy of the Schönsberger Passion in the Rosenwald/Dyson Perrins collection clearly demonstrate this stylistic continuity, showing typical traits from the early 1480s in their outlines. The contour lines, being slightly angular in shape, are emphasized, and few details appear in the inner drawing. Only a small number of parallel lines form accents in folds or shaded parts of the woodcuts. The faces, with their big eyes and half-moon eyelids show very little variety. (See item 3.)[21]

The composition of Christ Washing the Feet of the Apostles from Schönsperger's Passion shows a novel compositional arrangement. Apostles pour into the scene from both sides. Some figures are partly cut off by the borderline, a rather modern concept for the artist. He no longer needs to have the entire scene framed but is free to truncate parts of figures or background that seem unimportant. In addition, the composition has a central focal point in the hands of Christ, with different axes leading to it. The woodcutter uses these axes in a skilled way, with a confident artistic sensibility. It must be noted that this particular composition of Christ Washing the Feet was not included in Anton Sorg's original series of woodcuts made in 1480. Yet by 1490, in Schönsperger's woodcut, we see a new sense of iconographical composition begin to take form. Surprising in this image is the relatively crude cutting of the block, which contrasts with the more sophisticated sense of composition. This subtle woodcut offers an indication that the reading public of the late 1480s had begun to expect more from book illustration.

## Erhard Ratdolt and Color Printing

Augsburg was also the birthplace and home of one of the most enterprising and experimental printers of the 1480s and 1490s. At a very young age, Erhard Ratdolt moved from Augsburg to Venice, where he opened a printing shop in 1476. His early publications are renowned for their wood-block borders and decorative letters. In Ratdolt's Venetian edition of Regiomontanus's *Calendarium,* printed in 1476, one recognizes an undeniable Italian Renaissance influence in both the borders and initials. Gilbert Redgrave, in his work on Erhard Ratdolt, states that the title page of the *Calendarium* is the first title page ever to appear in a printed book.[22] The initial letter and border printed on the title page are composed of white vines on black grounds, and remind us of the precise work of a goldsmith or the gold engraving on armor of the famous Negrolli Mantuan school. One further senses an Arabic influence in the borders of the *Calendarium,* though it is less prominent in the borders for his editions of Appianus's *Historia Romana* and *De bellis civilibus,* both printed in 1477.[23] Here, a new harmony is achieved by Ratdolt's congruous design in both initials and borders, which seem to have been executed by the same cutter, resulting in some of the most beautiful borders ever included in a printed book.

It was in Venice that Erhart Ratdolt embraced scientific publishing and printed a few famous astronomical texts. His edition of Albumasar's *Flores astrologiae* printed on November 18, 1488, offers a series of woodcuts in clear outline style, with sparse parallel hatching and without background or borders (see item 1). The iconography of these cuts, gods and goddesses driving chariots decorated with zodiac signs, harkens back to subjects first encountered in Florence in 1460 and copied by Venetian artists in the decades to follow.

Ratdolt first used these famous wood blocks in his Venetian editions of Hyginus's *Poetica astronomica* printed in 1482 and 1485. He then reincorporated them in his two editions of Albumasar's *Flores astrologiae,* printed in Augsburg in 1488 and 1495, and later used parts of the same blocks in Leupoldus's *Compilatio de astrorum scientia,* which he issued in 1489.[24] It is significant that these wood blocks, with their Florentine and Venetian characteristics, were transported by Ratdolt to his new home in Augsburg. Thus, Ratdolt left Venice not only with the spirit of Italian Renaissance distilled in his soul, but also with the actual wood blocks securely packed in his luggage.

Another milestone established by Erhard Ratdolt involved his experimentation with printing in color. He chose an unprecedented design in black and red for his own well-known printer's mark. He was the first printer to introduce the use of astronomical diagrams printed in black, red, and shades of yellow-brown to illustrate Sacrobusto's *Sphaera mundi,* published in 1485. In Ratdolt's earlier edition of 1482, these planetary diagrams were still colored by hand.[25] The color-printed diagrams for his 1485 edition offer more intense tones when compared to the diagrams of the earlier edition, which are highlighted with watercolor and are less striking in their intensity.

Ratdolt's first figurative woodcut printed in color is the coat-of-arms of Bishop Johann II von Werdenberg. It is printed in black, red, and yellow, and Schramm suggests that this early color work was completed while Ratdolt was still working in Venice.[26] Rat-

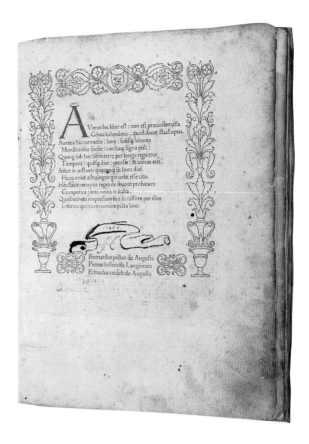

FIGURE 8. Johannes Mueller, Regiomontanus, *Calendarium,* printed in Venice by Erhard Ratdolt, 1476. Fol. [a¹]. (LC/R 221)

dolt's first color woodcut of a figure, a standing bishop, showing his new patron Friedrich II von Hohenzollern, is printed in black, yellow, red, and olive green. It appears in the first book he printed in Augsburg after his move from Venice, *Obsequiale augustanum,* published in February 1487. This publication also contains the first musical notes printed in woodcut.[27] Furthermore, Ratdolt had experimented with printing in gold during his stay in Venice, as can be noted in the dedicatory letter printed in gold in two luxury dedication copies of his well-known *Euclid* of 1486.[28] During the incunabula period, Erhard Ratdolt was the only printer widely recognized as having mastered the technique of printing in different colors.

After moving to Augsburg in 1486, Erhard Ratdolt began printing a larger number of liturgical books for various dioceses. Most of his missals are sumptuous productions printed in red and black, which often contain printed musical notes, woodcut illustrations, and large woodcut initials. Frequently, for these later publications, Ratdolt employed Hans Burgkmair, one of Augsburg's most important artists of the period, as artist-draftsman. The woodcut illustrations portray patron saints of the respective dioceses for which the books were being printed, as well as images of the Virgin Mary and the canon woodcut, or crucifixion scene, generally in full-page size. In the canon woodcut, one finds Christ on the cross in the center of the image, with Mary and Saint John standing to his right and left.

Hans Burgkmair (1473–1531) completed his apprenticeship with Martin Schongauer of Colmar around 1490. At the age of seventeen, he began to work for Erhard Ratdolt, who by that time was fully matured in the technical skills of printing. Burgkmair's first woodcut for Ratdolt depicts the Madonna and Child and dates from 1491. It reveals Schongauer's influence in its sensitive design and detail. A new departure is evident in the delineation of the image, created by the use of minute shading in the features of both figures.[29] Burgkmair provided Ratdolt with a succession of proficient woodcuts for patron saints, Madonnas, and Christ on the cross. Each woodcut shows finer expression in the faces and each captures the scene with in-

creased artistic sensibility. On several occasions, printing in different colors is used. As a consequence of his experience and exposure to color printing with Ratdolt, Hans Burgkmair later in his career was able to play an important role in the development of the chiaroscuro woodcut. His *Lovers Surprised by Death* is one of the great achievements in German Renaissance art.

In Ratdolt's *Missale Pataviense,* published in 1494, we encounter an absolutely exquisite full-page woodcut by Burgkmair of the patron saints of Passau, one of the rare existing title-page woodcuts printed in different colors.[30] Saint Stephen, with a palm twig, a book, and the stones of his martyrdom in his hands, stands beneath a three-part arch decorated with an ornamental white vine on a black ground. On either side of Saint Stephen stand two bishops, Saint Valentine and Saint Maximilian. The positioning of Saint Stephen with a slightly elevated right leg adds an unforeseen plasticity and physical presence to the figure. Burgkmair uses a black-line cut with four tone blocks in orange red, dark yellow, indigo, and brown to produce this stunning woodcut.

The use of a color-printed title page on the *Missale Pataviense* was unusual. Printing in color was normally too extravagant for title pages, because alternate versions with different patron saints were needed for the various dioceses that commissioned Ratdolt to print their liturgical publications. This was not the case for canon woodcuts, which could be reused in several different editions of a missal. Ratdolt's *Missale Pataviense* also contains a full-page canon woodcut on vellum by Hans Burgkmair, printed in black, orange red, dark yellow, dark blue, and olive. The canon woodcut possesses additional coloring by hand in the sky and in the drops of blood on Christ's body.[31] As Margaret Grasselli states, "All color blocks used in the woodcuts published by Ratdolt were cut so that the printed colors were separated from each other by the black outlines; thus the prints look very much like woodcuts that had been hand colored with stencils."[32] This color-printing technique was intended to create an impression like that of a hand-painted miniature, but its production consumed less time and the image could be reproduced in multiple copies. These two outstanding woodcuts from the *Missale Pataviense* may represent Hans Burgkmair's earliest examples of color printing.[33]

The supreme quality of these Burgkmair woodcuts demonstrates the progress achieved in the stylistic development of woodcut illustration since the early 1460s. The incorporation of an illustration by an artist, later renowned, clearly improved the beauty of Erhard Ratdolt's printed books. Burgkmair's full-page illustrations are among the most elegant and masterful woodcuts of the fifteenth and early sixteenth centuries. Significantly, here for the first time, woodcuts in books could be attributed to an individual artist based on stylistic expression.

FIGURE 9. Saint Valentine, Saint Stephen, and Saint Maximilian, fol. 20, from the *Missale Pataviense* printed in Augsburg by Erhard Ratdolt, 1494. Rosenwald Collection, National Gallery of Art, Washington, D.C. Image © Board of Trustees, National Gallery of Art.

ERHARD REUWICH AND *PEREGRINATIONES IN TERRAM SANCTAM*

In 1486 a Mainz printer issued one of the masterworks of book illustration, Bernard von Breydenbach's *Peregrinationes in Terram Sanctam.* The dean of Mainz cathedral, Bernhard von Breydenbach, set out in April 1484 for the Holy Land, accompanied by Count Johann zu Solm-Lich,

Knight Philipp von Bicken, and, among others, Erhard Reuwich, an artist from Utrecht who was engaged to make pictures of places the travelers visited en route. After their return from the long journey, which included a visit to the monastery of Saint Catherine on the Sinai Peninsula, Breydenbach had an account written in Latin of their perilous expedition, and Reuwich worked up his sketches. The *Peregrinatio* appeared in 1486 in Latin and in German-language editions and became the first "best-selling" travel book.

Reuwich's panoramic woodcut views of ports and cities represent the first instance where topographical scenes drawn from life were used to illustrate a book. For the first time, actual topographical places are shown as seen by the artist at that moment. Many of these city views were printed from multiple wood blocks, which were pasted together and folded to fit with the text. In the case of the view of Venice, the woodcut extends to nearly five feet in length and was printed from eight blocks. In addition to views of Venice, Jerusalem, the Holy Land, Corfu, Crete, and Rhodes, Reuwich provided pictures of the Temple of Solomon and the Church of the Holy Sepulcher and images of inhabitants of the Holy Land in their native costumes. Furthermore, exotic animals like giraffes, dromedaries, a unicorn, and an ape, as well as six woodcuts of oriental alphabets, were included. Overall, *Peregrinationes in Terram Sanctam* is a luxurious production, and it seems probable that Reuwich supervised all the various aspects of its publication.[34]

From the stylistic point of view, the most developed woodcut in the book is Reuwich's impressive frontispiece. It shows the figure of a woman in Venetian costume holding the coats-of-arms of the three most prominent participants in the journey to the Holy Land. The ex-pressive figure of the woman stands under an arch of flow-ing vines with putti. In fact, the vines appear to be prickly climbing rose bushes in whose branches naked children play, climb, or reach to grab for a rose. At the center, carefully concealed, the viewer discovers a bird's nest. The active scene, drawn with delicate outline and shading, shows well-rounded forms and has a three-dimensional quality. It is evident that such a complex design could be executed and so skillfully accomplished only by an expert wood block cutter.

The feathers of the heraldic beasts dominate the design of the woodcut. These feathered wings are precisely rounded and give both of the heraldic animals lively expressions. In the helmets of the crests, Reuwich reverses the normal black-line-on-white-background technique by using white lines on a black background. The design further plays skillfully with light. On the upper part of the coats-of-arms to the left and right, the artist applies a varied pattern of cross hatches and parallel hatches to create the impression of the shields being contoured. Very fine, short shading lines are used to modulate the woman's cheeks, neck, and décolletée. The woman's dress and decorated head attire are typically Vene-tian. The elaborate folds of her costume express richness and wonder for the exotic. A comparison with the drawing of a *Female Figure in Venetian Costume* by Albrecht Dürer in the Albertina in Vienna shows remarkable similarities in cos-tume and headdress.[35]

FIGURE 10. Bernhard von Breydenbach's *Peregrinationes in Terram Sanctam,* printed in Mainz by Erhard Reuwich, June 21, 1486. Frontispiece, fol. i verso. (LC/R 116)

Equally successful in Reuwich's design is the architectural structure of the woodcut. The columns at both sides are done in three-dimensional perspective, as is the pedestal where the woman stands. Here we see one of the earliest examples of solid ground accentuated by images of individual plant specimens. Single plants in the foreground are a typical feature of Martin Schongauer's engravings, which must have been known to Reuwich.

The varying density of lines adds to the liveliness of the whole scene. Reuwich's frontispiece uses uneven contour lines, and curved, long hatches depicting subtle shades not only to express dynamic energy but also to create a clear spatial concept. This ground-breaking woodcut exhibits a strong expressive line and a novel artistic complexity. Reuwich's woodcut does not need any coloring. It actually does not allow any coloring. Artistically conceived and realized, this frontispiece represents a major step forward in the stylistic development of the late medieval woodcut. This is the first time the artist of the illustrations is mentioned by name in a book. To our knowledge, this is one of the first times as well that a frontispiece is used to enrich the opening of a printed book.

This new development, where the artist expresses movement, perspective, and contrast with a variation in line density and sculptural modeling, may at first appear busy. Taking a closer look, however, we detect that wherever the drawing process had been reversed, and white lines are the drawing or contour lines, a controlled calmness enters the scene. A new level of nuance and expression is achieved; a technique that will be further advanced and perfected by Albrecht Dürer, who in the 1490s completely changed the art of woodcut for all time.

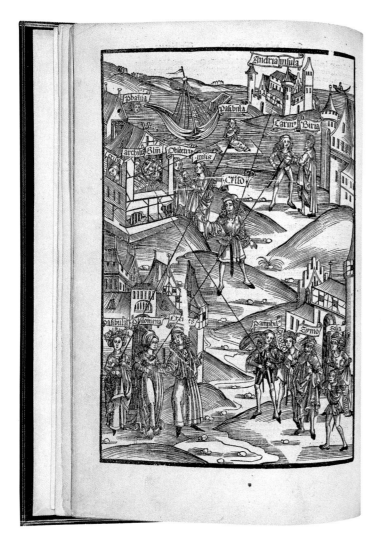

FIGURE 11. Terence's *Comedies* printed in Strasbourg by Johann Grüninger, 1 November 1496. Fol. b¹v. (LC/R 175)

## STRASBOURG, GRÜNINGER, AND URS GRAF

Apart from Augsburg, Ulm, and Nuremberg, the most important centers for printing books in the south of the German-speaking regions were Strasbourg and Basel. First printings for Strasbourg have been dated 1458/60 for works by Johann Mentelin. Mentelin produced his first and only illustrated book, the *Etymologiae* by Isidorus Hispalensis, which contained seven mostly schematic woodcuts, in about 1473.[36] A decade later, Strasbourg would become an important center for the production of illustrated books. The printer Johann Grüninger, active 1483–1531, was a vigorous promoter of illustrated books. He was Johannes Reinhardi from Grüningen but called himself Grüninger, and in his almost fifty years of active printing, he edited texts of all different sorts.

One of his earliest publications is a richly illustrated Bible, the Eleventh German Bible, published May 2, 1485. In its iconographical depiction, the choice of scenes illustrated, Grüninger generally follows earlier Bible editions. His conception of scenes, however, is imaginative. The woodcuts in the Eleventh German Bible foreshadow his later technique of combining

independent scenes within a single framed border.[37]
A distinctive Grüninger style of cutting wood block
illustrations began to develop over the next few years.[38]
In his editions of Terence and Horace, the woodcuts,
with multiple, dense, long fine parallel hatchings,
reach a hitherto unseen pictorial quality. Any coloring is superfluous in these images with their dark
strongly hatched backgrounds. Over successive publications, we see the cutters achieve a subtle softness
of form by reducing the density of the lines and changing them into finer, softer curved ones, without losing the appearance of precision. Frank Hieronymus
suggests that Grüninger, unlike the Basel printers, kept
a separate workshop with Reisser and Formschneider within his own printing shop.[39]

In his *Comedies* of Terence published 1496,
Grüninger perfected the technique of constructing
a single scene by mounting up to five separate woodcut blocks into one image. Each character is represented on a little woodcut resembling a slug of type.
These are designed to be grouped with other "character cuts" to express pictorially who is on stage in
each scene. Thus Grüninger was able, by producing
only 88 cuts, to illustrate his publication with 156
woodcut illustrations, evidently an important economical innovation. As a result, the reappearance of

the same human figures, sided by trees and houses as in stage sets, leads to a certain monotonous
feeling. Important for the development of iconography are the introductory woodcut, which
shows the inside of a theater, and the six full-page woodcuts at the beginning of each comedy.
One curious aspect is the attempt to connect the "dramatis personae" dispersed over the page
by the means of straight, naïve-looking lines.[40]

The year 1502 marks a key step forward in the quality of illustrations from the press of
Johann Grüninger. In the title and preface for his edition of Virgil's *Opera,* the humanist and
poet Sebastian Brant (1458–1521) is named as the designer of the illustrations, as well as the
editor of the work and the author of the commentary. The style of these woodcuts is characteristic of Grüninger's workshop and every block points to the hands of artists from that shop. In
them, the world of Greek gods and heroes has been transported to the late Middle Ages. Costumes, ships, buildings, and arms befit the fifteenth century. Most of the two hundred woodcuts are full page in size. Several different cutters used the same technique of applying thin,
slightly bent lines which give a round, smooth expression to figures and forms and allow fine
nuances in the shading from dark to light. Lively black and white nuances give physical presence
to the figures and spatial depth to the scenes. These dense arrays of parallel lines give the woodcuts an overall dark, even-toned, finish and achieve a pictorial effect. The images project the
impression of painterly differentiation.

This hatching style has generally been recognized as having its origin in the technique
of engraving. The attempt to copy the subtle nuances in the shades found in engravings was a
standard practice, but Grüninger achieved a better result in his Virgil than in the earlier edition

FIGURE 12. Publius
Vergilius Maro, *Opera,*
printed in Strasbourg
by Johann Grüninger,
1502. Fol. CCLXXr.
(LC/R 594)

of Terence published in 1496. In general, the images contain polyschematic scenes within a single woodcut. Landscapes are often depicted with perspective from an elevated point of view, and the picture surface seems densely filled. The compilation of different scenes from Virgil's text into a single woodcut adds a further visual tension for the onlooker.

Both Johann Grüninger and Johann Knobloch, another Strasbourg printer, published the sermons of Geyler von Kaisersperg, a prominent preacher of the period. In these books the illustrations show a quiet arrangement in composition, while never losing their typical stylistic complexity.

In 1506 Johann Knobloch issued a compilation of Geyler's texts on the passion illustrated with twenty-six full-page woodcuts by Urs Graf. The text was edited by a young humanist, poet, historian, and geographer, Mathias Ringmann Philesius (1482–1511). The woodcuts for the Ringmann Passion, as the book is also called, were Urs Graf's earliest important works and, according to Frank Hieronymus, must have taken the young artist several years to finish.[41] Of significance is their unusual size. One might assume that Urs Graf was influenced not only by Grüninger's edition of *Virgil* of 1502, but clearly also by Albrecht Dürer's *Apocalypse* published in 1498.

By dividing a scene into a foreground with dramatic action and a background with architecture or scenic landscape, Graf achieved a certain degree of monumentality. The woodcut of the Raising of Lazarus demonstrates Graf's attempt to organize a "multilayered" scene in different compartments. The composition, although it consists of multiple scenes in one, is strongly structured in a *Z* shape, which leads the eye into perspective depths toward the back. It finds its climax in the town of Jerusalem shown in the far upper background. Graf's technique in shading the woodcut is inspiring. He uses a varied line pattern, as well as cross-hatching, to emphasize the forms and to create liveliness and physical dimension. As Daniel De Simone points out, "His heads show individual characteristics and his method of using short accents to further define facial features is a technique reminiscent of Dürer's work." (See item 38.)

In Basel during the fifteenth century, we find a concentration of the production of religious, devotional, and erudite texts. First printings are dated to 1468 by Berthold Ruppel. In Basel, the earliest illustrated book is Alphonse de Spinas's *Fortalitium fidei,* published by Bernhard Richel around 1475 with one woodcut only. The earliest significant illustrated book was Richel's edition of a *Spiegel menschlicher Behaltnis,* richly illustrated with 278 woodcuts from 255 blocks, published in 1476.[42]

The vertical woodcuts illustrating the *Spiegel menschlicher Behaltnis* are enframed by a broad dominant borderline. The figures, depicted with admirable versatility and movement, dominate the scene, and short and longer parallel lines permeate the drawing style. Expressions in the features of figures are successfully achieved with finely cut lines, such as accents on eyebrows. Overall, the faces, with their prominent noses and oval eyes with black pupils, are economical in line but powerful in their emotional expression. The woodcuts for the *Spiegel menschlicher Behaltnis* can be associated stylistically with Günther Zainer's *Speculum humanae salvationis* published in Augsburg 1473.[43] A certain familiarity in the conception and character of the woodcuts of both works can be acknowledged. The iconographical sequence is followed, the accents in solid black are maintained, and the drawing of hair and beards confirms the overall similarity. The format of the Basel woodcuts, however, is vertical as opposed to horizontal, and one borderline—rather than the traditional double borderline of Augsburg and Ulm—is used.

The lively Basel series takes movement of figures and composition of scenes a distinct step further as well as amplifying the iconographical concept. A more energetic drawing line is combined with descriptive details in such scenes as those with elaborate floors. Complex floor tiles varying from square black and white, to plain white, to black and white dots, and to tiles striped diagonally enhance the scene's visual impact. The iconographical concept is also more decorative. On several occasions, God the Father is realized as a full or half figure rather than a mere symbol of a hand as found in the Augsburg series. Looking at the Annunciation woodcut, we are instantly reminded of Martin Schongauer's engraving of the same subject by the design of the flower in the vase and the checkered floor carpet. Altogether, the connection between the Basel and Augsburg cuts for the *Speculum* is clearly recognizable and points toward the direction of future stylistic development in woodcut illustration.

The same style can be found in Bernhard Richel's remarkable woodcuts for the popular saga *Melusine,* published in 1475, where a new spirit of lively Renaissance style is visible. The sixty-seven full-page cuts are comparable to those of the *Speculum,* but in *Melusine* the scenes exhibit a more immediate sensation of movement and a more concise spacial composition is realized.[44] The large-size *Melusine* illustrations transcend by far the visual experience of a mere *Volksbuch.*

Another of the early printers in Basel was Michael Furter, who came from Augsburg around 1486. His publications show a preference for illustration, unlike those of

FIGURE 15. Couldrette's *Von einer Frouwen genant Melusina* [Basel: Bernhard Richel, 1476]. Fol. 57v. (LC/R 356)

the great Basel contemporary of his time, Johann Amerbach, who published mainly learned texts. On behalf of Johann Bergmann von Olpe, Furter published the first illustrated edition of the famous letter of Christopher Columbus describing his discovery of America, *De Insulis in mari Indico nuper inventis,* printed after April 29, 1493.[45] The illustrations show Columbus landing on the island of Santo Domingo. The ship is not depicted after nature, but derives from Breydenbach's *Peregrinationes in Terram Sanctam.* The fine contour lines show an expert wood-block cutter at work. His accomplishment is readily seen in his ability to cut the lines with loose free movement to create the impression of live water. Winkler has attributed the design of these cuts to the Master of Haintz Narr.[46] The artist's efforts are less successful in delineating landscape, for little three-dimensional quality is conveyed. We again encounter the same stylistic traits in Methodius's *Revelationes divinae a sanctis angelis factae,* printed in Basel by Michael Furter in 1498 (see item 28).

Close in technique, but a distinct step ahead in composition and expression, are Michael Furter's illustrations for *Der Ritter vom Turn,* by Geoffroy de la Tour-Landry, published in 1493. An entirely new and much freer look can be detected in Furter's single scene images. The blocks further possess a superior artistic conception of composition. These woodcuts have been attributed to young Albrecht Dürer and might have been designed during his short stay in Basel. The uneven quality seen in the cutting of the blocks, however, gives cause to dispute this attribution.[47] A strong naturalistic touch permeates the depiction of the female cadaver lying on a table, her chest opened and exposed to the surrounding spectators. Striking details of composition, like the brick walls of the chamber or the man to the right wearing spectacles, remind us of Martin Schongauer's Death of the Virgin. The arches of the vault in which the scene is situated can be found later in Albrecht Dürer's *Life of the Virgin Mary* in manifold varieties.[48] It is of note that the knight in the woodcut Jephta Receives Her Father in the *Schatzbehalter* resembles in specific detail and in overall style the knight in the *Ritter vom Turn.*[49]

Johann Bergmann von Olpe published Sebastian Brant's *Narrenschiff* on February 11, 1494. The text by the renowned Basel humanist Sebastian Brant narrates the sea journey of 112 fools to the paradise of fools, "Narragonia."[50] Brant's moral, didactic satire became one of the most successful book publications of all times. Printed in quarto size, its every page is framed at the sides by two decorative borders, and each chapter of the text begins with a full-page woodcut.

Of the 105 illustrations, 73 woodcuts are attributed to the young Albrecht Dürer, who must have sojourned in Basel during his journey to visit Martin Schongauer in Colmar. Dürer's 73 cuts are discernible by the bells on the caps of the fools. Another 15 illustrations are attributed to the Master of Haintz Narr. His fools have coxcombs instead of Dürer's bells.[51] The woodcuts possess an increasing sense of and certainty for perspective and show a new understanding of the relationship of figures within space. Light coming from the side and the resulting shadows situate the figures solidly within their backgrounds. Extensive varying shade lines and dots serve to give the image a three-dimensional modeling. The contour lines are more strongly conceived than the inside drawing and hatching. Characteristic of Dürer's poignant scenes is a sophisticated composition, well balanced between the figures and their surroundings. Dürer understood a way of drawing that would best allow the cutter to transform his demands into the final woodcut. All he required was a wood-block cutter with refined technical ability. "This new black-and-white art renounces color, for it is able to form a picture through the means of graphics alone."[52]

The woodcut illustrations created for *Das Narrenschiff* are of immense density and tenseness. Since there was no iconographical tradition for this newly conceived text, the subjects and scenes of the illustrations had to be created entirely new. The images presented are of such convincing force that their equal in design had never before been seen. In addition, the technical and artistic quality of the woodcutting marks a distinct advance in the craft.

The ingenuity of text and illustrations owes to the providential meeting of two extraordinary characters, Brant and Dürer. Sebastian Brant, a canonical conservative and moralistic mocker, clearly was able to visualize the way that illustration could enhance the finished text, so that each would complement the other. His motto was to create understanding in the uneducated by adding pictures to a story: "nam quod legentibus scriptura, hoc et idiotis prestat pictura cernentibus."[53] The *Narrenschiff* is considered the fifteenth-century publication where text and illustration complete each other in an ideal way and are interwoven in a perfect manner.

FIGURE 17. Sebastian Brant's *Das Narrenschiff*, printed in Basel by Johann Bergmann von Olpe, 11 February 1494. Fol. c³v. (LC/R 361)

## NUREMBERG, KOBERGER, AND ALBRECHT DÜRER

Nuremberg, a wealthy mercantile center in south Germany, provided an environment propitious for the advancement of book illustration. Two illustrated books published in 1488 by different printers show the favorable and fruitful situation for the book printing business that resulted from the free access to many different Reisser and Formschneider from various workshops and regions. In the *Bruder Claus,* published 1488 by Marx Ayrer, and in the Latin edition of Bertholdus's *Horologium devotionis,* published by Friedrich Creussner, young Albrecht Dürer's hand has been repeatedly recognized, though also repeatedly questioned.

The illustrations in the *Horologium* show an unusual observation of nature and a graphic delineation of body. The figures are pictured in clearly organized relationships. Slanting diagonal lines emphasize space, and hatches delineate the forms of landscape. The variable delineations in the trees express a clear endeavor to render individual diversity. Not yet having mastered all aspects of his craft, the artist nevertheless tries to achieve a new, direct presentation of nature. Space is opening up and figures are grouped in connection to each other within their space, easily interacting within a single coherent picture.[54]

Unquestionably the most important Nuremberg printer, Anton Koberger built a large printing establishment over the period of several years. On December 5, 1488, he printed a luxury edition of Jacopo da Voragine's *Lives of the Saints* containing more than 250 woodcut illustrations that were narrow, rectangular in shape, and spread across both columns. Although

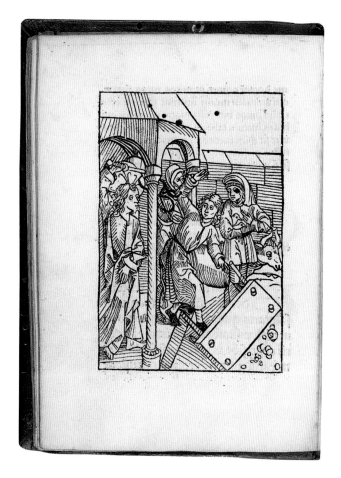

FIGURE 18. Bertholdus's *Horologium devotionis, Zeitglöcklein des Lebens und Leidens Christi,* printed in Nuremberg by Friedrich Creussner, 11 May 1489. Fol. c⁷v. (LC/R 139)

FIGURE 19. Jacopo da Voragine's *Legenda aurea sanctorum,* printed in Nuremberg by Anton Koberger, 5 December 1488. Fol. LXXXIIII. (LC/R 127)

the woodcuts convey a Gothic feeling, some of them show a new liveliness in the conception of the images. This early Koberger book gives a clear indication of the direction toward luxury publication that his printing house was to take. As Schramm confirms, the *Lives of the Saints* is a publication "which does great credit to its [Koberger's] printing establishment in terms of printing as well as illustrations."[55] The principal woodcutter for Koberger's *Lives of the Saints* was the Ulm Master, who was responsible for the magnificent illustrations of Thomas Lirer's *Chronicle* published in 1486.

Anton Koberger frequently employed the painters and sculptors Michael Wolgemut and Wilhelm Pleydenwurff and their workshop as designers for his publications. As an artist, Wolgemut was renowned in Nuremberg. Giulia Bartrum states that "he specialized in the production of elaborate painted and sculpted altarpieces," as well as stained-glass windows. His high altarpiece for the Marienkirche in Zwickau cost fourteen hundred gulden, "a fee considerably larger than any earned by Dürer for his painted altarpieces."[56] By the mid-1480s Wolgemut's artwork succeeded in forming a new, more convincing depiction of nature and space. Clearly, in his work a more accurate approach toward the composition of scenes began to prevail. Wolgemut's austere, functional style was suitable for the new necessities of imagery in Nuremberg at the time, and it was the foundation of his success. This clear eye for nature was one of the main sensibilities that he transmitted to his young apprentice Albrecht Dürer.

Around 1465 Wolgemut was joined by Wilhelm Pleydenwurff, his stepson, possibly as an equal partner. Pleydenwurff might have been active in the Netherlands before joining Wolgemut. Netherlandish influence represents an important element in the training of his father, the painter Hans Pleydenwurff, as it was for Albrecht Dürer's father as well. Wilhelm Pleydenwurff seems to have been the driving force behind book illustration in Wolgemut's workshop

until his death in 1494. Wolgemut and Pleydenwurff are considered "draftsmen with a strong sense of graphic layout both in the design of an individual composition and in the construction of a page."[57]

In Wolgemut's diverse, encompassing workshop young Albrecht Dürer started his apprenticeship on November 30, 1486. During the following three years he must have participated in all the tasks at hand. As the son of a goldsmith, Dürer was familiar with precise craftsmanship. It was during his apprenticeship with Wolgemut that he probably learned the craft of woodblock cutting. This invaluable skill later allowed Dürer to correct and help improve the cutters' work in actualizing his designs. Whether early on Dürer worked as a Reisser on some illustrations in Nuremberg, or later during his travel days in Basel, we will probably never know. It is likely, however, that Albrecht Dürer executed his drawings directly onto the wood blocks, which allowed the cutter to translate his designs into a lively, expressive, and artistic line. He was able to convey to the cutter his acute understanding of the woodcut lines as they would print on paper.

In connection with book illustration, the supportive interest of Dürer's godfather Anton Koberger was of decisive significance. A few of the woodcuts from the 1488 *Lives of the Saints* have been attributed to the extraordinary talent of the twelve-year-old Albrecht Dürer.[58] In 1491 Koberger published his exceptional *Schatzbehalter der wahren Reichtümer des Heils,* a richly illustrated devotional text.[59] Two years later, in 1493, Anton Koberger's best-known and most ambitious undertaking, Hartmann Schedel's *Weltchronik,* was published.[60]

The Nuremberg city physician and humanist Hartmann Schedel (1440–1514) compiled a history of the world from creation onward on behalf of two wealthy Nuremberg patricians, Sebald Schreyer and Sebastian Kammermeister. The *Weltchronik,* as it was called, achieved a level far superior to any previous publications with regard to its large-scale images, the unprecedented number of illustrations, and its large-size format. The book contains 1,809 illustrations, formed from 645 wood blocks, and the history of its production is well documented. It is recorded that the *Weltchronik* was "not meant for students of antiquity, but rather for the delight of the general public," a novel conception for the fifteenth century.[61] Such a statement implies that visually alert readers made up the public, and that this public was ready for the astonishing woodcuts of Albrecht Dürer's generation.

Michael Wolgemut and Wilhelm Pleydenwurff were contracted as designers for the *Weltchronik.* In their workshop, the wood blocks were also cut by as many as four different wood block-cutters. It should be noted that the actual cutting of the designs was a considerable expense, costing four times as much as the original invention and transfer of the images.[62]

The stylistic differences in the woodcut illustrations in the *Schatzbehalter* and those in the *Weltchronik* were evaluated by Landau and Parshall as showing a "significant shift in style and particularly in graphic sensibility. The cuts for the earlier text are engagingly rhythmical and graceful, the later ones staccato and angular. The compositions for the *Schatzbehalter* tend to weave over the whole surface of the block, whereas those in the *Weltchronik* are relatively liberal in their allowance of white, unprinted regions. Here priority is given to the arrangement of figures within a framed field, with greater stress on contrasting areas of dark and medium tone."[63] Whereas the *Schatzbehalter* offers a more artistic presentation in its illustration, the later *Weltchronik* represents an advancement in overall conception of design and, specifically, *mise-en-page.*

In regard to the expense and the overall financial risks involved in the making of the *Weltchronik,* one can assume Koberger chose Wolgemut and his workshop because it was the finest of its kind at the time. All stages of the project were planned on an ambitious level with a meticulous attention to detail. The quality of the design has been considered uneven, owing

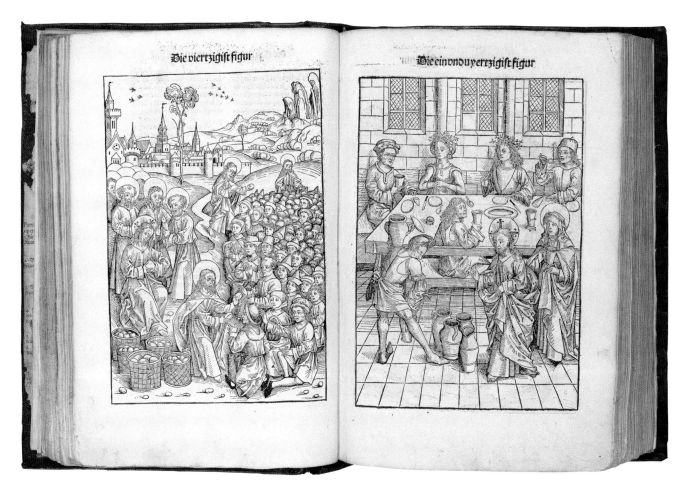

Die viertzigist figur                    Die einvnduyertzigist figur

Figure 20. Stephan
Fridolin's *Schatzbehalter,*
printed in Nuremberg
by Anton Koberger,
8 November 1491.
Fols. p⁴v–p⁵ r.
(LC/R 154)

to the sheer quantity of woodcuts that had to be executed.[64] Nevertheless, in general the figures are well defined with graphic modeling and with hatches in cross and parallel lines. An obvious effort was made to achieve uniformity in light.

The contribution of Albrecht Dürer to the illustrations of the *Weltchronik* has been discussed at length.[65] The plastic strength of the line in certain woodcuts or parts of them is extraordinary, as is the expression of the line in a few of the images. The dynamic is tense to the extreme. A fine example is found in the wind gods in the corners of the Seventh Day of Creation, which show a hand with excellent artistry executing a bold and creative design. Cramped in their corners, the four heads of the wind gods seem to burst the borderline of the woodcut. This dramatic effect is achieved by white-line drawing, which drastically augments the impact in plasticity.

The invention of the technique of white-line drawing was attributed to Albrecht Dürer first by F. Kriegbaum. Black contour lines adjoining shadows became white contour lines, thus creating a new artistic technique, which Kriegbaum attributed exclusively and solely to Dürer. In any case, the technique of white line is found in a number of illustrations in the *Weltchronik.*[66] Certainly, drawing in white line represents a more advanced and progressive style. We have noticed its use already in the remarkable frontispiece of Breydenbach's *Peregrinationes in Terram Sanctam* of 1486. A similar solution is notable in the compositions of the frontispieces of the *Weltchronik* and of the *Peregrinationes.* In both frontispieces, two architectural columns on either side of the composition are topped by a vine border. Both vines are subdivided into three parts and cut in white line on black background.[67]

The *Weltchronik* and the *Schatzbehalter* were the first two major printmaking projects of

Nuremberg with documented attributions to the designers of the illustrations. Together with Breydenbach's *Peregrinationes,* they are also the earliest books printed in Germany for which the responsibility for the designs can be assigned to known artists.

## DÜRER AND THE BIRTH OF THE ARTIST'S BOOK

In the year 1495, Albrecht Dürer returned from his first journey to Italy, and it was at this time that he may have begun his fabulous cycle of woodcut illustrations for the *Apocalypsis cum figuris.* The workshop of Wolgemut provided a vast source of experienced wood-block cutters, from which Dürer could draw for his woodcut projects of the mid-1490s onward. The question of Dürer's personal involvement in block cutting has been raised many times. If he did cut some of his early wood blocks then, as Eleanor Sayre states in her definitive exhibition catalogue on Albrecht Dürer, "later blocks, and documentary evidence reveal that this did not remain his method."[68] Later in his life, Dürer employed the cutter Hieronymus Andreae to cut the blocks for the Triumphal Arch of Emperor Maximilian dated 1515. Andreae was so well known in Nuremberg that he was called Hieronymus Formschneider. Here we see a Formschneider step out of anonymity to be individually named for the first time.

The *Apocalypsis cum figuris* was both designed and published by Albrecht Dürer. According to its colophon, it was printed by Albrecht Dürer, painter (in the) year of our Lord 1498. It is reasonable to assume that the book was printed by Dürer on one of Koberger's numerous presses, because the typeface used in the *Apocalypse* was designed by Koberger. Also interesting

is the similarity in the titles—*Apocalypsis cum figuris* and Schedel's world chronicle *Liber chronicarum cum figuris.* For the *Apocalypse,* two separate editions were published, one with Latin and the other with German text. The Latin version derives from the Vulgate of Saint Jerome; the source of the German edition is the Bible Koberger published in 1483.

The monumental format of the woodcuts reveals the artist's intention to take precedence over the author's text. Here, for the first time, illustration has priority over text. In several of the stunning images, Albrecht Dürer succeeded in unifying multiple textual sequences in a single pictorial composition. The text of the book of Revelations gave the artist ample material for his fantasy. In transposing the supernatural, visionary Revelations into understandable pictures, he incorporated numerous, direct observations after nature, and as a consequence, he succeeded in translating the mysteries of Saint John into realistic, powerful images. Albrecht

Dürer combined a new, artistically vibrant graphic style with the imaginative elements of the text to dazzle the eyes of the reader. The reader, on the other hand, becomes an observer, for there is so much more to see than to read. Dürer's artistic style displays a hitherto unseen dynamic graphic line, inspired by his recent exposure to Italian Renaissance art.

"Dürer's 1498 *Apocalypse* was a milestone in the history of book illustration. The fifteen large-scale woodcuts with their elaborate though unified compositions were unlike anything that had been seen before for intricacy of design and naturalism of detail," concludes Nancy Finlay.[69] Albrecht Dürer conceived his *Apocalypsis cum figures* principally as a bound portfolio of images accented by a text. As Erasmus of Rotterdam wrote about Dürer, "he knows to state the unstatable, like fire, rays, thunderstorm, lightning, weather, and fog . . . all passions . . . even almost the language itself."[70] Dürer's contemporaries recognized the *Apocalypse* as an extraordinary artistic achievement.

Albrecht Dürer's portfolio represents a decisive moment in the history of the woodcut and a culmination of the art of the woodcut in the Renaissance. Critical steps in this achievement marked fifteenth-century German illustrated books, which found their finest expression in the lavish imprints from Anton Koberger's printing press. A second Latin edition of the *Apocalypse* was published in 1511, with the addition of a woodcut of Saint John with the Virgin and Child on the title page. In the same year, Dürer issued two additional series on a scale similar to that of the *Apocalypse:* the *Great Passion* and the *Life of the Virgin.* Although many of the blocks had been cut and printed separately at an earlier date, the year 1511 marked their first appearance with a text. "These 'Three Great Books' of Albrecht Dürer, through their monumentality and sheer artistic quality, look ahead four centuries to modern '*livres de peintre.*'"[71]

NOTES

1. *Albrecht Dürer, Master Printmaker* (Boston: Museum of Fine Arts, 1971), xi. For a broader discussion of the *Reisser* and *Briefmaler,* see David Landau and Peter Parshall, *The Renaissance Print* (New Haven: Yale University Press, 1994), 10, 169.

2. Peter Amelung, *Der Frühdruck im deutschen Südwesten 1473–1500,* an exhibition catalogue (Stuttgart: Württembergische Landesbibliothek, 1979), p. 4.

3. John Harthan, *The History of the Illustrated Book: The Western Tradition* (London: Thames and Hudson, 1981), 60.

4. Gottfried Zedler, *Die Bamberger Pfister Drucke und die 36-zeilige Bibel* (Mainz: Gutenberg-Gesellschaft, 1911), 13.

5. For figures on publication of printed books during the incunable period, see S. H. Steinberg, *500 Years of Printing,* 3rd edition (Baltimore: Penguin Books, 1974), 158; Harthan, *History of the Illustrated Book,* 62.

6. Amelung, *Der Frühdruck,* pp. xv–xvi. For a discussion of Günther Zainer's move to Augsburg, see Arthur Hind, *History of Woodcut,* 2 vols. (London: Constable, 1935), 1: 91, 211, 279; David Landau and Peter Parshall, *The Renaissance Print* (New Haven: Yale University Press, 1994), 10n23, stating that Hind provides no primary source for his observation; and David Bland, *A History of Book Illustration* (Cleveland, Ohio: World Publishing Company, 1985), 105.

7. Albert Schramm, *Der Bilderschmuck der Frühdrucke,* 26 vols. (Leipzig: Verlag von Karl W. Hierse-

mann, 1920–43), 2: figs. 1–127, 129–231; Eduard Isphording, *Fünf Jahrhunderte Buchillustration: Meister-werke der Buchgraphik aus der Bibliothek Otto Schäfer,* an exhibition catalogue (Nuremberg: Germanisches Nationalmuseum, 1987), no. 4.

8. Schramm 2, fig. 232, p. 1.

9. Schramm 2, p. 5, my translation.

10. Amelung, *Der Frühdruck,* p. 40; Lilli Fischl, *Bilderfolgen im frühen Buchdruck: Studien zur Inkun-abel-Illustration in Ulm und Strassburg* (Stuttgart: Konstanz, 1963).

11. Amelung, *Der Frühdruck,* pp. 17–18, nos. 11, 9, 28; Schramm 5, figs. 8–98.

12. Philip Hofer, *A Catalogue of an Exhibi-tion of the Philip Hofer Bequest in the Department of Printing and Graphic Arts* (Cambridge, Mass.: Harvard College Library, 1988), 13, entry by Nancy Finlay.

13. Amelung, *Der Frühdruck,* nos. 9, 11.

14. Amelung, *Der Frühdruck,* figs. 42, 43, no. 10.

15. Amelung, *Der Frühdruck,* p. 78.

16. Amelung, *Der Frühdruck,* p. 61, fig. 42, no. 9; fig. 72, no. 22; Schramm 5, p. 5, fig. 100.

17. Amelung, *Der Frühdruck,* no. 110; Schramm 6, pp. 6–7, figs. 128–49; see also Amelung, figs. 163, 164, both reproduced from the partially col-ored copy in the Württembergische Landes-bibliothek, Stuttgart. See item 4, LC/R156.

18. Amelung, *Der Frühdruck,* p. 216, no. 111; Schramm 6, pp. 7–8, figs. 150–77.

19. Amelung, *Der Frühdruck,* p. 5; A. Hyatt Mayor, *Prints & People: A Social History of Printed Pictures* (New York: Metropolitan Museum of Art, distributed by the New York Graphic Society, 1971), no. 32.

20. Schramm 4, pp. 17–18, figs. 545–71.

21. Schramm 4, pp. 40–41, figs. 2,759–84. See item 3, LC/R146.

22. Gilbert R. Redgrave, *Erhard Ratdolt and His Work at Venice* (London: Printed for the Biblio-graphical Society, 1894), no. 1.

23. Redgrave, *Erhard Ratdolt,* nos. 3, 4.

24. Schramm 23, p. 11, figs. 119–25. See item 1, LC/R126.

25. Redgrave, *Erhard Ratdolt,* p. 17, nos. 57, 27; Robert Diehl. *Erhard Ratdolt: ein Meisterdrucker des XV. und XVI. Jahrhunderts* (Vienna: Herbert Reich-ner, 1933), 14.

26. Schramm 23, p. 4, fig. 12; Karl Schotten-loher, *Die liturgischen Druckwerke Erhard Ratdolts aus Augsburg, 1485–1522* (Mainz: Gutenberg-Gesellschaft, 1922), ix, 1.

27. Schramm 23, p. 4, fig. 11; Schottenloher, *Die liturgischen Druckwerke,* pp. ix, 2.

28. Schottenloher, *Die liturgischen Druckwerke,* vi; Diehl, *Ratdolt: ein Meisterdrucker,* 16; Redgrave, *Erhard Ratdolt,* 16.

29. Rolf Biedermann [and Tilman Falk], *Hans Burgkmair, 1473–1973: Das graphische Werk,* an ex-hibition catalogue (Augsburg: Städtische Kunst-sammlungen, 1973), no. 1.

30. Biedermann [and Falk], *Hans Burgkmair,* no. 3, fig. 4; Schramm 23, fig. 23.

31. Paul Heitz, *Christus am Kreuz* (Munich: Heitz, 1910), fig. 3.

32. Margaret Morgan Grasselli, *Colorful Im-pressions: The Printmaking Revolution in Eighteenth-Century France* (Washington: National Gallery of Art, 2003), 2.

33. Biedermann [and Falk], *Hans Burgkmair,* nos. 3, 4.

34. Schramm 15, figs. 1–17, 19–24; Harthan, *History of the Illustrated Book,* 63.

35. Leonhard Sladeczek, *Albrecht Dürer und die Illustrationen zur Schedelchronik* (Baden-Baden and Strasbourg: Heitz, 1965), p. 34, fig. 13.

36. Schramm 19, p. 3, figs. 1–7; Frank Hiero-nymus, *Oberrheinische Buchillustration,* an exhibition catalogue, 2 vols. (Basel: Universitätsbibliothek, 1984), no. 3, p. 4; François Ritter, *Histoire de l'im-primerie alsacienne aux 15e et 16e siècles,* vol. 1 (Stras-bourg: F.-X LeRoux, 1955), 19–20.

37. Hieronymus, *Buchillustration* 1, p. 81; Schramm 20, p. 3, figs. 4–112.

38. Paul Kristeller, *Die Strassburger Bücher-Illustration im XV. und im Anfange des XVI. Jahr-hunderts* (Leipzig: A. E. Seemann, 1888), defines three distinct Grüninger woodcut styles.

39. Hieronymus, *Buchillustration* 1, p. 5.

40. Schramm 20, figs. 240–338; Hieronymus, *Buchillustration* 1, p. 137.

41. Hieronymus, *Buchillustration* 2, p. 24, no. 29.

42. Hieronymus, *Buchillustration* 1, no. 3; Schramm 21, p. 13, fig. 553; Hieronymus 1, no. 4; Schramm 21, p. 6, figs. 18–272.

43. Schramm 2, figs. 351–526; Hieronymus, *Buchillustration* 1, no. 5; Isphording, *Fünf Jahrhunderte Buchillustration,* p. 12.

44. Schramm 21, p. 11, figs. 330–97.

45. Hieronymus, *Buchillustration* 1, p. 141; Schramm 22, p. 22, figs. 1,043–49.

46. Friedrich Winkler, *Dürer und die Illustrationen zum Narrenschiff* (Berlin, 1951), 90–91; *Albrecht Dürer, 1471–1971,* catalogue of an exhibition held at the Germanische National-museum in Nurem-berg from May to August 1971 (Munich: Prestel Verlag, 1971), no. 159.

47. Hieronymus, *Buchillustration* 1, p. 185;

Schramm 22, pp. 20–21, figs. 998–1,042.

48. Schramm 22, fig. 1028.

49. Schramm 21, fig. 998; Schramm 18, fig. 335, attributed to Pleydenwurff; *Albrecht Dürer, 1471–1971*, nos. 115, 153.

50. Schramm 22, p. 29, figs. 1,110–1,227; Hieronymus, *Buchillustration* I, pp. 110ff.

51. *Albrecht Dürer, 1471–1971*, no. 154; Hieronymus, *Buchillustration* I, pp. 9, 111, no. 192.

52. *Albrecht Dürer, 1471–1971*, no. 154 (my translation).

53. Hieronymus, *Buchillustration* I, p. 38; for Brant's motto, also see pp. 9, 110; Schramm 22, pp. 15–16.

54. *Albrecht Dürer, 1471–1971*, no. 109; Willi Kurth, editor, *The Complete Woodcuts of Albrecht Dürer*, with an introduction by Campbell Dodgson, German text translated by Silvia M. Welsh (New York: Dover, 1963), nos. 1–5, 13–14, pp. 7–8; Schramm 18, pp. 8–9, figs. 600–609, 297–320; Landau and Parshall, *The Renaissance Print*, 10–11.

55. Schramm 27, p. 3 (my translation), figs. 56–314.

56. Giulia Bartrum, *German Renaissance Prints, 1490–1550* (London: Published for the Trustees of the British Museum by British Museum Press, 1995), 17.

57. Landau and Parshall, *The Renaissance Print*, 38.

58. *Albrecht Dürer, 1471–1971*, 107; Sladeczek, *Dürer und die Illustrationen zur Schedelchronik*, p. 43, fig. 13, referring to woodcuts Schramm 18, figs. 119, 184.

59. Schramm 27, pp. 4–5, figs. 317–402.

60. Schramm 27, pp. 6–7, figs. 408–576.

61. Landau and Parshall, *The Renaissance Print*, 38. See also Adrian Wilson, *The Making of the Nuremberg Chronicle* (Amsterdam: Nico Israel, 1977)

and Elisabeth Rücker, *Die Schedelsche Weltchronik: das grösste Buchunternehmen d. Dürer-Zeit; mit e. Katalog d. Städteansichten* (Munich: Prestel, 1973) for a complete discussion of the subject.

62. Landau and Parshall, *The Renaissance Print*, 41; Bartrum, *German Renaissance Prints*, 18–19; Richard Bellm, *Wolgemut's Skizzenbuch im Berliner Kupferstichkabinett: Ein Beitrag zur Erforschung des graphischen Werkes von Michael Wolgemut und Wilhelm Pleydenwurff* (Baden-Baden: Heitz, 1959), 44–61.

63. Landau and Parshall, *The Renaissance Print*, 39.

64. Bartrum, *German Renaissance Prints*, 19; Landau and Parshall, *The Renaissance Print*, 39.

65. See Sladeczek, *Dürer und die Illustrationen zur Schedelchronik*, and Franz Stadler, *Michael Wolgemut und der Nürnberger Holzschnitt im letzten Drittel des XV. Jahrhunderts* (Strasbourg: J.H.E. Heitz, 1913) for a complete discussion of the subject.

66. Friedrich Kriegbaum, *Zu den graphischen Prinzipien in Dürers frühem Holzschnittwerk*, Goldschmidt-Festschrift "Das siebente Jahrzehnt," 1935, pp. 100ff.; Sladeczek, *Dürer und die Illustrationen zur Schedelchronik*, 28; Schramm 18, fig. 366.

67. *Albrecht Dürer, 1471–1971*, 117, 136.

68. *Albrecht Dürer, Master Printmaker* (Boston: Museum of Fine Arts, 1971), xix; Kurth, *The Complete Woodcuts*, 7–8.

69. Hofer, *Catalogue of an Exhibition*, 18, entry by Nancy Finlay.

70. See Erich Schneider, *Dürer, Die Kunst aus der Natur zu "reyssenn,"* an exhibition catalogue (Schweinfurt: Ludwig & Höhne, 1997), 54 (my translation).

71. Hofer, *Catalogue of an Exhibition*, 18, entry by Nancy Finlay; Landau and Parshall, *The Renaissance Print*, 42.

# CATALOGUE

FIFTEENTH-CENTURY BOOKS

*(Items 1–37)*

SIXTEENTH-CENTURY BOOKS

*(Items 38–75)*

# FIFTEENTH-CENTURY BOOKS

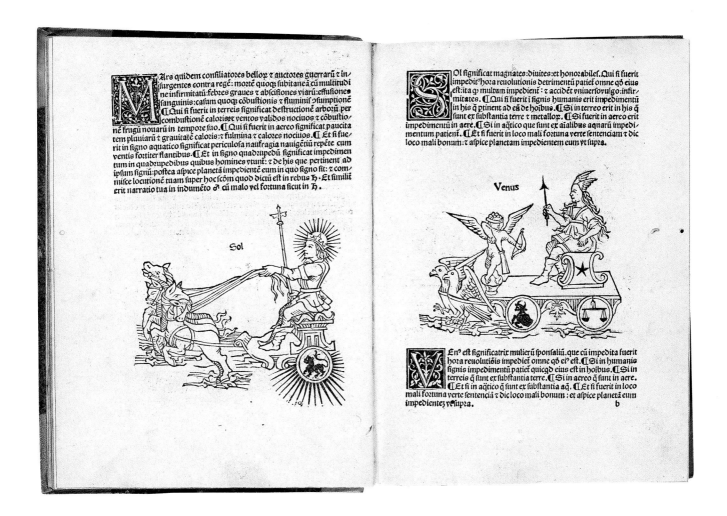

## I  ROSENWALD 126: DYSON PERRINS 541

ALBUMASAR WAS A NINTH-CENTURY ARAB ASTRONOMER, called by most scholars the father of medieval and Renaissance astrology. His systematic analysis of the heavens resulted in a creation theory based on the alignment of the seven known planets. Albumasar's *Flores astrologiae*, printed by Erhard Ratdolt in 1488, is illustrated with seventy-three woodcuts, including twelve small zodiac cuts, seven larger cuts of the planets, and numerous repeats. The cuts of the planets, two of which are illustrated here, originally appeared in Julius Hyginus's *Poeticon astronomicon*, printed in Venice in 1482, and in Johannes Angelus's *Astrolabium*, printed in Augsburg in 1485, both also by Ratdolt.

The career of the noted German printer Erhard Ratdolt spanned over forty years, beginning with his work in Venice from 1476 to 1486 and continuing in his native Augsburg from 1486 to about 1516, when his last imprint is recorded. The business then continued until 1520 under the imprint of Georg Ratdolt. In the context of the illustrated book, Ratdolt is remembered

1. ALBUMASAR.
*Flores astrologiae.*
Augsburg:
Erhard Ratdolt,
18 November 1488

as an innovator in the use of decorative initials, woodcut borders, printing in gold, and color printing, which he experimented with during his Venetian period and developed further during the 1490s when Hans Burgkmair worked in his shop. Ratdolt specialized in the publication of liturgical books, mathematical texts, and astronomy books, many of which were illustrated with simple line woodcuts, like those shown here. His edition of Regiomontanus's *Calendarium,* printed in Venice in 1476, with woodcuts printed in two colors, and his 1482 edition of Euclid's *Elementa geometriae,* also printed in Venice, are two of his most famous works.

Ratdolt returned to Augsburg, a major center of the German illustrated book, after ten years in Italy. The commingling of German and Italian styles, which began as early as the 1470s, was to have an enormous impact on the development of the woodcut in both countries. As the first German printer to use the wood block border and the decorative initial letter, Ratdolt has received near universal recognition as one of the first links between the German and Italian traditions. The simple lines of the cuts illustrated here are representative of German style, reflecting what David Landau and Peter Parshall characterize as "the simplicity and cleanliness" of Augsburg design. There is no background or border, and very little shading. The result is a clear narrative image created by broad contours with a minimum of embellishment.

In creating the images used in this edition of *Flores astrologiae,* the anonymous designer or woodcutter uses classical and medieval conventions to illustrate Albumasar's astrological text. The use of "triumphal cars," which in this case carry each of the seven planets, was a common motif well known during the late medieval and early Renaissance period. In the image on the left, Apollo the Sun God, depicted with a halo and staff, rides his golden chariot drawn by a team of horses galloping four abreast across the northern sky. On the right, Venus's triumphal car is guided by a pair of doves. She is dressed in her magic girdle, a symbol of her femininity, and is accompanied by her offspring Cupid, who is blindfolded and reaching for an arrow from his quiver. This image suggests the adage "love is blind." Both triumphal cars have symbols of the zodiac in their wheels, representing the power of the planets over specific signs.

This copy is bound with the next item, Albumasar's *De magnis coniunctionibus,* also printed in Augsburg by Erhard Ratdolt, in 1489.

4to. 200 x 145 mm, 7¾ x 5¾ in. Goff A-356.
*Morgan* 158. Pellechet 412. W. L. Schreiber 3073.
Hind, p. 299. Landau and Parshall, p. 34.
Hall, pp. 25–29, 310, 318–20.
Schramm 23, figs. 122, 123.

## 2   ROSENWALD 137: DYSON PERRINS 541

Erhard Ratdolt printed the first edition of Albumasar's thesis on the creation of the universe in March 1489. It is the only edition printed in the fifteenth century. The *Book of Conjunctions,* as this work is known, proposed that the world was created when the seven planets were in conjunction in the first point of Aries and that the end of the world would occur when the conjunction was repeated in the point of Pisces. Albumasar's predictions concerning the end of the world proved to be a topic of lively discussion among Western astrologers throughout the Middle Ages.

The book is illustrated with 268 woodcuts, most of which originally appeared in Ratdolt's

2. ALBUMASAR.

*Albumasar de magnis*

*coniunctionibus.*

Augsburg:

Erhard Ratdolt,

31 March 1489

previously published editions of Julius Hyginus's *Poeticon astronomicon,* printed in Venice in 1482, and Johannes Angelus's *Astrolabium,* printed in Augsburg in 1485. The woodcuts of Capricorn, the "goat with a spiral tale," and the water bearer, representing Aquarius, are good examples of the woodcuts produced for Ratdolt's press. They can be characterized by the thick contours or outlines used to define the image and the introduction of parallel lines to model the figures. These techniques, common to early German woodcuts of the period, offer the viewer a simple representation of an image, in this case the astrological sign. The clarity of the figures and the creative manner in which they are presented suggest that the designer and the woodcutter were skilled craftsmen.

The opening illustrated here also includes a woodcut initial, an innovation for which Ratdolt is well known. The initial letter *P* is a black-ground woodcut, decorated with branch work and flowers. This example is one of the more commonplace initials used by Ratdolt, where the letterform is finely cut but the vines and tiny flowers are not clearly articulated. By contrast, letters of the same size used in his 1482 edition of Hyginus are much more carefully cut, with both the flowers and the branches defined by thin lines, creating a more detailed background for the initial letter. His most impressive woodcut letters are the large foliated initials that he used in his Apianus's *Historia romana* of 1477 and Euclid's *Elementa geometriæ* of 1482.

4to. 200 x 145 mm, 7¾ x 5¾ in.

Goff A-360. *Morgan* 160. Pellechet 414. Fairfax Murray 26.

Hind, pp. 299–303, 458–64. Sander 6400, fig. 140.

Schramm 23, figs. 157, 158.

## 3 ROSENWALD 146: DYSON PERRINS 670

3. *Passio domini Jesu Christi.*
Augsburg: [Johann
Schönsperger],
22 February 1490

JOHANN SCHÖNSPERGER'S 1490 EDITION of the Passion of Christ, often referred to as the Teutsch Passion, is illustrated with a woodcut initial letter and twenty-four woodcuts colored by hand, with one repeated image. The designs were first used in 1480 by Anton Sorg for his edition of the *Passio domini* printed, like Schönsperger's edition, in Augsburg. In 1489 Sorg had new blocks cut of these images in a reduced size and used them in his *Horologium devotionis.* The following year, they appeared in Schönsperger's edition of the *Passio domini.*

It was Schönsperger's practice to use cuts already in circulation. Many of his books contain blocks borrowed from Sorg, Johann Baemler, Gunther Zainer, and other Augsburg printers. Occasionally, however, he commissioned new wood blocks to be designed after existing images, as he did with his *Herbarius latinus* printed in 1485, whose woodcuts were based on Schoeffer's Mainz edition of the same title published earlier that same year. Schönsperger is also remembered as one of the first printers to color his woodcuts using stencils, his *Herbarius latinus* being a noted example.

The twenty-four woodcuts in the Rosenwald/Dyson Perrins copy of the *Passio domini Jesu Christi* include the Old Testament image of the Sacrifice of Abraham followed by images of Christ's crucifixion, burial, and resurrection. The cuts are typical of the early 1480s, with the use of broad contours to outline the figures and parallel lines to model their forms. Also typical of German woodcuts of the period is a spare background and the lack of a decorative border. The varying styles and quality of the cutting of the blocks suggests that at least three hands were involved in their design and execution.

The woodcut Christ Washing the Feet of the Apostles illustrated here is one of the more successful in the suite. It communicates to the medieval viewer the sense of wonder expressed by Saint Peter and the other disciples as they watch Christ in supplication before them. Although there is a uniformity of line in the design, especially in the facial characteristics of the apostles, the raised arm of Saint Peter, the extended left hand of Christ, and the opened hand of Saint John convey the emotional quality of the event. Another characteristic of the woodcut is the variety of line which the woodcutter incorporates in the image. In addition to thick contours and parallel lines, the cutter uses hooked lines and looped lines to accentuate the garments and to create a physical presence beneath the folds. The use of color wash to highlight parts of the image was a common practice in Germany, especially to delineate foreground or background or to add an ornamental touch that the woodcutter was not able to supply with his knife.

According to Frederick R. Goff, this copy is a variant of the one described by W.L. Schreiber in his bibliography of German woodcuts. It differs in that it contains the woodcut Christ Washing the Feet of the Apostles, illustrated here, and lacks the cut of Jesus with Saint Anne which is repeated twice in the edition cited by W.L. Schreiber. The Rosenwald/Dyson Perrins copy also has different woodcuts in place of W.L. Schreiber numbers 11 and 12, which are repeats in the copy described in W.L. Schreiber's bibliography. The Rosenwald/Dyson Perrins copy is the only recorded copy of this issue in America and the only perfect copy extant.

8vo. 120 x 95 mm, 4¾ x 3¾ in.
Goff P-138. W.L. Schreiber 3744. Schramm 4, figs. 2765–83.
Hind, p. 298. Schiller, pp. 41–44.

## 4   ROSENWALD 156: DYSON PERRINS 608

A RARE BOOK OF HOURS DEVOTED TO THE BLESSED VIRGIN, *Dye Siben Cursz* is organized in seven chapters. Printed in Ulm by Conrad Dinckmut in 1491, the book begins with prayers to the Trinity and for the Repose of the Souls of the Faithfully Departed, and continues with a text on the Annunciation of Mary, sacramental prayers for confession and the eucharist, a commemoration of the passion of Christ, and prayers celebrating the feast of the Assumption. Seven original woodcuts, all but one of them colored, illustrate the book of hours. Bound in contemporary brown leather over oak boards and decorated with blind tooling in a traditional panel design, highlighted with a floral and star motif, the book still retains three of its four corner bosses and remnants of a metal clasp. A second edition appeared in 1493, and was illustrated with the original suite of seven cuts augmented by seven additional images.

Conrad Dinckmut of Ulm began his career in the 1470s printing block books. In *A History of the Woodcut,* Arthur M. Hind cites Dinckmut's block book edition of Donatus's *De octo partibus orationis,* printed at Ulm in 1475–80, and he illustrates a particularly impressive leaf which Dinckmut had decorated with a complex floral border and an initial letter *D* enclosing an image of a master teaching his students. Dinckmut's first illustrated book printed with metal type appeared in 1482. It was quickly followed by numerous other illustrated books, including two published in 1486 that are universally considered his most impressive printed works: Thomas Lirer's *Chronica* and an edition of Terence's *Eunuchus.* Dinckmut's last recorded imprint is dated 1499.

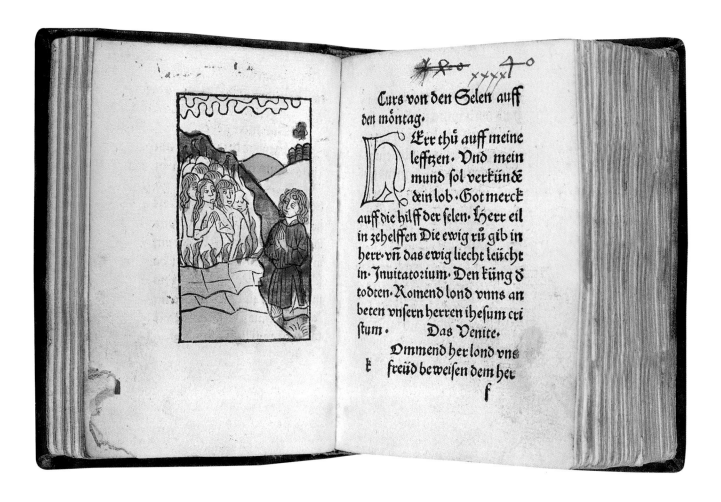

Cursz von den Selen auff
den montag.

Err thu auff meine
lefftzen. Vnd mein
mund sol verkünde
dein lob. Got merck
auff die hilff der selen. Herr eil
in zehelffen Die ewig ru gib in
herr. vn das ewig liecht leücht
in. Inuitatorium. Den küng d
todten. Komend lond vnns an
beten vnsern herren ihesum cri
stum. Das Venite.
Ommend her lond vns
freüd beweisen dem her

4. *Dye Siben Cursz.*
Ulm: Conrad Dinckmut,
1491

Ulm was the second important German center for the printing of illustrated books during the 1470s and 1480s. In addition to such important printers as Johann Zainer, Lienhart Holle, and Dinckmut, the city supported a number of highly skilled *Formschneider,* or block cutters, who worked for the printers and anonymously produced the wood blocks used to illustrate the books. Zainer's editions of Boccaccio's *De claris mulieribus* (1473), his Aesop (1476–77), and the *Geistliche Auslegung des Lebens Jesu Christi* (1485), to mention only three titles, are highly regarded for the complexity of their compositions and quality of their line. Lienhart Holle's *Ptolemy* of 1482, and his *Buch der Weisheit* of 1483, and Dinckmut's *Chronica* and Terrence's *Eunuchus* printed in 1486 are also highly regarded works. Late in the 1480s, financial difficulties hit the industry and Ulm lost much of the investment that fueled its printing trade. Hind suggests these troubles resulted from the plague, but other historians are less specific about the cause of the decline of the trade in Ulm. Zainer and Dinckmut stayed in business, but they were never again able to produce illustrated books of a similar caliber. Many of the woodcutters moved to Augsburg, Basel, or Nuremberg, where the trade in illustrated books was picking up momentum.

The woodcuts in this edition of *Dye Siben Cursz* are modest by comparison with some of Dinckmut's other, more complex illustrated works, which contain detailed landscapes or architectural renderings. The woodcut Prayers for the Repose of the Souls of the Faithful Departed illustrated here is typical of his modest cuts. The outlines are simple and clear, the facial expressions and folds of drapery crisp and precise but uniform and enhanced only by a hint of shading. The delineation of the landscape and sky, along with the hand coloring, add significantly to the appealing effect of this woodcut. Dinckmut further enhances the attractiveness of his book by using ornamental capitals in double line to complement the typographical design and the delicate contours of the figural woodcuts on the opposite page.

According to both Goff and the *Incunabula Short-Title Catalogue* (ISTC), this is the only known complete copy of the book and the only copy in America.

8vo. 190 x 130 mm, 5¼ x 3¾ in. Goff H-428. W.L. Schreiber 5, 3799.
Hind, pp. 258–60, 312. Schramm 6, figs. 642, 648, 638, 647, 640, 641, 643.
Dodgson *Early German and Flemish Woodcuts* 1, p. 23.

# 5 ROSENWALD 193: DYSON-PERRINS 563

JOHANN LANDEN'S COLOGNE EDITION published about 1498 appears to be the fifth edition of Bertoldus's Latin translation of the popular devotional work entitled *Zeitlöcklein des Lebens und Leidens Christi*. The work focuses on the life and passion of Christ, commencing with the Annunciation and ending with the Judgment Day. It is organized in twenty-four parts, or hours, with prayers specified for certain times of the day. Landen's edition is illustrated with eight woodcuts and twenty-seven metalcuts, including two repeated images. Four of the metalcuts are highlighted in red.

The ISTC cites twenty-two titles printed before 1501 that either carry Johann Landen's imprint or are attributed to his press. W.L. Schreiber, however, considers this edition of the *Horologium* as Landen's only worthwhile work, and it is the only one mentioned by Hind. Landen began printing in Cologne in 1496, and his last recorded imprint is 1521. Closely associated with the Cologne trade, he used Heinrich Quentell's type and some of Ulrich Zel's woodcuts and metalcuts in the early productions from his press. He made his living printing religious texts, hagiography, and schoolbooks, perhaps also doing job printing for the more established Cologne printers.

The metalcuts in Landen's *Horologium* are called "dotted prints," or images printed in the *manière criblée,* because of the use of the round metal punch to create texture and pattern in the image. Campbell Dodgson describes metalcuts as "white line engravings in relief." The outlines and contours appear in white surrounded by a black background. Ornamentation was added by punching stars or dots into the metal. The ornaments also read white, thus adding a white-on-black effect in the printed image. Like woodcuts, metalcuts were placed in the same form as the type and both were printed at the same time. Most historians of the early prints place the origin of the dotted print along the Upper Rhine, with Cologne being one of its centers.

Thirteen of the twenty-five metalcuts in this edition were originally used by Ulrich Zel in the first edition of Bertoldus, printed in Cologne around 1488. The use of the same borders and the consistent style of the images suggest that the twelve new metalcuts may have been produced for Landen from the same workshop as the original cuts produced for Zel about ten years earlier. Some of the Zel/Landen metalcuts may be traced to a series produced in or around Cologne between 1460 and 1480. The so-called Oxford Passion, a set of twenty-two prints in the Rosenwald Collection at the National Gallery of Art, Washington, D.C., is fully described and illustrated by Richard S. Field in his catalogue of the fifteenth-century woodcuts and metalcuts in that collection. A comparison of the two sets shows that twelve of the twenty-five Zel/Landen designs follow the exact composition of the Oxford Passion, though the facial features and drapery folds are not as refined.

Cb dulciffime deus qȝ crudeliter ⁊ abfcȝ mi♦
fericozdia miniftri tue mo2tis taȝ penofe te cõ♦
elauatum cruci cũ cruce te eleuauerũt.⁊ crucem cum
tuo cozpoze trunco ad boc factoviolenti potentia im
pofuerũt ⁊ intruferunt.qȝ oĩa membza ⁊ articuli diſ♦
iungebanf ⁊ collidebanf ⁊ oẽsvene ⁊ nerui ad ruptis
tã redebanf Acb õne ibu qȝ miferabilẽ vocẽ dabas
acb q̃ties p̃ magno doloze o ve ynd ve acclamabas

5. BERTOLDUS (fl. 1350).
*Horologium devotionis.*
Cologne: Johann Landen,
[ca. 1498]

The image Christ Nailed to the Cross illustrated here achieves the compositional density and decorative range that was characteristic of metalcuts produced during this period. The central image of Christ stands out against the dotted foreground and backdrop, as do his garment and the figures of his persecutors. The action of the event seems to vibrate, making it palpable and immediate. The addition of the city view of Jerusalem in the background fixes the image in space and time, adding narrative content to the image. Also notable is the decorative border, with its branches, vines, and flowers framing the entire event and focusing attention on the content of the cut. The two black dots in the center of the upper and lower borders are from impressions left by nails that were used to attach the metal plate to a block before printing.

The eight woodcuts in this volume are all small, simple line cuts probably by two different hands. The cuts are described in A. W. Pollard's catalogue of the Morgan collection as "rude and clumsy," but the woodcut Saint Christopher with the Christ Child is quite accomplished and suggests a more experienced hand at work.

Only four copies of Landen's edition of *Horologium* are located by ISTC in American libraries. This edition of Bertoldus is frequently bound as here, with two other works printed by Landen, *Meditationes de vita Jesu Christi* and *De spiritualibus asensionibus* by Gerardus de Zutphania, both also about 1498 and both unillustrated. This volume also includes a copy of an edition of Saint Bonaventure's *Stimulus amoris,* printed in Antwerp after 1500 by Adriaen van Berghen. The last is illustrated with a simple line woodcut Christ on the Cross between Mary and Saint John, framed by a four-part passe-partout border decorated with a floral design.

8vo. 135 x 95 mm, 5¼ x 3¾ in. Goff B-507. *Morgan* 112.
W.L. Schreiber 3446. Schramm 8, figs. 41–46, 50, 51, 67–71.
For additional information on the origins of the manière criblée,
see Henry Bradshaw's *Collected Papers,* pp. 239–43;
Dodgson *Prints in the Dotted Manner,* p. 7; Gascoigne 7a;
Field, figs. 296–315, 321–28; Mongan, pp. 53–60.

## 6 ROSENWALD 205: DYSON PERRINS 589

THIS SECOND LATIN EDITION of the *Revelations* of Saint Birgitta was published with the patronage of Emperor Maximilian, who urged the Nuremberg printer Anton Koberger to print both a Latin and a German-language edition. The former he completed on September 21, 1500, and the latter in 1502. An earlier Latin edition of *Revelationes* had been printed in Lübeck in 1492 by Bartholomaeus Ghotan, its text illustrated with fourteen full-page woodcuts, a few small woodcuts, and initial letters, all of considerable quality.

Maximilian's patronage was critical to making the cities of Augsburg and Nuremberg centers of the German printing trade during the first quarter of the sixteenth century. His commissions for woodcut illustrations were executed by renowned artists from all over Germany, including Albrecht Dürer, Hans Burgkmair, Albrecht Altdorfer, Leonard Beck, Lucas Cranach, and Hans Schäufelein. According to Landau and Parshall, "his patronage had much to do with the evolution of commercial print production in Germany, and particularly with the rise in importance of professional block cutters, many of whom passed through Maximilian's service at one stage or another."

The Koberger edition includes eighteen pages of woodcuts, loosely based on those from the Lübeck edition printed eight years earlier. Of these, five are full-page woodcuts, including one repeat, one is a half-page woodcut, and thirteen are illustrations composed of from two to eight blocks, some of which are repeated. In all, thirty individual woodcut blocks were used to illustrate these eighteen pages of images. Erwin Panofsky states that the woodcut Coat-of-Arms of Maximilian I as King, which appears in this edition, is probably by Dürer, but the "authenticity is not quite certain." He suggests that the remaining cuts are in the style of Dürer and "were probably designed in his workshop by the 'Benedict Master.'" More recent research by Friedrich Winkler and Ursula Frenzel suggests that those works designated as being by the Benedict Master are in fact by Dürer himself.

The full-page woodcuts Saint Birgitta Bestowing the *Revelations* on Monks and Nuns, Coat-of-Arms of Maximilian I as King, and the Crucifixion exhibit many of the qualities that distinguish the Nuremberg woodcut at the beginning of the sixteenth century. Building on the influences first seen in Michel Wolgemut's woodcuts produced for the *Schatzbehalter* (1491), and his work in collaboration with Wilhelm Pleydenwurff for Schedel's *The Nuremberg Chronicle* (1493), Nuremberg designers expanded the parameters of illustration by creating more complex compositions, by introducing shading and perspective to the image, and by emphasizing individual human expression.

6. SAINT BIRGITTA
(1302–1373). *Revelationes.*
Nuremberg:
Anton Koberger,
21 September 1500

# Reuelationes sancte Birgitte

*Revelationes.*
Lübeck, 1492.
From Fairfax Murray
*German* 1, no. 73

A comparison with the woodcuts in the 1492 Lübeck edition provides an excellent case in point. The uniformity of the 1492 cut of Saint Birgitta is all but abandoned in the Nuremberg image. Neat rows of nuns and priests, all of whom resemble one another in both posture and expression, are supplanted by two sets of congregations in motion, individually styled in both physiognomy and comportment. The modeling of the folds of the garments and the bodies beneath the vestments is achieved by the combined use of thin and thick parallel lines and some cross-hatching. The countenance of Saint Birgitta in the Nuremberg woodcut is womanly in its depiction, enhanced by its finely rendered eyes, nose, and mouth. This freer use of the carving tool points to a more skilled craftsman, who is successful in investing the image not only with meaning but also with beauty.

This is not to dismiss the qualities of the Lübeck image. For its time, it is highly successful in rendering the intention of the artist and displaying the skill of the woodcutter. The fanciful depiction of the heavens resembling a boiling surf provides a balance to the composition, so that all the elements of the image are in harmony. It is clear, precise, and thoroughly Gothic in style.

These same characteristics are true of the Nuremberg Crucifixion. But what strikes one most about the woodcut Crucifixion is the composition of the piece. It reflects the ambitions of contemporary painting in the positioning of the figures, the perspective, the landscape, and the addition of an architectural element in the background. This woodcut is Renaissance in style and has the feel of an old master painting. If it is by Dürer, as some have suggested, it contains elements of Italian art that he may have adopted during his first visit to Venice in the 1490s. If not, it nevertheless demonstrates the rapid advancement made in the art of the woodcut in Germany at the end of the fifteenth century.

Folio. 308 x 210 mm, 12 x 8¼ in. Goff B-688. W. L. Schreiber 3504.
Schramm 12 (Lübeck, 1492), nos. 16–29; (Nuremberg, 1500), nos. 600–617.
Fairfax Murray *German* 1, no. 73. Hind, pp. 379–90. Panofsky *Dürer* 2, nos. 372, 401.
Butts and Hendrix 12. For further details on Emperor Maximilian I and the
development of the Nuremberg print trade, see Landau and Parshall, pp. 206–16.

## 7    ROSENWALD 208: DYSON PERRINS 551

T HE *ARS MORIENDI, OR THE ART OF DYING,* is an important genre of book that reveals the medieval church's rituals surrounding the last rites of a dying Christian. The earliest known printing of *Ars moriendi* is a block book edition produced in the southern Netherlands around 1450, though this date is still under debate by historians. By 1500, more than eighty printed editions had been produced from presses in Germany, France, Italy, the Low Countries, Spain, and Great Britain. Hind wrote that the book's "popularity probably comes from the fact that it was intended as a guide to clergy in giving comfort and counsel to the dying."

This 1500 edition of *Ars moriendi* was printed by Melchior Lotter, son-in-law of the noted Leipzig printer Conrad Kachelofen. Lotter's career spanned over forty years, from 1495 to 1537, and his press continued to publish in Leipzig until 1556 under the direction of Michael Lotter. It was Kachelofen who commissioned the fourteen woodcuts used for his first edition of *Ars moriendi,* published in Leipzig in 1494. All the woodcuts except the first are based on block book images, the first having appeared previously in an edition of *Beichtebüchlein,* also printed by Kachelofen in 1494. In her book *The Art of Dying Well,* Mary Catherine O'Connor states that eight separate printed editions containing these woodcuts appeared before Lotter's edition of 1500. In his description of the Kachelofen edition of 1494 written in 1907, Robert Proctor describes the fourteen full-page cuts as "from the same hand, and of exceptionally fine quality."

Most printed editions of *Ars moriendi* follow a standard format. The first two woodcuts represent the sacraments of confession and extreme unction, events critical to the salvation of the soul of the dying man. They are followed by ten full-page cuts, issued in pairs, one illustrating man's struggle with temptation and the other depicting the intervention of angels and the saints to help the person to resist. The final two woodcuts illustrate the triumph of salvation through grace at the hour of death and the role of Saint Michael in determining, by the scale of justice, the disposition of the soul at death. Although these wood blocks were used on eight separate occasions before being used in the Lotter edition, the impressions are clear and dark, suggesting the great care taken by the printers in preparing and using these blocks.

The first illustration is from the Rosenwald/Dyson Perrins copy of the Lotter edition of *Ars moriendi.* The second shows a probable source for the Lotter image, a German block book from about 1465, also from the Rosenwald Collection (edition IV A, as described by W. L. Schreiber). The image represents the "temptation of impatience," where the dying man, having overturned the bedside table, is kicking his physician out of his way. His wife in the

7. *Ars moriendi.*
Leipzig: Melchior Lotter,
after 1500

background is pleading for patience, while the maid stands in the foreground ready to deliver supper, and the devil, who is off in the margin, expresses his pleasure at the success of his intervention.

The complex spatial composition of both images is almost identical, except that the woodcut used by Lotter prints in reverse, as is typical when a design is copied from an existing image and a new block cut. In both images, the border pattern is the same, the use of parallel lines to create shading is consistent, and the facial expressions are similar for all of the four characters. The only significant differences besides the size of the image and its reversed printing are the greater use of parallel lines in the later cut and a more complex floor pattern.

Determining the original sources for these images is a matter of debate. Some historians suggest that the woodcuts are based on illuminations from the medieval manuscript tradition, while others contend that the source was the engraver known as the Master ES, active in the Upper Rhineland from about 1450 to 1467. These differences of opinion go to the heart of the

question of attribution, where date, place, and authorship are extremely difficult issues to re- *Ars moriendi.*
solve for work done during the late medieval and early Renaissance period. Perhaps William Block book, ca. 1465.
Ivins, of the Metropolitan Museum of Art, said it best when he wrote, "The series of volumes LC/R20
of the *Ars moriendi* in the Museum collection thus opens up for the student almost as complicated
a series of questions as the history of prints has to show, and it also contains the material from
which one may learn to be very humble in matters of attribution and dating."

ISTC lists only four copies of the Lotter edition in American libraries.

4to. 200 x 143 mm, 7⅞ x 5¾ in. Goff A-1120.
W. L. Schreiber 5, no. 3375; 4, nos. 267–312.
Hind, pp. 224–30. O'Connor, pp. 48–60, 134.
Ivins "Ars moriendi," pp. 230–36.
For Robert Proctor's description, see *Morgan* 213, 214.

Quinquagesimusquartus
articulus est cristi vestimeto

## 8 ROSENWALD 209, 211: DYSON PERRINS 508

8. JORDAN VAN
QUEDLINBURG.
*Meditationes de vita et
passione Jesu Christi.*
[Magdeburg: Moritz
Brandis, 1500]

*bound with*

*Rosarium Beatae Virginae
Maria.* [Magdeburg:
Moritz Brandis, 1500]

Moritz Brandis, who printed both *Meditationes de vita et passione Jesu Christi* and *Rosarium Beatae Virginae Maria* in Magdeburg in 1500, began his career around 1483 in Leipzig, where he printed various editions of the lives of the saints, indulgences, and other religious works until 1490. In 1491 he moved his press to Magdeburg, a town on the Elbe River. References show that in Magdeburg he printed religious texts, missals, prayer books, and local council documents until about 1500, when no further imprints are recorded.

These two well-preserved copies of rare devotional works are illustrated with sixty-seven and sixty-four woodcuts respectively, including repeats. Many of the woodcuts that appear in his editions of the *Meditationes* and *Rosarium* repeat in both volumes, especially the series illustrating the passion. For the most part they are simple contour cuts where the characters are defined in outline and parallel lines are added for background. The woodcut shown here of the Guards Gambling for Christ's Garments is one of the more interesting in the suite. It captures the action of the scene and depicts Christ's persecutors as consumed with greed and oblivious to the significance of the events taking place around them. The rolling dice, the drawn weapons, the torn knee in the pants of the man in the foreground, and the determined expression of each of the men, suggest to the viewer the chaos surrounding the passion and the horror of the crucifixion.

An examination of the woodcuts reveals that at least four different hands were involved in cutting these images. There are a few, like the Guards Gambling for Christ's Garments, which display skill at composition and in the depiction of human nature. Another series of wood blocks is cut in pure outline without embellishment or artistic subtlety. A third group appears very similar in style and composition to those in the 1489 Antwerp edition printed by Leeu, described below. A few woodcuts are clearly based on images copied from dotted prints, where the foreground is black with a series of white dots systematically placed to create contrast. Manfred von Arnim's *Katalog der Bibliothek Otto Schäfer Schwienfurt* illustrates five images from the Brandis edition.

There is little doubt that these texts were meant to be bound together, and ISTC cites only two extant copies of the pair: the Rosenwald/Dyson Perrins copy and one at the Wolfenbüttel Library. The *Meditationes* is imperfect, having 104 of 112 leaves, with leaf 12 repaired with loss to the text. The book is bound in contemporary leather over wooden boards and is tooled in blind in a traditional panel format with floral decorations. It is in very good condition, although there seems to have been a repair to the original clasp. The book is remarkable for its size, the binding measuring just 4 by 2½ inches. In a description in the *Quarterly Journal of the Library of Congress,* Frederick Goff writes, "Incunabula of this diminutive size are, as one might expect, quite uncommon." He also suggests that this edition may be pirated from one printed in Antwerp by Gerard Leeu in 1489, a copy of which Rosenwald also purchased at the Dyson Perrins sale (item 33).

16mo. 103 x 65 mm, 4 x 2½ in. Goff J-475.
W. L. Schreiber 4399a. Campbell 1049.
Goff *LCQJ* 48. Arnim 198.

## 9   ROSENWALD 239: DYSON PERRINS 285

ONE OF SIX KNOWN COPIES, this is the fourth edition of Torquemada's *Meditationes,* thought to be the first illustrated book printed in Italy. Considered a cornerstone of Italian book illustration, Torquemada's work was originally printed in Rome in 1467 by the German printer Ulrich Han, a native of the city of Vienna. Subsequent editions by Han appeared in 1473 and 1478. The fourth edition, illustrated here, was printed in 1484 by Stephan Plannck, an apprentice in Han's shop who took over the business after his death. Plannck printed nearly three hundred titles during the incunable period, but only a few of them were illustrated with woodcuts.

Unlike Florence and Venice in the fifteenth century, Rome never became a center for the printing of illustrated books. After Ulrich Han's edition of Torquemada, it was fourteen years before J. P. de Lignamine was to print an illustrated book in Rome. His 1481 edition of Philippus de Barberiis's *Opuscula* is illustrated with 29 woodcuts from 23 blocks, and he followed it with Lucius Apuleius's *Herbarius,* illustrated with 131 woodcuts, thought to be the first printed herbal. In the 1490s Johann Besicken and Andreas Freitag were the only Roman printers other than Plannck who produced illustrated books of quality.

Plannck used thirty-three of Han's original thirty-four cuts in his edition of 1484. The quality of the designs of these woodcuts, though considered rough by some early critics, are distinguished by their spaciousness, clarity, and economy of line, all important characteristics of the Italian woodcut before 1490. The woodcuts of Adam and Eve in the Garden and The Annunciation shown here are simple in construction, graceful in execution, and eminently ac-

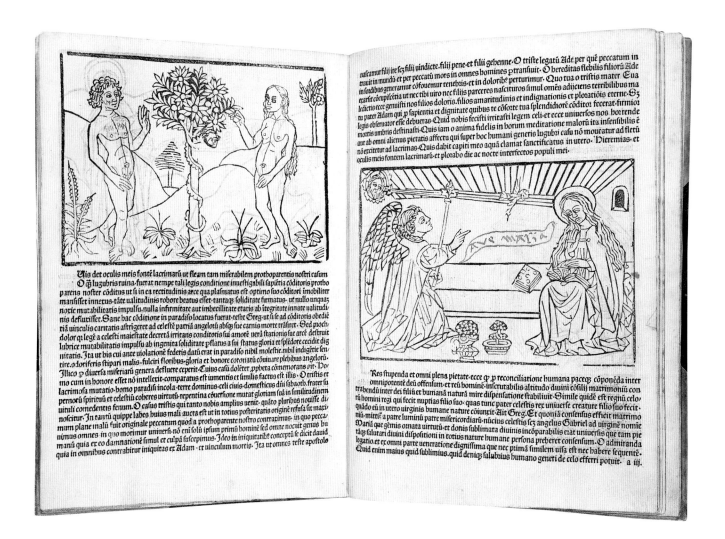

9. JUAN DE TORQUEMADA, CARDINAL. *Meditationes.* Rome: Stephan Plannck, 13 March 1484

cessible to the viewer. There is a sensuousness in the lines that defines Adam's torso and the fine turn of Eve's ankle, contours that demonstrate a developed sense of artistic possibility. This emphasis on the physical form suggests a new artistic awareness which was developing in the Italian woodcut during the early Renaissance period.

Over the years, a consensus formed attributing the cuts in Torquemada's *Meditationes* to German craftsmen and the design to an Italian source. Friedrich Lippmann, A. W. Pollard, and Arthur M. Hind all make this point, contrasting the coarseness of the cutting with the fine compositional elements attributed to the designer of the image. But attribution, as already pointed out, is a very difficult endeavor. A statement on the title page of the 1467 edition claims that the thirty-four original woodcuts were based on frescoes that were painted on the walls of the Church of Santa Maria de Minerva in Rome. This was taken to be true by bibliographers and art historians who studied this suite until 1980, when Franz Unterkircher attempted to link these illustrations to a now-lost illuminated manuscript. In an English-language summary of his article, Unterkircher writes, "It is improbable that the frescoes served as direct models for the woodcuts; rather it must be assumed that this was an illuminated manuscript that had existed somewhere north of the Alps and that might possibly still be lying unknown and be concealed in some library." Unterkircher declares that, based on the compositional elements of the woodcuts, the source of the manuscript was probably Bavarian or Austrian, a suggestion that locates the designer as coming from north of the Alps. Unterkircher challenged conventional wisdom as to the origin of the woodcuts, reinforcing the point about the difficulty of establishing geographical origins of woodcuts during the late medieval and early Renaissance period.

This copy includes a collation and note by C. W. Dyson Perrins, which reads in part, "This edition seems unknown and is not mentioned by Hain or Proctor. A copy was sold in the Trau Sale in Vienna in October 1905 to Mons. D. Morgand for 6020 Kroners. I bought this copy from Marinis, Florence, January 1907 for £250."

ISTC cites copies at the Huntington Library; the Scheide Library at Princeton; and the Library of Congress; as well as copies at the Bibliothèque nationale, Paris; Siena Biblioteca comunale, Italy; and Bibliothek Ecclesciastica, Hungary.

Folio. 276 x 198 mm, 10¾ x 7¾ in. Goff T‑540.
Pollard *Italian* 34. Hind, p. 396. Lippmann, pp. 9–10.
Sander 7407. Landau and Parshall, p. 162. Unterkircher, p. 516.

## 10    ROSENWALD 260: DYSON PERRINS 97

THE MARCH 1491 EDITION of the *Divine Comedy* printed in Venice is considered by many bibliographers to be one of the most important fifteenth-century illustrated editions of Dante's masterpiece. Bernardinus Benalius and Matteo Capcasa illustrated it with three full-page woodcuts introducing each of the books of Dante's poem and ninety-seven small cuts illustrating the action of each canto. The three large cuts are framed by a monumental architectural border which encloses a design illustrating a complex narrative that refers to a series of major events told in the canto. The images and borders are cleanly cut in outline in the popular style common to many Venetian woodcuts of the period.

The other two important fifteenth-century Italian editions of Dante are the Brescia edition of 1487 printed by Boninus de Boninis, illustrated with sixty-eight full-page woodcuts framed within black-ground borders, and the edition printed by Petrus de Piasiis in Venice in November 1491. This edition uses the same format as the edition printed by Benalius and Capcasa, but the ninety-seven blocks have been recut and exhibit a bit more clarity in the depiction of the narrative and the figures.

In the second half of the fifteenth century, Venice was the richest city in Italy and the economic center of the European publishing trade. According to Gerulaitis, nearly 13 percent of all books produced before 1501 were printed on Venetian presses. This activity drew printers from all over Europe as well as artists and craftsmen who could contribute their skills to this growing industry. Erhard Ratdolt, the Augsburg printer who worked in Venice for ten years in the 1470s and 1480s, was instrumental in developing printing techniques that would mimic the skill of the illuminator. He was the first to introduce the use of large ornamental woodcut initial letters and black-ground borders, innovations that became staples of the Venetian illustrated book of the period. William Ivins refers to the "sculpturesque style" of these borders and suggests that their design was influenced by the larger world of Italian painters and sculptors.

The Venetian woodcut of the last decade of the fifteenth century, like Italian woodcuts in general, is distinguished by a number of characteristics visible in the image reproduced here. In addition to its use of the border, the large woodcut exhibits a freedom of line that emphasizes

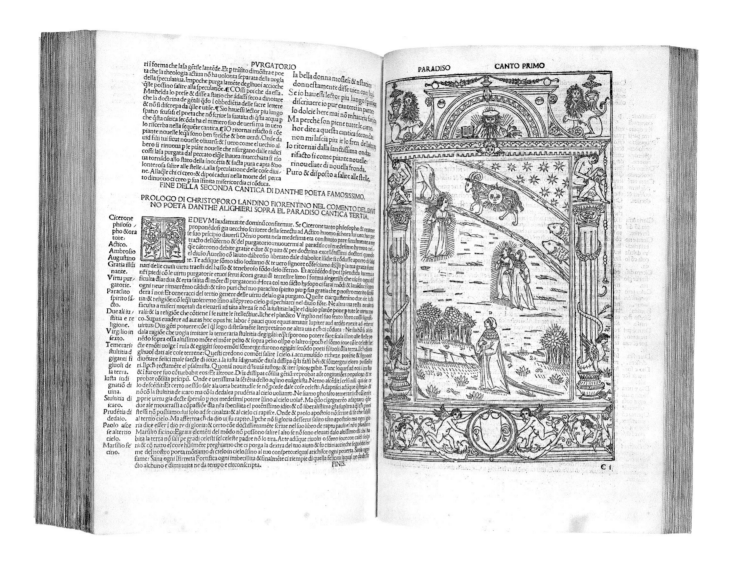

10. DANTE ALIGHIERI.
*La Commedia.* Venice:
Bernardinus Benalius and
Matteo Capcasa,
3 March 1491

the naturalness of the human figure and the ease with which it is set in motion. The folds of clothing, facial features, and expressiveness in the action of the hands are characteristics common to the Venetian cut. As mentioned above, this image exemplifies the popular style of Venetian woodcut, which gets its name from the designer's decision to dress characters in contemporary costume, to use playful images to decorate borders, and to populate the composition with animals, birds, and flowers. The designer gains much of this effect by using outline to construct forms rather than relying on shading or parallel lines. This keeps the image open and less formal and contributes to the popular nature of the design. Lilian Armstrong attributes the work of the leading practitioner of the popular style, the so-called Popular Designer, to the Pico Master, a miniaturist whose work in Venice spanned the years 1465 to 1495.

The large woodcut that illustrates the beginning of the *Paradiso* translates into pictorial form Beatrice's vision, transmigration, and ecstasy as she ascends from earth to paradise. The designer of the woodcut composes the image around the contemporary motif of the universe, following the medieval concept of the structure of the world, where the earth is at its center and spheres radiate out in concentric circles. Numerous books were printed on this subject and many were illustrated with woodcuts showing the demarcation of spheres. Editions of Sacro Bosco's *Sphera mundi* and Konrad von Megenberg's *Buch der Natur* were published in the later decades of the fifteenth century, and these texts trace the roots of this concept back to the early Middle Ages. Paintings from the period also document this vision of the world. An example is Giovanni di Paolo's *Creation of the World,* in the Metropolitan Museum of Art, New York.

The success of the woodcut shown here lies in the designer's ability to adapt the concept of the medieval world view to Dante's account of Beatrice's passage to heaven. By depicting Beatrice's path as passing from earth, through the circles of water, wind, and fire, up through the spheres of the seven planets signified by the zodiac signs, and into the realm of the "ethereal sphere," represented by the stars in the upper right, the artist translates the idea in a manner completely understandable to the contemporary viewer.

Folio. 300 x 205 mm, 12 x 8 in. Goff D-32. Pollard *Italian* 57, 59.
Lippmann, p. 88. Hind 482–84. Essling 531. Gerulaitis, pp. 1–19.
Ivins "Woodcut Books," p. 46. Ramsden, pp. 32–38.
Dixon, pp. 604–13. Lippincott, pp. 460–68.
Armstrong "The Pico Master," p. 270. Schäfer *Italian* 69.

## II    ROSENWALD 266: DYSON PERRINS 64

**L**ORENZO MORGIANI AND JOHANNES PETRI'S EDITION of Calandri's *Arithmetica* is recognized as an important example of a Florentine woodcut book because of the usefulness of its cleverly designed cuts as educational aids. David Smith calls this first edition "the first printed Italian arithmetic with illustrations accompanying problems, and the first to give long division in the modern form." The printers' careers spanned most of the decade of the 1490s. In addition to the *Arithmetica,* Morgiani and Petri printed religious tracts, an alchemical work by Panziera, sermons by Savonarola, and the works of Saint Augustine. The most important

11. FILIPPO CALANDRI.
*Arithmetica.* Florence:
Lorenzo Morgiani
and Johannes Petri,
1 January 1491/92

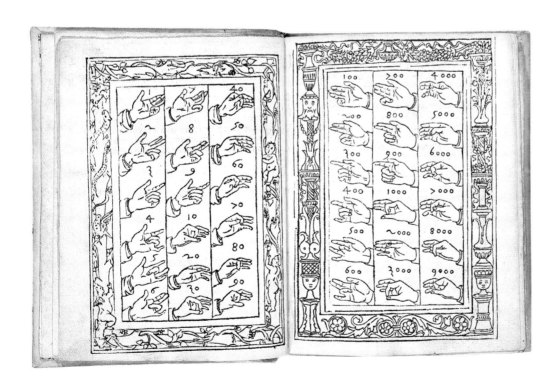

of their printed works is their 1495 edition of *Epistole et Evangelii,* also considered the most notable book in the Dyson Perrins collection and one purchased by Rosenwald (item 18).

Although modest in appearance, Calandri's *Arithmetica* contains many of the qualities one looks for in a Florentine book from the period. The three most apparent elements are the use of ornamental borders to frame an image; simple contours to elucidate content; and sensitive physical representations that depict human expression. In the example illustrated here, particular attention should be paid to the outline border, cut in a delicate yet casual style, and the fluid depiction of the hand in motion. The borders are composed of eight individual blocks, all of different designs, incorporating standard motifs of columns and urns, foliage, branch-and-leaf patterns, and cherubs and birds. A freedom of line and playfulness in imagery characterize the borders. The actions of the hands counting numbers are clearly expressed and the usefulness of the images as an educational device is clearly understood. The remainder of the volume is illustrated with woodcuts that help elucidate mathematical problems, including examples of use to builders, merchants, and farmers.

8vo. 195 x 130 mm, 7 ½ x 5 ¼ in. Goff C-34. Smith, pp. 47–49.
Hind, p. 537. Pollard *Italian* 56. Sander 1523. Ivins
"Early Florentine," pp. 14–23. Schäfer *Italian* 50.

## 12   ROSENWALD 271: DYSON PERRINS 161

LANDINO'S MANUAL DESCRIBING THE MANNER of writing letters provides standard forms for specific subjects and instructions for creating proper salutations for church officials, dignitaries, and members of the nobility. The author, one of the leading Florentine scholars of the period, is best known for his commentary on Dante's *Commedia,* which first appeared in the 1481 edition printed in Florence, illustrated with engravings after Botticelli.

The first edition of *Formulario di lettere,* printed by Ugo de Rugeriis in 1485, was the first illustrated book printed in Bologna. Rugeriis issued two editions during that same year, each illustrated with a single woodcut, the Visitation of Mary. Subsequent illustrated editions were printed in Florence by Bartolommeo di Libri in 1490 and, the fourth, by Miscomini in 1492, the edition shown here. Both the 1490 and the 1492 editions were illustrated with a woodcut entitled Master and Seven Students, but they were designed and cut by different hands. The cut that appears in the Miscomini edition was originally used by Bartolommeo di Libri in his edition of Perottus's *Regulae grammaticae,* Florence, 1490. It was used again in 1500 when Miscomini printed his edition of *Flores poetarum.*

The subject of the master with his students was a common motif used in Italy to illustrate educational or scientific books of the period, much the way portraits of saints were used for religious tracts or thinkers at their desks for humanist writings. What distinguishes this rendering of the Master with His Seven Students from other contemporary examples is what Pollard called "the little masterpiece of quiet drama," in which a teacher and his students, all in action and all perfectly comfortable in their environment, are depicted. One student takes notes, another reads, four are paying close attention to the teacher, and one is entering the room. The teacher is poised to make his point with his eyes directed at the young men, his arm raised, his finger pointed, and in the next moment he will utter the pearl of wisdom his students have been waiting to hear. This little drama is accomplished by an artist whose con-

summate skill at drawing and composition is perfectly matched in a woodcutter who is capable of creating fine line cuts that translate expression and motion in a natural and convincing manner. This is the essence of the best of the Florentine woodcut.

As we look more closely at the woodcut, other, more general Florentine characteristics emerge, especially the use of a border to frame the event. In this case the woodcut is framed by a thin black-ground border decorated with a ribbon pattern. This is a very common pattern, as are dart borders, floral borders, and chain borders. Antonio Miscomini's printer's mark, which appears at the end of this volume, illustrates another border style common to Florentine books. This mark is framed by a black-ground border made up of four wood blocks. The pattern is thicker and more decorative in style. The top blocks consist of two man-serpents holding a chalice on a pedestal. The bottom block shows two eagles guarding a wreath that encloses a blank shield. The two side wood blocks are decorated with a flower-and-branch motif, and the entire border encloses the initials *AM,* which are placed within a diamond that is within a circle and then a square. Both styles of thin and thick borders are important elements of the Florentine woodcut of the period.

Found in this copy of Landino's style manual is a manuscript coat-of-arms that appears both on the first leaf and in the printer's mark at the end of the book. This ownership mark— a shield decorated with a single ribbon and the letter *B,* which supports a sign of the cross—

12. CHRISTOFORO LANDINO. *Formulario di lettere & di orationi volgari.* Florence: Antonio di Bartolommeo Miscomini, 1492

has yet to be identified. It appears to be in a contemporary hand, as are the other marks in the margin of the text. This copy, bound in nineteenth-century straight grain morocco, also has the monogram bookplate of the Victorian collector Sir John H. Thorold and his plate for Syston Park, as well as bookplates of C. W. Dyson Perrins and Lessing J. Rosenwald, which appear in all the books in this collection. ISTC lists only three copies in American libraries.

4to. 195 x 135 mm, 7½ x 5¼ in. Goff L-41. Kristeller 230b. Pollard *Italian* 63.
Hind, p. 535. Sander 3836; figs. 522, 512, 464, 613, 640.

## 13   ROSENWALD 272: DYSON PERRINS 58

BONET DE LATIS DEDICATED HIS *Annulus astronomicus,* an elementary treatise on the use of the astrolabe, to Pope Alexander VI. Official physician to the pope, he describes himself in the introduction and the colophon as a "Hebrew" working under the patronage of papal authorities. The book is based on original observations and research and contains chapters from Sacro Bosco's *Sphaera mundi.* It is illustrated with a woodcut frontispiece and two woodcut diagrams, and it appears to be the only separately printed edition published in the fifteenth century.

The printer Andreas Freitag's first book appeared in Rome in 1482 and was an edition of *Fiore de virtue,* a popular guide to morality printed in the vernacular. His career spanned about fifteen years, and the last of his sixty-seven recorded books was published in 1496. Although most of his books appeared with a Roman imprint, Freitag printed two books in Naples, and between 1487 and 1492 nine of his books carried the imprint of Gaeta, at the time a small village on the coast between Rome and Naples. Toward the end of his career some of his books were printed in partnership with Johann Besicken of Basel, who did most of his printing in Italy.

The woodcut frontispiece, illustrated here, is based on a design that first appeared in Francesco del Tuppo's edition of Bernardus de Granollachs's *Sommario dell'arte di astrologia,* Naples, 1485. Del Tuppo's woodcut was copied in 1489 and used in an anonymously printed edition of Luca Pulci's *Driadeo d'amore,* probably printed in Florence. Morgiani and Petri copied it again for another edition of Granollach printed in Florence in 1491, this time using a simple Florentine-style dart border to frame the cut. For his edition of 1492/93, Freitag had this wood block made, using it again in 1493 for his edition of Anianus's *Computus cum commento.*

An examination of Freitag's woodcut reveals the use of simple lines to delineate the tools of the astronomer's trade and the architectural setting in which the two figures are placed. The man in the lower right, possibly the author, works a compass on an open tomb and holds a prism in his right hand, while the man in the portico holds a sphere that hangs from a balance and points to the heavens. The stars and planets are well defined according to contemporary understanding of the spheres of the heavens, but the meaning of the woodcut is difficult to discern. It could represent a variation on the theme of the master and student, with oblique references to early works of astronomy conducted by Arabian scholars, as represented by the oriental garb of both figures. Or, Freitag may very well have chosen to copy this cut because it represents a stock image used to illustrate a text on astronomy. The puzzling banner inscription, "Altior incubuit animus sub imagine mundi," reads, "The nobler mind would think in cosmic terms." If this translation is correct, it suggests a general statement about the study of astronomy and does not appear to be specific to Bonet de Latis's text.

In embellishing this woodcut, Freitag uses two sets of borders to frame the image. The first is the thin dart border common to many Florentine woodcuts of the period. This border is designed to be cut as part of the wood block and simply encloses the subject. The second is a passe-partout border, a device often used to increase the size of a woodcut in order to fill the entire page on which it was printed. Florentine woodcuts tended to be small images and this type of border was very effective in creating the illusion of a framed picture. Passe-partout borders are usually made up of four distinct wood blocks set around the central block. The passe-partout border Freitag uses is decorated with a hound-and-hare motif at the top, jousting cherubs riding pigs at the bottom, and candelabra on the two sides. This corresponds to Hind's border number 6, which he describes in his chapter on the Florentine woodcut.

13. BONET DE LATIS.
*Annulus astronomicus.*
[Rome: Andreas Freitag, ca. 1492/93]

4to. 209 x 144 mm, 8 ½ x 5 ½ in. Goff L-71. Pollard *Italian* 75.
Hind, pp. 403, 532–33. Kristeller, figs. 11, 13. Sanders 1210;
figs. 510, 767, 825. Gottheil, "Bonet de Latis," in *The Jewish Encyclopedia.*
Thanks to Svato Schutzner and Anna Bryan for help with translation.

Sermoni Volgari del Venerando doctore Sancto
& Aurelio Augustino:padre della regola
Heremitana/molto deuoti & spiri
tuali ad acquistare lagloria
del paradiso

THIS RARE, ANONYMOUS COLLECTION OF SERMONS, originally attributed to Saint Augustine, was at the time Rosenwald purchased it the only copy in an American collection. Today the ISTC locates only two other perfect copies outside Italy, one at Yale University and the other at the British Library. The *Sermones ad heremitas* printed in Florence in June 1493 appears to be the first use of the woodcut frontispiece designed and cut for the printer Antonio di Bartolemmeo Miscomini. Based on a woodcut of Saint Augustine in His Study that appeared in an edition of Augustine's *Soliloquii* printed by Morgiani and Petri in 1491, it appeared again in their edition of the *Confessionale* by Antonius printed in 1493. The cuts differ in the choice of border, the reversed orientation of the composition, and the architectural and decorative elements used by the artist. Lorenzo Morgiani and Johannes Petri included it again in an edition of the *Sermones* printed around 1500. Black-ground initial letters decorated with a branch-and-flower motif and Miscomini's printer's mark also illustrate the 1493 *Sermones*.

Like the woodcut of the Master with His Seven Students, this portrait of the Saint in His Study captures the essential elements of Florentine style during the 1490s. The distinctive decorative black-ground border, the finely cut contours, and the simple presentation of the author at work create an intimate scene appropriate to the text of the sermons. Augustine's halo, his monk's tonsure, and a bishop's miter resting on the edge of the desk each signify a stage of his life and signal his eventual canonization. The curtain, the hourglass, the apple, the books, and the partially drawn curtain create a comfortable setting for contemplation. Pollard calls this one of the "finest Florentine woodcuts in the large style," referring to those woodcuts usually used on the first leaf, which were normally larger than the standard size of woodcut used to illustrate a text.

As we follow the development of the Florentine woodcut, it is hard not to notice the interrelationships among printers and the images they used to illustrate their books. Wood blocks were passed from printer to printer, images were copied, and new blocks were produced. Documenting this relative freedom of movement of wood blocks and images within the printing trade has contributed greatly to our understanding of how the trade worked in fifteenth-century Florence. Yet, evidence with regard to the publication history of a text and image is in direct contrast to the anonymity of the artists, designers, and woodcutters who produced these images in the fifteenth and sixteenth centuries. Friedrich Lippmann, Paul Kristeller, Alfred W. Pollard, Arthur M. Hind, and other nineteenth- and early twentieth-century historians took great pains to identify those responsible for creating them. With so little specific information available about locality and authorship, however, they sometimes suspended good judgment to prove a point about national origins, character, or identity. Modern historians of the subject are wary of making similar missteps and in many cases refuse to address the question at all. Those who do address questions of attribution follow a more judicious approach, relying on a stricter analysis of the woodcut image and focusing on its evolution from illuminated manuscript and painting, before making attributions.

4to. 240 x 140 mm, 8 x 5 ½ in. Goff A-1322. Pollard *Italian* 69.
Kristeller 11c, fig. 20. Hind, p. 547. Sander 688. Panofsky, *Iconology,* p. 15.
Lincoln, p. 4. Landau and Parshall, pp. 33–38.

14. [SAINT AUGUSTINE.]
*Sermones ad heremitas.*
Florence: Antonio di
Bartolemmeo Miscomini,
28 June 1493

## 15   INCUN. X.A296: DYSON PERRINS 2

15. AESOP.
*Aesopus moralisatus.*
[Brescia: Boninus de
Boninis, ca. 1487]

THE ROSENWALD/DYSON PERRINS COPY of the undated Brescia edition of Aesop's fables printed in 1487 is the only copy known. This *Aesopus moralisatus* includes forty-three of the sixty-seven cuts that appear in another edition by the same printer, Boninus de Boninis, dated March 7, 1487. Each leaf illustrated here has been remargined, and there is considerable loss to both image and text in about one-third of the leaves. Of the March 7 edition, the only copy cited in an American library by ISTC is also at the Library of Congress, and it also is incomplete, with nine leaves in facsimile. Goff cites a second copy in the possession of H. P. Kraus who later sold it to Otto Schäfer. Pollard writes that the text setting and the borders are different in each of the 1487 editions but the woodcuts are the same.

Both editions contain a Latin text and Accio Zucco's Italian translation, which first appeared in a Verona edition printed by Giovanni and Alberto Alvise in 1479. The Veronese edition is also the first Italian illustrated edition of the *Fables,* and the woodcuts in many subsequent editions are based on the designs created for Alvise. In his study of the 1479 Verona edition,

Giovanni Mardersteig writes that for the 1487 edition, Boninis "copied the format, the text, and half the illustrations of the Veronese edition," with the remaining woodcuts designed by a local artisan from Brescia.

The image illustrated here is based on fable number 13, "The Country Mouse and the City Mouse." This well-known fable extols the joys of the pastoral life and warns of the risks inherent in urban living. In L'Estrange's translation, the moral of the fable reads, "The Difference of a Court and a Country Life: The Delights, Innocence, and Security of the one, compar'd with the Anxiety, the Lewdness, and the Hazards of the other."

What is most striking in the woodcut is the scale of the characters and the open environment in which they are placed. The setting is well defined but uncluttered and spacious. The steward, in contemporary costume, is simply drawn but effectively portrayed, and the mice, aware of the intruder, seem to be in motion. All this is accomplished with the sparse use of black line and no shading. The passe-partout border is a simple, rhythmic fish-scale pattern, enclosed in a double-line border.

In the undated edition of the Brescia Aesop, there are two border styles framing the forty-three woodcuts; one in outline as described above and another in black ground in a leaf-and-branch motif. These two borders also appear in the March 7 edition, along with a third border in an oak leaf pattern cut in outline. A comparison of the editions shows that the same wood block is not always framed by the same border, suggesting that the printer was not concerned with a standard application of the border to the image, but rather used the borders at hand when imposing his page layouts.

The undated copy of the *Fables* is lot number 2 in the Dyson Perrins sale, but was not purchased by Rosenwald and is part of the general incunable collection at the Library of Congress. An examination of Rosenwald's copy of the Dyson Perrins sale catalogue shows that Rosenwald placed an *X* through the lot number and wrote the word "Condition" in the margin. Another note in the margin states that A. S. W. Rosenbach, Rosenwald's agent at the sale, purchased the book over E. P. Goldschmidt for £260 for the Library of Congress but not for the Rosenwald Collection.

4to. 218 x 150 mm, 8½ x 6 in. Goff A-150. Pollard *Italian* 43.
Sander 54, figs. 118–21. Mardersteig, p. 274. *Aesop's Fables,* translated by
Sir Roger L'Estrange, p. 61. Schäfer *Italian* 4. Special thanks to Mary Ann Folter for
information about HPK's sale of the March 7, 1487, edition to Otto Schäfer.


## 16    ROSENWALD 280: DYSON PERRINS 3

ILLUSTRATED WITH SIXTY-SEVEN WOODCUTS, the Manfredus de Bonellis edition of *Aesop* provides an excellent example of the various influences that helped produce the Venetian woodcut during the final decade of the fifteenth century. Bonellis first published an illustrated edition of Aesop's *Fables* in January 1491, followed quickly by an edition in November of the same year. The copy illustrated here is the third edition, printed in 1493, and it is an exact reprint of two previous printings. Subsequent reprint editions were issued in 1497, 1502, and 1508, attesting to its success as a publishing venture.

Bonellis was active as a printer in Venice from about 1491 to 1508, with a few titles carrying his imprint between 1515 and 1516. He was noted for his editions of Italian literature in

Uſticus vrbanum mus murem ſuſcipit ede
r    Commodat ⁊ mentem menſamᶜᶫ mente minoꝛ
      Intenui menſa ſatis eſt immenſa voluntas
Nobilitat viles frons generoſa dapes
F acto fine cibis vrbanum ruſticus audit.
      Urbani ſocius tendit in vrbis opes.
Ecce penu ſubeunt. inſeruit amicus amico.
      Inuigilant menſe. ſercula menſa gerit.

the vernacular, and for reprinting books using the same wood blocks cut originally for other Venetian printers. His most important illustrated books include this edition of Aesop, his 1492 edition of Jacobus de Voragine's *Legenda aurea,* and his 1498 edition of Boccaccio's *Decameron.*

16. AESOP.
*Aesopus moralisatus.*
Venice: Manfredus de
Bonellis, 17 August 1493

The source for Manfredus de Bonellis's images and passe-partout borders was the first Venetian illustrated edition of the *Fables,* printed in Brescia by Bernardinus Benalius in 1487 (item 15). Giovanni Mardersteig states that half of the woodcuts in the 1493 edition are based on those printed by Benalius, and the "other half are original and are designed and cut by an able artist." The 1487 edition itself was significantly influenced by the composition of the characters that appear in the Verona edition of 1479 and the architectural borders from the Naples edition printed by Francesco Tuppo in 1485. These influences are apparent in the Country Mouse and the City Mouse illustrated here. The passe-partout borders, with their architectural motif, dramatically frame the woodcut and focus the attention of the viewer on the action of the image. The composition is clearly based on the 1487 edition, with the steward entering from the right, and the mice, in a well-stocked larder, frozen in fear of his entry.

On its own, this woodcut from the 1493 edition can be viewed as a well-arranged, easily read image in outline. The woodcut is successful in rendering the movement of the steward as he pushes open the door and the reaction of the mice to this impending danger. But when compared with the image designed and cut for the 1487 edition, the figures of the steward and the mice appear less well defined and much more conventional in their characterization. The steward is dressed in contemporary costume, but his facial features are more generic and lack the individuality of the steward in the Brescia design. The rendering of the mice is sketchy compared with the well-crafted mice in the 1487 edition.

Given the prominence of Venice as the center of printing and publishing in Italy during the last decades of the century, it is not unreasonable to expect influences from such towns as Naples, Verona, and Brescia to affect the artistic design of the Venetian illustrated book. The passe-partout border, the architectural headpiece, and the sparsely drawn line are all design elements that first appeared in other Italian printing centers but very quickly became part of the developing Venetian style.

8vo. 186 x 145 mm, 7⅜ x 5¾ in. Goff A-153. Pollard *Italian* 72.
Essling 362. Sander 63, 58; figs. 189, 190. Hind, p. 485.
Norton *Italian,* p. 131. Mardersteig, pp. 259–77.
Ivins "Woodcut Books," p. 49. Schäfer *Italian* 5.

## 17    ROSENWALD 289: DYSON PERRINS 46

PRINTED IN VENICE IN 1494, the third edition of LucAntonio Giunta's *Biblia italica* is considered by Alfred W. Pollard to be the "most important Venetian folio illustrated with small column cuts." Called the Malermi Bible, for the translator Niccolò Malermi, the first edition appeared in 1490 and was illustrated with 384 woodcuts designed in the popular style. It was reprinted in 1492 and in 1494, both editions illustrated with 430 woodcuts. Guilelmus Anima Mia printed an edition of Malermi's translation in 1493, basing his woodcuts on the 1490 edition, but using a series of passe-partout borders to frame his newly cut wood blocks.

LucAntonio Giunta was the most enterprising Venetian printer and publisher of the

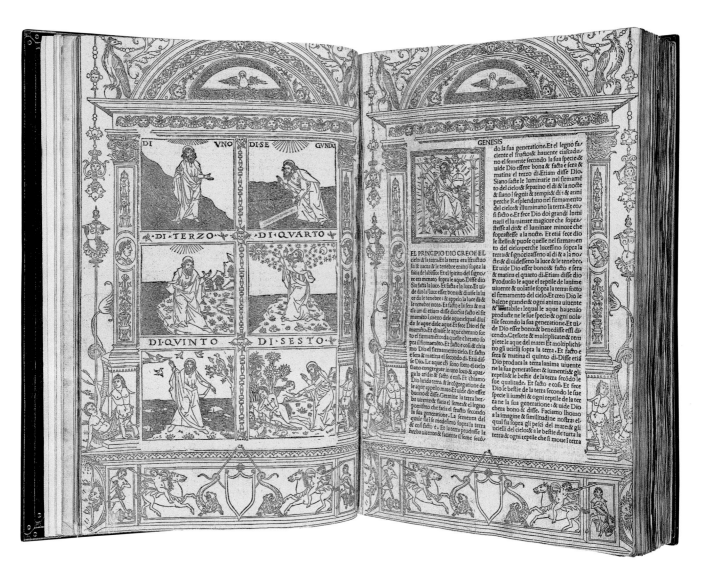

17. *Biblia italica.*
Translated by Niccolò
Malermi. Venice: Johannes
Rubeus Vercellensis for
LucAntonio Giunta,
June 1494

period, whose career continued from 1489 until his death in 1538. Lilian Armstrong has ascertained that 406 editions are linked to Giunta during this forty-year period. Besides printing titles of his own, he acted as a publisher, commissioning a number of important Venetian printers to produce books under his imprint. His relation with Johannes Rubeus, who began his printing career in Treviso in 1480 and moved to Venice in 1486, was particularly productive in the 1490s. Their collaboration produced some important illustrated books, including three editions of this Bible, an edition of Livy printed in 1493, and an edition of Ovid's *Metamorphoses* printed in 1497.

The first series of woodcuts designed for the *Biblia italica* appear at the opening of the Book of Genesis and illustrate the six days of creation. These woodcuts, larger than cuts that appear throughout the rest of the book, are square in shape and are set within a monumental architectural passe-partout border cut in outline. The top border block is decorated with the Holy Spirit in the form of a dove within a lunette framed by an arch, with eagles perched on either end of the structural pediment. The designs of the side borders include architectural columns decorated with vases and portraits. At the center of the base block is a shield held by cupids on horseback, with mythological creatures in the corners. This border is repeated on the following page, where it encloses the beginning text of Genesis, decorated with an elaborate wood block initial letter *N* showing God the Father surrounded by a choir of angels. The border is repeated a third time at the beginning of the Book of Proverbs, where the designer of the block substitutes God the Father for the Holy Spirit at the top and encloses a depiction of Solomon at his writing table and asleep in his bed. Hind designates this as "black line border A 1," and cites its use in three other titles published by Giunta. In all three examples, the choice of costume and decoration is clearly in the popular style, which Armstrong here attributes to the Pico Master.

The text of this volume is set in two columns, and each of the 434 woodcuts is designed in a small format to match the width of a single column. The wood blocks are mostly cut in outline and modeled with some cross-hatching. Unlike the woodcut in the 1491 edition of Dante (item 10), the small cuts in this work rarely attempt to depict more than one episode of a story. This, along with the clarity of the outline cuts, makes the woodcuts easier to understand and more intimate in their presentation.

Characteristic of the Malermi Bible is the thoughtful integration of the text and image. In addition to the large initial letter *N*, the book is filled with floriated and historiated initial letters, cut in two sizes. Although not as elaborate as Ratdolt's finest initial letters, they are carefully cut black-ground woodcuts that are dropped into the text at the beginnings of chapters and add greatly to the typographical harmony of the volume.

Folio. 303 x 207 mm, 12 x 8 ¼ in. Goff B-647. Camerini 17. Essling 136.
Sander 993. Hind, pp. 466–69; 503–4. Schäfer *Italian* 29.
Armstrong "Woodcuts for Liturgical Books," pp. 65–93. Armstrong
"The Pico Master," p. 271. Landau and Parshall, pp. 19–20. Ramsden, pp. 32–38.
Bliss, p. 75. Weitenkampf, pp. 779–88.

## 18   ROSENWALD 298: DYSON PERRINS 106

ONE OF TWO KNOWN COPIES of Piero Pacini's first publication to be fully illustrated with woodcuts, this copy of the *Epistole et Evangelii et lectioni volgari in lingua toscana* contains 144 large cuts in 205 impressions, 24 small cuts of saints and prophets used 297 times, and numerous decorated initial letters in branch-and-leaf patterns. Only 8 of the large woodcuts were used by Florentine printers and publishers before the publication of this July 27, 1495, edition.

The copious number of images, along with the quality of the wood blocks created for Pacini, make the *Epistolae et Evangelii* one of the greatest Florentine illustrated books of the period, and, as Pollard writes, it is the "most notable book in the [Dyson Perrins] collection." Rosenwald apparently agreed with this sentiment, because he paid £7,400 for the book, even though it has paper restoration to the first and last signatures, with some loss to the text, and leaf VII is wanting. It should be noted that, in addition to this title, Pacini was responsible for publishing two other fully illustrated books: an edition of *Aesop* printed by Francesco Bonaccorsi in 1496, illustrated with 66 woodcuts, and an edition of Pulci's *Morgante Maggiore* printed by Antonio Tubini in 1500, with 150 cuts. In all three cases, Pacini used different printers and a combination of new and previously used wood blocks to illustrate his books, attesting to the fluidity of the Florentine printing trade at the end of the fifteenth century.

The Florentine woodcut book evolved in two distinct styles during the period from 1490

to 1508. Both these styles were firmly based on the example of Florentine painters. One was a more dramatic style, influenced by Botticelli, Filippino Lippi, and Donatello. The second, which emphasized a more epic form, found its inspiration in the work of Ghirlandaio, Filippo Lippi, and Verrocchio. Paul Kristeller summarizes the differences between the two schools as follows: "In studying the Florentine woodcut we notice on the one part a conciseness of composition, dramatic vivacity, and energy of movement, or an expression of exalted sentiment characterized by Botticelli and his school. On the other side we have quiet storytelling and detailed compositions accompanied by great freedom of design, as represented by Ghirlandaio and his followers." In both cases, there is an emphasis on vigorously drawn lines, balanced composition, and careful draftsmanship and cutting.

The *Epistole et Evangelii* title leaf is one of the most striking of the period, with an elaborate black-ground border designed in the flower-and-vine motif, balanced by the four block cuts of the four evangelists. At the center is a roundel of Saint Peter and Saint Paul cut in simple contours set in a landscape punctuated by an ancient wall and a mountainous background also cut in outline, with some parallel lines to suggest shading. The ground plane is shaded in white on black, providing an emphatic contrast to the central images of the wood block.

The 144 large cuts that decorate the volume are framed by a series of fourteen borders in typical Florentine style. The cuts clearly fall into the school of Ghirlandaio, where the emphasis lies in depicting the essential message of the Gospels rendered in complex compositional format. The small blocks are filled with figures, landscapes, and architectural elements cut in fine con-

18. *Epistole et Evangelii et lectioni volgari in lingua toscana.* Florence: Lorenzo Morgiani and Johannes Petri, for Piero Pacini, 27 July 1495

tours and highlighted with shading produced by a white-on-black technique that provides depth to the images. They exhibit a convincing representation of the human body in motion and nearly always succeed in focusing the attention of the viewer on the dramatic action of the Gospel story.

An examination of the three small woodcuts from the *Epistole et Evangelii* illustrated here demonstrates the skill of the designer and the block cutter who created these woodcuts. The images of Manna from Heaven, Christ Entering Jerusalem, and Christ Teaching the Apostles all contain elements characteristic of the Florentine woodcut. The positioning of the cuts and the three initial letters also demonstrate the clever eye and skill of the printers, Lorenzo Morgiani and Johann Petri, whose choice of type and sense of composition add significantly to the beauty of the book.

In 1903 Bernard Berenson attributed the block designs in this work to Alunno di Domenico, a student of Domenico Ghirlandaio, who was later identified as Bartolommeo di Giovanni. In the same article, later expanded into the book *Drawings of the Florentine Painters,* Berenson attributes nearly all the designs for Florentine woodcuts of this period to this singular master. He writes, "and if, at the same time, it was he and no other who furnished the fascinating designs for nearly all the illustrated books that appeared in Florence for some fifteen years, then surely he was an artistic personality with which we have done well to become acquainted." Pollard and subsequent scholars have challenged this wholesale attribution, but Bartolommeo di Giovanni's name is still closely associated to the designs for the wood blocks in the Pacini edition of the *Epistole et Evangellii.*

Another edition of the *Epistole* with this series of woodcuts appeared in 1515, and subsequent use of the wood blocks from this work continued well into the third quarter of the sixteenth century.

Folio. 270 x 130 mm, 11 ¼ x 7⅝ in. Goff E-94. Pollard *Italian* 90.
Kristeller 135b; pp. xviii–xix, xxvii; fig. 79–96. Sander 2568.
Berenson *Burlington Magazine,* pp. 1–20.
Berenson *Drawings of the Florentine Painters,* pp. 128–29.
Pollard, Introduction to *Epistole et Evangelii,* pp. xxi–xxiii. Hind, pp. 533–34.


## 19   ROSENWALD 308: DYSON PERRINS 44

THE *PROTESTO ALLA SIGNORIA DI FIRENZE* was printed about 1495 by Bartolommeo Libri, whose career in Florence spanned forty years, his last imprint appearing in 1511. Although most of his work was unsigned, 209 editions have been attributed to his press. Libri is best remembered for the numerous religious pamphlets and Savonarola tracts he printed, many, like the one exhibited here, illustrated with only one woodcut. Francesco Berlinghieri's most important printed work is his monumental poetic adaptation of Ptolemy's geography printed in Florence in 1482 and illustrated with engraved maps.

The Master and His Disciple, illustrated here, is designed in typical Florentine style, with a black-ground border with a dart pattern. The two figures, caught in debate, are dressed in finely contoured costumes cut with considerable care, and the facial features of both figures are quite distinctive. The woodcut's architectural element, with its complex brick pattern and shading, defines the space and provides perspective. The free-spirited manner in which the lines of the floor are cut suggests a confident craftsman skilled at evoking fine details with the flick of his knife. Other than an opening initial letter, this woodcut is the only embellishment used by Libri in printing this tract. This eight-page pamphlet is one of four known copies, this the only example in an American library. The ownership mark of the shield within a wreath that is stamped below the woodcut is yet to be identified.

19. FRANCESCO BERLINGHIERI. *Protesto alla signoria di Firenze.* [Florence: Bartolommeo Libri, ca. 1495]

4to. 200 x 130 mm, 7⅞ x 5⅛ in. Goff B-343. Sander 928, fig. 534. Norton *Italian,* pp. 31–32. Ivins "Early Florentine," pp. 20–21.

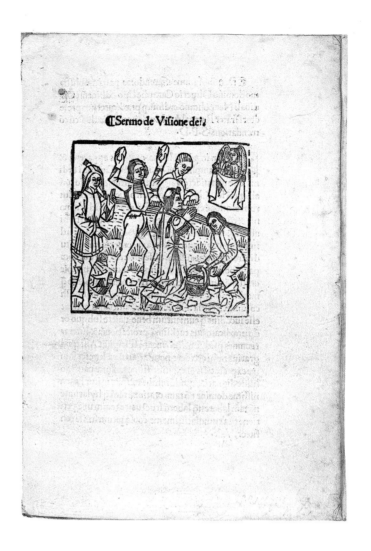

## 20    ROSENWALD 310: DYSON PERRINS 185

20. RAYNALDUS
MONSAUREUS.
*Sermo de visione Dei.*
[Rome: Johann Besicken
et Sigismundus Mayer,
after 26 December 1495]

THE WOODCUT ON THE TITLE PAGE of the first edition of Raynaldus Monsaureus's sermon illustrates the Stoning of Saint Stephen, the first Christian martyr. The sermon was
printed by Johann Besicken and Sigismundus Mayer in Rome sometime after December 26,
1495. This image clearly demonstrates the differences in style between the Roman woodcuts
of the late fifteenth century and those designed and printed in Venice and Florence during the
same period. Johann Besicken, Andreas Freitag, and Stephan Plannck were the leading printers
in Rome during the fifteenth century. All three were trained in Germany and it is not surprising,
therefore, that the first woodcuts designed to illustrate books printed in Rome reflect a German
style. Another difference is that in Rome, a secondary center for the Italian illustrated book,
print culture did not evolve from the fine arts traditions as occurred in its sister cities to the
north. No leading school of painting contributed its influence to the woodcutters and designers
at work there, and as a result, the Roman woodcut did not take on the fresh characteristics of
the Renaissance style until after the turn of the sixteenth century.

In the woodcut illustrated here, all the figures are cut in thick contours, on a single plane,
with parallel lines used for shading. The costumes are simple in design but contemporary in
style. The image of the young man carrying a basket of stones lacks the fluidity of motion or
the natural grace of its Florentine counterparts. This can also be said of the other characters in

the woodcut. The landscape is suggested by the use of varied parallel lines and blank space, without ornamentation, embellishment, or border to enhance the artistic quality of the image, as is often found in Venetian and Florentine cuts printed before 1500. The medieval style is still dominant here and it produces a much different effect than do the compositional arrangements, well-defined architectural and landscape motifs, black-ground borders, and white-on-black technique used in both Venice and Florence.

Although ISTC lists only two copies of the first printing in America, a copy recently appeared at the sale of the Italian books from the library of Otto Schäfer. In his description of the Schäfer copy, Paul Needham suggests that the design of the woodcut has Neapolitan origins, and that the work of this woodcutter "has been identified in several other very rare Roman illustrated incunables and post-incunables."

4to. 210 x 146 mm, 8½ x 5⅞ in. Goff M-811. Pollard *Italian* 115.
Sander 4869. Hind, pp. 402–4. Schäfer *Italian* 124.

## 21    ROSENWALD 313: DYSON PERRINS 121

THIS FAMOUS WOODCUT BINDING, produced in Ferrara during the last years of the fifteenth century, is one of only two known copies, and the only copy in an American collection. The woodcut for Battista Fregoso's *Anteros,* published by Leonardus Pachel in 1496, was designed specifically as a binding, printed and then pasted to boards that were used to bind the volumes. Mirjam M. Foot provides a detailed description of this binding and discusses the origins of the images of the Sacred Monogram IHS and the Saint George that appear on the covers. Foot attributes the wood blocks, as did Kristeller, to "one of the artists who worked for the printer Lorenzo de'Rossi," and she contrasts its stylistic qualities to the eight other known examples of this type of bookbinding produced in Ferrara during this period. The earliest examples were made in Augsburg in the 1480s and 1490s, where they were produced as publishers' wrappers for a specific book. Those produced in Italy "have no connection with the book they cover."

Lorenzo de'Rossi's career in Ferrara began in 1482 and continued until his death in 1521. He is best remembered for his illustrated editions of *De claris mulieribus* by Foresti and the *Epistles* of Saint Jerome, both published in 1497 and illustrated with woodcuts designed in both Venetian and Florentine styles. The Venetian influence is not surprising given Ferrara's geographical proximity to Venice. As early as the 1470s, fonts of type based on the Roman face created by the Venetian printer Nicholas Jenson were used for books printed in Ferrara, and Hind points to the production of woodcuts in the popular style as an example of the influence of Venetian taste on the Ferrarese illustrated book. The way in which the Florentine style came to Ferrara is not as clear. Landau and Parshall suggest that perhaps members "of one of the three Florentine workshops had moved to Ferrara" and established a connection with the local printing trade.

The border designs and patterned ornaments of this woodcut binding are produced in the black-ground manner, with the symbolic figures of the four evangelists on the front cover and Saint George on the back. The winged cherubs, palmettes, and garlands running up and down the sides and the composition of the central images in outline, flanked at top and bottom with repetitive ornaments and cornerpieces, were common devices used by Florentine designers to create balance and focus. A striking aspect of the woodcut binding is the effective use of black

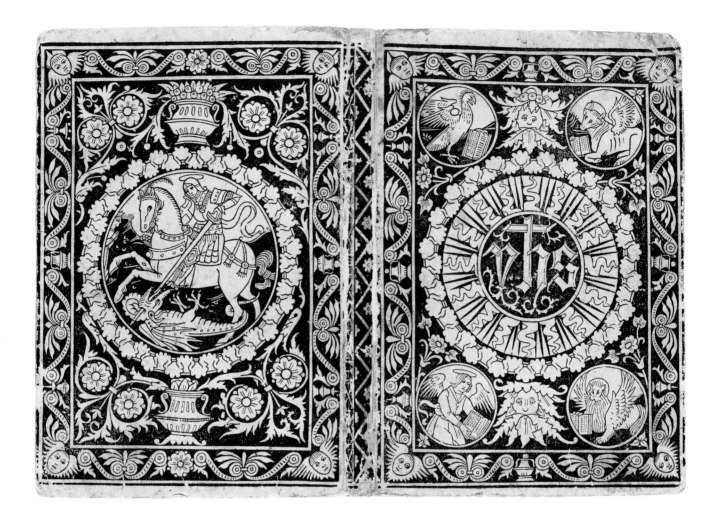

21. BATTISTA FREGOSO. *Anteros, sive Tractatus contra amorem.* Milan: Leonardus Pachel, 1496

and white to accentuate details and create rich contrast. The powerful presentation is executed with skill and imagination. Hind makes the comparison with the style of the frontispiece found in the *Epistole et Evangelii* (item 18).

The sacred monogram IHS, which appears on the front cover, may be linked to the monogram found on a single-leaf woodcut of Saint Bernardino of Siena produced in northern Italy between 1470 and 1480. In his catalogue of fifteenth-century woodcuts, Richard Field illustrates an image of Saint Bernardino holding the sacred monogram in his hand and lifting it to heaven. The initials *IHS* are placed within a circle surrounded by a larger circle with radiating tongues of fire and rays of light bursting out to the perimeter. It is cut in black ground with a very bold white-on-black presentation. Field also illustrates an image dated from the late fifteenth century, probably of German origin, which is similar in style but encloses the larger circle within a rectangular border and embellishes the woodcut with flowers and vines. Text is carved around the outer circle and at the base of the wood block.

The image of Saint George and the Dragon is likely based on a painting by the Ferrarese master Cosimo Tura. In 1469, Tura was commissioned to paint a fresco on the shutters to the great organ in Ferrara Cathedral, the subject of which was to be Saint George and the dragon set in a landscape. Adolfo Venturi illustrates this fresco, and Kristeller, Hind, and Gruyer all suggest that it may have been the inspiration for the woodcut binding illustrated here.

Yet the woodcut binding with its specific motifs has nothing to do with Fregoso's text, a treatise on the Greek god Anteros, brother of Eros and symbol of unrequited love. Printed

by Leonardus Pachel and illustrated with one woodcut, this appears to be the only incunable edition of the text. Pachel's career in Milan spanned thirty years or more, the first dozen or so in partnership with Uldericus Scinzenzeler. He was known for the use of metalcuts in his 1493 edition of Bernardino de Busti's *Mariale* and for a 1499 edition of the *Missale Ambrosianum*. Hind states that the metalcuts that appeared in *Missale* were based on Florentine engravings prepared in the broad manner, where thick black lines are used for contours and shading is created with parallel lines only, without cross-hatching. He goes on to say, "A considerable portion of Milanese woodcuts of the last decade of the XV century are characterized by heavy outlines, regular parallel shading, and crude somewhat angular design. It is German in manner, though often based on Venetian originals."

The woodcut frontispiece from this copy of *Anteros* seems to fit Hind's description quite well. The contours of the tree, the landscape on the left of the image, and the costumes of the characters are drawn with thick and unvaried lines. The use of parallel-line shading and the sharp facial features of the characters also seem to fit Hind's general statement about the German influence on the Milanese woodcut of the period. Unlike the binding, the allegorical woodcut succeeds in providing entrée into the nature of Fregoso's text. Cupid, blindfolded and tied to the tree, with his bow and broken arrows at his feet, is the central focus. With Cupid's powers arrested, the demons, signifying eternal death, rise to stifle the expression of love, creating a world where only want, jealousy, mockery, and sorrow flourish. The author sits in the lower left chronicling the misery of the four women bereft of life's most precious emotion. In his description of the copy in the Schäfer sale, Paul Needham suggests that the image may have a French origin, as Fregoso lived in exile in France after being "deposed as Doge of Genoa in the early 1480's."

This copy has a distinguished provenance, formerly having been a part of the F. Cortesi, Michele Cavaleri, Cernuschi, Charles Fairfax Murray, C. W. Dyson Perrins, and Lessing J. Rosenwald libraries.

8vo. 213 x 150 mm, 8½ x 5⅞ in. Goff F-329. Pollard *Italian* 106. Sander 2946.
Rogledi Manni 451. Hind, p. 521. Miner 193a. Foot, pp. 335−38.
Kristeller "Woodcuts as Bindings," pp. 249−51. Kristeller 160, p. 38.
Landau and Parshall, p. 71. Field 207, 261. Venturi 4, fig. 398.
Gruyer, pp. 89−102. Schäfer *Italian* 80.


## 22   ROSENWALD 316: DYSON PERRINS 70

22. [SIMON DE CASSIA.] *Esposizione sopra evangeli.* Edited by Giovanni da Salerno. Florence: Bartolommeo di Libri, 24 September 1496

THIS RARE FLORENTINE EDITION of the *Esposizione sopra evangeli* was published in Florence by Bartolommeo di Libri fourteen months after the Pacini edition of the *Epistole et Evangelii* (item 18). The only copy in America, it is one of only seven known copies cited by the ISTC. Many of the woodcuts in this Libri edition were originally used in the vernacular edition of Jacobus de Voragine's *Legenda Aurea* printed in Venice by Manfredus Bonellis in 1492.

The first leaf of the text is illustrated with a half-page woodcut of the Last Judgment, cut in outline and enclosed by a full-page, black-line architectural border in the Venetian style. The design includes a bottom border with eight children working in a vineyard, vertical columns with leaves and vines, and a top border of sphinxes flanking a lunette of the Holy Spirit. It is a well-known design, first used by Bonellis in his 1492 edition of Voragine and afterward by other Venetian printers, including Bernardinus Rizzus and Matteo Capcasa. The text is illustrated with 167 simple contour woodcuts, flanked by side borders cut in the black-ground manner of Venetian design.

A comparison of the images in this edition of the *Esposizione* with the woodcuts in the Florentine edition of the *Epistole* of 1495 printed for Pacini demonstrates some of the stylistic differences that distinguish the Venetian from the Florentine woodcut. Both these styles rely on finely carved contours and complex compositional formats, but the Florentine cuts give a greater emphasis to backgrounds and rely on the white-on-black technique to produce shading and perspective. Their simple black-ground borders also contribute a finished quality to Florentine woodcuts. Reproductions of the image Christ Entering Jerusalem from each of the editions demonstrate these stylistic differences.

The woodcut on the opening leaf of the *Esposizione* is signed in the lower right corner with the monogram *b.* Little is known about this Venetian artisan, but Hind proposes that the monogram belongs to the cutter rather than to the designer of the image, or to a particular workshop, even though the variations in the quality of cuts bearing this initial perhaps suggest that more than one person was involved in the cutting of the blocks.

Folio. 320 x 225 mm, 12¾ x 9 in. Goff S-523. Kristeller 135a. Essling 190.
Sander 2571. Hind, p. 503, border no. 4; p. 475.

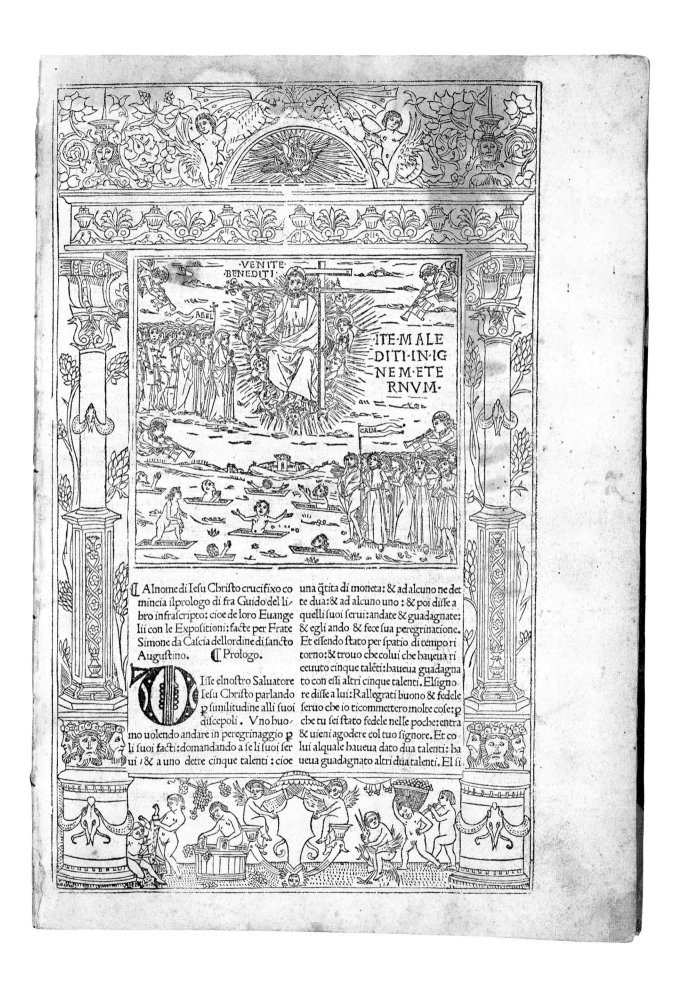

Al nome di Iesu Christo crucifixo comincia ilprologo di fra Guido del libro infrascripto: cioe de loro Euangelii con le Expositioni: facte per Frate Simone da Cascia dellordine di sancto Augustino. Prologo.

Isse elnostro Saluatore Iesu Christo parlando p similitudine alli suoi discepoli. Vno buomo uolendo andare in peregrinaggio p li suoi facti: domandando a se li suoi serui / & a uno dette cinque talenti : cioe una q̃tita di moneta: & ad alcuno ne dette dua:& ad alcuno uno : & poi disse a quelli suoi serui:andate & guadagnate: & egli ando & fece sua peregrinatione. Et essendo stato per spatio di tempo ritorno:& trouo che colui che haueua riceuuto cinque talẽti:haueua guadagnato con essi altri cinque talenti. Elsignore disse a lui:Rallegrati buono & fedele seruo che io ticommettero molte cose:p che tu sei stato fedele nelle poche:entra & uieni agodere col tuo signore. Et colui alquale haueua dato dua talenti: haueua guadagnato altri dua talenti. El si

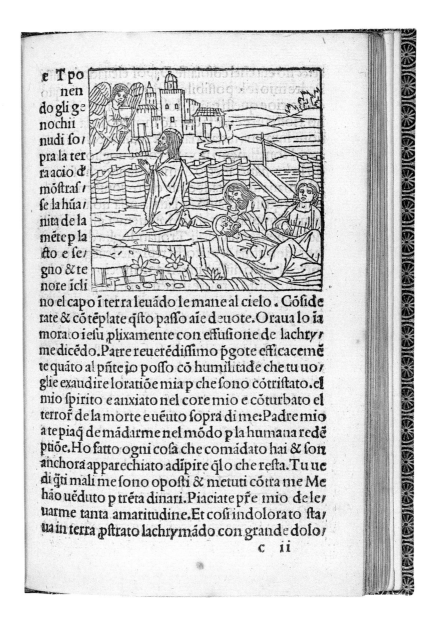

The woodcut image contains the following text:

e Tpo
nen
do gli ge
nochii
nudi for
pra la ter
ra acio d
moftraf
fe la húa
nita de la
mête p la
fto e fe
gno & te
nore ícli
no el capo í terra leuádo le mane al cielo . Cófide
rate & cótêplate qſto paffo aie d euote. Oraua lo ia
morato iefu plixamente con effufione de lachry
me dicédo. Patre reuerédiffimo pgote efficacemê
te quáto al pñte io poffo có humilitade che tu uor
glie exaudire loratióe mia p che fono cótriftato. el
mio fpirito e anxiato nel core mio e cóturbato el
terroř de la morte e uéuto foprá di me: Padre mio
a te piaq de mádarme nel módo p la humana redê
ptióe. Ho fatto ogni cofa che comádato hai & for
anchora apparechiato adípire qlo che refta. Tu ue
di qù mali me fono opofti & metuti cótra me Me
háo uéduto p trêta dinari. Piaciate přé mio de ler
uarme tanta amaritudine. Et cofi indolorato ſtar
ua in terra pſtrato lachrymádo con grande dolor

c    ii

## 23   ROSENWALD 320: DYSON PERRINS 56

23. [Saint Bonaventura?]
*Meditatione de la passione de
Christo.* Venice: Lazarus de
Soardis, 16 March 1497

ONE OF TWO COPIES IN AN AMERICAN COLLECTION, this is the second edition of *Meditatione de la passione de Christo* to contain this series of cuts. The original edition was printed anonymously in 1493 and attributed by Max Sander to the Venetian press of Guilielmus de Cereto. The March 16, 1497, edition printed by Lazarus de Soardis is illustrated with a title-page woodcut that differs significantly from the title cut in the 1493 edition and from the other eleven woodcuts in thirteen impressions that are from the original blocks. The text of this copy is incomplete as leaf h¹ is missing. The supposed author is Saint Bonaventure, but scholars disagree as to whether the *Meditatione* is actually his work.

The woodcut of the Agony in the Garden is one of the most complex in the suite. The spacious composition created on such a small scale reflects the influence of religious paintings on the print trade of the period. The fully developed landscape comfortably encompasses the five figures, with Christ as the focal point. The simple outlines are delicately cut and clearly convey the story of Christ receiving the cup of the passion while the three apostles sleep. Two other woodcuts from the series, Christ on the Cross and Christ's Removal from the Cross, show a similar sensitivity to the subject and complexity of compositional structure. The designs of the remaining woodcuts in the suite lack the perspective and shading that distinguish these three images.

The cuts illustrating this text are from at least three different hands and represent the varying quality of draftsmanship in Venetian woodcuts of the period. The mixed quality may be related to the nature of the publishing enterprise operated by Lazarus de Soardis. Known first as a publisher, then a printer, de Soardis began his career in Venice around 1490 and continued until 1517. He worked in partnership with many Venetian printers, including Bernardinus Benalius, Simon Bevilaqua, Bonetus Locatellus, Joannes Tacuinus, Jacobus Pentius, and Simon de Leure, and he had access to wood blocks from a variety of printers. Even his most famous illustrated book, the *Commoediae* of Terence, printed for him by Simon de Leure in 1497, contains woodcuts of varying merit, which are based on a series from the Lyon edition of 1493.

8vo. 145 x 100 mm, 5⅞ x 4 in. Goff B-913. Essling 413. Sander 1186.
Pollard *Italian* 118. Norton *Italian*, p. 152. Hind, p. 487.

## 24   INCUN. X.S197: DYSON PERRINS 261

A RARE ILLUSTRATED EDITION ON THE ART OF DYING by the Florentine priest and reformer Girolamo Savonarola, whose rhetoric and political philosophy challenged de Medici Florence in the 1490s, this is the second edition printed by Bartolommeo di Libri. It is one of five known copies in America, two of which are in the Library of Congress. Libri's printing of *Predica dell'arte del bene morire* came to the Library of Congress collection indirectly from the Dyson Perrins sale, where it was bought by A. S. W. Rosenbach over Maggs for £90, but not for Lessing Rosenwald, who already had a copy. An examination of the codes on the back pastedown indicates that this copy entered the Library of Congress in 1950 and was probably sold or given by Rosenbach to Frederick Goff, who needed it for his article "Four Florentine Editions of Savonarola's *Art of Dying*," published that year. At the time of the Dyson Perrins sale, the catalogue description noted that the book was in need of restoration, and in 1994 the book received extensive paper and binding conservation.

In his essay "Early Florentine Illustrated Books," William Ivins provides a summary of the historical events that contributed to the enormous demand by the Florentine public for copies of printed sermons and political tracts. In it he briefly outlines Savonarola's rise to power, his fervor for both civic and ecclesiastical reform, the power of his preaching style, and the impact of his sermons on the Florentine public. He discusses the manner in which Savonarola alienated the dying Lorenzo de Medici and describes his final arrest and excommunication by Pope Alexander VI. The text of Savonarola's *Predica dell'arte del bene morire* was delivered on November 2, 1496, when the city of Florence was under siege following Lorenzo's death.

Tracts by Savonarola are an extremely important source for Florentine woodcuts of the early Renaissance. Sander lists more than 130 separate editions, all of which are illustrated with at least one woodcut. The woodcut illustrated here, the Triumph of Death, is framed by a passe-partout border first used by Libri in his 1495 edition of Passavanti's *Speechio di Vera Penitensa*. The Triumph of Death is cut in simple contours without embellishment but with great imagination and flair. Screaming across the sky, death leaves nothing in its wake, not peasant,

¶Predica dellarte del Bene morire.

24. GIROLAMO
SAVONAROLA.
*Predica dell'arte del bene
morire.* [Florence:
Bartolommeo di Libri,
after June 1497]

patrician, pope, or nun. The remaining three woodcuts, framed by two different styles of Florentine border, reflect the content of Savonarola's sermon. The woodcuts depict man's choice of paradise or punishment, his struggle to take seriously the signs of approaching death, and the final moments of life when repentance may be too late. These themes, very well known to the Florentine public of the period, were illustrated by using conventional motifs from earlier editions of *Ars moriendi*. Devils, angels, congregations of saints, suffering souls in purgatory, and mourning family members are represented in clear outline, with generous use of white-on-black for backgrounds and complex renderings of Florentine interiors. All three woodcuts appear to be the work of the same designer and block cutter.

8vo. 190 x 150 mm, 7½ x 5⅞ in. Goff S-250. Pollard *Italian* 113. Kristeller 375c.
Sander 6815. Hind, p. 532. Goff "The Four Florentine Editions,"
pp. 286–301. Ivins "Early Florentine," pp. 14–23.
O'Connor, pp. 178–79. Schäfer *Italian* 170.

dolotis/filios amaritudinis z indignatiōis z ploxati
onis eterne · Sed tu pater Adam qui pxo fapientia et
dignitate quibus te confoxte tua fplendidioxez cōditox
fecerat/firmiox legis obferuatox effe debueras · Quid
nobis fecifti : irritafti legem celi i z ecce vniuerfos nos
bouēde moxtis vmbxis deftinafti· Quis iam o anima
fidelis in box meditatiōe maloz ita infenfibilis eftaut
ab omni alienus pietatis affectu qui fuper bochumani
generis lugubxi cafu nō moueaf ad fletum/non exciret
ad lachxymas· Quis dabit capiti meo aquam clamat
fanctificatus in vteroDieremias:z oculis meis fontez
lachxymaz:z ploxabo die ac nocte iterfectos pph̄ mei·

ORes ftupenda z omni plena pietate·Ecce cp pxo
reconciliatione humana pacecp componenda in
ter omnipotentem deum offenfum z reum hominem:
a 4

## 25   ROSENWALD 334: DYSON PERRINS 286

STEPHAN PLANNCK'S 1498 PRINTING of Torquemada's *Meditationes* is his second printed edition of the text, and this copy is one of only two in an American library. The original edition, printed in 1467 by the German printer Ulrich Han, who was working in Rome, was the first illustrated book printed in Italy. Plannck's first edition was issued in Rome in 1484 (LC/R239, item 9) and was illustrated with woodcuts from the original blocks used by Han in his 1467 edition. His 1498 edition is illustrated with thirty-three woodcuts that are based on images from the original edition but newly designed and cut for this smaller format.

The composition of the Annunciation illustrated here reflects the original design that appeared in the previous editions, but it is compressed to accommodate the quarto format of the publication. The interior setting is more detailed in the new cut, with its addition of double arches and windows and a screen in the background. The sloping floor provides a sense of perspective, an element missing in the original cut, made over thirty years earlier. In addition to the architectural features used by Plannck's designer, the image is enhanced by the ornamental

25. JUAN DE TORQUEMADA, CARDINAL. *Meditationes deu Contemplationes devotissimae.* Rome: Stephan Plannck, 21 August 1498

designs on the front of the kneeler on which Mary rests, the delineation of Gabriel's wings, the quality of Mary's hair, the folds of the garments, and the finely cut facial features of both figures. The judicious use of varied parallel lines to create shading and texture in the image gives the woodcut a dimensionality rarely found in other illustrated books from Plannck's press.

The first woodcut in the book, the Creation, is the only image set within two black-ground borders, decorated top and bottom in a leaf-and-vine pattern, with a cherub highlighting the bottom border in the center. Hind and Sander liken the style of the borders to that found in Tuppo's 1485 edition of *Aesop*. The remaining thirty-two woodcuts are printed without a border and are cut by at least two different skilled hands capable of rendering some compositional complexity along with detailed imagery. Not all are as refined as the image in the Annunciation, but each is cut in clear outline, with the additional use of white-on-black highlights to embellish the images.

4to. 205 x 140 mm, 8 x 5½ in. Goff T-541. Hind 397.
Sander 7409. Schäfer *Italian* 185.

# 26    ROSENWALD 345, 853, 854, 855: DYSON PERRINS 236

THIS BOUND COLLECTION of four *rappresentazioni,* or printed tracts and plays celebrating lives of saints and biblical stories, contains one first edition known in only this copy and three sixteenth-century reprints. These eight- to twelve-leaf pamphlets were a favorite of the Florentine public during the last years of the fifteenth century, and as the competition among publishers increased, woodcuts were added to bolster sales. As is the case in all four of the works in this sammelband, most rappresentazioni were printed anonymously. Bibliographers have attributed many, however, to two Florentine printers, Bartolommeo di Libri and Antonio di Bartolommeo Miscomini.

Illustrating the first leaf of the edition of *La rappresentatione di Joseph figluolo di Jacob* printed by Libri circa 1500 are two woodcuts, the ubiquitous Angel of the Annunciation, which appears in most editions of rappresentazioni, and the Old Testament hero Joseph being sold into slavery by his brothers. Each is framed by a dart-patterned black-ground border. The images are cut in outline and the landscape cut in white on black, creating a vigorous contrast. The tract contains three other illustrations, each cut with similar care and with attention to interior space and arrangement of figures.

The most striking of the three, illustrated here, depicts the scene Joseph and Potiphar's Wife. The image freezes the moment as Joseph turns from the advance of Potiphar's wife, who is clasping his cloak and pulling the young man toward her. The woodcut design is in perfect balance and conveys the desperation of the scene with both force and sensitivity. The shading near the woman's face, the use of parallel lines to bring reality to the movement of the characters, and the varied border styles create a simple but compelling image well suited to the text.

The woodcuts that appear in the reprinted editions of the rappresentazioni offer some interesting insights into the use and re-use of the blocks by Florentine printers a full half century after they were originally cut. The reprints combine original cuts created for a specific text with cuts from other sources and of various styles. The study of the reprinted editions is of special importance because they are, in many cases, the only link to original images used in earlier editions now lost.

In *La rappresentatione del Angelo Raffaello & Tobbia,* printed in 1554, with ten woodcuts, the text of the title page is enclosed by a black-ground passe-partout border. This is the same border used by Libri in his 1497 edition of Savoranola's *Predica dell'arte de bene morire* (item 24). Beneath the title of *Angelo Raffaello & Tobbia* is the Angel of the Annunciation and a woodcut representing Raphael and Tobia standing outside the house next to two storks, which originally appeared in the 1491 edition of *Fior di Virtu.* Another image from the *Fior di Virtu* appears in another title from this collection, *La rapresentatione d'uno miracolo di duo Pellegrini,* printed in Florence in 1554 and illustrated with the Angel of the Annunciation and six woodcuts.

*La rapresentatione de sette dormienti,* printed in Florence in 1554, contains the Angel of the Annunciation on the title page plus thirteen more woodcuts. One of these cuts comes from the *Fior di Virtu,* the rest from other sources. Each has a different border style and they are of differing quality of draftsmanship. In all cases, the freedom of line and compositional structure link them to their Florentine heritage.

The blank leaves between the four titles of this volume have bibliographical notes written by Rosenwald using purple ink, as was his custom.

8vo. 200 x 140 mm, 8 x 5 ½ in. Goff R-29. Pollard *Italian* 147, 280, 279, 283. Sander 6275, 6169, 6334, 6218. Kristeller, pp. xii–xiv; 208, 352e, and fig. 17. *The Florentine Fior di Virtu of 1491* (Washington, 1953).

26. *La rappresentatione divota di Joseph figluolo di Jacob.* [Florence, ca. 1500]

bound with

*La rappresentatione de sette dormienti: di nuouo mandata in luce.* [Florence, 1554]

*La rappresentatione del Angelo Raffaello & Tobbia. Di nuouo ristampata.* [Florence, 1554]

*La rappresentatione d'uno miracolo di duo Pellegrini che andauano a San Jacopo di Galitia. Nuouamente ristampata.* [Florence, 1554]

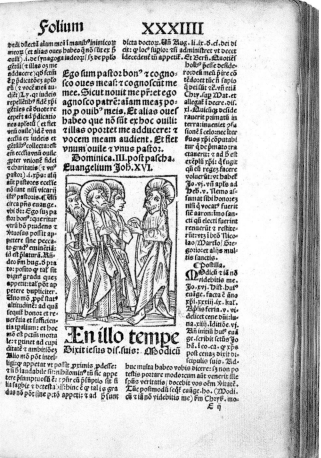

## 27  ROSENWALD 370, 376: DYSON PERRINS 625

27. GUILLERMUS
PARISIENSIS. *Postilla
super Epistolas et Evangelia.*
[Basel: Nicolaus Kesler,
not before 1497]

THIS PAIR OF NICOLAUS KESLER'S BASEL IMPRINTS are illustrated with woodcuts showing a distinctive northern influence and based on designs published by Michael Furter in
the early 1490s. Kessler first published an edition of the *Postilla* in 1495, and this is his first edition of the *Passio*. Both titles are rare. The Rosenwald/Dyson Perrins copy of the *Postilla* is the
only copy located in an American library. Two American holdings are listed for the *Passio*, but
the other copy is imperfect.

The first illustrated book containing woodcuts to appear in Basel was printed by Bernhard
Richel in 1476. In that year he published an edition of *Spiegel menschlicher Behältnis* decorated
with large woodcut initial letters and 273 woodcuts. Hind suggests Richel's woodcuts show
influences of both Gunther Zainer's Augsburg edition of the *Speculum humane salvationis* printed
in 1473 and the Netherlandish block book *Biblia pauperum,* of the 1470s. After Richel's death
in 1482, Nicolaus Kesler took over the business, and Victor Scholderer speculates that Kesler
was Richel's son-in-law.

Nicolaus Kesler is best remembered today for printing an edition of the *Epistolare* of Saint
Jerome, which contains the famous woodcut by Albrecht Dürer of Saint Jerome removing the
thorn from the foot of a lion. Dürer spent nearly two years in Basel, between 1492 and 1494,
and besides contributing this illustration to the *Epistolare,* he is reputed to have made some of
the woodcut designs for Michael Furter's edition of *Der Ritter vom Turn,* 1493, and Sebastian

Brant's *Das Narrenschiff,* printed by Johann Bergmann von Olpe in 1494. According to Talbot, "these woodcuts represent a style unequaled in book illustrations from Basel prior to Dürer's arrival or from anywhere else at this time." Erwin Panofsky states that the woodcuts in these books not attributed to Dürer carry evidence of the influence that he had on his Swiss collaborators.

An examination of the title leaf of the *Postilla* illustrated here bears witness to Panofsky's statement. The Christ Child and the Four Evangelists clearly shows Dürer's influence, especially when compared to the other fifty-three cuts used to illustrate the book. The woodcut first appeared in Furter's 1495 edition published after Dürer had left Basel for Strasbourg. It replaced a woodcut of the Crucifixion used by both Furter and Kesler in 1491 and 1492 and again by Kesler in his *Passio,* illustrated below.

The woodcut of the Christ Child and the Four Evangelists is executed in a robust manner, especially in its corporeal depiction of the child and in the garments of Saint John in the lower left. The body of the Christ Child is clearly rendered by round contours and the delicate use of variable parallel lines. The face of Christ is believable, and the spare use of black lines at the neck and shoulders suggests a reality completely lacking in the illustrations in the remainder of the book. The image Christ Teaching, also illustrated here, clearly harkens back to an earlier style. In this image, thick contours, angular cuts, repetitive parallel lines, and a uniform compo-

*bound with*

*Passio Domini Jesus Christi secundum quattuor Evangelia.* [Basel: Nicolaus Kesler, ca. 1500]

sitional plane dominate. The artistic repertoire of the designer and the technical skill of the woodcutter rely on suggesting form and expression rather than rendering it.

This medieval style can be seen again in the image of the Crucifixion that appears on the title leaf of Kesler's *Passio Domini Jesu Christi*. Though complex in its compositional format, the woodcut reflects a Netherlandish origin of around 1480, rather than the influence of the Nuremburg cut of the Crucifixion made for the *Revelationes* of Saint Birgitta printed in 1500 (item 6).

4to. 205 x 143 mm, 8 x 5⅝ in. Goff G-669, P-131.
W. L. Schreiber 4153, 4162, 4156. Schramm 21, pp. 21, 28, figs. 725–88, 790.
Hind, p. 326. Johnson, pp. 6–8, figs. 1–3, 9. Talbot, pp. 348–50.
Panofsky *Dürer* 2, pp. 54–55.

## 28   ROSENWALD 371: DYSON PERRINS 658

28. [METHODIUS?]
*Revelationes divinae a sanctis angelis factae.* Basel: Michael Furter, 1498

THIS WELL-ILLUSTRATED EDITION of the *Revelationes*, attributed to Methodius, was edited by Sebastian Brant, author of *The Ship of Fools*. Its printer, Michael Furter, was among Basel's first generation of printers. He spent his entire twenty-nine-year career in Basel, where his last imprint appeared in 1517, and he worked in cooperation with other local printers. His wood blocks can be found in books printed by Kesler and Johann von Amerbach, the Paris-trained scholar and printer whose 1492 Basel edition of Bertholdus shows a French influence. Basel's location and proximity to the cities of the Rhine to the north and Lyon to the west promoted the mingling of German, Dutch, and French styles that became a feature of book design and illustration there during the first decades of the sixteenth century. But as the woodcuts in this edition of the *Revelationes* reveal, reliance on the northern style and technique was a dominant feature of Swiss book illustration before 1500.

Furter's *Revelationes* is illustrated with fifty-five original woodcuts and four repeats. The images differ in quality, and it appears that at least two different hands cut the blocks. The woodcut Adam and Eve in the Garden is cut in a free, almost sensuous style, using a combination of round and angular contours to outline the figures. The rendering of the physical form of Adam and Eve is further enhanced by the use of varied parallel lines to model their figures, a Renaissance technique that focuses attention on the human body. Great attention is also paid to Adam's hair and Eve's flowing mane, a design that was cut with fine detail and which attests to the block cutter's skill. But the design is less successful when the focus turns to the rendering of the Tree of Knowledge and the limited detail devoted to the landscape and background, these stylistic elements more characteristic of the medieval image than of Renaissance design.

Some of the other woodcuts appearing in this book are more in the style of Ulm and Augsburg in the 1480s and early 1490s. There is very little detail in the images and large areas of white space dominate both foreground and sky. Figures are fashioned by thick contours and angular cuts, with no attempt at creating individual physical characteristics.

4to. 220 x 153 mm, 8⅝ x 6¼ in. Goff M-524. W. L. Schreiber 4648.
Schramm 22, p. 43, figs. 561–614. Johnson, p. 1

¶ De iniqua ſerpentis pſuaſione et
pzimozum parentum tranſgreſſione

Uidens autē diabolus ſe expulſum e celo: in magna ta-
men poteſtate relictum : Cogitauit quomodo poſſet diſ-
plicere deo et in omnibus ſibi contrariari: Et quia vidit
pzimum hominem Adam ſcilicet cum ſua vxoze in terre-
ſtri paradiſo collocatum: ſcilicet in locū voluptatis: inno
centia decozatum : ac omnium beſtiarum volatilium et

que interuale entre lefditz fi-
gnes le glozieulx faît hierofme
ne la point er prime ne declaire
ne les aultres Docteurs nen af-
ferment rien de certain/mais

le laiffent q remettêt en la bou-
lente de dieu le createur

Le premier figne côme la mer
fe lieue fur les montaignes

## 29  ROSENWALD 424: DYSON PERRINS 327

THE SECOND ILLUSTRATED EDITION of Antoine Vérard's *Ars moriendi,* printed in 1493/94, is illustrated with sixty-nine woodcuts, with a few images repeated. Many of the woodcuts are colored by a contemporary hand. The first edition appeared in 1492, printed for Vérard by Pierre Le Rouge, Gillet Couteau, and Jean Ménard. Only three copies of the second edition are known, and this is the only copy in America. The Rosenwald/Dyson Perrins copy is imperfect, with text leaf l⁸ in facsimile. The Bodleian Library copy also lacks one leaf. Vérard's edition of *The Art of Dying* is organized in four parts: "L'Art de bien mourir," "Laguillon de crainte divine," "L'Advenement de l'Antichrist," and "L'Art de bien vivre."

The source of many French woodcuts during the incunable period was the illuminated

manuscript. The highly developed French style of illumination was distinctive in its use of
contemporary French costume and uniquely styled border decoration. The style was also
notable for particular facial characteristics used to distinguish the numerous saints, heroes, and
historical figures represented in many woodcut images. Some of the earliest French printers
were trained as illuminators, including Pierre Le Rouge and Antoine Vérard, whose printed
books are illustrated with border designs and elaborate woodcuts in outline taken freely from
the manuscript tradition. In her book *Pen to Press,* Sandra Hindman makes the point that for
special copies of his books, especially copies for royal patrons, Vérard had illuminators over-
paint the woodcuts to give the book the appearance of an illuminated manuscript.

The *Paris Missal* of 1481 printed by Jean Dupré was the first illustrated book printed in France. The missal contained two full-page woodcuts, which appear in the text at the canon of the mass, one, God on His Throne and the other, the Crucifixion. Dupré quickly followed this in the same year with his *Verdun Missal,* illustrated with the large woodcut of the Celebration of the Mass and numerous smaller woodcuts representing stories from the Gospels, all enclosed in decorative borders. Over the next two decades, Dupré produced illustrated missals and books of hours for Angers, Arras, Besançon, Chartres, Meaux, Reims, Sarum, Troyes, and other major dioceses. In discussing the work of Dupré in his history of the woodcut, Hind writes, "Apart from the fine quality of the woodcut work which proceeded from his workshops, . . . his borders and decorative pieces, largely in outline, with designs of birds, beasts, branch and flowers, in the best tradition of medieval French illumination, are among the most beautiful productions of the time." Dupré's other important illustrated books include editions of Boccaccio's *Les cas et ruynes des nobles hommes et femmes* (1483/84) and *Les cent nouvelles* (1485), the *Vie des saints pères hermites* by Saint Jerome (1486), and Voragine's *Légende dorée* (1489).

Vérard came to the printing trade from the scriptorium, and he established one of the most successful publishing firms in Paris during the last years of the fifteenth century. More than 250 titles are linked to his name and until 1512, when his last imprint is recorded, Vérard dominated the illustrated book trade. Many of the most important Parisian printers made books for him, including Jean Dupré, Antoine Caillaut, Pierre Le Rouge, and Pierre Levet, and Vérard's influence on the style and quality of woodcut illustration was considerable.

Both Arthur M. Hind and John Macfarlane refer to two distinct styles of illustration that can be detected in Vérard's books over his twenty-seven-year career. The first style is very similar to that of woodcuts created for Dupré's missals, as described above. Based on the compositional structure and border styles of illuminated manuscripts, this style relies on the use of thick contours to define the outlines of the image. It was with the publication of the first edition of *L'Art de bien vivre et de bien mourir* in 1492 that Vérard's chief designer's new style emerged. As Hind writes, these woodcuts "show considerable independence of treatment and are powerfully designed and cut."

In addition to a number of small woodcuts throughout the text, *L'Art de bien vivre et de bien mourir* is illustrated with a large woodcut, the Author Presenting His Book, and three smaller but equally well designed cuts, namely, Christ Teaching His Disciples the "Our Father," the Saints Reciting the Confession of Faith, and Moses Presenting the Ten Commandments, which all appear in the first part of the work. Two more series of large woodcuts depict the seven sacraments and the seven deadly sins, following the block book tradition of the *Ars moriendi.* The fourth and final part includes fifteen woodcuts illustrating the signs of the Apocalypse and a large, full-page woodcut of the Joys of Paradise.

The large woodcuts in outline show figures draped in contemporary French costume, drawn in outline in rather thick contours, and shaded by parallel lines. The compositions are enhanced by borders in the manuscript tradition. The woodcuts of the sacraments are designed in a monumental style, the pivotal action enclosed in an architectural framework resembling the interior of a cathedral. A small vignette at the top of the cut depicts the rite being practiced in early Christian times. Directly below is the ritual scene of the faithful fulfilling their sacramental obligations. The large woodcuts of the seven sins are set in hell and vividly depict the terrors awaiting those who refuse to follow the commandments of Moses. Each woodcut occupies about half the page, with text below, and the whole is enclosed with three borders and corner pieces at the top.

Fifteen remarkable woodcuts describing the events of the Last Judgment illustrate *L'Art de bien vivre.* They are born of an imagination distinct from all the others that illustrated this book. Hind found them to be of a lesser quality than those thought to be by Vérard's chief designer, but the originality of most of these designs is considerable. The image exhibited here, the First Sign of Judgment Day, depicts the seas rising to the mountain tops, moments before they inundate the land and consume the earth. The form of the rising sea, cut in thick contours, is enhanced by the shading and the placement of the fish throughout the rising column of water. The figures of fish, an early Christian emblem for baptism or cleansing, was a readily recognizable motif to the late medieval viewer. The rough mountain landscape capped with two standing trees complements the vertical thrust of the image and successfully balances the composition. The sparseness of the background with its open sky also contributes to this powerful presentation.

The final woodcut in the book, the Joys of Paradise, is a large image illustrating the rewards of the faithful after the Judgment Day. It is a complex design, with Christ positioned at the top center of the image, seated on a throne surrounded by an oval of open space, creating a halo effect. He is encircled by a legion of angels and flanked by the Virgin and Saint John. The remaining area of the wood block is filled with the figures of saints, kings, popes, peasants, nuns, and queens, who surround the throne and point in prayer to Christ. The figures, arranged in a variety of positions, are clothed in various contemporary costumes. The entire woodcut is in outline and enhanced by shading. This copy is highlighted with red and blue wash, which further enhances the power of the image. A modest border of pillars with architectural elements at the top is incorporated into the body of the woodcut. Anatole Claudin characterizes this cut as exhibiting calm and serenity after the upheavals of the Last Judgment, and it illustrates the skills of Vérard's chief designer praised by Hind.

Folio. 267 x 192 mm, 10 ½ x 7 ½ in. Goff A-1123. Claudin 2,
pp. 427–49, 209–19. O'Connor, pp. 149–55. Hind, pp. 597–98, 660–64.
Hindman, pp. 135–39. Macfarlane, pp. iv–xxxi.

## 30   ROSENWALD 429: DYSON PERRINS 402

HENRICUS DE VRIMARIA's *Præceptorium divinæ legis* is a commentary on the Ten Commandments, originally attributed to Nicolaus de Lyra. It is known in only eight copies, this being the sole copy in America. Pierre le Dru printed the work in 1495, illustrating it with two woodcuts and the publisher's mark of Antoine Baquelier, all three of which are highlighted in parts with a yellow and, in one instance, blue wash. Le Dru flourished as a printer in Paris from about 1488 to 1515, but documentation of his early career is sparse. It is known that in 1488 he was arrested for assault and was named in the indictment as the leader of a group of twenty-five toughs. His occupation was listed as "printer of books" but no imprint information exists before 1494. His name is often associated with Etienne Jehannot, and one of the woodcuts in this book, the Crucifixion of Christ, was frequently used by both printers for the many religious tracts they published.

The woodcut Crucifixion, illustrated here, is cut in outline with shading produced by the use of parallel lines that gives form to the figures represented in the image. Le Dru's woodcuts are modest in ornamentation and in background setting when compared to the cuts in Vérard's *Ars moriendi,* but they are as cleanly cut and as clearly defined as the best blocks in that

**Præceptorium de lira.**

30. [HENRICUS DE VRIMARIA.] *Præceptorium divinæ legis.* Paris: Pierre le Dru for Antoine Baquelier, 11 August 1495

work. The halo of Christ on the Cross is accented with blue. Both of the scenes are framed by architectural borders designed as part of the wood block, which adds a decorative element common to many French woodcuts of the period. The clever use of a zig-zag pattern in the border directs the viewer's eye to the action of the central figures in the scene. The crucifixion scene is enhanced by the figure of the soldier in the right foreground. His costume, physical features, and facial expression are the most clearly defined of all the skillfully drawn figures in the image and suggest that a well-trained hand was responsible for the woodcut.

The publisher's mark of Antoine Baquelier that appears at the end of this little volume is an excellent example of the marks which were adopted by many French printers. The pillar-and-post styled decorative borders that frame the woodcut enclose the Tree of Knowledge, growing in a natural environment of flowers and birds. Following the standard motif, a Latin inscription is incorporated at the center: "Fear of the Lord is the beginning of wisdom." The design of the cut, especially the pillars and the tree motif, is very similar to the mark of Philippe Pigouchet, which he first used in 1491, and which in turn was greatly influenced by the device used by Gunther Zainer in Augsburg in 1477.

8vo. 135 x 93 mm, 5 ¼ x 3 ⅛ in. Goff N-142.
Claudin 2, pp. 57–66, 525–27. Davies 82

GUY MARCHANT PRINTED THIS FIRST EDITION of a mathematical text by the Archbishop of Canterbury in Paris in February 1495/96. Marchant is famous for his five editions of *Danse macabre,* the first of which he printed in 1485, and his numerous editions of *Compost et kalendrier des bergers,* which originally appeared in 1491. Marchant's illustrated books had an enormous impact on the French printing trade and his 1490 edition of *Dance of Death* is thought by many to be one of the finest illustrated books printed in Paris in the fifteenth century. The familiar pictures of chambermaids and matrons, merchants, farmers, priests, and lawyers, all of whom were subject to the same rules that govern all human mortals, were images that fueled the popular demand for his *Danse macabre.*

This edition of *Arithmetica speculativa* contains six woodcuts, all of which had appeared in previous books printed by Marchant, and none of which has any relation to the mathematical text. Four of the woodcuts are from his edition of *Compost et calendrier des bergers,* including the image of François Villon, the smaller of the two figures on the recto page illustrated here, which is used twice in this book and originally appeared in Marchant's edition of *Grand testament de Maistre François Villon,* printed in Paris in 1489. The woodcut of the Virgin and Saint Anne appears beneath the colophon; it and a cut of the Nativity on the recto of the last leaf are both from Marchant's 1494 edition of Petrus de Alliaco's *De anima.* A woodcut of Marchant's famous printer's mark, device number III as defined by Victor Scholderer, appears on the title page. It portrays Saints Crispin and Crispinian, the patron saints of shoemakers.

31. THOMAS
BRADWARDINE.
*Arithmetica speculativa.*
Paris: Guy Marchant,
February 1495/96

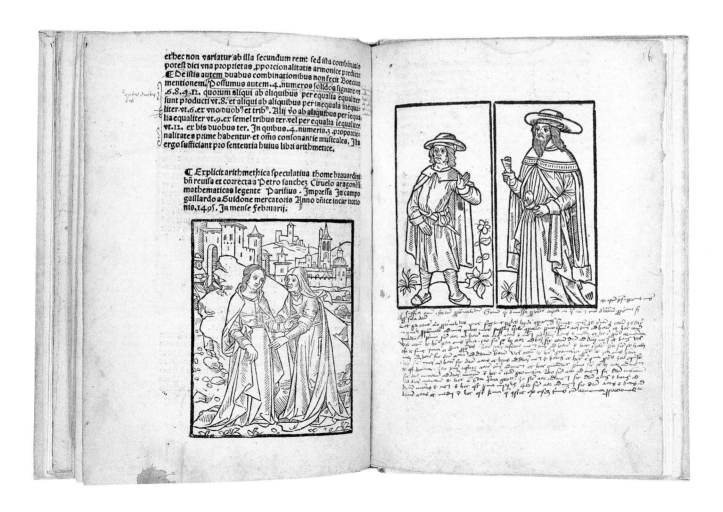

The three woodcuts illustrated here, the Virgin and Saint Anne, François Villon, and the Advocate, reflect a number of the elements that are characteristic of the French style. The highly developed landscape in the Virgin and Saint Anne is used to create the sense of space and perspective, a practice typical of the manuscript tradition, but also adds a complexity to the composition typical of the period. This detailed format is evident, too, in the cut of the Nativity and the printer's mark already mentioned. François Villon and the Advocate are cut in outline and with emphasis on the natural pose of the figures, their contemporary costume, and their distinctive facial characteristics.

This copy is one of only two copies of this edition in America, the other at the New York Public Library. There are four perfect copies in various English and European collections. This copy is annotated throughout with Latin script in a contemporary hand.

4to. 194 x 142 mm, 7⅝ x 5½ in. Goff B-1071. Claudin 1, no. 367.
Hind, p. 641. Davies 73.

## 32 ROSENWALD 501: DYSON PERRINS 491

SEVENTY-THREE EDITIONS OF *Cordiale quattuor novissimorum* were published throughout Europe during the incunable period. The popular text of eschatology contains Christian commentary on the four final stages of human experience: death, judgment, heaven, and hell. This Deventer edition by the Netherlandish printer Jacobus de Breda dated sometime between the beginning of August 1490 and the end of October 1492 is illustrated with a title-page woodcut and is rubricated in red with two- and four-line initial letters and paragraph marks.

Jacobus de Breda was one of two printers who published illustrated books in Deventer in the fifteenth century. Richardus Parfraet was the first, and his first recorded Deventer imprint appeared in 1477. William Martin Conway suggests that de Breda originally collaborated with Parfraet in the early 1480s, and by 1485 they were working simultaneously at their own presses, producing religious tracts and small classical texts. Jacobus de Breda's career in Deventer spanned three decades, with his last imprint recorded in 1512.

In addition to a few small woodcut ornaments, Jacobus de Breda repeatedly used three large woodcuts in many of his books. According to Conway, the Mass of Saint Gregory, the woodcut illustrated here, was used in at least nine different books during the years 1490 and 1491. In a more recent work on the Dutch woodcut, Ina Kok lists fourteen books in which this image appears. She also states that this is the first representational image used by de Breda, all his previous cuts having been strictly ornamental in nature.

The Mass of Saint Gregory is a complex image showing the saint kneeling before the altar witnessing the miraculous appearance of Christ. To his left is a bishop holding Gregory's miter and staff of office and to his right is his deacon, who is helping in the celebration of the mass. The transubstantiation of bread and wine into the body and blood of Christ is graphically represented by the blood flowing from Christ's pierced breast into the chalice below. Behind Christ appear the symbols of his passion and death: the cross, the ladder, and the Roman legionaries who put him to death. In his left hand, scarred by the stigmata, he holds the whip used during his scourging. A large spear, symbolizing the weapon that entered his body, stands on Christ's right, and the cock of Saint Peter stands on a pedestal in the upper right, signaling

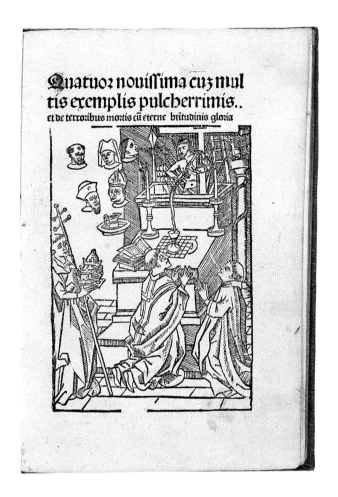

Peter's denial of Christ as his rabbi. The five heads and the pitcher and basin that float in the upper left are additional symbols of Christ's passion and give the woodcut a surreal quality.

During the late sixth century, Pope Gregory reformed the Roman liturgy and established a format for the mass that is still in use in part today. Gregory is most remembered for the symbolic celebration of the transubstantiation during the mass, and images showing the mass of Saint Gregory were well known in the late fifteenth century. Richard Field suggests that the earliest known woodcut image is Netherlandish from around 1462; it shows Saint Gregory before the altar with an angel acting as his acolyte and Christ appearing with many of the instruments and symbols of his passion.

Here the image is executed in the northern style, with the block cut in outline using thick contours and parallel lines for shading. The composition is all on one plane, with no ornamentation or embellishment used to decorate the image. The depiction of the deacon in the lower right, especially his head and the position of his body, demonstrates some skill on the part of the cutter in realizing the intention of the design. Conway suggests the influence of the Second Gouda Cutter, as some of his work found its way into books printed by de Breda in the late 1480s.

4to. 203 x 138 mm, 8 x 5 ½ in. Goff C-896. Thienen 622.
Campbell 1306=1312. Conway, pp. 158–60, 299–301. Kok, pp. 545–51. Field 230.

32. *Cordiale quattuor novissimorum.* Deventer: Jacobus de Breda [between 9 August 1490 and 31 October 1492]

Pater noster
Salue pijssima maria q̃ es filia
patris.dei filij mater. et sponsa
spūs sancti. tu enim ad hoc es a
deo electa vt esses aptissimum
scē trinitatis habitaculum.

Aue maria.
Qui in ortū cuz discipulis suis
intrauit. z plixius orando san=
guineū sudorem abūde sudauit
Amen.

Quinquagesimusquartᵃ arti
culus est christi vestimetor̃ di
uisio Matheus Postq̃t

crucifixerūt. diuiserūt vestimē
ta eius. z supra vestem miserūt
sortem

Orō

Domine ihū christe qui vesti=
menta tua int crucifixores tu
os diuidi z sup tunicā tuā incō
sutilem sortez mitti voluisti/da
mihi scōr tuor exempla cum
mādator tuor obseruantia p
ticipare z caritatem semp inte
gram seruare.

Gerard Leeu's illustrated *Rosarium* in its fifth printing and the fourth printing of the *Meditationes* contain fifty-seven and seventy-five woodcuts respectively, including repeated images. All the woodcuts are colored by a contemporary hand and the texts of both volumes are rubricated throughout. Three leaves of the *Rosarium* have paper repair with some loss of text. Both titles are rare, the *Rosarium* known only in this copy. The *Meditationes* has four locations listed in ISTC, this being the only copy in America. The volume is bound in contemporary tooled leather over wooden boards, decorated with corner pieces and a central floral motif, and measures 4¼ by 3 inches. This edition appears to be the source for the Moritz Brandis edition cited above (item 8, LC/R209, 211), the size, binding, and many of the illustrations of which seem in turn to be based on the edition printed by Gerard Leeu.

Leeu's career began in 1477 in Gouda, where he printed 62 titles before moving to Antwerp in 1484. Over the next nine years, Leeu produced more than 150 titles, many with woodcut illustrations. Netherlandish book illustration after the block book era of the mid-1460s to the early 1470s is distinguished by its simplicity in both design and cutting. It was not until the mid-1480s when Jacob Bellaert began using the images created by the Haarleem Designer that a complexity of composition and a liveliness of form began to characterize the Netherlandish illustrated book. Examples of the Haarlem Designer's work can be found in Bartholmaeus's *Boeck van den Proprieteyten der Dingen* and Raoul Le Fèvre's *Histoire van Jason,* both printed for Bellaert in 1485. After Bellaert stopped printing in 1486, his type fonts and many of his wood blocks found their way into Leeu's inventory and were used to illustrate Leeu's books over the next decade.

The miniature (16mo.) woodcuts from the *Rosarium* illustrated here were first produced in 1484 and used repeatedly in the four editions that followed the original printing. The image of the Rosary, containing symbols of Christ's physical suffering, and, on the right, Christ on the Mount of Olives, are simple in design and typical of many of the cuts from the series. These small images tested the skills of the woodcutter, who conveyed a clear message to the viewer. The thick contours of the outlines and the limited use of decoration and shading are consistent with Netherlandish style of the period.

The Guards Gambling for the Garments of Christ from the Leeu edition of the *Meditationes* (LC/R545), also illustrated here, appears to be by another designer and cutter. The black background and the bright colors of the figures contribute to a striking image of the guards fighting one another for the garments. Although the characters are not as well designed or as threatening as those that appear in the Brandis edition, the use of color and contrast is a very effective tool in conveying the ominous quality of this passion story.

16mo. 100 x 72 mm, 4 x 2⅞ in. Goff R-319, J-474. Theinen 1892, 1366.
Kronenberg/Campbell 1482a. Campbell 1048. Kok, pp. 245–58.
Conway, pp. 32–59. Schretlen, pp. 33–37.

33. *Rosarium Beate Virginae Maria.* Antwerp: [Gerard Leeu, 1489]

*bound with*

Jordan van Quedlinburg. *Meditationes de vita et passione Jesu Christi.* Antwerp: Gerard Leeu, 20 November 1488

THIS COPY OF *The Most Excellent Treatise of the Three Kings of Coleyne* appears to be the
only known complete copy. The British Library copy is missing the two woodcuts on
the recto and verso of leaf A¹, and the only other known copy, which is at the National
Library of Scotland, is wanting leaves 40–44. The book printed by Wynkyn de Worde in
Westminster after July 1499 is illustrated with two woodcuts at the beginning of the text and
Caxton printer's device on the final leaf. It is the first edition printed in English and Goff states
that it is "based on an abridged translation by Joannes von Hildersheim, a Carmelite friar who
died about 1375."

Wynkyn de Worde, Caxton's assistant and successor, took over the printing office after
Caxton's death in 1491 and printed more than eight hundred titles before his own death in
1534. Many of his early works were reprints of Caxton's publications, and over time he repeatedly used many of the wood blocks that came to him with Caxton's inventory. The Adoration
of the Magi, the first woodcut illustrating this text, is from a series of twenty-five cuts and was
first used by Caxton in his 1486 edition of the *Speculum vitae Christi.* He used this particular woodcut once again in a second edition of 1490, and de Worde used it three more times before 1500.
The woodcut of Christ on Calvary illustrated here was part of a series of images called the Fifteen
Oes and was used only once by Caxton. In his book on English woodcuts, Edward Hodnett
judges the Fifteen Oes series to be "the best cuts that Caxton ever used." Between 1493 and
1502, de Worde used this Christ on Calvary woodcut in twenty-four different publications.

Hodnett suggests that the two woodcuts, Adoration of the Magi and Calvary, that illustrate this book are probably both of Flemish origin. Hind states that some of the woodcuts
from the *Speculum vitae Christi* series are "reminiscent of the work of Bellaert's chief woodcutter
at Haarlem." In his book on Dutch and Flemish woodcuts, Schretlin describes the characteristics of the Haarleem Woodcutter in some detail. The cutter's use of thick lines for contour,
thin lines for shading, and dots for emphasis are all executed with "extreme delicacy." He at-
tempts to create a "plastic roundness" in his characters and applies "comb-like shading" to the
folds of the garments and the movements of his figures. His characters seem to float above the
ground, and they are very animated in their movements and "gesticulations."

Many of these characteristics are visible in the image of Christ on Calvary. The most
powerful is the cutter's ability to capture the human form in motion. Christ's body falling to
its right as it receives the thrust of the spear, the one thief with his dangling arms and legs, and
the other arched over his cross reflect this plasticity that Schretlin describes. The woodcut also
exhibits a very strong compositional element. The decision to expose the hind portions of the
horses out to the edge of the cut is a device that draws the viewer into the scene, as a participant
in the events of the crucifixion and not simply a bystander. The designer enhanced the composition by placing the circle of soldiers beneath the cross and balancing the figures of Saint John
and the Virgin on the left against the image of Christ to the right, showing him marching out
of Jerusalem to the hill of Calvary.

4to. 200 x 135 mm,  7⅞ x 5¼ in. Goff J-341. Hind, p. 713.
Goff *LCQJ*, p. 12. Hodnett 317, 374, pp. 5–7. Schretlen, p. 24.

⸿ Sacerdotalis instru-
ctio circa miſſam.

⸿Quotiéſcũqʒ eni mãducabitis

pané hũc τ calicé bibetis morté dñi ãnũcia

cũqʒ mãducauerit pané: vel biberit calicé

bitis donec veniat. Itaqʒ qui

RODRIGO FERNÁNDEZ DE SANTAELLA'S *Sacerdotalis instructio,* a book of instructions for priests and parishioners on the service of the mass, first appeared in this Seville edition in 1499 and was reprinted by Arnaldo Guillen de Brocar in 1503. The first edition was illustrated with a woodcut of the Mass of Saint Gregory, enclosed in a woodcut border, various rubricated initials in red and blue, woodcut initial letters, and a printer's device at the end of the book. Konrad Haebler states that the same image of the mass was first used in Iñigo López de Mendoza's *Tratado de las ceremonias de las misa,* printed in the same city by the Compañeros Alemanes, and dated June 7, 1499, just one week before this title was issued. The book is quite rare with only three copies located in America, two of which are in the collection of the Hispanic Society Library in New York.

Paulus de Colonia and the trio of printers called the Compañeros Alemanes (Johann Pegnitzer, Magnus Herbst, and Thomas Glockner) began printing in Seville in 1490. Although the printers were German, Haebler suggests, based on an analysis of the type, a Venetian origin of the press. By 1492 Paulus de Colonia had left the group, and the name of Johann Pegnitzer of Nuremberg assumed the first position in the imprint. The three printers continued to work together until the fall of 1499 when Thomas Glockner left the association. Pegnitzer and Herbst remained together until 1503. Between 1492 and 1503 the group printed mostly works of theology and law, but also some vernacular poetry and romances. It appears that many of their books were printed for booksellers or patrons, as is the case with this edition of the *Sacerdotalis.*

The Mass of Saint Gregory, illustrated here, has compositional similarities to the image in the *Cordiale quattuor novissimorum* printed by Jacobus de Breda in Deventer in 1490 (item 32). It contains many of the instruments of Christ's passion and illustrates the transubstantiation of bread and wine into the body and blood of Christ. A distinguishing feature of this woodcut is the vine-and-flower design that appears on the face and side of the altar, suggesting Arabic ornamentation. Also distinctive, the black-on-white design of the floor gives the image an Italian feel. The initial letters used to illustrate this work are very similar in style to Venetian black-ground letters, incorporating the familiar leaf-and-branch motif, the bursting floral design, and the shell pattern.

Black-ground borders, probably of Venetian origin, decorate the text. Borders of dissimilar design were often combined to frame Spanish woodcuts during the incunable period, reflecting the limited access to skilled cutters and the paucity of available wood blocks during the first two decades of book illustration in Spain.

8vo. 203 x 143 mm, 8 x 5⅝ in. Goff S-125. Haebler *Bibliografía* 2, no. 610.
Norton *Spain,* p. 8.

35. RODRIGO FERNÁNDEZ DE SANTAELLA. *Sacerdotalis instructio circa missam.* Seville: Johann Pegnitzer, Magnus Herbst, and Thomas Glockner, for Johannes Laurenti. 14 June 1499

# 36 ROSENWALD 587: DYSON PERRINS 303

THE FIRST SPANISH PRINTING OF *Tractatus super symbolum Athanasii* was published in Pamplona in 1499, four years after Henricus Mayer printed the first edition of the work in Toulouse. It contains Petrus de Castrovol's commentaries on the Athanasian Creed, a series of forty-four articles of faith, most of them devoted to the nature of the Trinity and the divinity

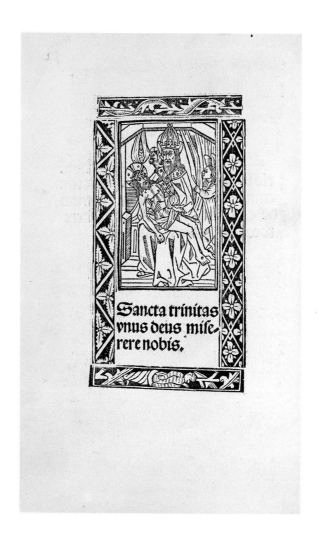

36. PETRUS DE
CASTROVOL. *Tractatus
super symbolum Athanasii:
Quicumque vult.* Pamplona
[Arnoldo Guillen
de Brocar, ca. 1499]

of Christ. Castrovol is best remembered for his commentaries on the works of Aristotle, first printed in Lérida by Heinrich Botel and in Pamplona by Arnoldo Guillen de Brocar. Brocar, the only printer in Pamplona during the incunable period, produced about a dozen works there, before moving to Logroño in 1501. In 1511 he was invited by Cardinal Ximénes to Alcalá, where he became printer to the university, a position he held until his death in 1524. He printed his most famous book, *Biblia complutense,* in Alcalá in 1514.

The woodcut of the Holy Trinity illustrated here depicts the crucified Christ in the arms of the Father, with the Holy Spirit as a dove, perched on the Father's right shoulder. The angel to the right is pulling back a curtain, revealing an open background. The wood block was cut in outline with a minimal use of shading to delineate the body of Christ and the gown of the Father. The clear and clean cut, straightforward in design, depicts the central theme of Castrovol's text without embellishment. The motto "Sancta trinitas unus deus miserere nobis" appears beneath the woodcut, and the whole is enclosed by four different floral borders, cut in black ground. Three initial letters cut in outline illustrate the remainder of the book. Initial letters and decorative borders are important elements of Spanish book illustration at the end of the fifteenth century, and more elaborate examples can be found in books printed in Valencia and Zaragosa at this time.

8vo. 204 x 133 mm, 8 x 5¼ in. Goff C-257. Haebler *Bibliografia* 1, no. 134. Hind, p. 742.
Norton *Descriptive Catalogue,* p. 159. Haebler *Early Printers,* p. 118; fig. 9. Lyell, p. 95.

Ricoldo da Montecroce, or Riccoldus Florentinus, as he was known, was a Dominican friar who traveled to the Middle East during the late 1280s and 1290s, spending considerable time in Palestine and Baghdad. He became fluent in both Arabic and the tenets of the Koran, and his *Improbatio Alcorani* was an influential source of information for western theologians on the laws of the Koran and Islam. His book, printed in Seville by Stanislaus Ponlonus in 1500, is illustrated with one woodcut, initial letters, and a printer's mark.

Polonus and Meinardo Ungut were Neapolitan printers, summoned to work in Seville by Ferdinand and Isabella. Both were of northern origins, and records indicate that while in Naples they worked for the printer Mathias Moravus, who himself was from Olmütz in Moravia. Polonus and Ungut were partners from 1491 until Ungut's death in 1499. Polonus carried on alone until 1503, when he took in Jacobo Cromberger as his partner.

German and Italian influences on the development of Spanish printing and illustration are important considerations. The Spanish style evolved by contributing its own scheme of ornamentation to compositional elements from the Italian and the use of thick contours and shading techniques common in German woodcuts. The Author Preaching to Five Arabs illustrates this evolution. The composition of the image is well balanced, with the figures and the interior setting both well defined, in a manner reminiscent of the Florentine woodcut of the

37. Ricoldo da
Montecroce.
*Improbatio Alcorani.* Seville:
Stanislaus Polonus, 1500

Master and His Seven Students found in Landino's *Formulario di lettere* of 1492 (item 12). The figures here are not as freely cut as those in the Florentine example, but the hand gestures of both the author and his listeners provide the image with a sense of movement, and their interaction is very clearly expressed.

Thick outline, looped and angular lines that define the garments, and consistent shading patterns are all techniques used by German block cutters. But the ornamentation of the image is distinctly Spanish. The designs of Arabic origin on the door, the distinctive style of the costumes, and the use of a Spanish type below the image are all elements of a Spanish woodcut style. Like many Spanish books of the period, the *Improbatio* is further decorated with woodcut initial letters and a printer's device. The large initial cut of the letter *P* on the verso of a³ is particularly decorative and well formed. The black-ground letter, set against a finely shaped tree that encompasses most of the wood block, is intertwined with the branch-and-leaf motif. The printer's device, also cut in black ground, incorporates a cross with two horizontal bars emerging from a double circle. The inner circle is bisected and the letter *S* is set in the lower half; the name "Polonus" appears at the bottom of the outer circle. The cross is enhanced with an oak leaf and acorn pattern design. The wood block is enclosed within three borders of floral designs, with a crown at the top, signifying Polonus's royal connections. Davies calls this printer's device "one of the best Spanish designs, or indeed of any of this type."

4to. 198 x 135 mm, 7⅞ x 5½ in. Goff R-190. Haebler *Bibliografía* 2, no. 577.
Norton *Descriptive Catalogue*, p. 275. Norton *Spain*, p. 9.
Hind, p. 752. Lyell, p. 68. Davies 158.

# SIXTEENTH-CENTURY BOOKS

### 38  ROSENWALD 602: DYSON PERRINS 687

*38. Passionis Christi unum ex quattuor Euagelistis textum.* [Strasbourg: J. Knobloch, 1506?]

THIS FIRST EDITION OF MATTHIAS RINGMANN'S COMMENTARIES on the *Passion of Christ* is illustrated with twenty-six full-page woodcuts designed by the Swiss artist Urs Graf. All but three of the woodcuts carry his initials *VG* cut into the block. According to Richard Muther, this is the first series of woodcuts designed and cut by Graf, a series that he started in 1503 and refined over the three years it took him to find a publisher. In this edition, printed by Johann Knobloch in Strasbourg, probably in 1506, the cut representing the Resurrection and the Visit to the Tomb is repeated. The final woodcut, representing the Man of Sorrows, appears in this and one other edition, being replaced in later editions by the Resurrection by Johann Wechtlin. The Rosenwald copy of the book is complete, including the final leaf containing an epistle by Ringmann, which is sometimes missing.

This series of woodcuts was used again by Knobloch in another Latin edition published in 1508, and in two German-language editions published in 1507 and 1509. Two other Strasbourg printers, Matthias Hupfuff and Johann Grüninger, also issued editions using Graf's wood blocks in 1513, 1514, and 1515. In 1512 Antoine Vérard copied twenty-one of these cuts for an edition of the passion that he published in Paris.

Urs Graf began his artistic career in Strasbourg around 1502, and in 1509 he left Germany

145

and returned to Basel, where he worked until his death in 1527 or 1528. He was born in Solu-thurn, Switzerland, in 1485, son of a goldsmith. The influence of his origins can be seen in the ornamental designs he created for woodcut borders, his title pages, and his thirty-eight known engravings and etchings. Graf's skill as a graphic artist has received considerable attention from bibliographers and art historians, in part because so many of his works can be identified by his signature. In addition, a significant number of his drawings have survived, and he was among the first artists to create these as independent works of art. He is well known for his images of secular life, but some of his best-known works are his chiaroscuro woodcuts of mili-tary life. These images deftly depict the swaggering bravado of soldiers, all of whom are dressed in highly detailed military costumes. F. W. H. Hollstein's attributions identify 384 large woodcuts, initial letters, and borders as Graf's work, in addition to the 85 engravings and single-leaf wood-cuts that are known to be by the Swiss artist.

The twenty-five original woodcuts Graf produced for Knobloch's edition of the *Passionis Christi* demonstrate remarkable skills for a young man under twenty years of age. The woodcut exhibited here, the Raising of Lazarus, is one of the more important in this remarkable series. It displays Graf's ability to design a composition combining many events described in the Gospels. The Gospel vignettes are organized in a *Z* pattern, which weaves its way through the image and leads the viewer from Jerusalem to the tomb of Lazarus. The woodcut shows Christ traveling to Bethany with his disciples, Martha's request that he save her brother, the whispering of the local Jews about Christ's activities, and Martha, Mary, and the apostles witnessing the miracle of Lazarus's resurrection. Graf creates balance in his woodcut design by integrating architectural elements and landscape motifs into this complex narrative image.

The shading seen in this image is another important element in Graf's woodcut style. The parallel lines he uses to model his figures are thinner than the outline contours, giving his forms a complexity that emphasizes physical dimensions. He uses a varied line pattern, with thin and thick parallel strokes, and cross-hatching to determine this form and to suggest motion. His heads show individual characteristics and his method of using short accents to further define facial features is a technique reminiscent of Dürer's work. Graf also dresses his figures in con-temporary costume, a characteristic of his work that reflects his interest in the norms and mores of everyday life in the early sixteenth century.

Folio. 300 x 210 mm, 11¾ x 8¼ in. Brunet 4, p. 422. Strauss, pp. 48–71.
Hollstein 11, pp. 68–72. Muther 1275. Johnson, pp. 13–15. Logan, p. 29.
Graf, *Die Holzschnitte zur Passion.*


## 39   ROSENWALD 738: DYSON PERRINS 181

LucAntonio Giunta's *Missale romanum* printed in November 1501 is illustrated with eighteen full-page woodcuts, nine of which are repeated from his *Officium beatae Mariae virginis,* which he published in June of the same year. In her essay "Woodcuts for Liturgical Books Published by LucAntonio Giunta in Venice, 1499–1501," Lilian Armstong attributes many of the designs of the full-page cuts to Benedetto Bordon and the cutting of the blocks to Jacob of Strasbourg. She associates these woodcuts with the so-called Classical Designer cited by Hind, whose work in the late 1490s "incorporated more classicizing figures than those of the Pico Master," who was the author of many of the popular designs of Venetian woodcuts done earlier in the decade. Armstrong's essay contains an analysis of the woodcuts that appeared in Giunta's *Graduale romanum* of 1499, the *Officium* of 1501, and this edition of the *Missale romanum.* She discusses the evolution of Bordon's work as an illuminator, which in style and technique was greatly influenced by another Paduan artist, Andrea Mantegna, and his contribution to the illustrated book in the first years of the sixteenth century. The essay, a model of its kind, carefully combines bibliographical detail and art historical analysis.

One of Giunta's achievements was his ability to incorporate the decorative elements of the medieval manuscript tradition for use in printing missals, prayer books, and choir books. The first leaf of the *Missale romanum,* printed in red, contains a six-line title and Giunta's printer's mark, the Florentine lily, set just below the text. Most of the text is set in two columns and is printed in black, with the addition of red ink for chapter headings, responses, and two- and four-line initial letters designed in the manuscript style. The text also contains numerous leaves of musical notations, with the staves printed in red and the musical notation and lyrics printed in black. In addition to the full-page woodcuts, Giunta illustrated his *Missale romanum* with numerous eight-line historiated initials, woodcut initial letters designed in floral patterns, and ten-line column cuts depicting biblical scenes and the lives of the saints. All of these decorative wood blocks were designed and cut in a clear yet simple style, and all were printed in black ink. The impact of this complicated combination of text, image, and color on the design and layout of his printed liturgical texts can be measured by the many editions of these books which were produced by his press over the following three decades.

39. *Missale romanum.* Venice: L. A. Giunta, 20 November 1501

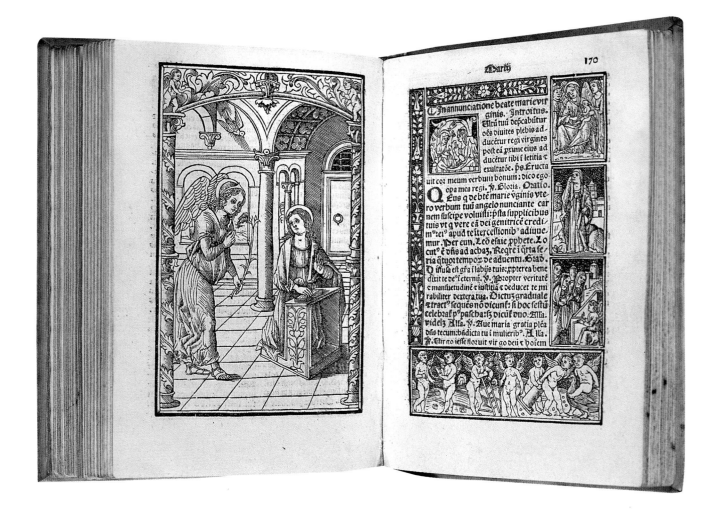

The woodcut of the Annunciation, a design not attributed to Bordon, recalls the interior design of the image used in the 1498 edition of *Meditationes* printed in Rome by Plannck (item 25, LC/R334). The overall composition of the image, the position of its figures, the three architectural columns, the ornamental designs on the kneeler, and the floor pattern are similar in both woodcuts. Yet in the 1501 design, the perspective, the complexity of the interior and its detailed ornamentation, and the modeling of the figures and their facial characteristics are more highly developed than in the design cut for Plannck. Focusing on the shading alone, we note the variety in the thickness and direction of the parallel lines, which are used to give greater dimensionality to the physical forms and a better sense of perspective in the interior view. This detailed shading technique results in an idealized rendering of the story of the Annunciation and reflects an important characteristic of Italian Renaissance style that emerged in the late 1490s. Armstrong suggests that the physical rendering of the two figures and the floor patterns are elements that are not characteristic of Bordon's style, and thus the author of this image remains anonymous.

On the page opposite the Annunciation, the text of the prayer to the Virgin is framed with three smaller border cuts depicting events from the Virgin's life, a lower border decorated with putti and cherubs in classical Venetian style, and two marginal borders ornamented with the vase-and-flower motif. These smaller blocks are well-developed compositions in themselves and are very finely cut, shaded, and highlighted in the criblé manner. The woodcut initial letter outlined against a black background reiterates the theme of the larger woodcut of the Annunciation scene, and the red and black type of the text brings all the elements of this two-page spread into a very satisfying whole. Much of the success Giunta enjoyed with his liturgical publications can be attributed to this formula of combining religious text with finely crafted images in a pleasing typographical design.

8vo. 160 x 110 mm, 6¼ x 4¼ in. Camerini 63. Essling *Missels* 59. Pollard *Italian* 158.
Mortimer *Italian* 305. Hind, pp. 465–71. Armstrong "Woodcuts," p. 77.

## 40 ROSENWALD 740: DYSON PERRINS 151

DOMENICO CAVALCA, A FOURTEENTH-CENTURY Dominican prelate and author of spiritual guides and books of religious instruction, translated into Italian this Venetian edition of the lives of the early saints and martyrs, attributed to Saint Jerome. The first edition of Cavalca's Italian translation was printed in 1474 without illustrations, and it was followed by twelve more Italian editions printed before 1500. Five of the twelve were illustrated editions printed in Venice, the most famous of which was printed for LucAntonio Giunta by Giovanni Ragazzo in 1491.

Otinus de Luna of Pavia began printing in Venice in 1496. He was responsible for about thirty titles under his own imprint, the last of which appeared in December 1507. According to Essling, only three of de la Luna's printed books contained illustrations, of which *Vita de sancti padri* was by far the most important. It was printed for Nicolò and Domenico Sandri, Fratelli dal Jesu, who were active as booksellers and publishers from 1501 to 1520. The title page bears their large circular publisher's mark printed in red and enclosed by a very elaborate black-ground, criblé woodcut border. The verso of the final leaf has a printer's mark set within a half-page roundel with six lines of text below.

Otinus de la Luna's 1501 edition of *Vita di sancti padri* is divided into six books, each chapter opening embellished with a full-page thick black-ground border enclosing a half-page roundel, an initial letter, and text. The six woodcut roundels, along with thirty half-page wood-cut roundels that appear throughout the text, are colored in a contemporary hand. The text is printed in two columns and decorated with about six hundred historiated initial letters in three sizes, including repeats, all cut in black ground and highlighted with criblé, or dotted backgrounds.

Four different thick black-ground borders are used to decorate the volume, all in monumental Venetian style. The border on the title leaf and three of the chapter headings is designed with four corner-pieces depicting sibyls surrounding the roundel, columns of vases and classical figures held aloft by putti, and illustrations of arms and armor intertwined with a leaf-and-branch motif. A second border, designed in a very formal style with vase, flowers, rosettes, and acanthus leaves surrounding the roundel and margins of the page, is used for the other three chapter openings. The thirty half-page roundels are enclosed by two different borders. The first contains dragons and grotesque figures and the second is decorated with a branch-and-leaf motif. These four borders appear to be original to this work, as do all the historiated initial letters and the designs that appear in the roundels. All are designed in a formal style and embellished with classical motifs.

The opening seen here illustrates the unique effect produced by the combined use of the circle and the square as design elements. On the left, the image depicts the capture and enslavement of Malchius by the Bedouins. It is of spacious design where all the figures are clearly differentiated and the drama of the forced march clearly depicted. But the roundel creates a telescopic effect, leaving the viewer with the impression that he is spying on the caravan as it moves across the landscape. The event becomes timeless and the woodcut takes on a quality of immediacy that is an important characteristic of Renaissance imagery.

The woodcut on the right depicts a series of events from the life of Saint Paul the Hermit, illustrated with symbols that anticipate the prose text to follow. The composition of the woodcut resembles the black-line design that appears in the 1491 Giunta edition, but the heavy shading pattern, the pose of the martyr at the pillar on the left, and the classical costume of the maiden distinguish the two woodcuts and demonstrate the rapid advancements in style that took place in the decade from 1491 to 1500. These design elements, along with the monumental architecture and landscape designs that appear in some of the cuts, forecast the emergence of the classical design that was to dominate Venetian woodcuts during the first decades of the sixteenth century.

Rarely do we find Italian woodcuts colored in a contemporary hand. In addition to the Rosenwald/Dyson Perrins copy, an incomplete colored copy of the 1501 *Vita di sancti padri* is part of the collections at the University of California at Los Angeles. The color in the two copies is very similar, especially in the density of the red and blue wash and in the placement of these colors throughout the book. Moreover, both copies were partially colored by stencil. A close look at the image of Malchius on the left shows color gaps at four points on the outer border where the stencil was placed. These gaps appear throughout both books, suggesting that they were colored at the same time by the same workshop. The Research Libraries Information Network (RLIN) records an uncolored copy at Princeton University.

40. [Saint Hieronymus] *Vita di sancti padri vulga[m] historiada.* Venice: Otinus de la Luna, 28 July 1501

Folio. 295 x 200 mm, 11⅝ x 8 in. Essling 574. Pollard *Italian* 156. Sander 3412. Norton *Italian* 151. Special thanks to David Slive, curator of rare books at the University of California, Los Angeles, for the description of their copy.

sempre di trouare la leona: & con quella pau
ra la sera uscissemo: & trouassemo li camel
li liquali per il ueloce suo camino chi chia
memo dromedarii: liquali li passati tempi ci
staueno a ruminare sopra quelli asciesi &
trouati alquanti cibi sopra quelli camelli si
confortassemo & metemosi in camino & in
diece giorni caminando per il deserto giose
mo nel campo de li Romani: & presentati
al tribuno: al quale tutto cio che ce intraue
ne per ordine li contamo e de quiui fossemo
mandati a sabiniano duca di Mesopotania
elqual uedete li camelli. Et perche haueua i
teso il mio Abbate esser gia morto: a gli mo
naci di quella patria macopagnai: & la mia
compagna racomadai a certe done religio

se uerzene. Amado quella come sorell
perho a quella in tuto come sorella m
fidaua. Queste cose a me garzonetto
ronimo narro il uechio Malco: & io
narrando in mia uechieza ui expono c
historia di castitade. Exortando gli ue
hauere custodia di la sua uirginitade.
narrate a tutti quelli che doppo uoi se
acio sapiano che la pudicitia ifra le spa
serti & le bestie mai potera pire. Et che
mo dedito a Christo ben potera mori
non potera essere superato.

Finisse la Vita di Malco Monaco
posta per il glorioso Sacto Hieron
elquale io prego lui prega per me.

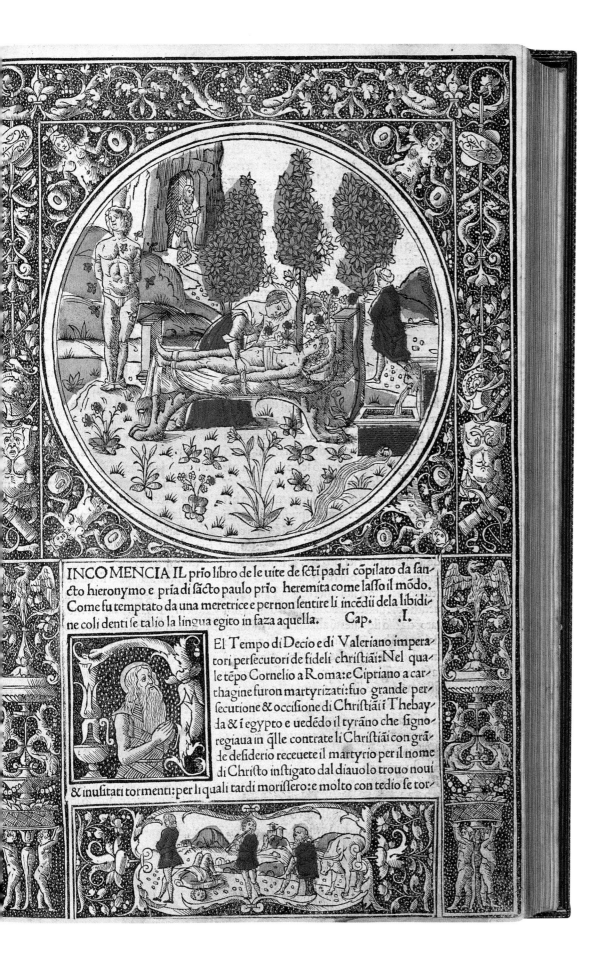

INCOMENCIA IL prio libro de le uite de sancti padri cõpilato da sancto hieronymo e pria di sãcto paulo prio heremita come lasso il mõdo.
Come fu temptato da una meretrice e per non sentire li incendii de la libidi-
ne coli denti se talio la lingua egito in faza aquella.     Cap.    .I.

El Tempo di Decio e di Valeriano impera-
tori persecutori de fideli christiãi: Nel quale tẽpo Cornelio a Roma: e Cipriano a car-
thagine furon martyrizati: fuo grande per-
secutione & occisione di Christiãi Thebay-
da & i egypto e uedẽdo il tyrãno che signo-
regiaua in q̃lle contrate li Christiãi con grã-
de desiderio receuete il martyrio per il nome
di Christo instigato dal diauolo trouo noui
& inusitati tormenti: per li quali tardi morissero: e molto con tedio se tor-

151

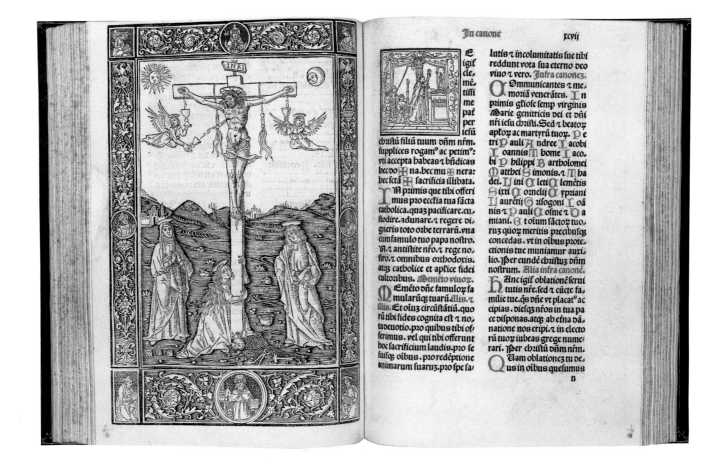

# 41 ROSENWALD 744: DYSON PERRINS 177

41. *Missale secundu[m]*
*ordinem carthusiensium.*
Ferrara: Carthusian
Monastery,
10 April 1503

THIS RARE AND BEAUTIFUL MISSAL appears to be the first and only book printed at the Carthusian Monastery in Ferrara during the sixteenth century. Norton suggests it may well have been printed by the Ferrarese printer Laurentius Rubeis de Valentia, because two of the three typefaces used to print the text are associated with his press. The text of the missal is printed in two columns in black ink and illustrated with a large woodcut of Saint Christopher and the Christ Child on the title leaf, a canon cut of the crucifixion placed at the beginning of the canon of the mass, and more than 150 initial letters in three sizes. The missal is rubricated throughout in red ink, and the musical notations and lyrics are printed in black on red staves.

The woodcuts have been attributed to an anonymous Ferrarese designer, who, with considerable skill, created two important woodcut images. The first is an image of Saint Christopher crossing the river with the Christ Child on his right shoulder. His figure is set front and center in the design and it dominates the composition of the woodcut. He is dressed in contemporary costume, and his face is well defined with expressive eyes and an aquiline nose. The saint's body is modeled by a few well-chosen lines, and the shapeliness of his bare legs, partially submerged in water, demonstrates that the artist was skilled at detailing the physical form. The Christ Child and the background are less well defined, but the wavy lines that define the river are effectively rendered.

The canon cut, which is illustrated here, is a full-page woodcut framed by a passe-partout border in the Venetian style. This cut is similar in composition to one found in a missal printed in Venice in 1498 by Johannes Emericas for Johannes Paep, which Victor Masséna, Prince d'Essling, illustrates in his bibliography on Venetian missals. Where the two differ is in the choice of background, which in this case is a landscape as opposed to an architectural view, and in the fact that the 1498 woodcut is executed in outline, whereas the Ferrarese cutter chose to use the white-on-black technique to create a dramatic presentation of the crucifixion.

This highly sculpted background where the contrast of black and white is so effectively applied is an interesting variation on the solid black with white of the black-ground style that was so much a part of Venetian taste. It gives the woodcut a lightness, almost a feathery quality, that is enhanced by incorporating the new shading techniques of the Venetian style for the modeling of the human form. The borders, which carry standard motifs, are also made lighter by the white-on-black technique and the use of the criblé method in the corner blocks. This beautifully printed Ferrarese *Missale* is also decorated with 9 ten-line historiated initial letters and 26 five-line historiated initials depicting biblical passages, and 120 four-line initial letters in the criblé manner. Hind suggests that this designer was inspired by the popular style of the Venetian woodcut.

Folio. 313 x 230 mm, 12 ¼ x 9 in. Pollard *Italian* 166. Bohatta *Katalog* 542.
Sander 4691. Mortimer *Italian* 306. Essling *Missels*, p. 159. Hind, p. 510.
Williamson, p. 220. Gruyer, part 4, pp. 153–54.

## 42   ROSENWALD 749: DYSON PERRINS 132

JACOBUS GUALLA'S LIVES OF THE SAINTS OF PAVIA and guide to the reliquaries in the churches of the city was printed after the author's death in early 1505. It was edited by J. F. Picius and printed for Paulus Morbius by Jacobus de Burgofrancho. It is illustrated with a woodcut portrait of the author, repeated twice, and sixty-seven small woodcuts from twenty-nine different wood blocks. The text is printed in black and is decorated with simple line and black-ground foliated initial letters of very fine quality and Burgofrancho's printer's device. This edition of *Papie sanctuarium* is described by Kristeller as "undeniably the most important of the Pavian books with woodcuts."

The woodcuts in Burgofrancho's *Papie sanctuarium* are well documented by Kristeller, who writes, "In them the characteristics of the style of woodcut as practiced at Pavia, and especially in the office of Jacobus de Burgofrancho, are seen in full distinction." The portrait of the author reproduced here is an excellent example of the Pavian style. It combines the influences of Milanese portrait painting with the thinly cut outline border designs of the Ferrarese masters. The portrait is delicately cut with lines of varied thicknesses resulting in a figure of individual character. The folds of the cloak incorporate curved lines, with loop and angle cuts, highlighted with parallel lines of varied lengths cut in different directions.

The border, cut in outline without shading, is distinguished by the thinness of the line and the clarity of the image. The use of roundels and curved-line designs for flowers and the figures of the putti with musical instruments and the two satyrs at the base of each column are in the popular style of Venetian design. The eyes of the figures in the roundels are quite large, with lids half closed and dark centers. The overall effect is a light, airy border of original character. This border first appeared in Laurentius Rubeis's edition of Francesco Negri's *Pullata*, printed in Ferrara earlier in 1505. The same border style is repeated here in another finely cut frame, surrounding a small portrait of Saint Jerome found at the end of the text.

42. JACOBUS GUALLA.
*Papie sanctuarium.* Pavia:
Jacobus de Burgofrancho,
10 November 1505

Of the remaining twenty-nine woodcuts, most are portraits cut in outline and highlighted with shading and some cross-hatching. The portrait of Saint Jerome was originally used by Laurentius Rubeis in his famous edition of *Vita epistole* of Saint Jerome printed in 1497. Two other cuts, Saint Siro and Statue of Regisole, appeared first in Burgofrancho's *Statuta* of Pavia, published in August 1505. They were copied, and in the case of the Regisole, the composition was reversed, and used in the November edition of *Papie sanctuarium.* A particularly well-conceived and well-executed portrait woodcut from this group of smaller cuts is the image Saint Symphorosa and Her Seven Sons. The composition is arranged with Saint Symphorosa standing at the center of the image with her arms outstretched, gathering her boys beneath her open cloak in order to protect them. All the figures are well defined, with individual facial characteristics and finely contoured costumes, and the cut is highlighted by the use of black space to define heavily shaded areas and thin parallel lines. Nine of the other smaller cuts in the book are of equal distinction, and all of them exhibit one or more of the characteristics of the Pavian style.

4to. 212 x 150 mm, 8¼ x 5⅞ in. Pollard *Italian* 174. Sander 3288.
Mortimer *Italian* 222. Schäfer *Italian* 84. Kristeller 176, p. 35.
Kristeller "Pavia," p. 361.

A VERY POPULAR COMMENTARY on the Epistles and Gospels by Guillermus Parisiensis, a mid-thirteenth-century bishop of Paris, this edition was apparently the first Italian printing. The work was first published in Augsburg in 1472, after which more than one hundred editions followed before LucAntonio Giunta commissioned this one in 1505. Giunta's edition was printed by Jacob Pentius de Leuco, a prolific Venetian printer, whose imprints appeared from 1495 until 1527, when he was succeeded by Hieronymus Pentius. The *Postilla* is organized in two parts. It is printed in a gothic type in two point sizes, with the commentary surrounding the biblical texts. The title page is printed in red, with the title set above Giunta's printer's mark. This is the only copy of the book recorded in an American library.

The first part is illustrated with a large woodcut of the Crucifixion, which previously appeared in Giunta's 1501 editions of the *Officium beatae Mariae virginis* and the *Missale romanum*. Giunta used it again for a 1509 edition of the *Missale Ordinis Carthusiensium*. The *Postilla* also includes thirty-seven woodcuts of biblical scenes from twenty-three original wood blocks and one initial letter in outline, with an image of Saint Matthew. The second part begins with a large woodcut, Saint Peter and Saint Paul, also from the *Missale romanum,* and a foliated initial letter. Both of these two large woodcuts have been attributed to Benedetto Bordon by Lilian Armstrong.

Mary Magdelene and the Other Marys at the Tomb is typical of the thirty-seven smaller cuts that illustrate the *Postilla*. This well-organized scene includes very delicately cut figures

43. GUILELMUS PARISIENSIS. *Postilla super Epistolas et Euangelia.* Venice: Jacobus Pentius de Leuco for LucAntonio Giunta, 6 November 1505

with thicker contour outlines and thinner parallel lines modeling the figures. The mountain and city views in the background are in proper perspective and the artist has introduced black space to define denser shaded areas and create contrasts. The woodcut is set within a frame of text, the commentary in the smaller type size and the Gospel story in larger, bolder type. The integration of the image and text is extremely well executed and the double-page spread produces a very satisfying typographical presentation, one of the hallmarks of Giunta's liturgical publications.

4to. 213 x 150 mm, 8⅜ x 6 in. Camerini 97. Pollard *Italian* 173.
Sander 3338. Essling 194 for 1515 reprint. Norton *Italian*, p. 146.
Goff "Postilla," pp. 73–77. Armstrong "Woodcuts," p. 83.

## 44 ROSENWALD 758: DYSON PERRINS 61

A LATER EDITION OF THE VENETIAN PRINTER LucAntonio Giunta's *Breviarium romanum*, this 1507 work includes 8 full-page cuts, 10 leaves with woodcut borders surrounding the text, 375 small woodcuts of biblical stories set throughout the text, and numerous initial letters, all used in previous editions of the work. The woodcut on the title leaf is printed in black and illustrates a priest kneeling before the cross contemplating the instruments of Christ's passion. Below, printed in contrasting red ink, are the title and Giunta's printer's mark. The

44. *Breviarium romanum.*
Venice: LucAntonio
Giunta, 26 March 1507

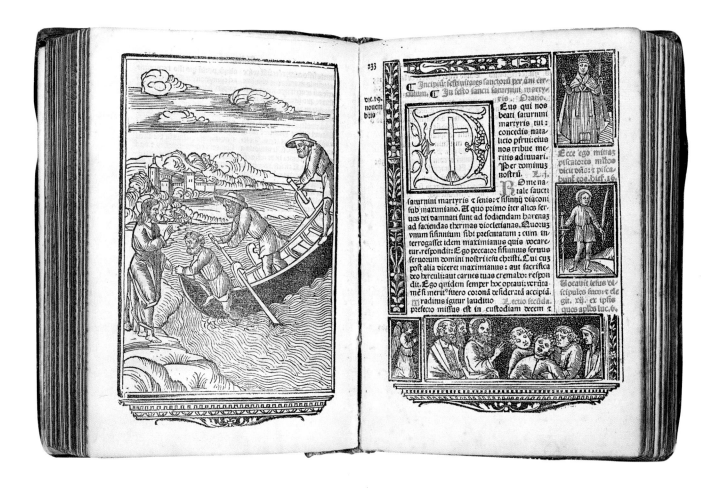

text of the breviary is printed in black, with chapter headings, initial letters, paragraph marks, and responses printed in red.

The opening illustrated here, the Calling of Peter and Andrew, is a design that Benedetto Bordon created for the *Missale romanum* printed in November 1501. It is distinguished from the original design used in that edition by a change in the border at the bottom of the image. In this woodcut, Bordon and the woodcutter Jacob of Strasbourg recreate the moment when Andrew recognized Christ as the Messiah and dedicated himself as Christ's first apostle. Peter witnessed his brother's commitment and followed as a disciple of Christ. One of the distinguishing characteristics of this woodcut is the highly developed use of shading to model the figures and background. The sea is equally well defined by the use of sculptured lines indicating the motion and direction of the water. The forward tilt of the boat and the bend in the knees of the oarsmen contribute to this sense of moving water. The powerful composition, classical costume, recognizable heads of the figures, and the use of a new, shaded style all point to the influence of the painter Andrea Mantegna and his circle on the emerging classical design of the Venetian woodcut at the end of the fifteenth century.

Here, as in the opening illustration for the 1501 edition of Giunta's *Missale,* the page opposite the large woodcut is decorated with an initial letter in outline, smaller woodcuts reflecting the life of Saint Andrew, and two marginal borders enclosing the red and black text. The woodcuts are not as clear or as evenly inked as those in the 1501 edition and reflect the continued use of these wood blocks by Giunta to illustrate his many editions of liturgical texts.

8vo. 146 x 100 mm, 5¾ x 4 in. Camerini III.
Pollard *Italian* 183. Sander 1351. Essling 937.

## 45    ROSENWALD 762: DYSON PERRINS 266

ZANOTO DI CASTELLIONE BASED THE TEXT and format of the 1508 Milan edition of *Libro de la ventura* by Lorenzo Spirito (d. 1496) on an edition printed in Milan for Johannes and Jacobus Legnano by Pietro de Mantegatiis in 1500. Like Mantegatiis, Castellione, a very successful printer whose imprints appeared in Milan from 1505 to 1523, often printed books for the publisher Johannes and Jacobus, Fratelli de Legnano, the most important publishing company in Milan during the first two decades of the sixteenth century. In his essay describing the illustrated editions of *Libro de la ventura,* Tammaro De Marinis points out that the woodcuts of the kings, the dice game, the prophets, and those set in the center of the wheels of fortune are the same in both editions, but the architectural woodcut border and the woodcut *IHS* that appear on the title leaf differ. He attributes the woodcuts to the Milan artist Giovanni Pagani and bases his attribution on a signed woodcut, the Assumption of Mary, that appears in the 1499 edition of *Vita de la Preciosa Vergine Maria,* also printed by Pietro de Mantegatiis.

The title leaf of this volume is illustrated with a full-page architectural border in outline enclosing the publisher's mark, the title, and instructions for playing the games. A parade of twenty woodcuts, including five repeats, follows, representing the kings who rule the game. Arranged on five pages, each is enclosed within the same full-page, thick black-ground passe-partout border. The border is decorated with columns of exotic floral and vase designs, a leaf-and-vine motif at the top border, and two putti flanking a wreath-and-shield motif in the bottom border. After the kings come twenty pages illustrating the game of dice. Each page is

45. LORENZO SPIRITO.
*Libro de la ventura.* Milan:
Zanoto di Castellione
for Fratelli Legnano,
23 August 1508

laid out in six columns to show dice combinations, and a few lines of text describe the result of the thrown dice. At the center of each page is a woodcut outline of either a symbol for one of the planets or a sign of the zodiac.

Following the game of dice are twenty wheels of fortune, each enclosed by a round black-ground border decorated with a branch-and-leaf motif. At the bottom of each wheel is a large border in one of four designs: a series of putti at play, a hunting scene, hounds catching a wolf, or a dragon brought to bay by hunters. The text describing the fortunes progresses from the outer border, and at the center of each wheel is a decorative woodcut representing a planet or a sign of the zodiac. The final twenty-five pages give predictions, illustrated with twenty woodcuts in outline of Old Testament prophets. Pollard provides a description of the rules to the game in his citation for the 1501 edition printed by Guillaume le Signerre in item 157 in his catalogue of the Dyson Perrins collection of Italian books.

Many of the designs are very well done, especially those that appear in the center of the wheels of fortune and in the woodcut borders below the wheels. In the opening illustrated here, the leopard on the left is cut in a thick outline and modeled with precise curved lines. The leopard's formal pose is particularly appealing as it projects a dignity commensurate with its position in the hierarchy of the animal kingdom. On the right, the dolphin is similarly cut, but it is set within a sea of curved lines against a well-defined architectural background. The dolphin's design is classical in origin and projects an aggressive attitude, one suggesting the dolphin's importance as protector of the city of Venice, denoted by the tower of St. Mark's in the background. The well-designed woodcut border of the hunt on the left and the putti at play on the right are symbols of the vagaries of life, where good fortune and calamity are equally possible.

The wheel of fortune and games of dice were common entertainments in the late Middle Ages and early Renaissance period. Most people considered personal fate to be as much dependent on good fortune and chance as on faith and good works. The spin of the wheel or the toss of the dice were tried and true methods of explaining how the unknown worked and gave meaning to what transpired in everyday life. Spirito's *Book of Fortune,* first published in 1482, went through more than a dozen editions by 1525 and was especially popular in Catholic countries like Italy. This edition appears to be very rare; the National Union Catalog (NUC) cites only the Rosenwald copy and a single copy at Harvard, which may be a mistaken identification. The Rosenwald copy was previously owned by Ambroise Firmin Didot and William Morris, and it carries their bookplates, along with the ownership plates of C. W. Dyson Perrins and Lessing J. Rosenwald.

Folio. 295 x 206 mm, 11 ⅝ x 8 in. Pollard *Italian* 187. Sander 7048.
De Marinis 5, 7, pp. 71–72. Kristeller 335, for the Milan,
1509 edition printed by Gotardo da Ponte.

## 46   ROSENWALD 770: DYSON PERRINS 114

THE FIRST EDITION OF THE FIRST ITALIAN writing manual was written by Sigismondo Fanti and printed in 1514 in Venice. It is illustrated with woodcut borders, initial letters, diagrams, and letterforms, accompanied by a text instructing in the art of handwriting. Fanti, a mathematician and astronomer from the city of Ferrara, published *Theorica et practica de modo scribendi fabricandique omnes litterarum species* with the thought that secretaries, copyists, merchants, and artisans could learn techniques of applying geometry to the construction of letterforms. His book is divided into four parts, beginning with information about paper, ink, and the proper way of holding a pen and applying it to paper. Fanti gives the history of various hands, describes in detail rotunda, textura, and roman alphabets, and explains the geometric method of forming both lowercase and capital letters. A. S. Osley writes, "In its way, Fanti's book is one of the most complete and systematic expositions of the art of calligraphy written in the sixteenth century."

Beneath the title on the first leaf is a woodcut in outline of a left-handed writer holding a pen and applying it to paper. The hand is extremely well drawn and highlighted with parallel lines. The subtle use of cross-hatching to shade the interior of the sleeve is used again in another woodcut showing the torso of a writer using both hands in the act of writing, the left hand to hold the pen and the right to secure the paper. A third woodcut in outline illustrates the tools of the writing trade. The pen, scissor, knife, inkwell, compass, and square are simply designed in outline and cut in black line. The finely cut contours and the clever application of the shading and cross-hatching in these three cuts indicate the work of an accomplished designer and block cutter.

The woodcuts of the capital letters *D* and *E* that appear here are examples of the way geometric patterns were used by Fanti in the design of his letters. The circle and the square,

Vando le medesime normæ de la pcedête serano obser-
uate:cioe cú li circuli magiori & minori iacéti in la potê
tia del qdro:& li diametri cú li possaméti & suæ diuisiõe:
si come in la lfa.c.apúcto fu istituito & ordiato. Excepto
che a la lfa.D.la qle intédiamo p forza geometrica al pñte descri-
re.Bisogna lasta naturale de manu sinistra ptrahere : Extendédo la
linea.u.x.ægdistâte da.s.t.si come.s.t.ægdista da.a.c.in potétia & in
lõgitudine:scdo il possaméto causato da la largheza de la péna.k.s.
Quãdo cosi hauerai ogni cosa diligentemête fabricato.Dico la lfa
D.Antiqua naturale essere p ragione pfectamête sortita:Chi igno.

rara le geometricæ normæ:& maxie le' Euclidiane isieme anchora
cú le Sigismôdane.Pronúciamo a qlli essere la uia recta acellata & p
lor la uia obliqua li sera manifesta & apta:Vñ te côsiglio o legéte:&
a uoi altri dilectari:nõ ue uogliati sopra de qlle lfæ che trouariti sot
li hauere piu gra asúdare:ne il senso li totalmête ponere.Impoche i
qllæ certamête mai nulla mesura atrouarai essere pfecta se nõ a ta
stoni:& se p caso li farai pmutare la magnitudie de la lfa: loro muta
rano noui modi & iuentiõe:& i qllæ li farano isinitæ lineæ & circu.
li & serano frustra.Ma sano pche apareno de piu artificio:tu intédi
&c.Multi sono che amensurano li terreni & Bottæ e non sano il p,
pter quid:ma dicono il præceptore cosi me ha insegnato.

A littera.E.antiqua certamente cauarse da le medesime
circústantiæ & modi de la præcedente nõ negamo.Quã
do adúque lasta naturale de qsta littera sera cú le medesi
me normæ,ptracta.Faciasse sopra il cétro.E. cômuno la
portiõe del circulo.x.y.secúdo la qtita de.e.x.tágendo lo diametro
i.d.in.y.dal qle puncto sia la linea.y.z.ppendiculariter extéduta so
pra il diametro.a.d.per la.xi. de Euclide:& de ditta lfa la gamba ise
riore hauerai fabricato:e se la supiore gâba uorai generare. Alhora
dal púcto.z.per la.xi.del Megarése sia la linea.z.&. ppendiculariter

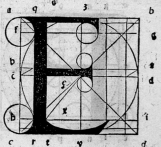

sopra lo lato.c.d.ptracta:secádo.f.g.in.o.Et qñ il circulo partio so
pra il centro.℟.o.sera descripto secúdo la qtita de.℟.o.la quale e po
sta essere æquale a li tri quarti de la largheza de la péna cioe de. f.a.
Et qsto fatto se la media asta.A.C.B.D.côtingéte al cétro.e. cômu,
no sera lineata il cui termio sia la linea.E.F.distâte da la linea.u.z.p
tri qrti de testa.Hauerai alhora la mediale gâba de dita lfa cú doctri
na erecta.Et maxie qñ p gra de qlla li serano li dui parissimi circu
li secúdo la qtita de media testa descripti.Se da poi li dui parui circu
li secúdo la qtita de.h.c.et de.f.a.cioe de la latitudine de la testa se
rano sopra li centri.f.et.h.descripti:ut supra iam ostensum est:la lit
tera.E. Antiqua sera cum perfectione instituita.

46. Sigismondo Fanti.
*Theorica et practica de modo
scribendi fabricandique omnes
litterarum species.* Venice:
Giovanni Rosso,
1 December 1514

the building blocks of classical architecture and the basis for letter designs that appear in Pacioli's *Divina proportione,* published in Venice in 1509, provide a starting point for Fanti. He, however, pushed past the limits of Pacioli's theory of proportion by applying principles of geometry to extend the lines of his letterforms beyond the limits imposed by the proportionality of the circle and the square.

Each of the four parts of *Theorica et practica* is introduced by a chapter page, each illustrated with the same full-page passe-partout border in black ground, and a large foliated initial letter. Sander suggests that the border and initial letter were copied from the 1505 edition of *Miracoli della Madonna* printed by Bartolomeo Zanni. The initial letters also resemble the black-ground woodcut in the *Commentaries* of Saint Jerome printed by Johannes and Gregorius Gregoriis in 1498. The bottom block of the border seems to be inspired by a border cut from the Giunta edition of *Regule ordinum* printed by Johannes Emericus de Spira in 1500.

One of the more curious aspects of Fanti's book is his discussion of the chancery letter. His work is the first to discuss how to write this letterform, but no examples were supplied even though space was provided for it in his text. It has been suggested that he was unable to find a block cutter able to produce samples of chancery design.

4to. 203 x 149 mm, 8 x 6 in. Pollard *Italian* 212. Bonacini 607. Sander 2652. Essling 1824.
Schäfer *Italian* 75. *2,000 Years of Calligraphy* 58. Becker 1. Osley, pp. 5–12.

THIS RARE EDITION OF ALEXANDRO DE PAGANINI'S *Apocalypse,* printed in Venice April 7, 1515/16, is organized in two parts. The first contains the text of the *Apocalypse* in Latin with commentaries in Italian by Federico Veneto, the early fourteenth-century Dominican friar and theologian. The second part comprises the Latin text of the *Apocalypse,* its title leaf illustrated with a large woodcut of Jesus Asleep in a Boat with His Disciples, and fifteen full-page woodcuts inspired by Dürer's monumental images, which were first printed in 1498 and reissued in 1511.

Enclosing the title of part 1 is an eight-piece woodcut border in black ground, designed with elaborate arabesque strapwork and highlighted with the systematic application of dots in the criblé manner. The large initial letter is similarly designed and printed in red, as is part of the text of the title. The remainder of part 1 is illustrated with four- and six-line initials decorated with floral patterns, strapwork, and criblé. The Italian text is printed in a beautiful roman font with an italic flair, first used by Paganini in his editions of Euclid and Pacioli printed in 1509. In this copy the first lines of the Italian commentary have been highlighted in brown wash by an early hand.

The illustrations that accompany part 2 have been variously attributed to Zoan Andrea and Domenico Campagnola, and one cut has even been attributed to Titian. As Mortimer

47. *Apocalypsis Jesu Christi.* Venice: Alexandro de Paganini, 7 April 1515/16

ALBRECHT DÜRER. *Saint Michael Fighting the Dragon.* 1511? Prints and Photographs Division, Library of Congress.

points out, eight of the cuts after Dürer and the woodcut on the title leaf all carry some form of the signature *ZA* or *IA*. One of the woodcuts is signed in full "Zova Adrae.," and their attribution to the fifteenth-century painter Zoan Andrea has been vigorously debated by art historians over the decades. Most recently, Suzanne Boorsch has proposed that the *ZA* and *IA* are probably the signatures of Giovanni Antonio da Brescia and not Zoan Andrea. Boorsch's essay is a useful introduction to the history of this controversy and to her methodology for establishing evidence for the attribution of the woodcuts to Giovanni Antonio da Brescia.

The woodcut Saint Michael Fighting the Dragon is signed *IA* in the lower right. About a third smaller than Dürer's original, it is cut in reverse. The landscape at the bottom of the cut looks more like an Italian hill town than a German village, and the figures in the image are more forward in the frame than they are in Dürer's design. Whereas Dürer used very little cross-hatching to shade his figures, the designer of the Italian woodcut darkens his backgrounds by freely using this method of colorization. Otherwise, the Italian cut follows Dürer's composition quite closely.

Yet it is the faces of the figures, the ornamentation of the shields and swords, and the detail of the robes and dragon's body that distinguish the original from the Italian copy. Dürer's flick of pencil, the use of varied thicknesses and patterns of line, and the sheer volume of detail bring a remarkable clarity and vibrancy to his cut. The Italian version, though successful in many respects, suffers from an application of uniform lines that fill in space rather than clearly define it. The Dürer woodcut also reflects the great skills of the Nuremberg craftsman who cut the block. This woodcutter was able to translate Dürer's flicks and dashes by executing exquisitely fine cuts in repetition, producing an exciting rendering of Dürer's image.

The Rosenwald/Dyson Perrins copy of Paganini's *Apocalypse* is marked on the title page with the ownership stamp of Josephi Martini Lucensis.

Folio. 300 x 205 mm, 11¾ x 8 in. Pollard *Italian* 214. Sander 3651.
Essling 205. Mortimer *Italian* 58. Norton *Italian*, p. 145. Boorsch, pp. 56–66.


## 48   ROSENWALD 828: DYSON PERRINS 115

THE SECOND EDITION OF THE STORY of the martyrdom of Faustino and Jovita, two saints of the city of Brescia put to death in A.D. 120, was printed in that city by Damiano and Jacobus Philippum fratres, dated April 4, 1534. The book is illustrated with a large woodcut of Saint Apollonius dressed as a bishop and seated between Saints Faustino and Jovita, who are dressed as priests. The image is deftly cut using thick lines for the contours of the forms, the folds of the garments, and a small amount of ornamentation applied to their robes. The most striking aspect of the woodcut is the emphasis the designer and the cutter have placed on the facial characteristics of the figures. Recalling in this way the Milanese interest in portraiture, the artist has focused on the eyes, nose, and mouth, providing each with individual characteristics, yet emphasizing the eyes by creating deep sockets and high cheekbones. The woodcut is framed by a four-piece passe-partout border designed in an arabesque style and cut in the white-on-black technique.

This little book also contains a portrait cut of Saint Afra, with a lion and dragon at her feet, illustrated here. Again, the facial features are emphasized, and particular skill is exhibited in the detailing of the eyes and nose of the saint. A cityscape in proper perspective contributes

Qua feguita la cõuerfiõe ð fãta affra moglíe ð Jtalíco cõte:e cõe
ãdo al deferto p volũta de dio e come li lioni la cõpagnozonoe fte
teno cũ lei p comãdamẽto ði fanctí:τ fimelmẽt cõe fãcto Apolõío
vefcouo de Breffa baptizo vna quantíta de bomíni.
Adõcha da fapere che aldẽdo affra moglíe de cõte italíco
cõe le fere baueuão mozto el fuo marito:ifpírata da dio fep
tete da cafa foua e vene doue er'a adrião che ftaua nel ãphiteatro:
p vedere la mozte ð li fácti martyri Fauftino e Jouita pche afpeta
ua pure de boza i boza chi foffino ðnozati e mozti. Quefta dða ef
fe doinãci ad adrião cõmicio a cridare e dire cũ vna grã voce. Et

to an overall balance of the compositional format. Simply cut with thick contour lines and
some shading, the image shows Saint Afra as well proportioned and sensitively portrayed. Mortimer suggests the woodcut of Saint Afra was executed by a different hand than the title cut of
the two saints, which she deems more coarsely executed.

4to. 198 x 142 mm, 8 x 5 ½ in. Pollard *Italian* 256.

Sander 2676. Mortimer *Italian* 181. Pasero 62.

48. *Legenda ouero passione
de li sancti martyri Faustino
e Jouita cavalieri de Christo.*
Brescia: Damiano and
Jacobus Philippum fratres,
4 April 1534

## 49  ROSENWALD 859: DYSON PERRINS 264

TITO GIOVANNI SCANDIANESE'S DIDACTIC POEM idealizing the chase, written in ottava
rima and illustrated throughout with woodcuts and initial letters, was first published in 1556.
The text in four parts describes the traditions of field sports, the pageantry of hunting, the hunt
with horse and hound, and the art of deer, boar, and rabbit hunting. This edition, published in
Venice by Gabriele Giolito et fratelli, also contains Giolito's translation of "Sfera," an essay by
Proclus, the fifth-century Neoplatonist and mathematician, its first translation into Italian.

   *Libri della Caccia* is illustrated with fifteen woodcuts in the text, some of which were

49. TITO GIOVANNI SCANDIANESE. *Libri della Caccia. Con la traduttione della Sfera di Proclo.* Venice: Gabriele Giolito et fratelli, 1556

originally designed for Lodovico Dolci's translation of Ovid's *Trasformazioni,* which Giolito printed in 1553. The work also includes woodcut headpieces and tailpieces, and foliated and historiated initial letters in three sizes. Giolito's large phoenix device appears on the title page of both works, and his smaller printer's mark of the phoenix rising is found on the verso of the final leaf. At the beginning of each part, Scandianese provides an eight-line "Argomento," the subject of the chapter, in verse, which is framed in a woodcut border illustrated with nymphs, grotesques, and satyrs, all of which are connected by an intertwined series of flowers, branches, urns, and vases. The detailed border is cut in outline, with parallel-line shading.

In the example offered here, the large cut is a well-composed and balanced image, set in classical times and illustrated with classical motifs. The woodcut shows Athena listening to Neptune, who gestures toward Arion, as he tells her the story of his union with Demeter and the creation of the first horse. Athena's costume and the figures of both Neptune and Arion are clearly articulated and expertly modeled by heavy shading. With the exception of the figure of Mercury winging its way across the sky, this is a very successful woodcut, pleasing in both its composition and its detail. The large historiated woodcut initial letter was designed to echo the story of Neptune and Demeter and is cut in the same style, and is of the same quality, as the larger narrative woodcut. This two-page opening is beautifully balanced, demonstrating the sensitive integration of text and image that is the strongest characteristic of the book.

By the mid-sixteenth century, the characteristics of the Italian woodcut had become well established. Reflecting the literary and antiquarian tastes of the previous five decades, classical subjects and images dominated Italian artistic output. The classical designs of woodcut images, which began appearing in the late 1490s, had become the standard, as had the heavy use of shading, which also began appearing in the Italian woodcut during the same period. By 1550 the techniques for creating perspective were universally understood by artists, designers, and woodcutters, an advancement that is seen clearly in the composition of Neptune and Arion.

4to. 207 x 144 mm, 8⅛ x 5¾ in. Pollard *Italian* 289.
Schwerdt 1, p. 207. Mortimer *Italian* 211.
Butler, "Gioloti and Their Press at Venice," pp. 83–107. Bongi I, pp. 485–87.

## 50   ROSENWALD 865: DYSON PERRINS 24

THE FIRST EDITION OF ARIOSTO'S TEXT for *Orlando furioso* was printed in 1516, after which it went through various editions, in ever growing numbers of cantos, until in 1532 the complete series of forty-six cantos was printed in Ferrara. The first illustrated edition, printed in Venice in 1530 by Zoppino, includes a crude portrait of the author and a series of undistinguished small woodcuts in the style of the 1491 Dante printed by Benalius and Capcasa. The Ferrara edition of 1532 is illustrated with a remarkable likeness of the author after a painting by Titian as well as a series of small cuts. The portrait was of such quality that it was used on the title pages of numerous editions of *Orlando* throughout the sixteenth century. In 1542

50. LUDOVICO ARIOSTO.
*Orlando furioso.* Venice:
Vicenzo Valgrisi, 1562

Gabriel Giolito of Venice printed an edition of *Orlando* and illustrated his book with larger woodcuts, which he placed at the head of each canto. Philip Hofer considers Giolito's production the "first worthwhile edition" and states that if it "were possible to give the artists who designed [the woodcuts] a name, he would rank among the best illustrators of the period." When Vincenzo Valgrisi first published an edition of *Orlando furioso* in 1556, he became the first printer to illustrate this text with full-page woodcuts. With its publication, Valgrisi entered a lucrative market and began competing directly with Giolito, who stopped publishing editions of *Orlando* in 1560, ceding the field to Valgrisi and to another Venetian printer, Giovanni Andrea Vavassore.

For his editions Valgrisi used an architectural title page containing the portrait of Ariosto after Titian and placed a large woodcut of his printer's device just below the text of the title. The text is illustrated with forty-six full-page woodcuts set within one of two border styles decorated with putti or grotesques. Two styles of woodcut borders frame the "argomento" that precedes each canto. All of these wood blocks were used repeatedly by Valgrisi, but Mortimer notes that there was some reworking of the original wood blocks before the publication of the 1560 edition. Valgrisi also decorated the book with historiated and foliated initial letters. A second, less elaborate printer's device appears twice, once on the section title page of "Annotationi et Avvertimenti" and again on the final leaf of the book.

The opening for canto 6, which is illustrated here, contains many of the elements Valgrisi used to decorate his text. The large narrative woodcut, the borders framing the large cut and each argomento, the historiated initials, and the arrangement in two columns of the text set in a small italic typeface combine to create a balanced and attractive typographical layout. Unfortunately, this arrangement is not used consistently throughout the entire volume, which may be the result of financial pressure caused by the competitive market in which this text was published.

All the cuts made for Valgrisi's book are cut in outline, with thicker lines used for contours and thinner lines and varied patterns of parallel lines for shading. In this image for canto 6, there are five separate events depicted in the block, beginning front forward and ending in a complex series of events depicted at the top. This running narrative format was first used by Giolito and became the standard for illustrating editions of *Orlando furioso* for almost two centuries. But unlike the clear narrative presented in the images created for Giolito, the compositions designed for Valgrisi, as well as for other later published editions of *Orlando,* are more difficult to decipher. Shaded areas dominate the cuts and the meaning of the narrative is obscured under the weight of the muddied figures and crowded spaces. To clarify the narrative, the designer labeled the figures and places in each image. Over time, the problem of discerning meaning was compounded by the wear to many of the wood blocks, which is apparent here in the weak printing of the border enclosing the large block.

The design of these blocks was originally attributed to Ariosto's friend Dosso Dossi, the painter, but modern historians have suggested, as did Hofer, that the woodcuts are "by a minor artist trained to draw intricate designs."

In addition to the bookplates of C. W. Dyson Perrins and Lessing J. Rosenwald, this copy also carries the bookplate of William Sneyd.

4to. 252 x 175 mm, 10 x 7 in. Pollard *Italian* 299.
Mortimer *Italian* 29. Hofer, pp. 27–40.

## 51   ROSENWALD 881: DYSON PERRINS 112

Ferdinando de' Medici established the Typographia Medicea, at the request of Pope Gregory XIII, and printed the first edition of the Gospels in Arabic, entitled *Evangelium sanctum*. Typographia Medicea was organized for the purpose of spreading Christianity by printing biblical texts and liturgical books in oriental languages. It also commissioned fonts of oriental type from some of the most important designers of the period, including the noted French printer Robert Granjon, who designed the typeface for this Arabic edition.

The *Evangelium* is illustrated with 149 woodcuts, using 67 repeated blocks. Fourteen of these blocks are signed with the monograms of the Florentine artist Antonio Tempesta and the block cutter Leonardo Parasole. Four of the blocks carry Parasole's initials alone. The opening pages of each of the Gospels are illustrated with a large headpiece in a leaf-and-vine pattern. The title page and all the text pages are ruled in a double-line border.

*51. Evangelium sanctum domini nostri Jesu Christi.* Rome: Typographia Medicea, 1591

On two occasions, Tempesta was commissioned to paint frescoes for the Vatican by Pope Gregory XIII, and his career in Rome lasted nearly forty years. He was trained by the Flemish artist Joannes Stradanus, whose influence can be seen in Tempesta's choice of everyday subjects and in his sweeping landscapes and urban backdrops. The opening illustrated here, Jesus at Jacob's Well Talking to the Samaritan Woman, reflects this influence, and although unsigned, it is undoubtedly Tempesta's work. The design is filled with Netherlandish characteristics, and its most charming quality arises from the artist's decision to make the Samaritan woman its focus. The casual setting and attitude of the figures, the flowing garments, the well-defined landscape, and the clearly delineated cityscape all speak to Tempesta's training and experience. The artist has created a brilliantly crafted woodcut, extremely well balanced in its composition and its space well defined and uncluttered. The perspective sweeps from right to left taking the viewer through all the elements of the Gospel story in a clear and complete manner.

Leonardo Parasole's ability to match in cutting the quality of Tempesta's design lifts the woodcut from the realm of craft into the realm of fine art. The Samaritan woman's finely contoured face and neck, the modest positioning of the left hand, the flowing garment and veil, and the strategic use of white space to highlight her hip and right leg, combine to present a sensuous and human quality. These artistic choices are rendered judiciously by the application of delicate shading and cross-hatching. These same qualities exist in many of the other woodcuts in the *Evangelium sanctum,* especially the image of John Evangelist, which is signed by both Tempesta and Parasole.

Folio. 336 x 230 mm, 13 ¼ x 9 in. Pollard *Italian* 319.
Mortimer *Italian* 64. Darlow and Moule 1636. Schäfer *Italian* 30.

## 52   ROSENWALD 889: DYSON PERRINS 537

JACOB WOLFF'S SECOND EDITION OF AESOP, his *Esopi appologi siue mythologi,* was printed in Basel in 1501 and is the first edition to contain the commentary of Sebastian Brant. It is organized in two parts, the first of which contains Rinuccio's translation of *Vita Aesop,* books 1–4 of Romulus's prose version of the *Fabula,* and books 1–3 of the metrical version of the Anonymous Neveleti. The second part includes the fables of Avianus, Rinuccio, and others, with additions and commentary by Brant. Part 2 is a collection of fables that Brant adapted from various authors.

Part 1 is illustrated with 194 woodcuts, copied in reverse from the originals that first appeared in Johann Zainer's Latin and German editions of Aesop's *Vita et fabulae* printed in Ulm, 1476–77. Most apparent of the stylistic choices in these woodcuts is the preponderance of white space in the sky and foreground. Also characteristic is the use of thick-line contours to outline the landscape and figures, the minimal shading and detail, and the addition of a simply designed tree and flowers to suggest a setting. As is the case with many of the better woodcuts from Ulm, the narrative is well defined and clearly reflects the text. Many of the woodcuts in the first part of the Rosenwald/Dyson Perrins copy are colored by a contemporary hand.

Part 2 is illustrated with 141 woodcuts that were first used by Jacobus Wolff for his circa 1489 edition of the *Vitae et fabulae* printed in Basel. They are much more complex in style than the cuts designed for Zainer in the mid-1470s and show an evolution in the content as well as the style of the woodcut over a twenty-year period. This new style of woodcut design that originated in Basel can also be seen in images that first appeared in Michael Furter's 1493 Basel edition of *Der Ritter vom Turn* and Bergmann von Olpe's 1494 Basel edition of Brant's *Das Narrenschiff*.

The distinctive images illustrating part 2 introduce contemporary content as an artistic element, something not seen in the Ulm blocks. Although the narrative remains simple, the images are more fully developed and clearly represent the life and customs of the sixteenth century. The Bird Catcher, on the left, depicts a figure dressed in contemporary costume, from the hat on his head to his britches and knee socks. The woodcut shows a trap and its construction, its placement in a clearing near a stand of trees, and the method used to control the trap, by pulling two ropes. The woodcut of the Ingenious Beavers, on the right, illustrates a different contemporary scene, including an allegorical representation of the vexing problem of river management that affected rural life at the time, as well as a different contemporary costume.

In addition to the development of content, the method of cutting the blocks here is very different from the examples designed in Ulm in 1476. The two woodcuts from the 1501 edition almost appear to be cut on metal. The careful execution of the thin, closely spaced parallel lines that shade the figures and the landscape appear at first glance to shimmer with movement,

52. A E S O P. *Esopi Appologi siue mythologi cum quibusdam carminum et fabularum additionibus Sebastiani Brant.* Basel: Jacobus Wolff de Pforzheim, 1501

an effect usually associated with metal cuts. Also, the landscapes of both images are more completely formed, with well-developed trees, clumps of tall grass, and a moving stream. These elements are also created by the methodical cutting of parallel lines in varying patterns of thicknesses and lengths. The designer and block cutter also took great care in depicting the lunging canine teased by the wily beavers. The facial features of both characters are well defined and contain individual characteristics.

Wolff also illustrated this edition with seven-line foliated black-ground initials and a fine series of four-line calligraphic initial letters. A portrait of Brant appears on the verso of the title leaf of part 2. The portrait is a fully realized rendering of the author kneeling in prayer, with his face clearly articulated and his gown, the landscape, and the distant city view all clearly defined and shaded.

Folio. 293 x 200 mm, 11½ x 8 in. Fairfax Murray 20.
Abrams 131. Heckethorn, pp. 62–68.

## 53   ROSENWALD 946: DYSON PERRINS 373

POPULAR LITERATURE OF THE LATE FIFTEENTH and early sixteenth centuries is notorious for its scarcity, and Pierre Gringore's works are no exception. Noted for his satire and humorous accounts of human relations, Gringore chronicles the battle for dominance in domestic affairs that pits vice against virtue. Editions of his earliest works are often known today in only one or two copies. This 1510 edition of *Le chasteau de labour* printed in Paris by Jean Tréperel is cited by Pollard as the ninth printed edition, but only two copies of any of these nine editions are in American libraries, this one at the Library of Congress and a copy of the 1505 edition at the New York Public Library. The Rosenwald/Dyson Perrins copy is incomplete, wanting leaf C¹, and it also has some minor paper repair to the title page.

The Parisian printer of Gringore's satire, Jean Tréperel, is best known for publishing popular tracts in the French language. Claudin suggests that Tréperel also edited many of these texts, playing a significant role in the development of early French literature. His imprint appeared in the early 1490s, but bibliographers find it hard to create a chronology of his work because many of his printed books were not signed. His son-in-law was the printer Michel Le Noir. It is thought that Le Noir, along with Tréperel's widow, kept the imprint alive after Tréperel's death in the early part of the sixteenth century.

Tréperel illustrates Gringore's *Le chasteau de labour* with the large woodcut of the Author in His Study, designed in a medieval style, and twenty images, including six repeats, that illustrate domestic life and labor in late medieval France. He also uses five black-ground woodcuts decorated in the criblé manner to illustrate the battle between vice and virtue in domestic and commercial affairs, common themes in French vernacular literature of the period. The woodcut on the left, the Workroom, is a good example of the half dozen images that depict the everyday life of the early modern tradesman. Cut in outline and highlighted with shading, this interior image is filled with information about the activities and division of responsibilities in an artisan's shop. Tools are displayed, work stations are defined, and the craftsmen's skills at pattern design, burnishing, and assembly are clearly articulated. The workroom is a well-defined interior space. The craftsmen, each given an individual facial expression, are attired in contemporary costume. Other images in this series of fully defined interior and exterior views of everyday life include

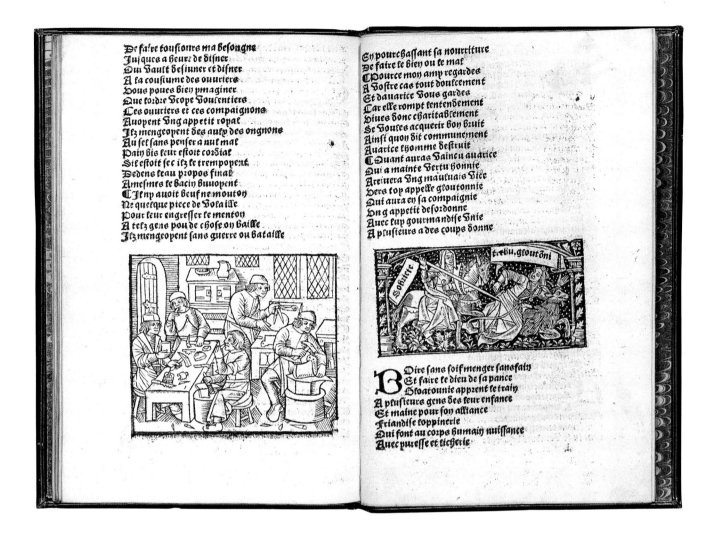

two market scenes, a second workshop scene, and a kitchen scene that shows a woman preparing a meal for a man seated at a table.

The black-ground woodcut on the right is from another of the series of images, representing the battles of virtues over vices, in this case Sobriety versus Gluttony. Other cautionary woodcuts in this format depict charity and envy, chastity and promiscuity, kindness and avarice, and humility and pride. The white-on-black style of these cuts, highlighted with dots, shading, decorated columns, and a floral foreground, creates a powerful contrast for representing the combat of good and evil.

This copy is from the library of Firmin Didot and is cited in the auction catalogue of June 1878, lot 178, as the "only known" copy, which is still true today.

> 8vo. 193 x 130 mm, 7⅝ x 5⅛ in. Pollard, Introduction to *The Castell of Labour*, p. 9.
> Firmin-Didot 1878. Hind, pp. 674–75. Claudin 2, pp. 511–16.
> Fairfax Murray *French* 205, for a description of the first edition of 1499.
> This edition not cited by Brunet or Rothschild.

53. PIERRE GRINGORE.
*Le chasteau de labour.*
Paris: Jean Tréperel, 1510

54. [SIMON BOUGOUYN]
*L'espinette du jeune prince,
conquerant le royaulme
de bonne renommee.* Paris:
Michel Le Noir, 1514

BOUGOUYN'S POEM WRITTEN IN THE FORM of a dialogue that describes the education of a prince was originally printed in Paris in 1508 by Vérard and was illustrated with sixty-five woodcuts from many sources. The second, 1514 edition was printed by Michel Le Noir, a Parisian printer whose imprint first appeared in 1492, and who continued to publish books well into the sixteenth century. Le Noir was Jean Tréperel's son-in-law and sometime partner, and on certain occasions both their names appear as printer of a book, one in the imprint and the other by his printer's mark. Because of the similarities in the type used, their habit of publishing titles without dates, and the fact that both their imprints reflect the choice of similar subjects, it is difficult to distinguish who actually printed which books. Scholderer has suggested that Le Noir, recorded as a stationer and bookseller in French records of the period, may not have been a printer at all, and that either Tréperel or other Parisian printers printed his books, using his device at the end of the text.

Le Noir's edition of Bougouyn is illustrated with fifty-two woodcuts, including the large representation of the Young Prince on the title page. Another large woodcut, Five Scribes, is on the verso of the title page. Three half-page woodcuts and forty-seven small images, cut in outline with some minor shading, are also included. Like Vérard, Le Noir took his woodcuts from various sources. The Young Prince had first appeared in his 1502 edition of *Beuves de Hanstone.* Two of the larger cuts with black borders are from Jean Bonhomme's 1484 edition of the *Destruction de Troie,* and many of the small cuts are from Vérard's 1485 edition of Caesar's *Commentaires* printed by Pierre Levet.

The Cultivators, illustrated here, is distinguished by its finely carved figures placed in a clearly defined rural setting. This image first appeared in Jean Bonhomme's 1484 edition of *Ruraulx Prouffitz,* and like so many French woodcuts, it captures a contemporary view of everyday life, where sowing seeds, tending the young growth, and harvesting the crop make up the cycle of the growing season and set the pace of life in the countryside. The woodcut contains significant contemporary content, from the style of medieval costume and farm architecture to the tools of the farmer's trade and the method of controlling root growth of a fruit tree.

The final leaf of Le Noir's *L'espinette du jeune prince* has his second printer's device, which Davies suggests was executed by the same artist who made devices for Vérard, Marnef, and Le Rouge. The image contains the name "M. Lenoir" at the top left, set next to a Moor's head with a black face and contrasting white turban. The Moor's head is set on a crown, poised above a shield in black, surrounded by a leaf-and-branch pattern, that floats above a setting of birds and flowers. This image is framed by a border carrying the motto: "My desire is to serve God so as to receive his lasting pleasure."

Purchased by Michael Wodhull from the sale of John Monro's library in 1792, this copy contains Wodhull's acquisition notes and was probably bound by him. The 1886 auction catalogue of the Wodhull library states that the binder's name was Johnson. The book brought £16.10 and was probably purchased by William Morris, who was an important buyer at the sale and whose bookplate is pasted to the front cover of this copy.

Both the 1508 and the 1514 editions of *L'espinette du jeune prince* are extremely scarce, and this is the only copy of either edition cited in an American library.

4to. 260 x 197 mm, 10¼ x 7¾ in. Fairfax Murray 62. Brunet 2, no. 1063.
Claudin 2, pp. 163 ff. Scholderer in BMC 8, pp. xxxv–xxxvi.
Davies 20, 21. Wodhull 478.

De tel il est/ et quil soit bien loyal  
Auoir le tiens vng bon cueur et royal  
Mais peu en a/ comme ie puis entendre  
Combien doit on de marchandise estendre  
Et estaller ou maint homme est deceu  
Trop y en a/ comme iay apperceu  
De vendre ainsi/ nest dung marchant le fait  
Mais dung trompeur/ et dung desloyal homme  
Ce qui ne vault que vingt soulz/ en effect  
Vendu sera/ plus de trente de fait  
Quest larrecin grande pour toute somme  
Cest tresmal fait/ que telz gens on ne assomme  
Du quau gibet tous pendre on ne les maine  
Car sont larrons qui est chose inhumaine  
Pour asseurer leur larcin et mensonge  
Tu les verras dieu follement iurer  
Penser ne fault que mon dit soit vng songe  
Mais dangier a que dieu ou feu les plonge  
Depuis denfer/ pour mieulx les coniurer  

Iurer ne font que dieu/ et pariurer  
Donner au dyable leurs corps aussi leurs ame  
Et desauouent les sainctz et nostre dame  
Mais que deuroit on faire de telz gens  
Les deust on pas par rigueur les pugnir  
Veu quilz sont tant actifz et diligens  
Dacquerir ors/ par larcin/ et argens  
Et regnier dieu pour dor eulx munir  
Certes on les deust du pays forbanir  
Et confisquer toute leur marchandise  
Pour droit en faire/ quoy que marchant dise  
Daultres marchans lon voit aller courir  
Par plusieurs pays et mainte seigneurie  
Pour marchander q voulroyent mieulx mou  
Et de laisser plus tost leurs biens pourrir (rit  
Que voulsit faire aulcune tromperie  
Telz gens qui naympent faire tel piperie  
Tout le clerge les deuroyent supporter  
Noblesse aussi deuroit leur droit porter  

### Des laboureurs

Apres marchans voy tous les laboureurs  
qui nupt et iour por nous nourrir trauaillet  
Ce sont les piedz qui en paine et douleurs  
Le corps soubstienent/ le plus souuet en pleurs  
yeulx/ bouche et bras nutz ne sen esmerueillent  
Les poures piedz/ de nupt et de iour veillent  

Pour mieulx nourrir les membres et le corps  
Cest le commun/ mon filz soys en recors  
Les piedz sont mys au lieu dhumilite  
Pres de la terre/ com tu peulx droit a loeil  
Sont laboureurs/ par leur subtillite  
A nous tous font tresgrant vtilite  
Car aux champs sont/ a vent/ pluye et soleil

## 55  ROSENWALD 963: DYSON PERRINS 357

55. *Le cuer de philozophie,*
*translated de Latin en*
*Francoys a la requeste de*
*Philippes le bel roy de France.*
Paris: Jean de la Garde,
[1515]

JEAN DE LA GARDE'S 1515 PRINTING OF *Le cuer de philosophie* is the second edition of this
collection of astrological and hermetic texts. It includes partial translations of *Placides
et Timoe, Sphaera mundi,* and *L'ordonnement du compost et du kalendrier* and was originally published
by Vérard in 1504. The translator is thought to be Simon Gréban, secretary to the comte d'Anjou,
comte du Maine. Both Vérard's edition and the 1515 edition printed for the bookseller La
Garde are illustrated with sixty-two woodcuts and diagrams, including repeats. It appears that
both editions carry many of the same images, including one of Adam and Eve that is decidedly
northern in style and differs from all the other woodcuts in the book.

This edition is also embellished with a series of foliated and calligraphic initial letters in
various sizes, many decorated with a variety of flourishes and fanciful facial profiles. The title
page is printed in red and black and is designed with a large grotesque letter *L* and the printer's
mark of Jean de la Garde, which also appears on the final leaf. This printer's device, similar to
one used by Simon Vostre, is of classical French design, featuring the Tree of Knowledge flanked
by two spotted foxes, standing on their hind legs, holding a shield cut with the printer's initials.

A ribbon at the bottom of the device carries the name "Jehan de lagarde." The background of the image is cut in criblé style and gives the impression that it was cut in metal.

The woodcut Cycle of Life illustrated here is one of the more complex images in the book. In a series of small spaces, the designer and cutter were able to accomplish a lot, from the depiction of the zodiac signs in the outer ring to the inner ring where more elaborate renderings illustrate the seasonal labors of man. The central image of the woman holding flowers against her womb suggests a fertility rite, while in the lower half of the circle, the man confronts the winter season in a barren landscape, comforted by fire alone. The clarity of each ring of the woodcut is enhanced by the amount of white space used to delineate the finely cut black lines. This black-on-white effect allows the parallel lines of the landscape and the scant shading of the garments to stand out and gives a dimensionality to the figures, especially those in the central roundel.

In a second layout illustrated here, La Garde decorates his text with nearly a dozen different initial letters of various forms and designs. This combination of large and small black-ground initial letters, early German style black-on-white letterforms decorated with large leaves and vines, calligraphic initials, and various other forms of grotesque letters, decorates the entire text. This rather striking layout, combining text and ornament, is one of the more beautiful aspects of the book and illustrates some of the letter designs common to French books of the period.

4to. 260 x 187 mm, 10¼ x 7⅜ in. Brunet 2, no. 438.

Fairfax Murray 97 (for the 1504 edition).

¶Comment leciel ⁊ la terre furent crees
et tous les autres elemens. ¶Chap.i.
**A**Ⴎ commencement crea Dieu le ciel et
la terre La terre estoit baine ⁊ buide et
tenebres estoiēt sur la face de labisme
⁊ les esperitz de nostre seigneur estoiēt
portez sur les eaues.

¶Lhystoire sur ceste partie de genesis
**A**Ⴎ cōmencement fut le filz. Et le filz
estoit le commencement par lequel et
en quel le pere crea le monde. Le mon
de estidit en trois manieres. Aucunes
fois est le mōde appelle le ciel empire pour sa net
tete Aucunesfois est il appelle sentable. Auctlesz
A.ii.

176

THE COLOPHON OF VOLUME I of this rare edition of the illustrated French-language Bible records its completion date as October 19, 1517, and although Antoine Vérard died in 1512, his name as printer is cited in the colophons of both volumes of the set. At the time Rosenwald purchased this edition, it was the only known copy. Other editions of the *La bible en francoiz* appear to have been printed during Vérard's lifetime, and, based on the collation and the placement of images, Ruth Mortimer dates the Hofer copy as about 1505 and suggests that it may be the second Vérard edition. The editions described in the Brunet, Macfarlane, and Fairfax Murray catalogues record the date of their respective copies as about 1510. As Mortimer explains, *La bible en francoiz* evolved from Guyard des Moulin's French translation from the Latin of Petrus Comestor's *Historia scholastica,* which Vérard published in 1498 under the title *La bible historiée.* By order of Charles VIII, Vérard expanded the text of *La bible historiée* into a full French translation of the Bible and in his later editions changed the title to reflect the expanded scope of the work.

The Rosenwald/Dyson Perrins copy of the 1517 French Bible contains 215 woodcuts, including repeated images. Many of the cuts are from Vérard's inventory of wood blocks, and were originally designed and used for such important French illustrated books as Jean Dupré's editions of *Cité de Dieu* printed in 1486 and Pierre Le Rouge's *La Mers des Hystoires* of 1488–89. Six of the woodcuts, repeated in ten examples, are nearly full-page in size, and thirty are about one-third of a page in size. The remaining are column cuts, which take about one-quarter of a column. The title page of each volume has a large initial letter *L* with a double grotesque head and Antoine Vérard's later printer's device, which Davies states he began using in 1489. The text is printed in lettres bâtardes and is decorated with foliated initials in the criblé style and grotesque and calligraphic initial letters in various sizes. The title page of volume I of the Rosenwald/Dyson Perrins copy is restored, and part of the text and image of the verso of folio ā¹ is in facsimile.

The large Adam and Eve in the Garden illustrated here is considered by Hind to be the most interesting cut to appear in the French Bible. Claudin states that it was created for Vérard for the 1498 edition of *La bible historiée,* but in a footnote Hind suggests it may have first appeared in *Mistère du viel testament* printed by Le Dru for Vérard about 1495. In any case, the references to the various editions cited above all mention this image, so it must have been used to illustrate the opening book of Genesis in all the known editions.

The woodcut Adam and Eve is a complex image that symbolizes the root of human existence and the fall from grace that marked mankind. The Garden of Eden, where man and animals coexist in peace, harmony, and abundance, is well defined and clearly depicted, as are the compositional elements—the Tree of Knowledge, the serpent in the guise of a woman, and the apple held by both Adam and Eve. The sudden embarrassment experienced by Adam and Eve as they recognize their nakedness is effectively rendered in the woeful expression on Eve's face and Adam's penetrating stare at his partner.

As stated, the original design of this image was executed in the 1490s, possibly by Vérard's Chief Designer, who was responsible for so many of the monumental woodcuts Vérard used in his illustrated books. The circular composition of the woodcut set at the base of the Tree of Life is an effective device to connect the story of the fall of Adam to future generations of mankind. The bodies of the figures are well proportioned and expertly modeled in pre-Renaissance style, with thick contours and some shading to give definition to the physical

*56. La premier [-second] volume de la bible en francoiz.* Paris: Antoine Vérard, 19 October 1517

form. Each has been given individual facial characteristics. The heads of the animals in the foreground are well defined and sympathetically carved. The background, alive with activity, is an amalgam of plants, trees, and birds. No line or contour seems to be wasted or lost in the complexity of the image.

Two volumes. Folio. 294 x 218 mm, 11 ⅜ x 8 ½ in. Hind 671.
Claudin 2, p. 482. See Mortimer *French* 59 for ca. 1505 edition.
See Brunet 2, no. 138, Macfarlane 156, and Fairfax Murray 38 for ca. 1510 edition.

## 57  ROSENWALD 999: DYSON PERRINS 329

THIS IS THE SECOND EDITION OF Raoul de Presles's French translation of Augustine's *City of God,* which first appeared in the famous Abbeville edition printed by Jean Du Pré and Pierre Gerard in 1486. The title page of Savetier's edition, printed in red and black, is decorated with a large initial letter *L* in the grotesque style, a small woodcut representing the evangelists, and an ornament composed of three shields with crowns. The second volume has the same large initial letter, with Jean Petit's printer's device in place of the other woodcuts.

The text and woodcuts of each title page are enclosed by a full-page architectural border of columns and vases with putti at the top holding a pediment with portrait roundels in each corner. In the center of the pediment, the hand of God holds a copy of Augustine's text. The bottom border also has portrait roundels in each corner, and in the center, a shield with a white horse in full trot. The border is cut with thick contours and is heavily shaded. It does not display the contrasts that black-ground or outline borders created in the earlier part of century do, but rather presents a cooler, less demonstrative introduction to the book. The border also carries the signature of the publisher Gaillot du Pré set above the bottom block. The same border was used by Savetier in his folio editions of Josephus and Livius also printed in 1530 and 1531.

Four woodcuts in five impressions and black-ground initial letters in three sizes, decorated in the criblé style, illustrate the text of this edition. One of the full-page woodcuts is very similar in design to the cut of the Joys of Paradise that first appeared in Vérard's 1493 edition of *Ars moriendi.* Goff writes that the recut image used by Savetier first appeared in Julyan Notary's 1503 edition of the *Golden Legend* printed in London and was used again in Paris by Wolfgang Hopyl in his Dutch-language edition of the same text printed in 1505. The woodcut passed into the hands of Hopyl's son-in-law Benoît Prevost and then to Savatier, who used it in this edition. The other three woodcuts in the book include an image of the author at work at his desk, which is ornamented with a flourish of acanthus leaves, an image of the Judgment Day cut in simple outline, and a full-page woodcut Christ Enthroned, which Goff suggests is original to this edition of the book.

The full-page illustration exhibited here, God Enthroned, is an excellent example of the development of the woodcut into the second quarter of the sixteenth century. The border, decorated with a leaf-and-branch motif and grotesques, is cut in a simple outline with a few flicks and parallel lines to heighten the forms. This simple pattern lacks the detail of the complex border structures that evolved from the manuscript tradition of the medieval period. The central panel of the woodcut, with God on the throne surrounded by the symbols of the four evangelists and a choir of angels, is well designed but offers little originality. Its compositional structure is formulaic. The image in the upper right, where the angel holds the banner of Mat-

thew, is likewise well designed and executed, but the presentation of the overall composition is flat and devoid of many of the artistic impulses that characterize the art of the French woodcut from earlier in the century.

This copy contains the inscriptions on the title pages of Lilias Lady Drummond and her son Patrick Lord Drummond, dated 1582, and the eighteenth-century engraved bookplate of Thomas Gage of Hengrave Hall, Suffolk. The binding appears to be English, probably from the late sixteenth century.

57. SAINT AUGUSTINE. *La Cité de Dieu.* Paris: Nicolas Savetier for Jean Petit, 22 April 1530, 7 June 1531

Two volumes. Folio. 333 x 213 mm, 13 x 8 ¼ in. Brunet 1, no. 560.
Goff *LCQ J* 5, no. 3 (May 1948), no. 32. Hodnett 2028.

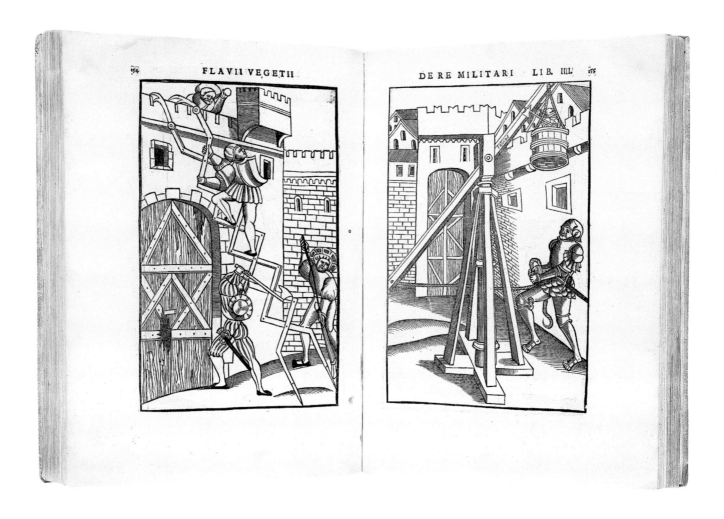

## 58    ROSENWALD 1005: DYSON PERRINS 428

58. FLAVIUS RENATUS
VEGETIUS. *De re militari
libri quatour.* Paris:
Christian Wechel,
23 August 1532

THE FIRST EDITION OF CHRISTIAN WECHEL's printing of *De re militari,* sometimes listed under the heading *Scriptores re militaris,* contains four texts, Vegetius's *De re militari,* Aelinus Tacticus's *De instruendis aciebus,* Sextus Julius Frontinus's *Strategematicon,* and Modestus's *De vocabulis rei militaris.* Wechel published this edition in Paris, August 23, 1532, about a month after his illustrated edition of Valturio's work of the same title appeared. All four of the texts in the Vegetius were edited by the noted French librarian and antiquarian Guillaume Budé, who became a counselor to the French monarchy. Wechel illustrated his edition with a woodcut on the title page showing a military encampment, a half-page woodcut of a soldier loading a canon; one diagram, and 119 full-page woodcuts depicting the art of war, the machinery of war, and some fantastic concepts for underwater assault. Two sizes of initial letters in outline also ornament the text. In Aelinus's *De instruendis aciebus,* Wechel uses creative patterns of individual letter fonts to show military formations and demonstrate troop movements.

Ruth Mortimer points out that the woodcuts for this edition are nearly identical to the cuts found in the edition printed by Heinrich Steiner in Augsburg in 1529. Steiner's images in turn were inspired by the woodcuts in Hans Knappe's edition printed in Erfurt in 1511, but are cut in reverse. The woodcuts exhibit northern characteristics, especially in the costumes and facial expressions of the figures, and are thought by Hugh Davies, in his description for the Fairfax Murray catalogue, to derive from either Swiss or Burgundian sources.

The two full-page woodcuts illustrated here are typical of the images that complement these texts. Their designs are purposeful in depicting the methods of war and providing significant content for the viewer. They show military machinery, inventions, assault tactics, weapons, and costumes of various orders of the military. The use of thick lines for both the contours and shading and the liberal use of white space harken back to the late medieval style and clearly demonstrate that these images are copies of much earlier designs. The skill of the woodcutter is not marked by innovation in this 1532 edition, which instead shows his ability to translate earlier designs in an efficient and predictable manner. Much of the history of the mid-sixteenth-century woodcut followed this formula, especially as more scientific and technical texts demanded clarity and precision from the image.

An inscription on the title page of this copy reads, "Ex dono P. Francisci de Nigro Genu-ens. Concionatoris Apostolice."

Folio. 333 x 215 mm, 11 ⅞ x 8 ½ in.
Mortimer *French* 486. Abrams 216. Brun 318. Fairfax Murray *French* 563,
and Brunet 5, no. 1162, both citing the 1534 edition.

## 59 ROSENWALD 1015: DYSON PERRINS 422

IN THIS WELL-ILLUSTRATED FRENCH-LANGUAGE edition of the *Comedies* of Terence, the text is presented in both prose and verse. Although scholars are not sure who did the trans-lations, it is probable that the prose text is by Guillaume Rippe and the verse by Gilles Cybile. A woodcut border in Venetian style, which Mortimer notes was copied from a design used by Jodocus Badius Ascensius for his Paris edition of Thucydides published in 1527, illustrates the title page. This 1539 Paris edition is printed in a lettre bâtarde typeface, set in two columns. The work contains a large woodcut repeated 4 times and 299 impressions of 155 half-page cuts originally used in the 1493 edition of Terence printed in Lyon by Jean Treschel. Hind considers the cuts used by Treschel as "the high watermark of book illustration in Lyon in the fifteenth century" and goes on to suggest that they were probably made by a German or Netherlandish designer. This copy has the printer's device of Guillaume le Bret on the title page; other copies are recorded displaying the shield device of Thielman Kerver.

The format of the half-page woodcuts includes one of a number of backgrounds illustrat-ing various set designs and curtained arches plus a cast of actors reciting their lines. Each of the characters is identified, by his or her name appearing above the curtained wall. The archi-tectural stage setting is often decorated with shell, floral, or harvest motifs. Perhaps the most remarkable aspect of the half-page woodcuts is the success that the designer and cutter achieved in bringing the action of the stage to life. The actors are not simply posing. They are made to be seen as expressing the action of the play in their posture, their movements, and their facial expressions. One has the sense that the designer of the images was intimately familiar with the works of Terence and translated this understanding to the designs he created.

A major difference between the 1493 printing of the woodcuts and the cuts as they appear here is the addition of a newly cut wood block of a city view. The view is placed either to the right or the left of each of the original half-page wood blocks to fill out the page and to create a balance between text and image. Otherwise, the images printed by Bossozel in 1539 are as they appeared in Lyon in 1493.

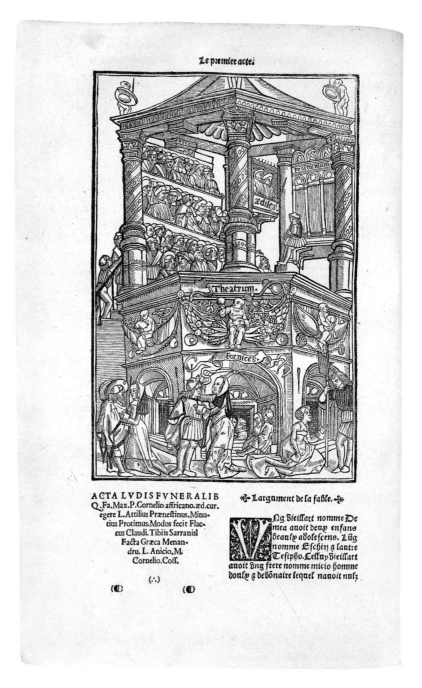

ACTA LVDISFVNERALIB
Q.Fa.Max.P.Cornelio africano.æd.cur.
egere L.Attilius Præneſtinus,Minu-
tius Protimus.Modos fecit Flac-
cus Claudi.Tibiis Sarraniſ
Faɕta Græca Menan-
dru. L. Anicio,M.
Cornelio.Coſſ.

(∴)

❧ L'argument de la fable. ❧

Vng vieillart nomme De
mea auoit deux enfans
beaulx adolefcens. L'ûg
nomme Eſchin̄ʒ e l'autre
Teſipħo.Ceſtuy vieillart
auoit vng frere nomme micio homme
doulx q debōnaire ſequel nauoit nuļʒ

59. Publius Terentius
Afer. *[Comoedia.] Le grant
therẽce en francoys tãt En Rime
que en Prose.* Paris:
Guillaume de Bossozel for
Guillaume le Bret, 1539

The large woodcut illustrated here shows the late medieval theater, complete with an interior view and a street scene in front of the theater where courtesans ply their trade. The interior view shows the stage with a lone musician to represent the orchestra, box seats, and three tiers of seats filled with theatergoers of various classes. The costumes are medieval in style, and their design demonstrates a developed skill at creating contour, shading, and motion, especially in the figures in the foreground. Some of the facial characteristics are repetitive but the designer varies the figures by emphasizing an individual's eye or nose and differentiating them by adding beards, varying hairstyles, or headdresses.

The architectural component of the composition is equally well executed, and demonstrates the designer's ability to use perspective as a tool. The delineation of the arched windows on the street level, the decorative elements on the façade and columns, and the ornamental design of the interior ceiling provide a nearly complete picture of medieval theater structure. The result of combining the architectural design, the interior view, the costumes, and the street life with the content provided in the half-page woodcuts is an enormous repository of historical information as well as a series of well-designed images.

This work is also decorated with initial letters in various sizes, cut either in the black-ground manner with a leaf-and-branch motif or in the criblé style. This copy contains a six-teenth-century inscription, "Collegi Bisuntini (Besançon) Societīs catalogo inscriptus, 1599" and the bookplates of George Goold, Walter Sneyd, and C. W. Dyson Perrins.

Folio. 320 x 210 mm, 12½ x 8¼ in. Brunet 5, no. 720.
Mortimer *French* 511. Goff *LCQJ* 33. Brun 309–10. Hind 609.
Claudin 4, pp. 67–77, for the 1493 edition.

## 60 ROSENWALD 1020: DYSON PERRINS 462

THIS VERY WELL-KNOWN COPY OF Olivier Mallard's 1542 printing of this Tory Book of Hours, originally thought to be from the library of Demetrio Canevari, contains eighteen large woodcuts, five small woodcuts, decorative woodcut borders, and woodcut initial letters after designs by Geoffrey Tory. A few of the woodcuts are highlighted with light watercolor, now dulled by cleaning, and a few corners have been repaired. The title page is printed in red and black and illustrated with a woodcut of Tory's *pot cassé* printer's device, set beneath the title

60. *Horæ in laudem beatissimę virginis Mariæ ad usum romanum.* Paris: Olivier Mallard, 1542

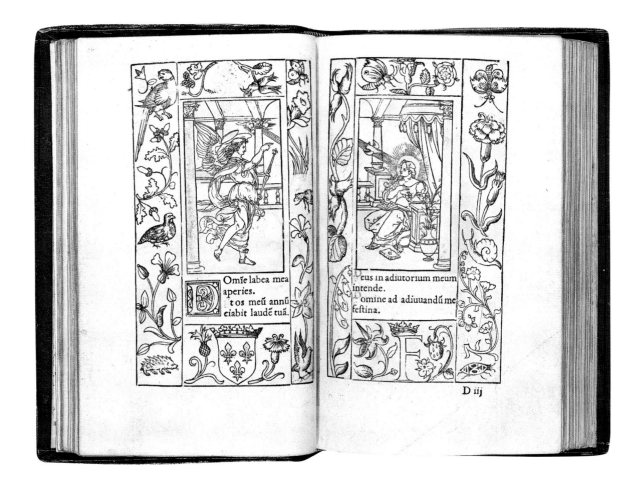

and above the imprint. Bernard designates this device as number 4 out of the ten devices Tory used throughout his career.

Mallard's 1542 title page is enclosed within a four-part woodcut border used by Tory in his 1527 octavo edition of the Hours for the Use of Paris. Based on woodcut designs first created for Jean du Pré in the 1490s, the border is in the medieval manuscript tradition. Du Pré's style relies on the use of flowers, birds, insects, and animals for decoration rather than the more formal architectural style that incorporates human figures, vases, and a branch-and-vine motif that developed during the early Renaissance period. A border based on various patterns created from thirty-two different border blocks encloses the text of every leaf in the book.

Alfred W. Pollard discusses the complicated combinations of woodcuts that make up this volume and tells us that the eighteen woodcuts that illustrate the text are from Tory's rare miniature (16mo.) edition printed in 1529. The borders and woodcuts illustrated here indicate the unique contribution Tory made to woodcut design during the first half of the sixteenth century. The artistic rendering of the borders and the pair of woodcuts of the Annunciation are defined not only by exceptional clarity of line and the precise use of shading but also by a skill at translation that transforms a well-known image into a tiny masterpiece. Tory created at least three other pairs of images of the Angel Gabriel and the Virgin for his various editions of the book of hours. But in the rendering first used in 1529 and again in this rare edition of 1542, the compositional structure, the physical representation of the figures, and the beauty of the two portraits present refinements that are only hinted at in his other designs. Here, Tory combines characteristics of Renaissance painting learned during his tours of Italy at the beginning of the century with the French manuscript tradition of animated borders decorating missals and prayer books.

This edition was unknown to Jacques-Charles Brunet and Auguste Bernard, and although Lacombe and Robert Brun cite it, their bibliographical descriptions are confusing enough to suggest that they never examined a copy. Pollard provides a more complete description, based on the copy he examined in the Bodleian Library. Philip Hofer and Otto Schäfer had copies of Mallard's 1541 edition, which contains different woodcut borders and illustrations. The Rosenwald/Dyson Perrins copy appears to be the only copy of the 1542 edition in an American library.

This copy is bound in full red morocco, lavishly tooled in gilt with floral design and interlaced borders, and decorated with a medallion of Apollo and Pegasus in the center of both boards. This binding and dozens like it were thought to have come from Demetrio Canevari, the Genoese book collector whose library was formed in the late sixteenth century. G. D. Hobson, however, summarizing research by Giuseppi Fumagalli, suggests that this particular binding is a forgery of a style originally created for Pier Luigi Farnese in the 1540s, and was probably made in the late nineteenth century by an Italian binder from Bologna.

8vo. 151 x 100 mm, 6 x 4 in. Lacombe 424.

Pollard *Bibliographica* I, pp. 114–22.

Mortimer *French* 305 and Schäfer *Parisian* 114, for descriptions of the 1541 edition.

Bernard, p. 45. Hobson, pp. 120–72.

## 61    ROSENWALD 1026: DYSON PERRINS 370

CHARLES ESTIENNE'S MONUMENTAL WORK on the human body was first published in Latin, followed by a French-language edition in 1546. Simon de Colines's 1545 Paris edition contains fifty-six full-page woodcuts in sixty-two impressions, initial letters in various sizes printed in black ground and decorated in the criblé manner, and scores of small woodcut diagrams of blood vessels, muscles, organs, and tissue. *Corporis humani* was printed by Simon de Colines, whose printer's device number 1 appears on the title page. The woodcuts in this well-documented work are attributed to the workshop of Geoffrey Tory, and seven carry the mark or signature of François Jollat. The first woodcut is signed with the initials *S R* for Étienne de La Rivière, who is also credited with having designed the smaller wood blocks depicting internal organs that are inset within the larger woodcuts.

The two full-page woodcuts of the female form illustrated here are representative of the images that Charles Estienne used to document his anatomical studies. They also display some of the characteristics of Renaissance woodcuts from the middle of the sixteenth century, which combine an emphasis on the artistic rendering of the human body with the exactitude demanded by modern scientific investigation. Though cloaked in classical format, with well-defined draperies, ornaments, and interior settings, these woodcuts are exceptional for the detailed anatomical descriptions they provide of the vascular and muscular systems of the human body.

61. CHARLES ESTIENNE.
*De dissectione partium
corporis humani libri tres.*
Paris: Simon de Colines,
1545

The design of the torsos of these two figures, with the abdomen exposed, are based on physical evidence observed during the dissection of the body. A close look reveals a white line where a smaller block, cut independently, was carefully fitted into the larger woodcut.

The sensual, almost erotic poses of the female figures highlight the influence of Italian Renaissance style on French design of the period. The sources of the female forms are engravings by Gian Giacomo Garaglio after drawings made in the late 1520s by Perino del Vaga, a student of Raphael. The designs of the male forms in the book are after drawings by Giovanni Battista Rosso, the Florentine painter who worked in France during the 1530s and who is known for his revival of Michelangelo's style. Rosso was one of the principal artists of the so-called Fontainebleau school, which developed around the decoration and artwork prepared for the chateau in Fontainebleau in the 1530s and later.

The robust proportionality of the female form is one of the most important characteristics of these mid-sixteenth-century images. The woodcuts are painterly in their conception, with the head, torso, arms, and legs fitting together in a coherent whole, and the rendering of the hair and facial features demonstrates a sensitivity for portraiture. The shading and cross-hatching that defines these figures is highly detailed. The white space boldly illuminates the muscles of the legs and torso, and the image beams with color and tone in the manner of an engraved print.

This copy is water-stained in the lower margin and has a repair to one leaf; a few wormholes penetrate the whole book, causing some minor defects.

Folio. 385 x 258 mm, 10 x 15 in. Brun, p. 198. Renouard *Colines,* pp. 409–10.
Bernard, pp. 223–26. Choulant, pp. 152–55. Norman 728.
Mortimer *French* 213 and Schäfer *Parisian* 78, for the 1546 French edition.

## 62   ROSENWALD 1060: DYSON PERRINS 404

THE FIRST EDITION OF OVID's *Metamorphoses* illustrated with woodcuts and borders attributed to Bernard Salomon contains 176 cuts, each set within one of twenty-six full borders. The text of the title page and the imprint are enclosed by an arabesque style border in the white-on-black manner. Ruth Mortimer describes Salomon's borders as "ranging from pure arabesque," to white-on-black or black-on-white, "to fully historiated" styles. The Lyon painter, sometimes referred to as Le Petit Bernard, worked closely with the book trade and, besides making designs for this 1557 edition of Ovid, is known to have produced images for a 1551 edition of Aesop and a 1553 edition of the history of the Bible. Salomon's images for this edition of Ovid were used many times over the next half-century and became models for other woodcut artists working in Lyon.

The small woodcut images of the Creation of Man and the Golden Age, both fully realized designs even in their small format, exhibit clearly defined figures freely drawn in contour lines with heavy shading. Classical references in the style of the period surround the focus of each —the laying of hands by the Creator on the left and the Tree of Life on the right—as they do in all of the woodcuts Salomon designed to illustrate Ovid's world view. One of the most distinctive design elements in these two pages is the ornamental border that Salomon had cut for this book. Certainly the parade of actors and grotesques at the top and bottom of the border on the right and the decorative motifs of candelabra and vase on the left are French in character

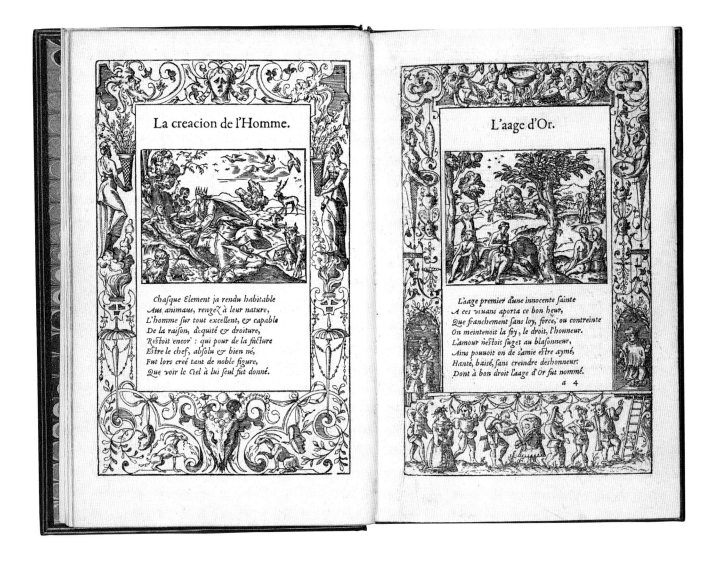

La creacion de l'Homme.

Chasque Element ja rendu habitable
Aux animaux, rengez à leur nature,
L'homme sur tout excellent, & capable
De la raison, d'equité & droiture,
Restoit encor` : qui pour de la facture
Estre le chef, absolu & bien né,
Fut lors creé tant de noble figure,
Que voir le Ciel à lui seul fut donné.

L'aage d'Or.

L'aage premier d'une innocente sainte
A ces viuans aporta ce bon heur,
Que franchement sans loy, force, ou contreinte
On meintenoit la foy, le droit, l'honneur.
L'amour n'estoit suget au blasonneur,
Ains pouuoit on de s'amie estre aymé,
Hanté, baisé, sans creindre deshonneur:
Dont à bon droit l'aage d'Or fut nommé.
a 4

and tradition, but the style is new. Overblown ornamentation, exaggerated heads, hanging crabs and fish, and the jeweled quality of the interlocking pieces represent a formalization of the Renaissance style and reflect an aspect of the burgeoning school of mannerism that was developing in Fontainebleau and influencing artists all over France.

62. OVID. *La metamorphose figurée.* Lyon: Jan de Tournes, 1557

8vo. 158 x 103 mm, 6¼ x 4⅛ in. Mortimer *French* 403.
Fairfax Murray *French* 420. Brun 276. Cartier 376.

## 63   ROSENWALD 1114: DYSON PERRINS 481

MANY EDITIONS OF *QUAESTIONES NATURALES,* a collection of works by Aristotle, Hippocrates, Theophrastus, and others, were printed during the incunable period. Matthias van der Goes published two editions in Antwerp before his death in 1491, but neither one was illustrated. In 1492, Govaert Bac married Van der Goes's widow and continued the business for about twenty years, using the first printer's supply of type and some of his wood blocks. This 1505 edition of the *Quaestiones naturales* is the first edition of this text printed by Bac.

**63. ARISTOTLE.**
*Quaestiones naturales.*
Antwerp: Govaert Bac,
ca. 1505

Two large woodcuts and a very attractive printer's device on the final leaf illustrate Bac's edition. The woodcut on the title page, a Scholar in the Tree and a Dreamer Lying on the Ground, was copied with variations from one used by Bellaert in his 1484 edition of Jacobus de Theramo's *Der Sonderen Troest,* printed in Haarlem. Hind thinks the image was originally created by the Haarlem Designer, who worked for Bellaert and who probably moved to Antwerp with Gerard Leeuw around 1486. Bac used the block again in 1511 for his edition of *Den Herbarius in dijetsche.*

The Writer Offering His Book to the Prince, illustrated here, was first used by Bac in his edition of Albertus Magnus's *Liber aggregationis* printed in 1498. M. F. A. G. Campbell attributes the cuts to the Third Antwerp Woodcutter and describes his style as "frightful." On closer analysis, the cuts offer an important reminder of the difficulty both designers and woodcutters faced in creating perspective before Dürer revolutionized the art form. In this woodcut, all the architectural elements of the interior are askew, including the bookshelves, the circular window, the ceiling and arch, and the windows to the right. The woodcutter attempted to create proper relationships but was simply not able to successfully calculate the proportional space effectively. Yet if one looks to the floor, it moves gracefully from front to back, and the lines of the two central figures are well drawn and shaded, though not all the faces are well delineated.

The printer's device that Bac used around 1500 is a playful design depicting two naked boys holding a birdcage, with the shield of Antwerp hanging from a rung and the initials *G B* set in the lower corners. As in the other cuts in the book, the perspective is weak, but the shading and black background create a vivid contrast to the cage, the shield, and the two figures.

4to. 178 x 140 mm, 7 x 5½ in. Goff A–1037. Rosenwald *Livres anciens* 102.
Thienen 274. Nijhoff-Kronenberg 1, no. 140. Campbell 182. Conway, pp. 309–11.
Nijhoff 2, p. 1, figs. "Anvers" 1–13.

## 64    ROSENWALD 1119: DYSON PERRINS 504

HENRICK ECKERT'S PRINTING OF THE first edition of Henricus van Santen's rare little devotional work, completed in about 1510, is illustrated with two woodcuts and two decorated initial letters, one in a manuscript style and the other in black ground. The work is printed in black letter, with red paragraph marks and some responses underlined in red. Henrick Eckert of Homburg began his printing career in Delft around 1498 and moved to Antwerp shortly thereafter. He appears to have succeeded the Delft printer Christian Snellaert, as Eckert used some of Snellaert's type and ornaments in the books he printed in both Delft and Antwerp.

64. HENRICUS VAN SANTEN. *Die collaciē vander eewaerdigē.* Antwerp: Henrick Eckert van Homberch, ca. 1510

Most of his publications were devotional tracts like this one, but he also printed some law and medical books as well as some works of literature and romances.

The woodcut on the title page is a familiar cut where Christ, dressed in full regalia and holding a globe with a cross at the top, stands with his right hand raised in the sign of peace. It is cut in the medieval style, with a background of white space, thick contours, and some heavy shading defining Christ's robe. The same image was used in an anonymously printed edition of Thomas à Kempis, probably published in Leiden in 1505.

On the verso of the title page is a more interesting cut that shows the risen Christ reaching into the mouth of hell and offering salvation to repentant figures, the first two of whom possibly represent Adam and Eve. The large opening to hell, a well-crafted design that resembles a beast with piercing eyes and a large bulbous nose, fills nearly half the image. This motif, with variations, derives from the block book tradition, especially the visions of hell that appear in editions of the *Apocalypse.* The image of a rat running out of the mouth of hell adds a playful touch.

This woodcut also displays a few of the stylistic advancements seen in Nederlandish images at the beginning of the sixteenth century. The introduction of an architectural element in the background, the limited use of white space, and the distinctive facial characteristics of Christ and the figures of the saved are sixteenth-century artistic elements that enhance this well-known medieval image. Wouter Nihoff illustrates Christ in Hell in his *Supplement* and suggests that it was first used by Eckert in his 1507 edition of Saint Bonaventure's *Boek van die vier oeffeningen,* printed in Antwerp.

8vo. 135 x 90 mm, 5¼ x 3½ in. Nijhoff-Kronenberg 1, nos. 1855, 2012.
Rosenwald *Livres anciens,* 112. Nijhoff 2, pp. 2–3, figs.
"Anvers" 33–34. Nijhoff *Supplement,* fig. xix.

## 65   ROSENWALD 1135, 1050: DYSON PERRINS 505

In 1516, Peter de Keysere printed what appears to be the second edition of this neo-Latin poem on the birth, passion, and resurrection of Christ by the thirteenth-century English chaplain to Queen Eleanor, John of Hoveden. The poem runs more than four thousand lines, written in rhyming quatrains. The original title on a manuscript of this work in the British museum is *Philomela, sive meditacio de nativitate, passione, et resurrectione Domini nostri Jesu Christi,* and the poem is often referred to as *Philomela.*

The first edition was thought to have been printed in Antwerp by Matthias van der Goes between 1485 and 1490, but Gerard van Thienen, in his study of early printing in the Low Countries, suggests that it may actually have been printed in Louvain by Aegidius van der Heerstraten between 1486 and 1488. This 1516 edition is known in only three copies, this copy being the only one in an American library. Peter de Keysere, or Petrus Caesar, as he is referred to in the imprint, was a bookseller and printer in Ghent, whose books appeared from 1516 to 1547. He produced much of his work for the Ghent booksellers Victor van Crommbrugghe and Victor de Dayn.

The *Carmen rithmicu* is printed in gothic type with the line capitals lightly highlighted with a sepia wash. A lovely woodcut of the nativity, designed with a rich interior background of the stable and well-designed and carved figures of Mary and Joseph, ornaments the title page.

The cut is heavily shaded, giving the small image clear contrasts, and it evokes a feeling of serenity appropriate to the scene. On the verso of the title page is a hand-colored woodcut of Mary standing on a crescent moon, holding the infant Jesus in her right arm. It is a well-known image based on a verse from the Apocalypse of Saint John, describing his vision of the Madonna and Child. This striking portrait depicts the Virgin with long blond hair, dressed in flowing pink and blue robes, and wearing a crown of precious stones. A halo surrounds her entire form and the corners of the woodcut are decorated with different types of flowers, also hand colored. This image of the Virgin, which appears in Peter de Keysere's edition of Hoveden, was copied by the Delft printer Corn. Henricz. Lettersnijder about 1520 and used as his printer's device.

    The woodcut illustrated here appears on the final leaf of Hoveden's poem. Saint Stephen is portrayed wearing a dalmatic over a long tunic to indicate his position of deacon in the church. He holds the palm of martyrdom in his right hand and a stone, the instrument of his death, in his left. This remarkable work of originality and craftsmanship is designed and cut with such delicacy that it appears to be cut on metal. The design of the sleeves of both the tunic and the blouse and the folds at the neckline are rendered with the style and grace of a painter with a palette full of colors. The oval of Saint Stephen's face is like nothing we have encountered before, with its deep brows and contoured mouth and chin. Its whiteness contrasts sharply with the black and white lines of hair that seems to be woven and perfectly set in place. The architectural background and the starry space behind is cut in white on black and introduces a dreamy quality to the portrait of the martyred saint. All these effects are heightened by the

65. JOANNES HOUDEN.
*Carmē rithmicū de passiōe
Dño.* Ghent: Peter de
Keysere, [1516]

*bound with:*

*Calendarium fratrum
minorum.* Toulouse:
J. Colomies, ca. 1550

applied red wash that decorates the dalmatic and lends a dramatic touch to a wonderful wood-cut portrait.

Bound with Hoveden's poem is *Calendarium fratrum minorum,* an eight-leaf calender of feast days prepared for the Franciscan order at Albi for the year 1551. It was printed by Jacques Colomies, who, along with his son, maintained a printing business in Toulouse for over forty years. He printed numerous religious tracts and works on language and was noted for his zeal in promoting the Catholic faith. He printed his *Calendarium* in red and black throughout and illustrated it with a woodcut on the title page that depicts Saint Francis receiving the stigmata. Some of the instruments of Christ's crucifixion, including the Hill of Calvary in the background and the crown of thorns, enclose the entire scene. Cut in a simple style of the medieval period, the figures highlighted with shading but without embellishment or careful attention to detail, this image appears to be a copy of the woodcut of Saint Francis that Jan van Westfalen used in about 1500 in his edition of Dirk van Munster's *Spieghel der kestenen menschen* printed in Louvain. This rare Toulouse imprint is thought to be the only copy in an American collection.

These two books are bound together in nineteenth-century straight grain morocco, and the book carries the label of the bookbinder James Faulkner and the bookplates of J. B. Inglis, C. Inglis, Prince Oettingen Wallerstein, C. W. Dyson Perrins, and Lessing J. Rosenwald. On the rear pastedown there is a one-by-two-inch woodcut of the Mass of Saint Gregory, probably removed from a fifteenth-century book and pasted into this copy.

Together two volumes bound in one. 8vo. 125 x 90 mm, 5 x 3 ½ in.
Nijhoff-Kronenberg 1142. Rosenwald *Livres anciens* 128.
Goldschmidt, pp. 31–33. Nijhoff 2, pp. 34–35, figs. "Gand" 1–13.
Thienen 1350, 594. Holtrop, p. 50, plate 120.

## 66  ROSENWALD 1154: DYSON PERRINS 487

WOODCUT DESIGNS BY LIEVEN DE WITTE illustrate the first edition of Guilielmus de Branteghem's compilation of stories from the New Testament. The title is set within a full-page border, and the book is illustrated with 184 half-page woodcuts, 43 small woodcut vignettes, and 44 border pieces, including repeats. These wood blocks were used again in numerous editions of the Bible and Bible histories, including Miles Coverdale's revision of William Tyndall's New Testament printed by Matthaeus Cromme in 1538. Lieven de Witte was a painter, architect, and designer of woodcuts and stained glass whose career spanned the middle half of the sixteenth century. His images for Branteghem's *Life of Christ* were to become his most famous series of woodcuts. A Dutch-language edition of *Jesu Christi vita,* published simultaneously with this Latin edition, contains four additional images.

The woodcut used for the opening of John 7 illustrates De Witte's skill at creating a fully realized composition that combines a highly detailed background with the narrative of John's Gospel story. Hollstein entitles this image Christ with His Doubting Brothers in Galilee, and it presents a simple rendering of the narrative of Christ uttering the words, "My doctrine is not mine, but his that sent me." The woodcut captures a world in motion around Christ as he preaches to those who are about to judge him. This picture of a world rich in landscape and architectural detail portrays a city on the sea and evokes the lives of its inhabitants. The wood-cutter successfully translates De Witte's composition by cutting the wood block with a freedom of line that suggests detail by the flick of the knife, investing the image with the liveliness, motion, and activity true to its design.

On the right are two border blocks representing the Soul of Lazarus and the Chains of Hell. Although the upper block is quite conventional in its depiction, the lower block is an image of some originality. It almost presages Blake in its design, with the contorted, oversized figure dominating the space and a fan of fire splayed in the background. The grotesque figures pulling at the chains are as muscular as the central figure, and the positions they hold reveal a sensitive understanding of the human form in motion. As in all of the woodcuts in De Witte's series, the finely cut lines, the delicate shading, and the classical costume suggest an Italian influence on a highly developed Flemish passion for detail.

66. GUILIELMUS DE BRANTEGHEM. *Jesu Christi vita, iuxta quatuor Evangelistarum narrationes.* Antwerp: Matthaeus Cromme for Adriaen Kempe de Bouchout, 24 December 1537

8vo. 155 x 95 mm, 6⅛ x 3¾ in. Nijhoff-Kronenberg 486.
Rosenwald *Livres anciens* 153. Delen 2, pp. 55–57.
Hollstein 53, "Lieven De Witte," fig. 87.

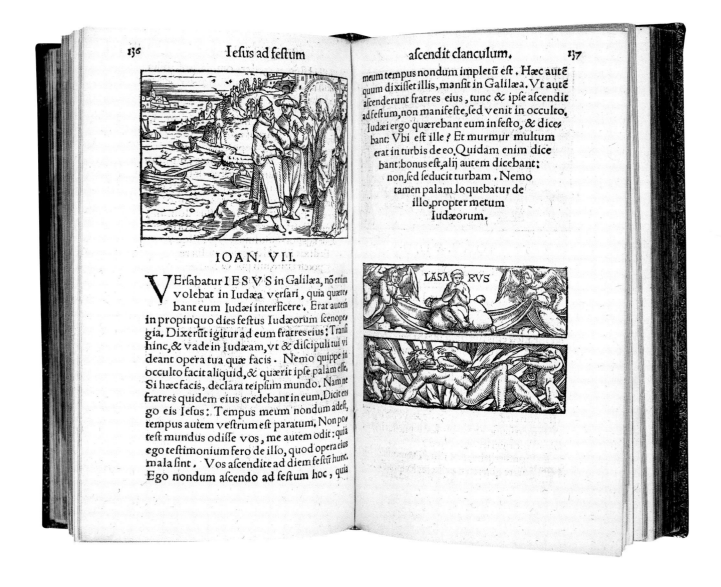

C HRISTOPHER PLANTIN'S 1572 EDITION of the *Humanae salutis monumenta* is one of two
books with engravings that Rosenwald purchased at the Dyson Perrins sale. Arias Montanus's *Humanae salutis monumenta* appeared at the same time that Plantin was finishing the
printing of the final volumes of his monumental *Biblia polyglotta*. It contains seventy-two engraved plates, with sixty-five designs by Pierre van der Borcht IV and seven by Crispin van
den Broeck. Thirty-two of the designs were engraved by Abraham de Bruyn and Pieter Huys,
thirty-eight by Jan and Jerome Wierix, and one by Crispin van den Broeck. One engraving
is unsigned. All of these designers and engravers were part of Plantin's stable of artists who designed and engraved images for him during his peak years from 1570 to his death in 1589.

The Virgin and Elizabeth, illustrated here, was engraved by Pieter Huys after a design
by Pierre van der Borcht, both artists' initials appearing at the bottom corners of the plate.
Van der Borcht was a painter, engraver, and draftsman who was a student of Pierre Bruegel.
Many of his engravings, like the paintings of his teacher, illustrate popular subjects, especially
the social relations of different classes of people celebrating at country fairs, at weddings, and
on sacred holidays. This predilection for the commonplace is apparent in the plate of the Virgin
and Elizabeth, which captures their emotional meeting and focuses on their rush to embrace.

67. BENEDICTUS ARIAS
MONTANUS. *Humanae
salutis monumenta.* Antwerp:
Christopher Plantin [1572]

The image is further enhanced by the heavily designed garments and the extremely detailed view of the city in the background. Though the subject is classical, the view resembles a mid-sixteenth-century townscape and reflects the Dutch and Flemish tendency to use contemporary content to embellish pictorial narratives.

This plate offers a wonderful example of how cutting images on metal offers the artist the opportunity to create details and tones not possible when working with wood. The first quality that leaps off the plate is the extensive use of cross-hatching to create subtle tones and rich colors in the costumes of the two women. Cross-hatching was not unknown to the wood-cutter, but the very fine lines that appear in the architectural setting—visible in the buildings in the right background—demonstrate how the burin can cut or scratch the surface of the metal plate to create closely spaced series of line patterns. The extensive detail, the richness of the tones and colors, and the ability to create very fine lines to emphasize a form or a facial feature, drew sixteenth-century artists to the intaglio process. Intaglio remained the dominant medium for artists for three centuries.

This copy is bound in nineteenth-century straight grain morocco and has the arms of J. Gomez de la Cortina on both boards, as well as his bookplate, and a note in ink that states that the book was purchased at the sale of the Marquis de Morante in 1872.

8vo. 160 x 100 mm, 6¼ x 4 in. Brunet 1, nos. 421–22. Hollstein 4, p. 8. Rosenwald *Livres anciens* 188. Voet 1, pp. 62–65. Funck, pp. 181–203.

## 68   ROSENWALD 1207: DYSON PERRINS 512

THE FIRST EDITION of Nicolas de Nicolay's travels to Turkey, North Africa, and Asia Minor was published in a folio edition in Lyon in 1567. Sixty full-page woodcuts designed by the author and cut by Louis Danet illustrate the volume. In 1576, Guillaume Silvius of Antwerp printed a quarto edition with sixty plates reduced in size from the folio edition. Many of these wood blocks carry initials thought to belong to woodcutters Anthony Van Leest, Hans Cressone, Corneille Muller, and perhaps Gérard Jansen van Kampen. F. W. H. Hollstein attributes the cuts with the initials *AVL* and many of the unsigned cuts to Van Leest. The 1586 edition printed by Arnould Coninx contains images from the same blocks used in 1576 by Silvius, with one addition, making a total of sixty-one woodcuts.

Nicolay's designs concentrate on the dress and costumes he saw on his travels, thus providing considerable information for European viewers about the various strata of Turkish, Armenian, Greek, and North African societies. He focused mostly on women but also included images of the military, merchant classes, and religious groups as well as peasants. A few of his images of women, renderings meant to pique interest in the exotic nature of the East for his European readers, are particularly revealing, and suggestive. His designs contain no architectural or landscape backgrounds and are decorated only by a series of arabesque style borders of considerable charm. The woodcut illustrated here, the Turkish Mother and Her Children, is typical of the quality of the designs Nicolay created for his book. The figures are well proportioned and ideally spaced so the costumes of mother and children could be developed in full. The highly ornamental designs of the children's costumes are carefully drawn, though the right foot of the young boy is poorly positioned, suggesting the difficulty the cutter had fitting the foot into the frame.

76

꒐§Femme Turcque menant ſes enfans.

68. NICOLAS DE NICOLAY.
*Discours et histoire véritable
des navigations, pérégrinations
et voyages, faicts en la Turquie.*
Antwerp: Arnould Coninx,
1586

The skill of the woodcutter can be seen in the facial characteristics and hands of the figures, renderings accomplished by the application of very fine lines and delicate shading. The folds of the head wrap and the gown of the mother's costume are also well cut, and the use of cross-hatching and fine parallel lines effectively conveys a natural draping of the material. But it is the costumes of the young girl and boy that best demonstrate the state of the woodcut during the last quarter of the sixteenth century. The complex floral patterns are delicately cut and highlighted with an over-layer of parallel lines that brings a texture to the garments. This technique, along with the amount of cross-hatching used by the cutter, resembles the intaglio process and suggests that the woodcutter is applying methods developed on copper to embellish his wood block. Certainly by 1576, when this block was made, the intaglio process was beginning to supersede the woodcut as the preferred method for creating images. This example shows the high degree of skill the block cutter exercised to execute this very detailed image.

This copy contains the bookplate of Walter Sneyd.

4to. 186 x 155 mm, 8¼ x 6¼ in. Brunet 4, no. 67.
Rosenwald *Livres anciens* 197. Funck 368. Hollstein 10, p. 43.

THE 153 ILLUSTRATIONS IN THIS EDITION of Hieronymus Natalis's *Adnotationes* are considered to be one of the high points of Flemish engraving during the Renaissance period. They were first executed in 1593 and issued with only five preliminary leaves of text under the title *Evangelicae historiae imagines*. The 1594–95 edition printed by Martinus Nutius includes 595 pages of text, inspired by the life of Ignatius of Loyola, most of which was written by Natalis, finished by Cardinal Ximenes. An engraved architectural title page with representations of the four evangelists and four fathers of the church, dated 1594, is followed by a second architectural title page illustrating Christ in the Heavens, set above the title *Evangelicae historiae imagines* and dated 1593. A colophon on the verso of the final leaf is dated 1595.

The 153 full-page engravings are based on stories from the New Testament. Most of the designs are by Bernardino Passeri, a Roman painter and engraver, and six are after drawings by Marten Vos, the noted Antwerp painter and draftsman. Passeri enjoyed the patronage of Cardinal Ximenes who, along with Christopher Plantin, was intimately involved in the publication of this book. In a monograph published in 1985, Maj-Brit Wadell claims that the engravings are based on a series of anonymous ink drawings found in the Bibliotheca Nazionale in Rome, which are attributed to the Italian artist Livio Agresti.

Though the designs are for the most part Italian in inspiration, the engraving of the plates was executed by the most important Flemish artists of the period, including Carl van Mallery and the two families of artists Anton, Jerome, and Jan Wierix and Adrian and Jan Collaert. This fabled group of engravers worked for Plantin before the printer's death in 1589, as well as for other important Antwerp publishers, including Phillip Galle and Hans Liefrinck, to name only two. The engravings in this text are a testament to the contributions this group of Antwerp artists made to the art of engraving at the end of the sixteenth century.

The image of Christ Descending into Hell by Anton Wierix after a design by Passeri illustrates the characteristics that distinguish the work of these masters. The composition of the fully developed cityscape and sky is constructed to create a very gradual slope from the center of the image to the borders. The church tower and hills sit directly above the image of Christ and Lucifer, creating a deliberate vertical thrust in contrast to the soft round layers of the landscape and the circles of hell. Yet it is not the design that makes this image so powerful. It is the exquisite detail that results from the flexibility that the copper plate offers the artist in rendering clarity and tone to the image. This relative freedom to apply very fine lines of varying depths to the plate, a practice impossible with the woodcut, controls the amount of ink that is transferred to the paper during the printing process and offers a variety of possibilities for varied levels of darkness, light, and detail.

69. HIERONYMUS NATALIS. *Adnotationes et meditationes in evangelia in sacrosancto missae sacrificio toto anno leguntur.* Antwerp: Martinus Nutius, 1594–95

Folio. 320 x 210 mm, 12 ½ x 8 ¼ in. Brunet 4, no. 18.
Rosenwald *Livres anciens* 198. Funck, pp. 366–67. Wadell, p. 70, fig. 129.

A. Christi anima nulla mora interposita, venit in Limbum Patrum.
B. Omnium sanctorum Patrum animæ, animam IESV supplices venerantur.
C. Anima latronis, paulo post mortui, portatur ab Angelis ad Limbum.

D. In Limbo infantü nulla pars huius lætitiæ.
E. E Purgatorio multæ animæ liberantur, quod significant radij lucis inde ad limbum Patrum prodeuntes.
F. In inferno inferiori Lucifer cum suis, ipsoque Iuda grauiter fremit.

## 70  ROSENWALD 1269: DYSON PERRINS 320

COMPILED BY ANTONIO DEL RINCON, Antonio de Medina, and Francisco de Ledesma, *Monumenta ordinis minorum* contains documents, rules, and privileges regulating the Franciscan order in Salamanca. This copy, printed by Juan de Porras on both vellum and paper, contains two manuscript statements of authenticity signed by Petrus del Enzina, public notary of Salamanca. Goff writes that "The legal representative of the Order, Antonio de Medina, appeared before the notaries to testify to the truthfulness of the text and undoubtedly had this copy with him at the time."

Juan de Porras was a well-known bookseller and printer whose activity in the book trade is first documented in 1491, when he published an edition of *Siete partidas* that was printed in Seville by Meinard Ungut and Stanislas Polonis. In 1494, in partnership with Rodrigo de la Pesara, he published an edition of the *Missale auriensei* in Monterrey, for the local clergy. After 1500 he established a press in Salamanca and continued to issue books until 1516. Many of the titles he published were issued anonymously, and Konrad Haebler suggests that even those that carry his imprint may have been printed by the German printer Hans Gherling, whom he first met in Monterrey.

70. *Monumenta ordinis minorum.* Salamanca: Juan de Porras, July 1506

His *Monumenta ordinis minorum* is illustrated with one full-page woodcut of the Crucifixion, two large initial letters, and two sizes of foliated initial letters. The image of the Crucifixion is cut in outline with some shading to the garments, but without background or embellishment. It seems to be a copy of a woodcut that appeared earlier in Juan Varela de Salamanca's edition of Durandus, printed in Granada in 1504. The initial letter opening the second volume is a woodcut of Saint Francis receiving the stigmata, set within a large letter *D* cut in the criblé manner and embellished with a branch-and-vine pattern. The image of Saint Francis is cut in fine line with some shading, and the letter *D* is outlined with an alternating pattern of decorated half-rounds.

The woodcut of the initial letter *S* illustrated here is a variation on similarly styled letters used by Pedro Brun and Juan Gentil in Seville in the 1490s. They differ in that the two segments of the letter *S* are in the form of fish meeting at the center of the initial, rather than half-round designs cut in outline without embellishment. This highly stylized letterform is cut in black ground and decorated with acanthus leaves that mimic the shape of the fish. The deep black of the contours and central ovals is set against the translucent white of the vellum, creating a richness in the image that illuminates the finely cut lines and shading of the fish scales. As in other examples of Spanish woodcuts of the period, the distinctive image reflects the influences of Arabic patterns and design.

Three parts in two volumes. 4to. 200 x 140 mm, 8 x 5¾ in.
Norton *Descriptive Catalogue* 478. Palau y Dulcet 5, p. 235.
Goff *LCQJ* 72. Lyell, p. 250.
Haebler *Early Printers,* pp. 74–5, fig. 20.

## 71  ROSENWALD 1270: DYSON PERRINS 310

THIS RARE EDITION OF GUILLERMUS PARISIENSIS'S *Postilla,* printed by Georg Coci in 1506, is illustrated with sixty-six woodcuts, including repeats. All but two of the cuts are small designs in outline that function as chapter headings for the commentary on Christ's life. Black-ground initial letters designed in various floral patterns and a printer's device also embellish the text. This appears to be the only copy of the book in an American library; it is one of three complete copies cited by F. J. A. Norton.

Georg Coci, a printer of German origin whose career spanned the years 1499 to 1538, was one of the leading Spanish printers of the period. He succeeded Pablo and Juan Hurus, also German printers who emigrated to Saragossa, whose illustrated editions of Aesop, Boccaccio, and *Spejo de la vida humana* are some of the finest illustrated books printed in Spain in the fifteenth century. Like his predecessors, Coci worked in partnership with numerous printers in Saragossa and was very closely associated with ecclesiastical authorities for whom he printed numerous missals, breviaries, and religious tracts. Many of Coci's books are illustrated, and although this edition is not one of his finest efforts, his editions of *Carcel de amor, Aurea expositio hymnorum,* Livy's *Las quatorze decadas,* and Pedro de la Vega's *Flos Sanctorum* are cited by J. P. R. Lyell as containing some of his most important illustrations.

The small woodcut of Jesus Presented at the Temple is cut in simple outline with some parallel lines used for shading. The simplicity of its design and the uniformity with which the figures are rendered reflects a northern style based on medieval models. The contours of the image

are clearly cut and the garments of the high priest and Mary are well defined, but in this image there is none of the detail, flourish, or individual characteristics that appear in many Spanish woodcuts of the same period. In addition to reflecting its origins, the quality of the image suggests that its purpose was as a marker to the text rather than as an artistic element meant to enhance the narrative.

The printer's mark, a device made up of three individual blocks enclosed by a flower-and-vine border that appears on the recto of the final leaf, is based on the design first used by Pablo Hurus in 1494. The central block is a large initial letter *C* bisected by a cross and surrounded by two rings decorated with a Greek chain design, connected by a Latin motto. At the base of the central block are two lions in aggressive postures and at the top, acanthus leaves set in each corner. To the right of the central block is an image of a pilgrim, and on the left a depiction of the martyrdom of Saint Stephen.

71. GUILLERMUS
PARISIENSIS. *Postilla
sive expositio epistolarum et
evangeliorum.* Saragossa:
Georg Coci, 1506

4to. 210 x 150 mm, 8 ¼ x 6 in. Norton *Descriptive Catalogue* 615.
Norton *Spain*, pp. 69–77.

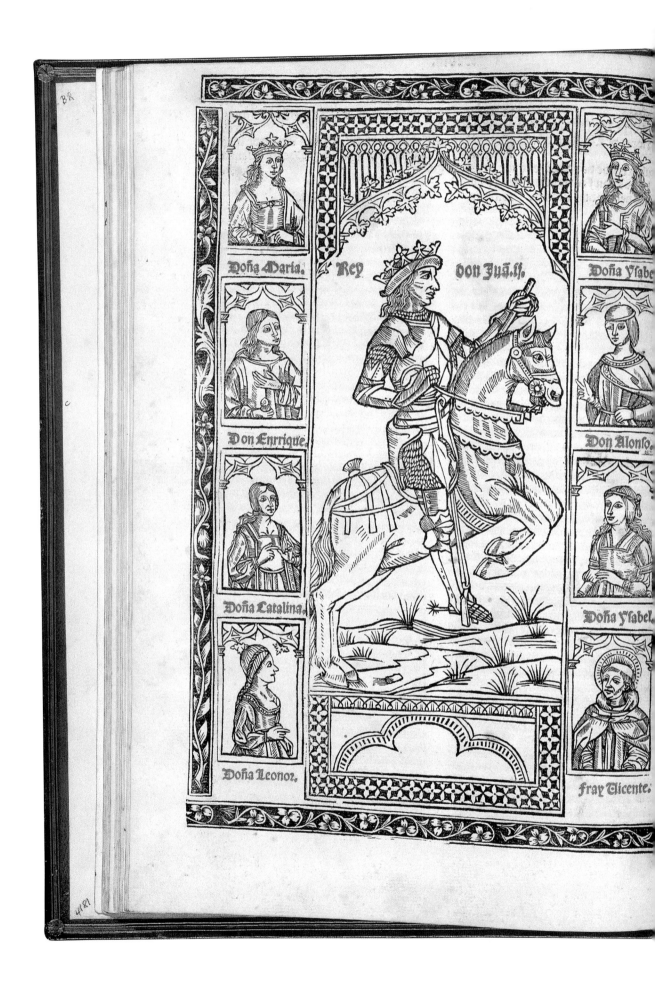

Doña Maria.

Rey don Juã.ij.

Doña Ysabe

Don Enrrique.

Don Alonso.

Doña Catalina.

Doña Ysabel.

Doña Leonor.

Fray Vicente.

¶Comiença la Cronica del serreniſſi-
mo principe don Juan ſegundo rey deſte nom-
bre:en Caſtilla y en Leon eſcrita por el noble τ
muy prudente cauallero fernan perez de guz-
man ſeñor de Batres del ſu conſejo.

## Prologo.

Ran traba
jo tomaró los
ſabios Anti-
gos en eſcre-
uir las baza-
ñoſas τ nota-
bles coſas he
chas por los
illuſtres prin
cipes:ḡ gran
parte del mú
do ſojuzgaró:
entre los ḡles
Plutarcho elegantemente eſcriuio dela vida
y obras de algúos claros varones aſſi griegos
como romanos. Suetonio de los doze ceſares
eſcriuio. Laercio delos filoſofos τ poetas. Juá
bocacio delos aſperos τ duros caſos general
mente acaecidos a muchos grádes enel mun
do. Lucano del gran ceſar τ pompeio. Tito li-
uio de roma. Omero de troya. Trogo pompeo
del orbe vniuerſo. Uirgilio de eneas. Quinto
curcio de alexandre. En que no ſolamente per
petuaron para ſiempre la memoria de aḡllos τ
la ſuya:mas dieron exemplo a todos los ḡ deſpues vinieron:para virtuoſa mente biuir τ ſa-
berſe guardar delos peligroſos caſos dela for-
tuna. Porque a todo principe cóuiene mucho
leer los hechos paſſados:para ordenança de
los preſentes/τ prouidencia delos venideros.
que ſegun ſentencia de Seneca:quien las coſas paſſadas no mira/la vida pierde:y el que en
las venideras no prouee entra en todas como
no ſabio. E los que tal cuydado tomaron:ſin
dubda ſon dignos de eterna memoria:τ ſonles
deuidos ſoberanos honores. E auñḡ yo no ſea
ſemejáte de aḡllos:determine de eſcreuir aſſi
verdaderamente como pude la vida/τ obras τ
coſas acaecidas enel tiempo del Illuſtriſſimo
principe don Juan/ſegundo rey deſte nombre:
en caſtilla/y en leon. Aſſi ruego alos que la pre
ſente Cronica leyeren:quieran dar ſe alo que
en ella ſe eſcriue:porque de lo mas ſoy teſtigo
de viſta:τ para lo ḡ ver no pude:vue muy cier-
ta y entera informacion de hombres prudétes
muy dignos de fe.

¶Capitulo. j. Dela genealogia deſte inclito
rey don Juan:τ del ſu naſcimiento.

Ste preclariſſimo rey don Juá ſe-
gúdo deſte nóbre fue hijo del chri
ſtianiſſimo principe dó Enriḡ ter
cero y dela muy eſclarecida price
ſa doña catalina:ḡ fue hija del du
que dó Juá de alécaſtre:τ dela duḡſa doña ma
ria hija del rey dó Pedro de caſtilla/τ de doña
Maria de padilla:τ fue nieto del rey don Juan
primero τ dela reyna doña Leonor hija del rey
dó Martin de aragó:τ fue viznieto del muy ex
celéte rey dó Alóſo onzeno:ḡ vécio la grá bata
lla de Belamarin:y regano las algeziras:τ de
la reyna doña Maria hija del rey don Pedro
de aragó. E fue deſcédiéte en ſeteno grado del
rey ſan Luys de francia τ del rey don Alóſo de
zeno ḡ fue elegido por empador. E naſcio enel
moneſterio de ſant Elefonſo dela cibdad de to
ro en martes a medio dia/a ſeys de março del
año dela encarnació de nfo Redéptor de Mil
τ. cccc. τ. v. años. E començo a reynar el dia de
nauidad del año de Mil τ. cccc. τ. vij. años. de=
ſpues del falleſcimiéto del xpianiſſimo rey dó
Enrique ſu padre:ſeyendo de hedad de. xxij.
meſes:τ reyno quarenta τ ſiete años. E fueron
ſus tutores τ gouernadores del reyno la ſeñora
reyna doña Catalina ſu madre:y el ſeñor infan
te don Fernando ſu tio. E dexo por teſtamenta
rios a don Ruy lopez de aualos condeſtable de
caſtilla:τ a don Pablo obiſpo de cartajena ḡ
deſpues fue de burgos:τ a fray Juan enriquez
miniſtro dela orden de ſan fráciſco:τ a fray fer
nando de yllescas ſu confeſſor.

¶Cap. ij. De como la reyna doña Catalina
eſtaua enel alcaçar de ſegouia:τ cóella el rey ſu
hijo τ las ifantas doña maria τ doña catalina.

Echa la concordia entre la ſeño
ra reyna doña Catalina τ Juan
de velaſco τ Diego lopez de eſtu
ñiga como dicho es. La ſeñora
reyna eſtaua enel alcaçar de ſe-
gouia:τ cóella el ſeñor rey τ las
ſeñoras infantas ſus hijas doña Maria τ doña Catalina. E los principales ḡ dentro enel al
caçar poſauan:eran Gomez carrillo de cuéca/
el qual la reyna auia pueſto para doctrinar al
principe:τ Alonſo garcia de cuellar contador
mayor del rey:τ ſu theſorero τ alcayde dl dicho
alcaçar:τ otros muchos oficiales ſuyos:τ aſſaz
géte de armas τ vaſſallos pa la guarda del alca
çar. E como quiera ḡ la ſeñora reyna tenia con
ſigo a doña Leonor hija del duḡ de benauente
muger del adelantado Pero márique:τ ala có

a

ONE OF THE MASTERPIECES of early Spanish printing is the first edition of *Cronica del serenissimo Rey Don Juan II* printed by Arnao Guillen de Brocar in 1517. It chronicles the turbulent political history of Spain during the reign of Juan II, 1406–54. The work describes the ceremonies, festivals, tournaments, and other public events organized by Juan II and so much loved by the Spanish public. It was long attributed to Fenán Pérez de Guzmán and Lorenzo Galíndez de Carvajal, but their authorship is now in doubt, and the work is thought to be a compilation of numerous authors. Brocar, a noted printer of Pamplona, Alcalá, and Logroño, used five narrative woodcuts and two sizes of historiated, foliated, and grotesque initial letters cut in black ground to illustrate the book. The title page and many of the text pages are printed in black and red.

The woodcut on the title page shows the author giving a copy of his book to Charles V, who was instrumental in its publication. The scene is outlined in thick contour lines and shaded with a regular pattern of parallel lines, giving the image some sense of perspective. Ten black-ground border blocks, all of different floral-and-branch designs, surround the image, and a historiated initial letter on the page is printed in red.

Illustrated here is a monumental rendering of Juan II, with portraits of his family on either side, which appears opposite the text of the Prologo to this chronicle. The woodcut depicts Juan II on his horse, with eight surrounding woodcut portraits that include an image of his daughter, who was to become Queen Isabella of Spain. The care taken in rendering a horse and rider in motion suggests a skilled designer and cutter at work. Although the proportion of the rider to the horse is not quite right, the anatomy of the horse is well rendered, and the depiction of reins, harness, saddle, and stirrup indicates a knowledge of equestrian equipment. Equally well executed is the posture of the rider on the horse, as well as the rendering of his crown, gloves, and armor. His facial features are depicted with care, especially the eyes, lips, and structure of the nose, which gives Juan II a particularly imperial presence.

The facial features of the eight members of his family are more repetitive in design but the various costumes that are illustrated provide significant information on the dress of the Spanish court in the early sixteenth century. The placement of the illustration opposite the two-column text printed in red and black, which is further embellished with a woodcut initial letter showing Juan II on his throne, creates the well-balanced and pleasing typographical arrangement that makes this two-page opening a highlight of Spanish printing from this period.

Another of the large woodcuts is the Crucifixion signed by the Spanish Master ID. Hind discusses this designer's woodcuts, concluding that his workmanship—"clear in design, hard in cutting, with strong outline and great regularity of shading, parallel series of short lines being often used in background."—resembles the Netherlandish style. Hind thinks this woodcut was probably executed by the Spanish Master ID around 1500. In both composition and the quality of the cutting, the Crucifixion is very similar to woodcuts that appear in the 1506 *Monumenta ordinis minorum* printed at Salamanca by Juan de Porras, and the 1504 edition of Durandus printed by Juan Varela de Salamanca of Granada. Anne Anniger states that Brocar first used this image in an edition of his *Missale* printed in Pamplona in 1501, and Lyell includes a facsimile of Brocar's Crucifixion woodcut in his history of early Spanish book illustration.

The final woodcut in the *Cronica* is Brocar's printer's device, which appears on the final leaf. It is a large woodcut incorporating two images separated by the printer's motto. The top image shows a man, probably the printer, kneeling before a cross that carries symbols of the passion of Christ. An ornamental ring embellished with the vases and floral arrangements encloses the scene. Below the motto, two angels stand on either side of an oak tree holding a shield illustrated with a boar, perhaps referring to the surname Brocar, and the intertwined initials *AG*.

This copy has damage to a few leaves and contains early repairs. There is a tear to the title page and two leaves of the text have also been mended. The final leaf was mutilated and was repaired with a facsimile of most of the text, part of the colophon, and the upper right corner of Brocar's printer's device. The text has some underlining in an early hand and contains marginal notes.

Folio. 310 x 230 mm, 12 x 9 in. Norton *Descriptive Catalogue* 427.
Norton *Spain,* pp. 44–45. Anninger 50.
Palau y Dulcet 2, no. 332. Salvá 3117. Lyell 287. Hind, pp. 616, 754. Davies 48.

## 73   ROSENWALD 1279: DYSON PERRINS 299

T HIS APPEARS TO BE the only known copy of Jacob Cromberger's 1521 edition of Aesop. Neither Brunet nor Salvá cite it, but it is listed by Antonio Palau y Dulcet, from the Huth sale catalogue, which describes this copy. Illustrated with 196 impressions of 192 woodcuts, woodcut initial letters, and woodcut scrolls with pointing hands in the margins, the text consists of a life of Aesop and 167 fables from Aesop, Avianus, Alfonso di Pogio, and other sources. The first leaf is illustrated with a series of 4 woodcuts from the life of Aesop set beneath the text, and enclosed within a three-part woodcut border. Each of the fables is illustrated with a single woodcut and an initial letter, and a scroll that contains the moral of the story, set in the margin.

*73. AESOPUS. Libro del sabio y clarissimo fabulador Ysopo historiado y annotado. Seville: Jacob Cromberger, 1521*

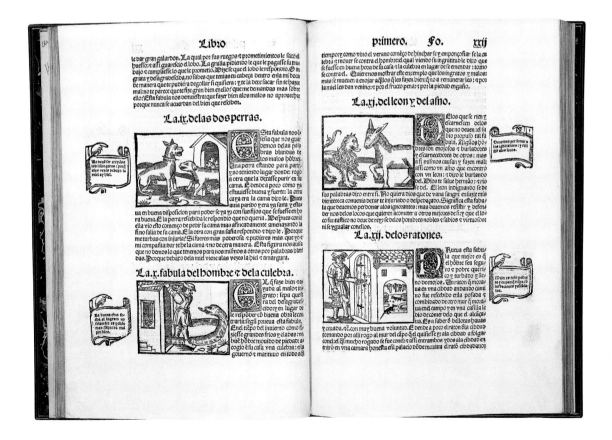

Over the course of his twenty-five-year career, Jacob Cromberger was to become the most important printer in Seville, establishing loose partnerships with printers and booksellers all over Spain and garnering for himself royal privileges and commissions. Norton notes that between 1504, after closing his partnership with Stanislao Polono, and 1520, Cromberger printed nearly two hundred titles of theology, law, popular romances and chronicles, and school texts. Most of his work was printed in the Spanish language. In the colophon of many of his books, his name is followed by the appellation "Aleman" or German, and his printing types, typographical layouts, and illustrations show a definite northern style.

Fables 9 through 12 from book 1, illustrated here, provides a good example of the woodcuts that appear throughout the volume. All are well-designed narratives, cut with thick contour lines and repetitive parallel lines for shading, but with little embellishment, background, or borders. Both the dominant use of white space for background and the flat white of the architectural structures recall the late medieval style of German woodcuts, and the lack of detail suggests the work of a local cutter working from earlier designs. Fable 12, "The Country Mouse and the City Mouse," at the bottom of the recto page, is illustrated with a familiar image of the steward entering his larder. While the figure of the steward and the architectural design of the larder are convincing, the interior of the larder and the figures of the two mice are very poorly designed and cut. It almost appears as if two hands were involved in cutting this block, or perhaps the cutter used a stock design for the steward and the building but had no guide for the contents of storeroom and did not try very hard to create credible images. This woodcut demonstrates the difficulty many local craftsmen had cutting small, detailed figures into a surface of wood.

Folio. 300 x 214 mm, 12 x 8½ in. Huth 1, no. 65. Palau y Dulcet 3, p. 140.
Norton *Spain,* pp. 8–19.

## 74   ROSENWALD 1284: DYSON PERRINS 317

74. Miquel Pérez.
*La Vida y excellencias y milagros dela sacratissima Virgen Maria.* Toledo: Miguel de Equia, 29 November 1526

THIS FIRST EDITION OF *LA VIDA* printed in Catalan was translated by Juan de Molina from the Valencian dialect. The original edition of Miquel Pérez's text in Latin was printed in Valencia in 1495 by Nicolas Spindeler, without illustrations. Miquel de Equia, son-in-law of Arnao Guillén de Brocar, published this edition in Toledo in 1526, after succeeding his father-in-law, who had died in the early 1520s.

The Toledo edition of 1526 is illustrated with a full-page title-page woodcut and sixteen smaller cuts in the text, including one repeat. The smaller cuts are all narrative images illustrating events in the life of Mary and Christ. Complex spatial relationships characterize these compositions, and each of the figures is well defined, with distinctive facial characteristics and costumes. The designs are cut in simple outline with heavy shading, and two different hands were probably involved in the creation of the wood blocks.

The image Mary of the Apocalypse illustrated here is based on the vision recorded by Saint John, in Revelation 12:1, a passage that took on great significance as the cult of Mary emerged during the late medieval period. In the passage, a woman appears to Saint John holding a child in her left arm. She is wearing a crown surrounded by twelve stars and is standing on a crescent moon with the sun at her back. The rays of the sun burst forth to create a circle of light around the woman and child. By the medieval period this woman and child were

¶La vida y excellécias ⁊ milagros dela sacratissima virgen
Maria nr̃a señora. Agoranue-
uaméte corregiday emédada.

understood to be Mary and the Christ Child, and the image of Mary of the Apocalypse was embellished with the descriptions from John's text. Richard Field records a woodcut image of Mary of the Apocalypse from as early as the 1460s, and this conception of the Virgin was reinterpreted by numerous artists and woodcutters well into the sixteenth century.

As with many of the smaller cuts in *La Vida,* the cutting in this woodcut of Mary of the Apocalypse is very well executed. Motifs such as the crown, stars, moon, and sun described by Saint John are clearly defined. The most striking aspect of the woodcut, however, inheres in the precise and expressive facial characteristics given to the two figures. These details, combined with the sensitively formed hands of the Virgin and her flowing gown, highlighted with parallel lines and cross-hatching, reveal the hand of a highly capable cutter, skilled at translating the details of an intricate drawing into wood.

4to. 200 x 140 mm, 7¾ x 5½ in. Norton *Descriptive Catalogue,* p. 33.
Lyell, pp. 225–28. Field 162.

## 75   ROSENWALD 1286: DYSON PERRINS 323

ALFONSO DE LA TORRE WROTE THIS allegorical work about knowledge and a liberal education around 1440, and the first printed edition was published in Barcelona in 1484. It was followed quickly by three other editions before 1500. The edition of *Visión delectable dela philosophia et artes liberales* illustrated here was printed in 1526 by Jacob Cromberger and his son Juan, whose name began appearing with his father's in 1525. Juan Cromberger continued the press after his father's death until the early 1540s, and his son, Jacome Cromberger, carried on the family business until 1557, when his final imprint is recorded. According to Haebler, this family of printers, the most notable in Spain during the first half of the sixteenth century, is best known today for printing vernacular editions of romances and ballads. The Crombergers played a significant role in the development of early Spanish literature.

Jacob Cromberger illustrated this edition of Torres's *Visión* with 118 woodcuts, including repeats, and numerous black-ground and fine-line initial letters. He embellished the title page with a large woodcut of an academy enclosed within four different woodcut borders. One of the characteristics of Spanish book illustration is the seemingly random use of different styles of borders. The structure of the Italian borders used to decorate title pages, with their monumental design and precise symmetry, is often set aside by Spanish printers, who freely use wood block borders of different sizes and designs to frame their text or image, as in the example illustrated here. Another characteristic of Spanish printing is the use of thick contour cuts and heavy use of parallel lines of the same dimension for shading and to give contrast and form to the image. This can be seen in all the woodcuts in Torres's *Visión,* which all seem to have been executed by the same local craftsman.

The large title-page woodcut shows an academy with the muse at the center of the image, surrounded by philosophers, poets, rhetoricians, and other symbols of the liberal arts. These characters, who appear throughout the text, provide instruction over the course of a young man's education. The woodcuts trace the progress of this education and, in the second example illustrated here, show the young boy being taught a lesson in the mysteries of the natural world. Five other woodcuts illustrate the lessons the boy may learn in music, rhetoric, and astronomy. As in the woodcut on the title page, each is cut with thick contours and highlighted with heavy

subitamente les aparescio vna donzella con tanta excellencia de alegria
enla cara:que bien representaua el lugar de donde venia. Aquesta don
zella era clauera de vna puerta:por la qual entrauan alsagrado monte.
Y la celica donzella tenia enla mano vna vihuela:y ela otra mano vnos
organos manuales. Y desque aqui fueron llegados:y por la donzella re
cebidos:despues que deletable reposo ouieron recebido los dos senti
dos mejores:preguntaua la causa de su oficio y morada:la donzella les
hablo enla siguiente forma. Ya aueys sabido como las cosas naturales
son encadenadas y ligadas por vna muy ingeniosa armonia :assi las co
mixtas(conuiene asaber las congeladas)como todas las otras comple
xionadas y organizadas:pues como los elemetos sean ligados por esta
manera:y los cuerpos de todas las cosas copuestas: necessario fue pre
ceder el artificio de saber las proporciones semejantes. Tanta es la ne
cessidad mia:que sin mi no se sabria alguna sciencia o disciplina perfeta
mete.Aun la esphera voluble o todo el vniuerso : por vna armonia de
sones es trayda:y yo soy refecio y nudrimiento singular del alma del co
raço y de los sentidos:y por mi se excitan y despierta los coraçones enlas
batallas y se anima y prouocan a causas arduas y fuertes :por mi son li
brados y releuados los coraçones pesosos dela tristura:y se oluidan de
las congoxas acostubradas. Y por mi son excitadas las deuociones y
afeciones buenas para alabar a dios sublime y glorioso:y por mi se leua
ta la fuerça intellectual a pesar transcediendo las cosas spirituales : bien
aueturadas y eternas. Y esto acabado de desir:fizo fin por vna tacitur
nidad y mirable silecio.El entedimieto vio enla supficie dela pared pin
tados primero a fabula:hallador y inuetor primero de aquesta arte:y
despues vio a Lino thebeo y amphio:a Zeco admirables casesuiosos en
el proferir dela modulacio.E vio alli a Rebrot q no era ra viuir. Edul
çura y teplamiento de su bos:que la fuerça y antiguad giganresce bieru
erpo. Alli pitagoras q cosideraua el son de los ferreros co los m.por las

produzido:y el caymiento delas gotas sobre el agua . Consideraua los
primeros d aqueste dulce artificio. Alli el gregorio que aunque viniesse
enlos postrimeros en tiempo:parescia ser delos primeros en grado. Y
luego dela otra parte vio las tres partes dela musica. Couiene asaber la
armonica:la organica:la metrica. Alli la diuersidad delos instrumetos
ala conuenecia delos sones:y la modulacio delas bozes:y la proporcio
y distacia delos numeros de aqllas . Y assi le fue abierta aquella puerta
y vino a otra puerta mas alta y mas ardua de pujar que aquesta.

¶ Capitulo.vij.que tracta dela astrologia breue
mente:porque lo entiende tratar enla philosofia natural.

Enbios ala septima masion:ya no auia cosa de subir del mo
te sino sola la donzella q ay estaua que quisiesse abrir la puer
ta.La ql aunque parecia delas hermanas passadas:mucho
mas moraua detro dela cerca que de fuera. Y por tato ella
desque vio el entedimieto:Ala aficio suya de entrar recono
cio:co piedad mouida fue ala reyna soberana de aquel mote glorioso y
bienaueturada habitacion:la qual era la verdad : y estauan co ella la sa
biduria y la naturaleza y la razon:y esso mesmo el colegio delas eroycas
inteletuales y morales virtudes. Y la donzella le fizo suplicacion por la
entrada del entendimiento :el qual tanto trabajo auia sostenido enlas
passadas jornadas:y que bien seria que la merced diesse licencia que en
trasse pues con tanta aficion lo desseaua : y que no era venido alli dias
auia huesped semejante:y a todas las señoras inclinando las a beniuo
lencia dixo que ella auia visto en su agudeza de ojos:y en su disposicion
de cara dio curaurian por su venida gradissimo gozo: y tomaria plazer
granna dera lanera de su fablar.La reyna enemiga de bestialidad le re
sponto enlos sa cosejo co las otras hermanas sobre la etrada d este hobre:
y asa:memando ala donzella q se tornasse:y lo detuuiesse hasta q ouiesse

shading. These woodcuts are distinguished not by their cutting but rather by their detailed designs, backgrounds, architectural settings, interiors, and costumes.

This book is also notable for the text that appears on its final leaf, which states that printing was invented in the city of Mainz in 1425 by Peter Fust. For years, this note was cited by the Fust family as one of the principal pieces of evidence to claim the invention of printing for Peter Fust. All the editions of Torres's books are rare, and the Rosenwald/Dyson Perrins and the Hofer copies of the 1526 edition of *Visión delectable* are the only copies in American libraries. This copy has a few headlines trimmed and some ancient wormholes, but is otherwise in fine condition.

4to. 245 x 180 mm, 9⅝ x 7¼ in. Brunet 5, no. 886. Salvá 2434.
Palau y Dulcet 7, p. 47. Anninger 14. Haebler *Early Printers*, pp. 55–67.

75. ALFONSO DE LA TORRE. *Visión delectable dela philosophia et artes liberales.* Seville: Jacob and Juan Cromberger, 1526

# BIBLIOGRAPHY & ABBREVIATIONS

Abrams

Abrams, George. *The George Abrams Collection*. London: Sotheby's, November 16, 1989.

*Aesop's Fables*. Translated by Sir Roger L'Estrange. London: Harrap, 1936.

Alexander, Jonathan J. G. *The Painted Page: Italian Renaissance Book Illumination, 1450–1550*. New York: Prestel Verlag/Royal Academy of Arts/Pierpont Morgan Library, 1994.

Anninger

Anninger, Anne. *Spanish and Portuguese 16th Century Books in the Department of Printing and Graphic Arts: A Description of an Exhibition and a Bibliographical Catalogue of the Collection*. Cambridge: Houghton Library, Harvard College, 1985.

Armstrong "The Pico Master"

Armstrong, Lilian. "The Pico Master: A Venetian Miniaturist of the Late Quattrocento." In *Studies of Renaissance Miniaturists in Venice*. 2 vols. London: Pindar Press, 2003.

Armstrong, Lilian. *Renaissance Miniature Painters & Classical Imagery: The Master of the Putti and His Venetian Workshop*. London: Harvey Miller Publishers; Philadelphia: Distributed by Heyden, 1981.

Armstrong "Woodcuts"

Armstrong, Lilian. "Woodcuts from Liturgical Books Published by LucAntonio Giunta in Venice, 1499–1501." *Word and Image* 17, nos. 1–2 (January–June 2001).

Arnim

Arnim, Manfred von. *Katalog der Bibliothek Otto Schäfer, Schwienfurt*. Stuttgart: E. Hauswedell, 1984.

*2,000 Years of Calligraphy*

Baltimore Museum of Art. *2,000 Years of Calligraphy: A Three-Part Exhibition Organized by the Baltimore Museum of Art, the Peabody Institute Library, the Walters Art Gallery, June 6–July 18, 1965*. Baltimore, 1965.

Becker

Becker, David. *The Practice of Letters: The Hofer Collection of Writing Manuals, 1514–1800*. Cambridge, Mass.: Harvard College Library, 1997.

Berenson, Bernard. "Alunno di Domenico." *Burlington Magazine* 1 (1903).

Berenson, Bernard. *Drawings of the Florentine Painters*. New York: Greenwod Press, 1969.

Bernard

Bernard, Auguste. *Geofroy Tory, Painter and Engraver*. Translated by George B. Ives. Cambridge, Mass.: The Riverside Press, 1909.

Bliss, Douglas Percy, *A History of Wood-Engraving,* London: J.M. Dent and Sons, 1928.

Bohatta *Katalog*

Bohatta, Hanns. *Katalog der Liturgischen Drucke des XV. und XVI. Jahrhunderts*. 2 vols. Vienna, 1910–11.

Bonacini

Bonacini, Claudio. *Bibliografia della arti scrittorie e della calligrafia*. Florence: Sansoni Antiquariato, 1953.

Bongi, Salvatore. *Annali di Gabriel Giolito de'Ferrari da Trino di Monferrato Stampatore in Venezia*. 2 vols. Rome: Presso i Principali Librai, 1890–95.

Boorsch

Boorsch, Suzanne. "Mantegna and His Printmakers." *Andrea Mantegna*. Edited by Jane Martineau. New York: Metropolitan Museum of Art, 1992.

BMC

British Museum. *Catalogue of Books Printed in the XVth Century Now in the British Museum*. 10 vols. in 12. London, 1908–85.

Brun

Brun, Robert. *Le livre illustré en France au XVIe sècle*. Paris: Librairie Félix Alcan, 1930.

Brunet

Brunet, Jacques-Charles. *Manuel du libraire et de l'amateur de livres*. 6 vols. Paris: Firmin Didot Frères, 1860–65.

Butler "Gioloti and Their Press at Venice"  Butler, A.J. "Gioloti and Their Press at Venice." *Transactions of the Bibliographical Society* 10 (London, 1910): 83–107.

Butts and Hendrix  Butts, Barbara, and Leigh Hendrix. *Painting on Light: Drawings and Stained Glass in the Age of Dürer ana Holbein.* Los Angeles: J. Paul Getty Museum, 2000.

Camerini  Camerini, Paolo. *Annali dei Giunti.* 2 vols. Florence: Sansoni, 1962–63.

Campbell  Campbell, M.F. A.G. *Annales de la typographie Néerlandaise au XVe siècle.* 5 vols. The Hague: M. Nijhoff, 1874–90.

Cartier, Alfred. *Bibliographie des éditions des Tournes, imprimeurs Lyonnais.* 2 vols. Paris, 1938.

Choulant  Choulant, Ludwig. *History and Bibliography of Anatomic Illustrations.* New York: Hafner, 1962.

Claudin  Claudin, Anatole. *Documents sur la typographie et la gravure en France.* London: Maggs Brothers, 1926.

Conway  Conway, William Martin. *The Woodcutters of the Netherlands in the Fifteenth Century.* Cambridge: University Press, 1884.

HC  Copinger, Walter A. *Supplement to Hain's Repertorium bibliographicum.* Berlin: J. Altmann, 1926.

Darlow and Moule  Darlow, T.H., and Horace Frederick Moule. *Historical Catalogue of the Printed Editions of Holy Scripture in the Library of the British and Foreign Bible Society.* 2 vols. in 4. London: Bible House, 1903–11.

Davies  Davies, Hugh William. *Devices of the Early Printers, 1457–1560: Their History and Development.* London: Grafton & Co., 1935.

Fairfax Murray *French*  Davies, Hugh William, compiler. *Catalogue of a Collection of Early French Books in the Library of C. Fairfax Murray.* 2 vols. London: Privately printed, 1910.

Fairfax Murray *German*  Davies, Hugh William, compiler. *Catalogue of a Collection of Early German Books in the Library of C. Fairfax Murray.* 2 vols. London: Privately printed, 1913.

Delen  Delen, A.J. J. *Histoire de la gravure dans les anciens Pays-Bas et dans les provinces belges des origines jusqu'a la fin du XVIe siècle.* Paris: F. De Nobele, 1969.

De Marinis  De Marinis, Tammaro. *Appunti e ricerche bibliografiche.* Milan: U. Hoepli, 1940.

Dixon  Dixon, Laurinda. "Giovanni di Paolo's Cosmology." *Art Bulletin* 67: 604–13.

Dodgson *Early German and Flemish Woodcuts*  Dodgson, Campbell. *Catalogue of Early German and Flemish Woodcuts in the British Museum.* 2 vols. London: British Museum, 1903, 1914.

Dodgson *Prints in the Dotted Manner*  Dodgson, Campbell. *Prints in the Dotted Manner.* London: British Museum, 1937.

Essling  Essling, Victor Masséna, [duc de Rivoli,] prince d'. *Les livres à figures vénetiens de la fin du XV siècle et du commencement du XVI siècle.* 3 vols. in 6. Florence: Olschki, 1907–14.

Essling *Missels,* Rivoli  [Essling,] Victor Masséna, duc de Rivoli, [prince d']. *Les missels imprimés à Venise de 1481 à 1600.* Paris: J. Rothschild, 1896.

Field  Field, Richard. *Fifteenth Century Woodcuts and Metalcuts from the National Gallery of Art, Washington, D.C.* Washington: Publications Department, National Gallery of Art, 1965.

Firmin-Didot, Ambroise. *Catalogue des livres précieux imprimés faisant partie de la bibliothèque de M. Firmin-Didot.* 6 vols. in 3. Paris, 1878–84.

*The Florentine Fior di virtu of 1491.* Translated into English by Nicholas Fersen. Philadelphia: Published for the Library of Congress; printed by E. Stern, 1953.

Foot  Foot, Mirjam M. "Battista Fregoso." In *Vision of a Collector: The Lessing J. Rosenwald Collection in the Library of Congress.* Washington: Library of Congress, 1991.

Funck  Funck, Maurice. *Le livres belge à gravures.* Paris: Van Oest, Éditeur, 1925.

Gascoigne  Gascoigne, Bamber. *How to Identify Prints.* New York: Thames and Hudson, 1995.

GW      *Gesamtkatalog de Wiegendrucke.* 8 vols. Leipzig: K. W. Hiersemann, 1925–40.

Glorieux, Geneviève. *Belgica typographica, 1541–1600.* Nieuwkoop: De Graaf, 1968.

Goff *LCQJ*      Goff, Frederick R. "A Catalogue of Important Recent Additions to the Lessing J. Rosenwald Collection." *Library of Congress Quarterly Journal of Current Acquisitions* 5, no. 3 (May 1948): 3–51.

Goff "The Four Florentine Editions"      Goff, Frederick R. "The Four Florentine Editions of Savonarola's *Predica dell'arte del Bene Morire.*" In *The New Colophon: A Book Collectors' Miscellany 1950.* New York: Limited Editions Club, 1950.

Goff      Goff, Frederick R. *Incunabula in American Libraries. A Third Census.* Millwood, New York: Kraus Reprint, 1973.

Goff "Postilla"      Goff, Frederick R. "The Postilla of Guillermus Parisiensis." *Gutenberg Jahrbuch.* Mainz, 1959.

Goldschmidt      Goldschmidt, E. P. "Medieval Texts and Their First Appearance in Print." London: Bibliographical Society, 1943.

Graf      Graf, Urs. *Die Holzschnitte zur Passion: Mit einer Einführung von Wilhelm Worringer.* Munich: R. Piper, 1923.

Gruyer      Gruyer, Gustave. "Les livres à gravures sur bois publiés à Ferrara." *Gazette des Beaux-Arts.* Published in four parts, Paris, 1888–89.

Haebler *Bibliografia*      Haebler, Konrad. *Bibliografia ibérica del siglo XV.* 2 vols. Leipzig and The Hague: Hiersemann and Nijhoff, 1903–17.

Haebler *Early Printers*      Haebler, Konrad. *The Early Printers of Spain and Portugal.* London: Bibliographical Society, 1897.

H, HR      Hain, Ludwig. *Repertorium biblographicum in quo libri omnes ab arte typographia inventa usque ad annum MD . . . recensentur.* 2 vols. in 4. Stuttgart: J. G. Gotta, 1826–38.

Hall      Hall, James. *Dictionary of Subjects and Symbols in Art.* London: J. Murray, 1974.

Heckethorn      Heckethorn, Charles William. *The Printers of Basle in the XV & XVI Centuries.* London: Unwin Brothers, 1897.

Hind      Hind, Arthur M. *An Introduction to a History of Woodcut.* 2 vols. London: Constable and Company, 1935.

Hindman      Hindman, Sandra, and James Douglas Farquhar. *Pen to Press: Illustrated Manuscripts and Printed Books in the First Century of Printing.* College Park, Md.: Art Department of the University of Maryland, 1977.

Hobson, G. D. *Maioli, Canevari, and Others.* Boston: Little, Brown, and Company, 1926.

Hodnett      Hodnett, Edward. *English Woodcuts 1480–1535.* Oxford: Oxford University Press, 1973.

Hofer, Philip. "Illustrated Editions of 'Orlando Furioso.'" In *Fragonard Drawings for Ariosto.* New York: Published for the National Gallery of Art, Pantheon Books, 1945.

Hollstein      Hollstein, F. W. H. *Dutch and Flemish Etchings, Engravings, and Woodcuts, ca. 1450–1700.* 60 vols. Amsterdam: M. Hertzberger, 1949–2003.

Holtrop      Holtrop, Jan Willem. *Monuments typographiques des Pays-Bas au quinzième siècle.* The Hague: M. Nijhoff, 1868.

Huth      Huth, Henry. *Catalogue of the Famous Library of Printed Books, Illuminated Manuscripts, Autograph Letters, and Engravings Collected by Henry Huth.* 9 vols. London: Dryden Press, J. Davy and Sons, 1911–20.

ISTC      *Incunable Short-Title Catalogue.* CD-ROM. London: British Library, 1980–.

Ivins "Ars moriendi"      Ivins, William. "The Museum's Editions of the Ars moriendi." *Bulletin of the Metropolitan Museum of Art* 18 (October 1923).

Ivins "Woodcut Books"      Ivins, William. "Some Venetian Renaissance Woodcut Books." *Bulletin of the Metropolitan Museum of Art* 29 (March 1934).

Ivins "Early Florentine"      Ivins, William. "Early Florentine Illustrated Books." *Bulletin of the Metropolitan Museum of Art,* n.s., 3 (Summer 1944).

Johnson   Johnson, A. F. *The First Century of Printing at Basle.* London: Ernest Benn Ltd.; New York: Scribner, 1926.

Kok   Kok, Clazina Helena Cornelis Maria. *De houtsneden in de incunabelen van de Lage Laden, 1475–1500.* Amsterdam: C. Kok, 1994.

Kristeller "Pavia"   Kristeller, Paul. "Books with Woodcuts Printed in Pavia." In *Bibliographia* 1, 347–72. London: Kegan Paul, Trench, Trübner, 1895.

Kristeller *Early Florentine Woodcuts*   Kristeller, Paul. *Early Florentine Woodcuts.* London: Kegan Paul, Trench, Trübner, 1897.

Kristeller   Kristeller, Paul. *Lombardische Graphik der Renaissance.* Berlin: Bruno Cassirer, 1913.

Kristeller "Woodcuts as Bindings"   Kristeller, Paul. "Woodcuts as Bindings." In *Bibliographia* 1, 249–51. London: Kegan Paul, Trench, Trübner, 1895.

Kronenberg/Campbell   Kronenberg, M. E. *Campbell's Annales de la Typographie Néerlandaise au XV. Siècle; Contributions to a New Edition.* The Hague: Nijhoff, 1956.

Lacombe   Lacombe, Paul. *Livres d'heures imprimés au XVe et au XVIe siècle.* Paris: Imprimerie nationale, 1907.

Landau and Parshall   Landau, David, and Peter Parshall. *The Renaissance Print, 1470–1550.* New Haven: Yale University Press, 1994.

Rosenwald, LC/R   *The Lessing J. Rosenwald Collection: A Catalog of the Gifts of Lessing J. Rosenwald to the Library of Congress, 1943 to 1975.* Washington: Library of Congress, 1977.

  Levarie, Norma. *The Art and History of Books.* New York: James H. Heineman, 1968.

Lincoln   Lincoln, Evelyn. *The Invention of the Italian Renaissance Printmaker.* New Haven: Yale University Press, 2000.

Lippincott   Lippincott, Kristen. "Giovanni di Paolo's Creation of the World and the Tradition of the Thema Mundi in Late Medieval and Renaissance Art." *Burlington Magazine* 132: 460–68.

Lippmann   Lippmann, Friedrich. *The Art of Wood-Engraving in Italy in the Fifteenth Century.* London: B. Quaritch, 1888.

Logan   Logan, Carolyn. "Urs Graf, Bust of a Bearded Old Man." *Bulletin of the Metropolitan Museum of Art* 55, no. 2 (Fall 1997).

Lyell   Lyell, James Patrick Ronaldson. *Early Book Illustration in Spain.* London: Grafton & Co., 1926.

Macfarlane   Macfarlane, John. *Antoine Vérard.* London: Printed for the Bibliographical Society by the Chiswick Press, 1900.

  Mardersteig, Giovanni. "Epilogue." In *The Fables of Aesop Printed from the Veronese Edition of MCCCCLXXIX in Latin Verses and the Italian Version by Accio Zucco,* 259–77. Verona: Officina Bodoni, 1973.

Mongan   Mongan, Elizabeth. *The First Century of Printmaking, 1400–1500.* Chicago: The Art Institute of Chicago, 1941.

Mortimer *French*   Mortimer, Ruth. *Harvard College Library Department of Printing and Graphic Arts Catalogue of Books and Manuscripts.* Part 1, *French 16th Century Books.* 2 vols. Cambridge, Mass.: Harvard University Press, 1964.

Mortimer *Italian*   Mortimer, Ruth. *Harvard College Library Department of Printing and Graphic Arts Catalogue of Books and Manuscripts.* Part 2, *Italian 16th Century Books.* 2 vols. Cambridge, Mass.: Harvard University Press, 1974.

Muther   Muther, Richard. *German Book Illustration of the Gothic Period and the Early Renaissance (1460–1530).* Translated by Ralph R. Shaw. Metuchen, N.J.: Scarecrow Press, 1972.

Nijhoff   Nijhoff, Wouter. *L'art typographique dans les Pays-Bas pendant des années 1500 à 1540.* 2 vols. plus a supplement. The Hague: Martinus Nijhoff, 1926.

Nijhoff-Kronenberg   Nijhoff, Wouter, and M. E. Kronenberg. *Nederlandish bibliographie van 1500 tot 1540.* 3 vols. in 7. The Hague: Nijhoff, 1923–61.

Norton *Descriptive Catalogue*   Norton, F. J. *A Descriptive Catalogue of Printing in Spain and Portugal, 1501–1520.* Cambridge: At the University Press, 1978.

Norton *Italian*      Norton, F. J. *Italian Printers, 1501–1520*. London: Bowes and Bowes, 1958.

Norton *Spain*      Norton, F. J. *Printing in Spain, 1501–1520*. Cambridge: At the University Press, 1966.

Nuyts, Corneille Joseph. *Essai sur l'imprimerie des Nutius*. Brussels: J. Vandereydt, 1856.

O'Connor      O'Connor, Mary Catharine, Sister. *The Art of Dying Well: The Development of the Ars moriendi*. New York: Columbia University Press, 1942.

Os, H. W. van. *The Art of Devotion in the Late Middle Ages in Europe, 1300–1500*. Translated from the Dutch by Michael Hoyle. Princeton: Princeton University Press, 1994.

Osley      Osley, A. S. *Luminario: An Introduction to the Italian Writing-Books of the Sixteenth and Seventeenth Centuries*. Nieuwkoop: Miland Publishers, 1972.

Palau y Dulcet      Palau y Dulcet, Antonio. *Manual del librero hispano-americano*. 7 vols. Barcelona: Libreria Anticuaria, 1923–27.

Panofsky *Dürer*      Panofsky, Erwin. *Albrecht Dürer*. 2 vols. Princeton: Princeton University Press, 1945.

Pasero      Pasero, Carlo. *Le xilografie dei libri bresciani dal 1483 alla seconda metà del XVI secolo*. Brescia: Scuola tipografia Istituto figli di Maria immacolata, 1928.

Pellechet      Pellechet, Marie Léontine Catherine. *Catalogue général des bibliothèques publiques de France*. Nendeln, Liechtenstein: Kraus-Thomson Organization Ltd., 1970.

Pettas, William A. *The Giunti of Florence*. San Francisco: B. M. Rosenthal, 1980.

Pollard *Bibliographica*      Pollard, Alfred W. "The Book of Hours of Geoffrey Tory." In *Bibliographica* 1, 114–22. London: Kegan Paul, Trench, Trübner, 1895.

Pollard Introduction to *Le Castell of Labour*      Pollard, Alfred W. "Introduction." In Pierre Gringore, *The Castell of Labour*. Translated from the French by Alexander Barclay. Edinburgh: Roxburghe Club, 1905.

Pollard Introduction to *Epistole et Evangelii*      Pollard, Alfred W. "Introduction." In *Epistole et Evangelii lectioni volgari in lingua toscana. The Woodcuts of the Florentine Edition of July 1495 Reproduced in Facsimile with the Text from a Copy in the Library of C. W. Dyson Perrins*, xxi–xxiii. London: Roxburghe Club, 1910.

Pollard *Italian*      Pollard, Alfred W. *Italian Book-Illustration and Early Printing: A Catalogue of the Early Italian Books in the Library of C. W. Dyson Perrins*. Oxford: The University Press, 1914.

Proctor, Robert George Collier. *An Index to the Early Printed Books in the British Museum*. 4 vols. London: Kegan Paul, Trench, Trübner & Co., 1898–99.

Ramsden      Ramsden, E. H. "Early Venetian Illustrated Books: The Essling Collection." *Apollo Magazine* 104 (July 1976).

Reichling, HCR      Reichling, Dietrich. *Appendices ad Hainii-Copinger Repertorium bibliographicum*. Munich: J. Rosenthal, 1905–11. *Supplement*, Münster, 1914.

Renouard *Colines*      Renouard, Philippe. *Bibliographie des éditions des Simon de Colines*. Paris: E. Paul, L. Huard et Guillemin, 1894.

Rogledi Manni      Rogledi Manni, Teresa. *La tipografia a Milano nel XV secolo*. Florence: Olschki, 1980.

Rosenwald *Livres anciens*      Rosenwald, Lessing J. *Livres anciens des Pays-Bas: La Collection Lessing J. Rosenwald provenant de la Bibliothèque d'Arenberg*. Brussels: Bibliothèque Royal de Belgique, 1960.

Salvá      Salvá y Mallen, Pedro. *Catálogo del la Biblioteca de Salvá*. 2 vols. Barcelona: Porter-Libros, 1963.

Sander      Sander, Max. *Le livre à figures italien depuis 1467 jusqu'à 1530*. 6 vols. New York: Stechert, 1941.

Schäfer *Italian*      Schäfer, Otto. *The Collection of Otto Schäfer*. Part 1, *Italian Books*. New York: Sotheby's, December 8, 1994.

Schäfer *Parisian*      Schäfer, Otto. *The Collection of Otto Schäfer*. Part 2, *Parisian Books*. New York: Sotheby's, June 27, 1995.

Schramm        Schramm, Albert. *Die Bilderschmuck der Frühdrucke.* 23 vols. Leipzig:
                Deutsches Museum für Buch und Schrift, 1920–23; K.W. Hierse-
                mann, 1924–43.

               Schreiber, Fred. *The Estiennes: An Annotated Catalogue.* New York:
                E. K. Schreiber, 1982.

W. L. Schreiber  Schreiber, W. L. *Handbuch der Holz- und Mettalschnitte des XV. Jahr-
                hunderts.* Leipzig: 1901–11; reprint ed., Stuttgart: A. Hiersemann;
                Nendeln, Liechtenstein: Kraus Reprint, 1969.

Schretlen      Schretlen, M. J. *Dutch and Flemish Woodcuts of the Fifteenth Century.*
                London: E. Benn, Ltd., 1925.

Schwerdt       Schwerdt, C. F. G. R. *Hunting, Hawking, Shooting, Illustrated in a
                Catalogue of Books.* 4 volumes. London: Privately printed for the
                author by Waterlow & Sons, 1928–37.

               Silver, Larry. "Nature and Nature's God: Landscape and Cosmos of
                Albrecht Altdorfer." *Art Bulletin* 81, no. 2 (June 1999).

               Silver, Larry. "Forest Primeval: Albrecht Altdorfer and the German
                Wilderness Landscape." *Simiolus* 13 (1983): 4–43.

Smith          Smith, David Eugene. *Rara Arithmetica.* New York: Chelsea Publish-
                ing Co., 1970.

Strauss        Strauss, Walter L. *Sixteenth Century Artists.* The Illustrated Bartsch 13.
                New York: Abaris Books, 1981.

Talbot         Talbot, Charles W. *Dürer in America: His Graphic Work.* Washington:
                National Gallery of Art, 1971.

Thienen        Thienen, Gerard van, and John Goldfinch. *Incunabula Printed in the
                Low Countries: A Census.* Nieuwkoop: De Graaf Publishers, 1999.

Unterkircher   Unterkircher, Franz. "Der erste illustrierte italienische Druck und
                eine Wiener Handschrift des gleichen Werkes (Hain 15722,
                Cod. Vindob. 3805)." In *Hellinga Festschrift: Feestbundel, Forty-three
                Studies in Bibliography Presented to Prof. Dr. Wytze Hellinga,* 498–
                516. Amsterdam: Israël, 1980.

               Urbini, Silvia. "Marcantonio as Book Illustrator." *Print Quarterly* 16,
                no. 1 (March 1999): 50–56.

Venturi        Venturi, Adolfo. *Storia dell'arte Italiana.* Milan: U. Hoepli, 1901.

               Vindel, Francisco. *Manual gráfico-descriptivo del bibliófilo hispano-
                americano, 1475–1850.* 11 vols. in 12. Madrid: Direccion General de
                Relaciones Culturales, 1930–34.

Voet           Voet, Léon. *The Golden Compasses: A History and Evaluation of
                the Printing and Publishing Activities of the Officina Plantiniana
                at Antwerp.* 2 vols. Amsterdam: Van Gendt; New York: Abner
                Schram, 1969–72.

Wadell         Wadell, Maj-Brit. *Evangelicae historiae imagines: Entstehungsgeschichte
                und Vorlagen.* Göteborg: Acta Universitatis Gothoburgensis;
                Atlantic Highlands, N.J.: Distributed in the U.S.A. by Humanities
                Press, 1985.

               Walters Art Gallery. *The History of Bookbinding, 525–1950 A.D.:
                An Exhibition Held at the Baltimore Museum of Art, November 12,
                1957, to January 12, 1958, Organized by the Walters Art Gallery
                and Presented in Cooperation with the Baltimore Museum of Art.*
                Baltimore: The Trustees of the Walters Art Gallery, 1957.

               Weitenkampf, Frank. "The Malermi Bible and the Spencer Collec-
                tion," *Bulletin of the New York Public Library* 33 (1929), 779–88.

Williamson     Williamson, G. C. "The Books of the Carthusians." In *Bibliographica* 3,
                213–31. London: Kegan Paul, Trench, Trübner, 1897.

               Winn, Mary Beth. *Anthoine Vérard: Parisian Publisher, 1485–1512.*
                Geneva: Librairie Droz, 1997.

Wodhull        Wodhull, Michael. *Catalogue of the Extensive and Valuable Library.*
                London: Sotheby, Wilkinson & Hodge, 1886.

# INDEX

Page numbers in *italics* refer to illustrations; page numbers in **boldface** type indicate main catalogue entries.

*Der Ackermann aus Böhmen*, Bamberg, 1462: 48
Adam and Eve: 52, *67*, 91–92, 126, *127*, 175, *176*, 177, *189*, 190
*Adnotationes et meditationes in evangelia in sacrosancto missae sacrificio toto anno leguntur*, Antwerp, 1594–95: **197**, *198*
Adoration of the Kings: *33*, 36, 138
Aelinus Tacticus: 180
Aesop's *Fables*: 22; Basel, 1492: 168; Basel, 1501: **168–70**, *169*; Brescia, 1487: **102–3**, 105; Florence, 1490: 107; Huras editions: 200; Seville, 1521: **205–6**; Tuppo's 1485 edition: 122; Ulm, 1476–77: 50–52, 53, 80, 168; Venice, 1493: **103–5**, *104*; Verona, 1479: 102–3, 105
Afra (saint): 162–63
Agony in the Garden: *118*, 136, 137
Agresti, Livio: 197
Alberti, Leon Battista: 36
Albertus Magnus: 188
Albumasar: 54–55, 75–77
Alcalá: 142, 204
Alliaco, Petrus de: 133
Altdorfer, Albrecht: 83
Alverthorpe: 1, 5, 6, 7
Alvise, Alberto: 102
Alvise, Giovanni: 102
Amerbach, Johann von: 62, 126
Andrea, Zoan: 161–62
Andreae, Hieronymus: 67
Andrew (saint): *28*, *37*, 45n42, 156, *157*
angels: *36–37*, 87, 120, *129*, 131, *140–41*, *142*, *161*, 162, 178, *179*, 204–5 (*see also* Annunciation)
Angelus, Johannes: 75, 77
Anima Mia, Guglielmus de: 42, 105, 118
Anne (saint): 79, *133*, 134
*Annulus astronomicus*, Rome, 1492/93: **98–99**, *99*
Annunciation: *36–37*, 60, 61, 79, 81, 91, *92*, *121–23*, *147*, 148, *183*, 184
anonymity of artists and designers: 101
*Anteros, sive Tractatus contra amorem*, Milan, 1490: **113–16**, *114*, *115*
antiphonary of San Nicolo dei Frari, Venice, 1490–1500: *37–39*
Antonio da Brescia, Giovanni: 162
Antwerp: 137, 187–90, 192–98
*Apocalypsis*: 190; Nuremberg, 1498: 60, 67–69, *68*, 161; Nuremberg, 1511: 69, 161; Venice,

1515/16: **161–62**; Virgin and Child on Crescent Moon: 191, 205–8, *207*
Apollonius (saint): 162
Appianus: 54, 77
Apuleius: 91
Arabic, gospels in: 167–68
Arabic ornamentation: 54, 141, 144, 162, 200
architectural elements: *26*, *27*, 29, *36*, *42*, *52*, *53*, *58*, *62*, *64*, *66*, 98, 106, 110, *111*, 116, *117*, 121, *129*, 131, 132, *147*, 148, 153, 157, 158, 166, *171*, 178, 182, 190, 191, 192, 197, 206, 209
Arias Montanus, Benedictus: 194
Ariosto, Ludovico: 165, 166
Aristotle: 142, 187, 188
*Arithmetica*, Florence, 1491/92: **95–96**
*Arithmetica speculativa*, Paris, 1495/96: **133–34**
Armstrong, Lilian: 25–45, 94, 106–7, 146–48, 155
Arnim, Manfred von: 91
*Ars moriendi (The Art of Dying)*: 10, 87, 89; Florence, 1497: **119–20**, 123; Leipzig, after 1500: **87–89**, *88*; Paris, 1492: 128, *130*; Paris, 1493/94: **128–31**, 178
Ascensius, Jodocus Badius: 181
Assumption: 79, 157
*Astrolabium*, Augsburg, 1485: 75, 77
attribution, author: 39, 59, 101, 126, 131, 148, 204
attribution, designer: 33, 35, 49, 59, 83, 88–89, 92–93, 101, 110, 113, 125, 146–47, 152, 157, 161–62, 166, 185, 188, 195; Bordon: 146–47, 155; Burgkmair: 56; Pico Master: 94, 107; Reuwich: 58
attribution, printer: 81, 110, 118, 122
attribution, wood cutter: 67, 146
Augsburg: 47, 49, 50, 53, 54, 60, 61, 76, 113, 126
Augustine (saint): *34*, *35*, 37, 95, *100*, 101, 178, *179*
Avianus: 168, 205

Bac, Govaert: 187–88
Bamberg: 47, 48–49
Bämler Master: 49
Bämler/Baemler, Johann: 49, 78
Baquelier, Antoine: 131, 132
Barberiis, Philippus de: 91
Basel: 47, 49, 59, 60, 61–63, 124–25, 126, 168–70
*Bay Psalm Book*, Cambridge, Mass., 1640: 18
*Beichtebüchlein*, Leipzig, 1494: 87
Bellaert, Jacob: 137, 138, 188
Bembo, Pietro: 40
Benalius, Bernardinus: 28, 29, 93, 94, 105, 119, 165
Benedict Master: 83

Berghen, Adriaen van: 83
Bergmann von Olpe, Johannes: 62, 125, 169
Berlinghieri: 34, 110, 111
Bernard, Auguste: 174, 183
Bernardino of Siena (saint): 114
Bertholdus/Bertoldus: 63, 81, 82, 126
Besicken, Johann: 91, 98, 112
*Beuves de Hanstone*, Paris, 1502: 172
Bevilaqua, Simon: 119
*La bible en françoiz*, Paris. 1517: **176–78**
*Bible historiée*, Paris: 1498: 177; 1517: 20
Bibles: 25, *33*, 48, 124, 142, 192, 194 (*see also* Gutenberg Bible)
Bibles, German: 28, 58, 68
*Biblia italica*, Venice: 1477: *27*; 1490: 43n5; 1493: 42; 1494: 14, 17, 25–29, *26*, *28*, 38, 42, 105–7, *106*
bindings: 11–12, 113–15, 137, 172, 179, 184, 192, 195
Birgitta (saint): 83–87, *84*, *86*, 126
black background: 30–31, 34, *35*, *36*, 37, 40, 77, 93, 97, 101, 103, 107, 109, 110, 113, 114, 116, 122, 123, 141, 142, 144, 149, 153, 157, 158, 160, 170, 171, 178, 182–83, 185, 189, 200, 204, 208
black space, use of: 31, 34, 51, 53, 61, 113–14, 154, 156, 200
black-on-white technique: 57, 141, 175, 186, 200
Blevdenwurff, Wilhelm: 83
block books: 1, 10, 79, 87, 124, 137, 190
Bocard, André: 128
Boccaccio: 14, 50–52, 130, 200; *De claris mulieribus*, Ulm, 1473: 50–52, *51*, 80
Boccaccio Master: 49
Bodleian Library: 128, 184
*Boek van den Proprieteyten der Dingen*, Antwerp, 1485: 137
*Boek van die vier oeffeningen*, Antwerp, 1507: 190
Bonaccorsi, Francesco: 107
Bonaventura (saint): 31, 83, 118, 190
Bonellis, Manfredus de: 103–5, 116
Boner, Ulrich: 48
Bonhomme, Jean: 172
Boninis, Boninus de: 93, 102–3
Borcht, Pierre van der, IV: 194
borders: 30–31, 34, *35*, 37, 40, 48, 50, 52, 54, 61, 76, 82, 83, 88, 93, 96–99, 101, 103, 105–7, 109, 110, 113, 116, 122, 123, 129–32, 141, 142, 148, 149, 152, 153, 157, 158, 160, 162, 164, 166, 168, 178, 181, 183, 184, 186, 192, 193, 204, 206, 208
Bordon, Benedetto: 38, 40, 146–47, 148, 155, 157

rappresentazioni, Florence, 1500 and 1554: 12, **122–23**

Ratdolt, Erhard: 54–56, 75–77, 93, 107

Ratdolt, Georg: 75

Regiomontanus, Johannes: 64, 76

*Regulae grammaticae,* Perottus, Florence, 1490: 96

*Regule ordinum,* Venice, 1500: 160

Reinhart, Johannes, of Grüningen: 58–60

Reisser: 47–48, 59, 65

religious works, Venetian and Florentine woodcuts for: 25–45; *Biblia italica,* Venice, 1494: 25–29; early 16th-century Venetian woodcuts: 35–40; *Epistole et Evangelii,* Florence, 1495: 29–35; *Espositione sopra Evangeli,* Simon de Cassia, Florence, 1496: 41–42

repair and rebinding: 11–12

resurrection: 36, 78, 144

reuse of woodcuts: 15th century: 75, 76, 78, 87–88, 90, 96, 98, 101, 110, 116, 118, 119, 121–23, 125, 126, 131, 133, 134, 137, 138, 141; 16th century: 144, 146, 153–55, 157, 160, 164–66, 168, 170, 172, 175, 177, 178, 180, 181, 184, 188, 189, 191, 192, 195, 200, 204, 206, 208; German woodcuts: 53, 54–55; religious works, Venetian and Florentine: 31, 42, 43n5

Reuwich, Erhard: 56–58

*Revelationes,* Saint Birgitta: Lübeck, 1492: 83, *86;* Nuremberg, 1500: **83–87,** *84–85,* 126

*Revelationes divinae a sanctis angelis factae,* Methodius (?), Basel, 1498: 62, **126–27**

Revelations of Saint John, *see* Apocalypsis

Rham, Henry: 11, 12, 14, 15, 17

Richel, Bernhard: 60, 61, 124

Rimini Ovid Master: 28

Rincon, Antonio del: 199

Ringmann, Matthias: 60, 144

Rinuccio/Rinucius: 50, 168

Rippe, Guillaume: 181

*Der Ritter vom Turn,* Basel, 1493: 21, *62,* 124

Rivoli, duc de, *see* Essling, Victor Masséna (duc de Rivoli), prince d'

Rizzus, Bernardinus: 116

Roman woodcuts: 91–93, 98–99, 112–13, 121–22, 167–68

Romulus: 50, 168

*Rosarium Beatae Virginae Maria:* Antwerp, 1489: **136–37;** Magdeburg, 1500: **90–91**

Rosenbach, A. S. W.: bibliographical notes: 123; Dyson Perrins sales: 11, 14, 20, 103, 119; Library of Congress exhibition catalogue: 21; prices: 17–18; Rosenwald and: 1–2, 4–6

Rosenwald, Julius: 2–4, 5, 6

Rosenwald, Lessing J.: 1–22; bookplate: 98; early collecting of: 4–7; family and early life: 2–4; Inventory Book, July 1946: *16, 17;* Library of Congress, relationship with: 21–22; portrait: *xiv;* purchases at Dyson

Perrins sales (*see* Dyson Perrins sales); views on collecting: 1

Rosselli, Francesco: 33

Rossi, Lorenzo de': 113

Rosso, Giovanni Battista: 160, 186

roundels: *124, 125,* 149–51, 153, 178

Rubeis de Valentia, Laurentius: 152, 153, 154

Rubens, Johannes: 26, 28, 106

Rugeriis, Ugo de: 96

Ruppel, Berthold: 61

*Rureaux Prouffitz,* Paris, 1484: 172

*Sacerdotalis instructio circa missam,* Seville, 1499: **140–41**

Sacrobusto/Sacro Bosco, Joannes de: 55, 94, 98

saints, *see under* individual names, e.g., Peter (saint)

Salamanca: 199

Salerno, Giovanni da: 116

Salomon, Bernard: 186

Samaritan Woman at Well: *167,* 168

San Nicolò dei Frari antiphonary, Venice, 1490–1500: *37, 38,* 39

Sandri, Domenico: 149

Sandri, Nicolò: 149

Santen, Henricus van: 189

Saragossa: 50, 200–201

Saturninus (saint): 37

Savetier, Nicolas: 178, 179

Savonarola: 11, 15, 18, 21–22, 95, 110, 119–20, 123

Scandianese, Tito Giovanni: 163, 164

Schäfer, Otto: 17, 19, 102, 113, 116, 184

*Schatzbehalter,* Nuremberg, 1491: *46,* 47, 62, 65–67, *66,* 83

Schäufelein, Hans: 83

Schedel, Hartmann: 65, 67, 68, 83

scholar at his desk: *34–35, 100, 101,* 170, 178

Schongauer, Martin: 55–56, 58, 61, 62

Schönsberger, Johann: 54, 78

*Schwäbische Chronik,* Ulm, 1486: *52,* 64, *79,* 80

Scinzenzeler, Uldericus: 114

sculpture and reliefs: 30, 31, 44n21, 64, 93

Second Gouda Cutter: 135

*Sermo de visione Dei,* Raynaldus Monsaureus, Rome, 1495: **112–13**

Sermon on the Mount: *28*

*Sermones ad heremitas:* Florence 1493: *34,* 36, **100–101;** Florence, 1500: 101

Sessler, Charles: 4

Seville: 141, 143–44, 199, 205–6, 208–9

shading: 110, 138, 142, 143, 144, 148, 149, 154, 157, 165, 168, 170, 171, 175, 177, 178, 181, 182, 186, 189, 190, 196, 200, 206 (*see also* cross-hatching; parallel-line shading); chiaroscuro woodcuts: 56; German woodcuts: 57, 60, 62; shaded style: 35, 37, 153

*Ship of Fools, see* Narrenschiff

Sienna, Biblioteca comunale: 93

*Siete partidas,* Seville, 1491: 199

Signerre, Guillaume le: 158

Silvius, Guillaume: 195

Snellaert, Christian: 189

Soardis, Lazarus de: 118, 119

*Soliloquii,* Saint Augustine, Florence, 1491: 101

Solomon: 28, *33,* 33–34, 107

*Der Sonderen Troest,* Haarlem, 1484: 188

Sorg, Anton: 53–54, 78

Spanish Master ID: 204

Spanish woodcuts: 20, 141–44, 199–209 (*see also* specific towns)

*Speculum humane salvationis,* Augsburg, 1473: *60, 61,* 124

*Speculum vitae Christi,* Westminster, 1486 and 1490: 138

*Spejo de la vida humana:* 200

*Sphaera mundi,* 1482 and 1485: 55, 94, 98, 175

*Spiegel menschlicher Behaltnis,* Basel, 1476: *60, 61,* 124

*Spieghel der kestenen menschen,* Louvain, 1500: 192

Spinas, Alphonse de: 61

Spindeler, Nicolas: 206

Spira, Johannes Henricus de: 160

Spirito, Lorenzo: 157, 159

*Statuta,* Pavia, 1505: 154

Steiner, Heinrich: 180

Steinhöwel, Heinrich: 50

stencils: 149

Stephen (saint): 34, *56, 112,* 191, 201

*Stimulus amoris,* Antwerp, after 1500: 83

Stradanus, Joannes: 168

Strasbourg: 47, 49, 50, 58–60, 146–48

Stuttgart Library: 52

*Summario dell'arte di astrologia,* Florence, 1491, and Naples, 1485: 98

Sweynheym, Conrad: 25

Symphorosa (saint): 154

Tacuinus, Joannes: 119

tapestries: 44n21

teacher and student: *97,* 101, *111*

Teaching of Apostles by Christ: *30–32,* 34, 44n16, *109,* 110, *124, 125,* 130

Tempesta, Antonio: 167–68

Temple: Expulsion of Money-Changers from: *41;* Presentation of Jesus at: 200–201

Terence, *Commoediae: Eunuchus,* Ulm, 1486: *53, 79,* 80; Lyon, 1493: 119, 181; Paris, 1539: **181–83,** *182;* Strasbourg, 1490: *58–60;* Venice, 1497: 119

theatrical performances: 181–82, *182*

Theophrastus: 187

*Theoretica et practica de modo scribendi fabricandique omnes litterarum species,* Venice, 1514: **159–60**

Theramo, Jacobus de: 188

Thienen, Gerard van: 190

Third Antwerp Woodcutter: 188

Thomas (saint): 44n21

Titian: 161, 165, 166

Toledo: 206–8

Tomb of Christ, Three Marys at: *36, 38,* 39, 144, *155*

Torquemada, Juan de: 14, 18, 19, 91–93, 121